ARCO

INTERNSHIPS

| A Directory for | Career-Finders |

SARA D. GILBERT

MACMILLAN • USA

First Edition

Macmillan General Reference
A Prentice Hall Macmillan Company
15 Columbus Circle
New York, NY 10023

An Arco Book

MACMILLAN is a registered trademark of Macmillan, Inc.
ARCO is a registered trademark of Prentice-Hall, Inc.

Library of Congress Cataloging-in-Publication Data

Gilbert, Sara D.
    Internships a directory for career-finders/
Sara D. Gilbert—1st ed.
    p. cm.
    At head of title: Arco.
Includes bibliographical references (p.) and indexes.
ISBN 0-02-860013-4
1. Internship programs—United States—Directories.
2. College students—Employment—United States—Directories.
I. Arco Publishing. II. Title.
LC1072.I58G55   1994   94-3621
331.25'922—dc20   CIP

Manufactured in the United States of America

10   9   8   7   6   5   4   3   2

ACKNOWLEDGMENTS

Whether you are a career-finder or career-changer, to get into an internship and to get the most out of one, you must first *find* the optimum internship opportunities.

And for *that* we go to the sources.

Thanks are owed, therefore, to the resources themselves—to all the internship coordinators, public affairs directors, human resource managers, and others who took the time to respond by mail, telephone, fax, and e-mail to the individual and networked requests for information about their internship opportunities, and who provided details on, and invited reader inquiries about the thousands of individual openings listed in, ARCO's internship guide.

* * *

Thanks also to the crew of callers, mailers, and inputters who helped to pull it all together: Lisa Abrams, Vivian Avila, John Cancel, Julie Cruz, Richard Marshall, Onix Ramos, and Maria Riera.

Contents

▪▪

I. WHY INTERN NOW

WHY INTERNING IS *IN*

Interning is *IN*—as demonstrated by the enthusiastic response to requests for information for this book from the hundreds of cultural, business, public, and service organizations that invite you here to take note of their thousands of openings.

Interning is in for new groups of people:

- for career-finders in a job market that is tight and demanding for the foreseeable future
- for career-changers in an era when career paths are shifting under their feet
- for employers who are sending the word back from the workplace that "it's the interns who get the jobs!"

Statistics gathered by the National Society for Internships and Experiential Education (NSIEE), which show internships are up by 37 percent in five years, demonstrate that the value of interning as a two-way learning tool is as great as in the earliest days of apprenticeships, the very first kind of job training. In both classrooms and boardrooms, recent interest in internships as a means to education and experience continues to intensify. The kind of hands-on learning that is the original kind of job training is now all new.

WHY THIS BOOK WAS WRITTEN

The need arose for a *new* kind of interns' directory—one that encourages the thoughtful attention any internship requires, especially now, when good internships are in such demand:

College students line up for internship interviews as though they were full-paying jobs, since competition for those jobs is stiff and "work-experience" has become a necessary addition to any education. Interns have a jump on the jobs-race: not just from the direct-contacts advantage, but from the demonstration any internship provides of willingness to work and learn.

Such a directory should recognize the following new facts of the successful work life.

1

That it's not only students who need to keep learning; it's all of us at any age who want to stay ahead of change—careers are open today that didn't even exist when we were getting our classroom training. To the ten million working adults who, according to the Labor Department, change careers each year, interning provides a powerful boost toward their new goals.

That it is not only youngsters who are students: *seven million* of those college students are *adults*, most of whom are in class part-time and seeking ways to refine their resumes to fit the 10 million jobs predicted to open in entirely new fields by the early 21st century. In fact, adults form the majority of the nation's undergraduates—and we adults learn better by doing (and have a *lot* to contribute while we do it).

Plus, it's not just students who are interning today! With career change an accepted and necessary aspect of success in today's changing work force, interning opens doors to new careers for workers of every age and position. In short, in the volatile job market of the 1990s, interning is one of the few consistently sure bets—for employers as well as for potential employees.

According to the National Society for Internships and Experiential Education (NSIEE), an *internship* is "any carefully monitored work or service experience in which an individual has intentional learning goals and reflects actively on what s/he is learning throughout the experience."

This book sifts out the best opportunities provided by public, private, corporate, government, and nonprofit operations, and also guides you toward valuable referral sources in each field: associations, agencies, and in-print and on-line advice about career-area specifics in the arts, business, communications, culture and education, the environment, government, health care, international groups, public affairs, science, social services, and associations.

In these pages, you will find fully detailed listings from nearly a thousand selective internship sponsors, as you might expect. But you will also find strategies and techniques for targeting and landing the optimum internship anywhere—*and* for making the most of the experience.

Experienced interns know that an internship is better than an entry-level job, since, when it is successful, it provides the chance to do substantive work in significant positions. You will note in this guide, too, that the call for interns is greatest in high-demand, newly-opening career paths, including environment, health care, communications, and international occupations.

The book is arranged according to the primary function of the organizations listed, with summaries derived from the respondents' own descriptions of themselves. Selections focus on internship opportunities that are the most flexible and broad-based; that seem willing to accept older career-changers as well as more traditional interns; and that, if possible, offer some kind of payment. In addition to the specific internship listings, career-related associations and other resources are included here to let you make an even wider search.

Each of the listings sections opens with an overview of the section's field and closes with referral resources. The book ends with lists cross-referenced by career category, geographic location, stipend, and such special status as ethnicity, gender, and age.

Why intern now? It is an effective way to explore the professional fields you think may interest you, testing your interest against the reality of the job. It is also a practical and efficient way of developing skills in your field and making yourself a more attractive candidate when you are conducting your real search for employment. The following chapter offers more specific, step-by-step techniques for securing the kind of internship you want.

II. How To Intern

■■

> ***Profile of a Successful Intern:*** *Martha, an intern at*
> Newsweek, *is past "normal" student age but is getting, she*
> *says, more out of her ongoing internship at the magazine*
> *than she would as an entering employee. With some journal-*
> *ism experience already to her credit, and with a graduate*
> *degree in Latin American studies, she wanted to secure a*
> *position with a more prestigious publication and decided*
> *that an "internship was the vehicle" for that. And because of*
> *the internship, she is with an automatic "support group" and*
> *gets "good treatment" at the magazine where she and the*
> *other interns sit in on editorial meetings and get worthwhile*
> *article assignments.*
>
> *She gets paid (minimally, with no benefits)—and suggests*
> *that even small pay is an important criterion for choosing*
> *an internship. "It shows they respect you," she comments,*
> *"and you're more likely to get valuable work."*

How to Be a Successful Intern

First, keep in mind that an internship is not just *like* a job; an internship *is* a job. You are most likely to succeed at an internship if you remember that it may be the most important job you will ever have:

> It will place you firmly within the kind of network of career contacts that is repeatedly shown to be the most successful path to career satisfaction.
>
> It will give you the credentials and contacts you need when you are just starting out to find your career.
>
> It will provide the firsthand experience you need to determine whether the career you are considering is one you will enjoy, *before* you make a commitment.

How to Get an Internship

Approach your interning experience as you would the most important job you will ever do.

You will need to explore, to apply with a well-done résumé, letter, and interview—and it will be up to you to optimize your opportunities. This guide will help you do that, in as *complete* a fashion as possible, with listings of and leads to thousands of opportunities and resources to follow up for more.

This book starts you on your search. Each entry in the listings sections contains the information that you will need to evaluate each internship opportunity. For each opening you find, you will need to answer the following questions:

LOCATION: Can you *be* there?

ORGANIZATION'S ACTIVITIES: Does this group do something you can relate to, now or in the future?

Number of Internships: The more there are, the better your chances to be accepted and the more likely the program is to be formalized and well organized. If only a few formal internship spots are open, offer to create one that suits your needs, or consider turning volunteer work into an internship by offering to make a formal commitment.

Type: Are the "type" and "function" things that you *can* do and/or would like to *learn*?

Function/Duties: Do you have the skills required? Does the work seem substantial enough to meet your learning needs?

Schedule: Can you manage the schedule, given your other responsibilities for school, work, or family?

Stipend or Pay: Can you afford this opportunity? Does it allow time for a supplemental job?

Academic Credit Offered: If you want to put an internship toward a degree, will your school approve this specific one? Be sure before you start!

ELIGIBILITY REQUIREMENTS: In terms of status or skills, can you meet the eligibility requirements for this job?

APPLICATION PROCEDURE: Follow the rules that each internship sponsor requires. Note that most request applications well in advance.

Now that you are ready to start an active internship search, follow this schedule:

- You should make your lists of targets from this book about *one year* before your internship starts.
- Call for information about *9 months* ahead.
- Get your résumé, references, and other material ready to send about *6 months* ahead of time.
- Have application finished by *3 months* at most before you want to start.
- Then, follow up at least once, and do what you can to make a personal pitch to your prime targets: Offer to come in for an interview even if it is not required, or at least try for a telephone conversation about your qualifications.

Landing an internship is exactly like landing a job—except you have the advantage of using the listings in this book to know just what criteria you must meet.

You can follow the entries' information point by point to target your résumé and cover letter in order to gain an interview. At the interview, the format provides an outline for your presentation of why you and this internship are a perfect match. Be prepared to present the benefits you can provide to the employer—and to state why this opportunity is something you have always sought. If you are in school, show how this work dovetails with your studies. If you are a nonstudent (or an older undergraduate), you will need to explain your goals and motivations.

TIP: In addition to the specific openings listed here that you can apply for, you can use this book to *create* your own internship in several ways: If you find a listing here that appeals to you but that does not match your qualifications exactly, go for it anyway. Find all the reasons that make you the right candidate for this internship, and let the employer know them. Or, let the entries here give you a sense of what might be available in your own community, and seek out firms or associations in your own area that could most likely use interns. You may present yourself as an intern, or turn a volunteer stint into a formalized learning experience. However you proceed, use the format above as a checklist for success.

How to Get the Most out of an Internship

A job involves primarily an exchange of work for pay; an internship involves primarily an exchange of work for learning. Since *learning* is less concrete than *pay*, the making of specific arrangements is critical if both parties involved in the internship are to get from it what they expect.

Agree. Begin with putting into writing the details of the exchange, along the lines of the same points outlined above.

The more organized internship sponsors have their own agreement forms for you to sign, but remember to make certain *your* needs are met, too. At least produce an informal note, setting forth what you expect to learn from the commitment and what you promise to perform; both you and the sponsor should sign this agreement. Many schools require this kind of documentation. If there is none, however, or if you are doing this on your own, having the work-learning "contract" in writing can prove very valuable in keeping the proper balance between the work you give and the learning you receive.

Evaluate. While you are working, the same checklist will help you to maintain an ongoing evaluation of your experience: in terms of "type...," "function...," "duties...," "schedule...," "stipend...," and "credit ...." Is it all that was promised?

This kind of evaluation is especially critical when what you gain is nothing so simple as a piece of paper marked "paycheck." Your rewards are less tangible and, thus, harder to measure. Arrange for regular review sessions during your internship to be sure you are meeting your goals. How does your experience stack up against the definition "Any carefully monitored work or service experience in which an individual has intentional learning goals and reflects actively on what s/he is learning throughout the experience"?

Follow up. Since your internship's primary goal is likely to be a boost in a new career, one of your main rewards is a supervisor's praise. Therefore, be sure to:

Leave with a (good, if possible) recommendation letter. If you are a student, your school will require this—and you will surely want it for your job search.

Since contacts are at least as valuable as that good report, be sure to:

Keep in touch—this is the heart of your networking. If you have discovered from your internship experience that this is indeed the field where you want to stay, this is critical.

How to succeed at interning? Get *into* an internship that promises what you need. Get *out* of it all the benefits possible: ***learning, contacts,*** and ***credentials.***

An internship is a success if you have learned the general information and the specific skills you sought, and if you have gained the career contacts and other credentials you need.

The opportunities to gain those benefits begin in the next section.

III. Internship Listings

■■

Here are 13 sections, arranged by field of interest and endeavor, where you can find the work-and-learn arrangement that best fits your needs, for now and for your future, followed by a further section on finding more information.

Each section presents a group of sponsoring associations, agencies, businesses, or organizations (including one section on opportunities for people with special eligibilities), offering anywhere from one to hundreds and even thousands of internships to qualified people at virtually any given time. Each begins with a paragraph describing general opportunities in the field and their characteristics, and includes tips and personal observations by interns; each closes with resources, such as placement, publication, or information services, for referral to even more opportunities.

Following the internship listings is a section of resources and references: clearinghouses, placement services, and other organizations to contact for a wide range of opportunities. The final section consists of indexes that cross-reference the internship offerings by category or content.

It is a good idea first to browse through the entire book—even those sections you think are not to your liking. Opportunities are in most cases listed according to the primary activity of the employer or sponsoring organization, and you may find work of interest in an area you would not have considered.

You can do science-related work for the government, for example, or learn management in a science organization. You can do public relations for a video group, or learn video with a PR firm. You can focus the general skills you are learning or have just learned in school by getting practice in some specific areas that you will only find or think of if you consider *all* the options. And career *change* is more successful when you take the skills you know into an area you want to enter. Take your computer expertise into a theater company where it is needed to streamline ticket sales, for instance—and you have an entree backstage. Or take your acting skills into a teaching, sales, or PR role, where they will give you a natural boost into a new career.

How to Read the Internship Entries

The internship listings in the following sections are organized in a standard format with headings outlining the key information about the organization offering the internship, its requirements, and the conditions of the internship. On the following page is an outline of a regular entry showing all the elements that may appear.

Name: Organization   **Phone:**

Address: Of principal headquarters   **FAX:**

* * *

ORGANIZATION'S ACTIVITIES: A concise description derived, or directly quoted, from the organization's description of itself.

Number of Internships: The usual number of openings; often varies due to projects, need, or quantity of applicants.

Type: Generic description of available internships, e.g., clerical, advertising, photography, editorial, public relations, etc.

Function/Duties: Specific duties required.

Schedule: Yearly periods, hours, days required, with minimum time commitment if supplied.

Stipend or Pay: Remuneration, if offered, and its form, e.g., salary, transportation costs, housing, etc.

Academic Credit Offered: Indicates if employer has a formal learning program or if credit must be arranged by the intern through the academic institution. *Plus* additional opportunities or perks internship may bring or lead to.

ELIGIBILITY: Categories or groups for whom internship is available; may include students, non-students, career-changers. *Special eligibilities:* Indicates when particular invitation is offered to special groups, e.g., minorities, women, handicapped. Most state they are equal opportunity groups.

REQUIREMENTS: Specific restrictions of position, i.e., whether applicant must be enrolled in academic program, how competitive internship is, etc. A few, select groups are included that ask a fee.

APPLICATION PROCEDURE: Formal method for initiating application. Includes person or office to contact and date by which application process must be completed.

Each of the following entries covers these points.

INTERNSHIP SOURCES IN THE ARTS

■■

Notes on Interning in the Arts:

Often the only way to open the door to a career in the creative arts is by interning in art, music, dance, or theater. Not surprisingly, these are among the kinds of groups *most* likely to offer internships and to treat them seriously. Also, as you might expect, competition is stiff for openings in these areas, which are in effect working apprenticeships in the arts. The good news: Every community has an abundance of arts organizations that need interns even if they do not know it until you convince them of it.

TIP: All arts organizations need all kinds of skills, so career-changers have a good chance of making a successful pitch.

> *Nick makes $100 a week interning at the League of American Theaters and Producers. In the theater world, he says, many companies take on summer apprentices to do lighting and other chores, printing brochures to attract apprentices and paying for the work. Since Nick gets paid, he is especially happy—despite the ten-hour days.*

AMERICAN CONSERVATORY THEATRE

450 Geary Street   **Phone:** 415/749-2226
San Francisco, CA 94102   **FAX:**   415/771-4859

* * *

ORGANIZATION'S ACTIVITIES: A resident theater company that presents a variety of works throughout the year.

Number of Internships: 12.

Type: Production and stage management.

Function/Duties: Assist professionals in all aspects of backstage work, including lighting and design.

Schedule: Full-time +, September–May.

Stipend or Pay: Yes.

Academic Credit Offered: Per student's own arrangements with academic institution.

ELIGIBILITY: Students and non-students.

REQUIREMENTS: Interest in pursuing a career in the theater.

APPLICATION PROCEDURE: Send inquiries *to* Intern Coordinator in February; submit application *by* May deadline.

ARENA STAGE

6th Street and Maine Avenue SW   **Phone:** 202/554-9066
Washington, DC 10024   **FAX:**   N/A

*   *   *

ORGANIZATION'S ACTIVITIES: One of the nation's leading regional theaters, a nonprofit residential repertory presenting a varied selection of works year-round.

Number of Internships: 25.

Type: Production and stage management and theater administration.

Function/Duties: Work with directors, designers, administrators in capacities suiting intern's skill.

Schedule: Full-time, 2- to 12-month commitment, year-round availability.

Stipend or Pay: May be arranged.

Academic Credit Offered: Per student's own arrangements with academic institution.

ELIGIBILITY: Consideration given to students, non-students, or career-changers with appropriate qualifications.

REQUIREMENTS: Interest in pursuing a career in the theater.

APPLICATION PROCEDURE: Send inquiries *to* Intern Coordinator in time to submit application *by* 3 months prior to availability date.

ART INSTITUTE OF CHICAGO

Adams Street and Michigan Avenue   **Phone:** 312/443-3600
Chicago, IL 60614   **FAX:**   312/443-0849

*   *   *

ORGANIZATION'S ACTIVITIES: A major cultural center for the collection, preservation, exhibition, and interpretation of one of the "finest art collections in the nation."

Number of Internships: Varies; numerous.

Type: Education, conservation, architecture, collecting, public relations, accounting.

Function/Duties: Professional-level assistance in departments suited to intern's abilities and interests.

Schedule: Full- and part-time, summers only or year-round.

Stipend or Pay: Some are paid.

Academic Credit Offered: Per student's own arrangements with academic institution.

ELIGIBILITY: College students and/or some non-students and career-changers with appropriate degrees or experience.

REQUIREMENTS: Strong interest in art.

APPLICATION PROCEDURE: Request application form *from* Internship Coordinator. *Deadline:* Ongoing.

THE ARTS AND EDUCATION COUNCIL OF GREATER ST. LOUIS

3526 Washington Avenue	**Phone:** 314/535-3600
St. Louis, MO 63103	**FAX:** 314/535-3606

* * *

ORGANIZATION'S ACTIVITIES: Fundraising for arts and cultural organizations in the St. Louis bi-state area.

Number of Internships: 1 per semester.

Type: Public relations.

Function/Duties: Writing and assisting in special projects.

Schedule: Part-time during the winter, spring, and summer.

Academic Credit Offered: If arranged by intern.

Stipend or Pay: No.

ELIGIBILITY: All students as well as non-students welcome to apply.

REQUIREMENTS: Interests, goals, skills, and/or experience relevant to available assignments.

APPLICATION PROCEDURE: Submit résumé and cover letter *to* Renee Bazin, Communications Coordinator.

ARTS EXTENSION SERVICE

602 Goodell Building	
University of Massachusetts	**Phone:** 413/545-2360
Amherst, MA 01003	**FAX:** 413/545-3351

* * *

ORGANIZATION'S ACTIVITIES: AES is a national arts service organization that works to achieve access to and integration of the arts communities through continuing education for artists, arts organizations, and community leaders.

Number of Internships: About 4.

Type: Program and promotion assistants.

Function/Duties: Research related to arts administration.

Schedule: Full-time and part-time, September–May; occasional summer internships; minimum 3-month term.

Stipend or Pay: No.

Academic Credit Available: Yes.

ELIGIBILITY: College and graduate students. Non-students and career-changers welcome.

REQUIREMENTS: Interns must work in AES office a minimum of 12 hours a week, depending on the position.

APPLICATION PROCEDURE: Submit letter of inquiry or make phone call *to* Pam Korza. *Deadline:* August and November.

BERKELEY REPERTORY THEATER

2025 Addison Street   **Phone:** 510/841-6108
Berkeley, CA 94704   **FAX:**   N/A

* * *

ORGANIZATION'S ACTIVITIES: A resident theater company that presents 7 shows annually during its 10-month season.

Number of Internships: Varies; fairly numerous.

Type: Technical, management.

Function/Duties: Aid in preparing costumes, lighting, scenery, etc.

Schedule: Full-time August–May.

Stipend or Pay: $300 per month; housing provided.

Academic Credit Offered: Per student's own arrangements with academic institution; *Plus* internship may lead to regular employment.

ELIGIBILITY: Students and non-students with appropriate credentials.

REQUIREMENTS: Especially interested in students with theater experience.

APPLICATION PROCEDURE: Request application materials *from* intern coordinator for submission *before* April 1.

BISHOP MUSEUM

P.O. Box 19000-A   **Phone:** 808/847-3511
Honolulu, HI 96817-8968   **FAX:**   808/841-8968

* * *

ORGANIZATION'S ACTIVITIES: Collection of art and artifacts renowned for its depth and breadth; a cultural center for the Pacific region.

Number of Internships: Varies according to need.

Type: Curatorial, communications, education, marketing.

Function/Duties: Assist curators and researchers.

CHICAGO CHILDREN'S MUSEUM

435 East Illinois Street   **Phone:** 312/527-1000
Chicago, IL 60611   **FAX:**   312/527-9082

* * *

ORGANIZATION'S ACTIVITIES: The city's "only museum exclusively dedicated to the needs and interests of children."

Number of Internships: 12.

Type: Education, programming, public relations.

Function/Duties: Provide professional assistance to staff members in various departments, dealing with exhibitions and with public.

Schedule: About 20 hours per week for 15 weeks.

Stipend or Pay: No.

Academic Credit Offered: Per student's own arrangements with academic institution; *Plus* training provided.

ELIGIBILITY: Primarily college students, though others considered.

REQUIREMENTS: Interests, goals, and/or experience relevant to available assignments.

APPLICATION PROCEDURE: Send résumé, cover letter, and writing samples *to* Director of Intern Services. *Deadline:* Ongoing.

CINCINNATI BALLET

1216 Central Parkway   **Phone:** 513/621-5219
Cincinnati, OH 45210   **FAX:**   513/621-4844

* * *

ORGANIZATION'S ACTIVITIES: A classical ballet company giving about 38 local performances a year and about 10 each year in its sister city (Knoxville). Major staff functions are marketing, fundraising, special events, and development.

Number of Internships: 2 or more.

Type: Public relations, marketing, some management aid.

Function/Duties: Writing, researching, planning promotions and events.

Schedule: Part-time and full-time, year-round; term at least 3 months long.

Stipend or Pay: No.

Academic Credit Offered: Yes.

ELIGIBILITY: College students; majors preferred: marketing, public relations, development, and arts management.

REQUIREMENTS: Excellent communications skills; interest in arts.

APPLICATION PROCEDURE: Submit résumé and cover letter *to* Director of Marketing and Development. *Deadline:* April 1 for summer; August 1 for fall/winter, and November 1 for winter/spring.

CINCINNATI OPERA

1241 Elm Street	**Phone:** 513/621-1919
Cincinnati, OH 45210	**FAX:** N/A

* * *

ORGANIZATION'S ACTIVITIES: A nationally known regional company whose activities feature a major Summer Festival.

Number of Internships: Numerous.

Type: Technical and artistic.

Function/Duties: Assist with production and design for Summer Festival presentations.

Schedule: Full-time + in summer.

Stipend or Pay: Honorarium, plus repay of travel costs from home cities.

Academic Credit Offered: Per student's own arrangements with academic institution.

ELIGIBILITY: Consideration given to students, non-students or career-changers with appropriate qualifications.

REQUIREMENTS: Musical and/or technical backgrounds preferred.

APPLICATION PROCEDURE: Request application, send *to* Administrative Office Manager *by* March 1.

COLUMBUS MUSEUM OF ART

480 East Broad Street	**Phone:** 614/221-6801
Columbus, OH 43213	**FAX:** 614/221-0226

* * *

ORGANIZATION'S ACTIVITIES: Preserve and present visual arts; serve as regional cultural center.

Number of Internships: Varies.

Type: Public relations, development, curatorial, education.

Function/Duties: Multifaceted, hands-on.

Schedule: Part-time and full-time, quarterly term.

Stipend or Pay: No.

Academic Credit Offered: Yes.

ELIGIBILITY: Students in junior and senior years in college, graduate students.

REQUIREMENTS: Interview required.

APPLICATION PROCEDURE: Submit letter of intent and résumé to Department Head *by* 3 months prior to desired start date.

CRAFT AND FOLK ART MUSEUM

5800 Wilshire Boulevard	**Phone:** 213/937-5544
Los Angeles, CA 90036	**FAX:** 213/937-5576

* * *

ORGANIZATION'S ACTIVITIES: "Promotes cross-cultural understanding through a wide variety of exhibitions, education programs, and activities associated with the International Festival of Masks."

Number of Internships: Varies.

Type: Education, research, curatorial, events, public relations.

Function/Duties: Varies by department and intern's interest.

Schedule: Full-time or part-time, year-round or seasonal.

Stipend or Pay: No.

Academic Credit Offered: Per student's own arrangements with academic institution; *Plus* internship may lead to full-time position.

ELIGIBILITY: Consideration given to students, non-students, or career-changers with appropriate qualifications.

REQUIREMENTS: Minimum 3 months' commitment; prefer college majors related to internship duties.

APPLICATION PROCEDURE: Send letter of interest with résumé *to* Executive Director's Assistant *by* at least 60 days prior to internship.

DANCE IN AMERICA

356 West 58th Street	**Phone:** 212/560-2956
New York, NY 10019	**FAX:** 212/560-2099

* * *

ORGANIZATION'S ACTIVITIES: Dance in America is the only American television dance series that produces year-round on a major network station. Dance in America brings dance documentaries and the works of major choreographers to public television.

Number of Internships: 2–3.

Type: Production internships.

Function/Duties: Assist in production, research, office support.

Schedule: Full-time and part-time, 4 hours a day minimum.

Stipend or Pay: $10 a day.

Academic Credit Offered: Yes.

ELIGIBILITY: Undergraduate and graduate students (majors preferred: television, journalism, dance). Non-students and career-changers welcome.

APPLICATION PROCEDURE: Send résumé and cover letter *to* Internship Coordinator at least two months prior to starting date.

DANCE THEATER WORKSHOP

49 West 19th Street   **Phone:** 212/691-6500
New York, NY 10011   **FAX:** 212/633-1973

*   *   *

ORGANIZATION'S ACTIVITIES: Currently in its twenty-ninth year, DTW is a nonprofit, tax-exempt Presenting and Services organization that provides artist sponsorship programs, related promotions, and administrative and production services to the community of independent dance and other performing artists in New York and across the country, facilitating concert performances for choreographers, composers, and theater artists across the U.S. and abroad, and stimulating the development of new audiences.

Number of Internships: Varies by need and project.

Type: Clerical, administrative, production.

Function/Duties: Depending on the department—mostly office work and administrative assistance.

Schedule: Part-time and full-time; very flexible—depends on intern's schedule.

Stipend or Pay: No.

Academic Credit Offered: Yes.

ELIGIBILITY: All students, non-students, and career-changers.

REQUIREMENTS: Typing skills are helpful, but not necessary.

APPLICATION PROCEDURE: Submit a letter and résumé *to* Shoshana Hellerstein, Director of Services.

DAVID FINLEY JR. FINE ART

19 East 81st Street   **Phone:** 212/472-3590
New York, NY 10028   **FAX:** 212/472-4376

*   *   *

ORGANIZATION'S ACTIVITIES: American 19th- and 20th-century painting and sculpture gallery.

Number of Internships: 12.

Type: Varies.

Function/Duties: Working on projects like research, filing, inventories, catalogue, layouts, etc.

Schedule: Part-time and full-time, one-month term.

Stipend or Pay: No.

Academic Credit Offered: No.

ELIGIBILITY: All college and graduate students.

REQUIREMENTS: Must have good attitude.

APPLICATION PROCEDURE: Submit résumé and cover letter *to* Lee Finley, Cherokee Station, Box 20080, New York, NY 10028-0050.

FOUNDATION FOR INDEPENDENT VIDEO AND FILM (FIVF)

625 Broadway
Ninth Floor   **Phone:** 212/473-3400
New York, NY 10012   **FAX:**   212/677-8732

* * *

ORGANIZATION'S ACTIVITIES: Support of independent film and video makers through programs; publication of *Independent Film and Video Monthly;* festival bureau, publications, activities, seminars, consultations.

Number of Internships: 5.

Type: Clerical.

Function/Duties: Assist in all office work.

Schedule: Part-time.

Stipend or Pay: $100 per month.

Academic Credit Offered: Yes.

ELIGIBILITY: All students (majors preferred: film and communications). Non-students and career-changers welcome to apply.

REQUIREMENTS: Goals, interests, skills, and/or background related to group's activities.

APPLICATION PROCEDURE: Submit résumé and cover letter *to* Kathryn Bowser.

FRANKLIN FURNACE ARCHIVE

112 Franklin Street   **Phone:** 212/925-4671
New York, NY 10013   **FAX:**   212/925-0903

* * *

ORGANIZATION'S ACTIVITIES: Franklin Furnace is a not-for-profit arts organization that specializes in presenting installation and performance art and has a collection of artists' books.

Number of Internships: Varies.

Type: Production, public relations.

Function/Duties: Assist staff in setting up programs, marketing institution.

Schedule: Full-time.

Stipend or Pay: No.

Academic Credit Offered: Yes.

ELIGIBILITY: Undergraduate and graduate students. High-school students and non-students also welcome to apply; *Plus* equipped (at this time) for the disabled.

REQUIREMENTS: Interests, goals, skills, and/or experience relevant to available assignments.

APPLICATION PROCEDURE: Submit résumé and cover letter *to* Anita Chao.

J. PAUL GETTY MUSEUM

17895 Pacific Highway   **Phone:** 310/459-7611
Malibu, CA 90265   **FAX:** 310/454-6633

* * *

ORGANIZATION'S ACTIVITIES: Major private art museum specializing in Greek and other ancient classical collections.

Number of Internships: 20 graduate internships.

Type: Educational, administrative, curatorial, public relations.

Function/Duties: Assist in research and presenting exhibitions; planning programs and events.

Schedule: Full-time for 9-month or 12-month commitment.

Stipend or Pay: $18,000 for full-year and $12,500 for 9-month internship.

Academic Credit Offered: If applicable, per student's own arrangements with academic institution.

ELIGIBILITY: Graduate students or those who have recently completed graduate degrees; *Plus* internships may lead to career positions.

REQUIREMENTS: MBA, arts and related majors, or communications majors preferred.

APPLICATION PROCEDURE: Contact graduate intern program director for application details and deadlines.

GUGGENHEIM MUSEUM

1071 Fifth Avenue   **Phone:** 212/423-3500
New York, NY 10128   **FAX:** 212/423-3640

* * *

ORGANIZATION'S ACTIVITIES: Major private art museum concentrating on modern painting and sculpture in its exhibitions.

Number of Internships: 20 summer internships; more year-round as needed.

Type: Research, administrative.

Function/Duties: Assist in research and presenting exhibitions; some clerical work.

Schedule: Full-time in the summer; year-round according to need of particular project.

Stipend or Pay: May be arranged for summer openings.

Academic Credit Offered: Per student's own arrangements with academic institution.

ELIGIBILITY: College junior and senior and graduate students; *Plus* participation in regular seminars and field trips.

REQUIREMENTS: Arts and related majors preferred; must be available for full-time work in New York City.

APPLICATION PROCEDURE: Call for application; submit with letter, résumé, references, and transcript *to* Personnel Office *by* March 16 for summer program.

HIGH MUSEUM OF ART

1280 Peachtree Street NE
Atlanta, GA 30309

Phone: 404/892-3600
FAX: 404/898-9578

* * *

ORGANIZATION'S ACTIVITIES: Visual arts museum serving Georgia and the Southeast with permanent collections of decorative arts and 20th-century European and American art, with branch at Georgia-Pacific Center for folk art and photography.

Number of Internships: Varies; several each season.

Type: Available in most departments.

Function/Duties: Aid permanent staff with museum work as well as administrative duties.

Schedule: Full-time and part-time year-round.

Stipend or Pay: No.

Academic Credit Offered: Per student's own arrangements with academic institution.

ELIGIBILITY: Consideration given to students, non-students, or career-changers with appropriate qualifications.

REQUIREMENTS: Computer literacy, research skills; need 8-hour commitment minimum per week.

APPLICATION PROCEDURE: Send résumé and cover letter *to* Internship Coordinator *by* several months prior to start date.

HOUSTON MUSEUM OF FINE ARTS

P.O. Box 6826   **Phone:** 713/639-7540
Houston, TX 77265   **FAX:**   713/639-7399

* * *

ORGANIZATION'S ACTIVITIES: A museum "dedicated to serving all people by pursuing excellence in art through collection, exhibition, and instruction."

Number of Internships: 6.

Type: Various—teaching, curatorial, public relations.

Function/Duties: Assist full-time staff as needed, according to intern's interests.

Schedule: Full-time, summers (10 weeks, June–August).

Stipend or Pay: $2,500.

Academic Credit Offered: Per student's own arrangements with academic institution.

ELIGIBILITY: Undergraduate college students. *Special Eligibilities:* 5 internships open preferentially to minorities.

REQUIREMENTS: Interests, goals, and/or experience relevant to available assignments.

APPLICATION PROCEDURE: Write for application materials *to* Beth Schneider, Education Director, *by* late January (application materials available in October).

JACOB'S PILLOW DANCE FESTIVAL

P.O. Box 287   **Phone:** 413/637-1322
Lee, MA 01238   **FAX:**   413/243-4744

* * *

ORGANIZATION'S ACTIVITIES: America's oldest dance festival. Presents 10 weeks of dance performances and conducts a professional dance school each summer.

Number of Internships: 9.

Type: Technical theater/production.

Function/Duties: Interns will gain professional experience working as running crew for over 25 productions (over 100 performances), for the Pillow's two theater spaces and informal outdoor stage. Participants will work closely with the resident professional staff, as well as with visiting designers, stage managers, and artists. In addition to exposure to production and stage management techniques, responsibilities will include most aspects of production, including general theater maintenance, hanging and focusing lights, operating light boards and sound equipment, and general stage carpentry.

Schedule: Seasonal—3 months.

Stipend or Pay: $100 a month.

Academic Credit Offered: Per student's own arrangements with academic institution.

ELIGIBILITY: College and graduate students; *Plus* internship may lead to career position.

REQUIREMENTS: A strong interest in dance-related production is desirable.

APPLICATION PROCEDURE: Submit résumé and cover letter *to* Jackie Thomas. *Deadline:* March 4.

LINCOLN CENTER FOR THE PERFORMING ARTS

70 Lincoln Center Plaza   **Phone:** 212/875-5610
New York, NY 10023   **FAX:**   212/875-5414

* * *

ORGANIZATION'S ACTIVITIES: One of the nation's leading arts complexes, comprising the Metropolitan Opera, the New York Philharmonic Orchestra, the Vivian Beaumont Theatre, and the New York State Theatre.

Number of Internships: Varies; 12 or more.

Type: Arts administration.

Function/Duties: Assist professionals in education, finance, planning, public relations, and other departments on management and special projects.

Schedule: Full-time, 12 weeks in summer.

Stipend or Pay: $400 a week.

Academic Credit Offered: Per student's own arrangements with academic institution; *Plus* housing available.

ELIGIBILITY: First-year graduate students in appropriate studies.

REQUIREMENTS: Excellent communications skills and art experience.

APPLICATION PROCEDURE: Send résumé and cover letter, including discussion of career interests, *to* Vice President of Marketing *by* as early in academic year as possible.

LOS ANGELES PHILHARMONIC

135 North Grand Avenue   **Phone:** 213/972-7300
Los Angeles, CA 90012   **FAX:**   213/972-7300

* * *

ORGANIZATION'S ACTIVITIES: One of the nation's leading regional orchestras, with national and international reputation.

Number of Internships: Varies (numerous).

Type: Marketing, administrative.

Function/Duties: Varies, depends on projects.

Schedule: 20 hours per week minimum; year-round availability.

Stipend or Pay: No.

Academic Credit Offered: Per student's own arrangements with academic institution; *Plus* internships may lead to career positions.

ELIGIBILITY: Primarily undergraduate and graduate students, but non-students or career-changers with appropriate qualifications may be considered.

REQUIREMENTS: Studies and/or experience in marketing and/or music; positions are very competitive.

APPLICATION PROCEDURE: Send inquiries *to* Internship Coordinator. *Deadline:* Ongoing.

MANHATTAN THEATRE CLUB

453 West 16th Street **Phone:** 212/645-5590
New York, NY 10011 **FAX:** 212/691-9106

* * *

ORGANIZATION'S ACTIVITIES: A not-for-profit off-Broadway theater institution that provides a forum for the finest authors and artists in the U.S. and abroad, producing 8 plays per season with an emphasis on new plays and new playwrights.

Number of Internships: Up to 36, in at least 16 separate areas.

Type: Management, technical, press, artistic, production, and others.

Function/Duties: Hands-on, full involvement with activities of theater on-stage, backstage, and in the front office, depending on intern's skills and interests.

Schedule: Full- and/or part-time, both year-round and seasonal, with a minimum commitment of 3 months; must be available for long hours, evenings, and weekends.

Stipend or Pay: Some stipends are available, and some expenses may be covered.

Academic Credit Offered: Per student's own arrangements with academic institution; *Plus* well-organized, well-established internship program.

ELIGIBILITY: Primarily undergraduate and graduate students, but non-students or career-changers with appropriate qualifications may be considered.

REQUIREMENTS: Those with interest and/or experience in any aspect of theater are preferred.

APPLICATION PROCEDURE: Contact Internship Coordinator for details. *Deadline:* January and February, depending on program.

METROPOLITAN MUSEUM OF ART

1000 Fifth Avenue   **Phone:** 212/879-5500
New York, NY 10028   **FAX:**   212/570-3879

* * *

ORGANIZATION'S ACTIVITIES: One of the world's leading repositories and exhibitors of art of all types and eras as well as cultural artifacts and other treasures.

Number of Internships: Up to 36, in at least 4 special programs.

Type: Research, teaching, writing, curatorial assisting at the Cloisters collection and in the main building.

Function/Duties: Leading tour groups, conducting workshops; researching and writing about the collections.

Schedule: Some summer internships; some throughout academic year.

Stipend or Pay: Yes; ranging from $2,000 to $2,500 for summers; $1,500 per month for academic year; unpaid internships also open year round.

Academic Credit Offered: Per student's own arrangements with academic institution.

ELIGIBILITY: Undergraduate students for summer programs; graduate students for special summer programs. *Special Eligibilities:* Graduate and undergraduate minority students for 9-month positions.

REQUIREMENTS: Majors in art history, arts administration, or cultural history preferred.

APPLICATION PROCEDURE: Contact Internship Coordinator for details. *Deadline:* January and February, depending on program.

MUSEUM OF ART, INC.

1 East Las Olas Blvd.   **Phone:** 305/525-5500
Ft. Lauderdale, FL 33301   **FAX:**   305/524-6011

* * *

ORGANIZATION'S ACTIVITIES: Art museum designed by Edward Larrabee Barnes; the largest repository of William Glackens' work and owner of the largest collection of CoBrA (post–World War II expressionistic art) in the Americas. Also offers traveling exhibitions such as works from the Metropolitan Museum of Art, photographs by Annie Liebovitz and sculpture by Willa Shalit.

Number of Internships: Varies according to need.

Type: Public relations assistant.

Function/Duties: Writing, desktop publishing, clerical.

Schedule: Full-time and part-time from September to June.

Stipend or Pay: $6 per hour.

Academic Credit Offered: Per student's own arrangements with academic institution.

ELIGIBILITY: College and graduate students (majors preferred: journalism or public relations).

REQUIREMENTS: Must be good typist, detail-oriented; creativity and desktop publishing training are plusses.

APPLICATION PROCEDURE: Submit résumé, cover letter, and articles written *to* Cynthia Hancock, Manager of PR/Publications.

MUSEUM OF PHOTOGRAPHIC ARTS

1649 El Prado
Balboa Park **Phone:** 619/239-7559
San Diego, CA 92101 **FAX:** 619/238-8777

* * *

ORGANIZATION'S ACTIVITIES: Dedicated to presenting world-class exhibitions of the photographic arts (photography at present, film and video programs to be developed this decade). Award-winning international reputation.

Number of Internships: Flexible; varies with need.

Type: Development, education, and registrar.

Function/Duties: Assist staff of specific departments according to intern's skills and interests. Interns should offer commitment, dedication, flexibility, initiative, curiosity, creativity, excellent communication skills, people skills, and a desire to learn and grow on the job.

Schedule: Year-round, full-time and part-time internships available.

Stipend or Pay: None.

Academic Credit Offered: Per intern's arrangement with academic institution.

ELIGIBILITY: Undergraduate and graduate students are encouraged to apply; open to non-students and career-changers. *Special Eligibilities:* Minorities and women are particularly encouraged.

REQUIREMENTS: Must provide a cover letter expressing areas of interest, a résumé, and three references along with an application. (Preferred majors: Art History, Photography, Museum Studies, Arts Administration.)

APPLICATION PROCEDURE: Submit full application *to* Cathy Silvern Boeuer, Assistant to Director.

NATIONAL GALLERY OF ART

6th Street and Constitution Avenue NW   **Phone:** 202/737-4215
Washington, DC 20565   **FAX:**   202/842-2356

* * *

ORGANIZATION'S ACTIVITIES: A federally run, publicly funded institution housing the art collections belonging to the United States.

Number of Internships: Varies; numerous.

Type: Curatorial, educational, administrative, publications-related, guides.

Function/Duties: Assist professional staff and participate in areas of intern's special interests.

Schedule: Full-time summers.

Stipend or Pay: Yes.

Academic Credit Offered: Per student's own arrangements with academic institution; *Plus* may lead to career positions; includes special seminars.

ELIGIBILITY: Graduate and undergraduate students.

REQUIREMENTS: Enrolled in art history or related graduate or undergraduate programs; may NOT be offspring of Gallery employees.

APPLICATION PROCEDURE: Send inquiries *to* Summer Employment Coordinator. *Deadline:* Spring.

NEW YORK STATE THEATRE INSTITUTE

1400 Washington Avenue   **Phone:** (518) 442-5825
Albany, NY 12205   **FAX:**   N/A

* * *

ORGANIZATION'S ACTIVITIES: Publicly funded working/learning organization, operating in performing arts/education center.

Number of Internships: 75.

Type: Performance, production, education.

Function/Duties: Work in technical theater production, arts management, performing, and education.

Schedule: One semester, full- or part-time; year-round openings.

Stipend or Pay: Yes.

Academic Credit Offered: Per intern's arrangement with academic institution.

ELIGIBILITY: Undergraduate and graduate students are encouraged to apply. Non-students and career-changers are considered if qualified.

REQUIREMENTS: Majors preferred: Communications, Theatre Arts, Education.

APPLICATION PROCEDURE: Send inquiries *to* Internship Coordinator *by* 3 months prior to availability.

NORTH CAROLINA ARTS COUNCIL

Department of Cultural Resources   **Phone:** 919/733-7897
Raleigh, NC 27601   **FAX:**   N/A

*   *   *

ORGANIZATION'S ACTIVITIES: Coordinates and supports activities of local arts councils.

Number of Internships: Various, numerous openings statewide at local offices and operations offices.

Type: Planning, fundraising, financial management, programming, publicity, marketing, promotion.

Function/Duties: Aid professionals as needed and interested.

Schedule: 3 months, full-time, September–June.

Stipend or Pay: May be arranged.

Academic Credit Offered: Per intern's arrangement with academic institution.

ELIGIBILITY: Undergraduate and graduate students are encouraged to apply; non-students and career-changers are considered if qualified.

REQUIREMENTS: Varies with institution assigned. Majors preferred: Communications, Theater Arts, Education.

APPLICATION PROCEDURE: Send inquiries *to* Internship Coordinator *by* March.

OPERA COMPANY OF PHILADELPHIA

One Penn Square West   **Phone:** 215/981-1450
Philadelphia, PA 19102   **FAX:**   215/981-1455

*   *   *

ORGANIZATION'S ACTIVITIES: A nonprofit agency that runs Philadelphia's Opera Company and Theater Company.

Number of Internships: 12.

Type: Public relations, fundraising, education, production, administration.

Function/Duties: Assist professional staff in managing agency's affairs and companies' activities.

Schedule: Full- and part-time year-round.

Stipend or Pay: Yes.

Academic Credit Offered: Per student's own arrangements with academic institution; *Plus* may lead to career positions.

ELIGIBILITY: Graduate and undergraduate students.

REQUIREMENTS: Interests, goals, and/or experience relevant to available assignments.

APPLICATION PROCEDURE: Send résumé and cover letter *to* Internship Coordinator. *Deadline:* Ongoing.

PEARL THEATRE COMPANY

125 West 22nd Street   **Phone:** 212/645-7708
New York, NY 10011   **FAX:**   212/645-7709

* * *

ORGANIZATION'S ACTIVITIES: The Pearl Theatre produces a season of 5 classical plays in repertory with a resident company of professional actors. The internship program is connected to the Equity Membership candidate programs.

Number of Internships: 12.

Type: Acting, stage managing, technical, management.

Function/Duties: Participate in activities of 6 separate areas of theater and help out with box office, ushering duties as well.

Schedule: Full-time; season runs from late August to early May, with internships available for the full 5-show season, or for 3 shows. A summer internship is available for an administrative intern.

Stipend or Pay: $75 per week.

Academic Credit Offered: Yes.

ELIGIBILITY: All students (high school, college, and graduate); nonstudents and career-changers also considered; *Plus* minorities and special constituencies are encouraged to apply.

REQUIREMENTS: Interests, goals, skills, and/or experience relevant to available assignments.

APPLICATION PROCEDURE: Submit a letter of interest and résumé *to* Shepard Sobel, Artistic Director.

PERFORMING ARTS RESOURCES, INC.

270 Lafayette Street, #809   **Phone:** 212/966-8658
New York, NY 10012   **FAX:**   N/A

* * *

ORGANIZATION'S ACTIVITIES: PAR is a not-for-profit organization which offers assistance to individuals and companies seeking technical and administrative information in the performing arts. Established in 1981 as the Technical Assistance Project, and restructured in 1987 as PAR, it is an essential resource to anyone concerned with bringing live performance to the stage. PAR's services are offered through a Personnel Network, Consultation Services, Set Recycling Hotline, Seminars, Workshops, Publications, and its Resource Center.

Number of Internships: Varies with season and project needs.

Type: Administrative.

Functions/Duties: Assist executive director.

Schedule: Part-time or full-time, flexible.

Stipend or Pay: No.

Academic Credit Offered: Through intern's school.

ELIGIBILITY: Undergraduate and graduate students; career-changers and non-students also welcome to apply.

REQUIREMENTS: Prefer computer-literate, but will train.

APPLICATION PROCEDURE: Submit résumé and reference *to* Donna C. Brady.

PHILADELPHIA INSTITUTE OF CONTEMPORARY ART

118 South 36th Street   **Phone:** 215/898-7108
Philadelphia, PA 19104   **FAX:**   215/898-5050

* * *

ORGANIZATION'S ACTIVITIES: A national center for the exhibition and study of modern art.

Number of Internships: 7.

Type: Curatorial, education, business, fundraising.

Function/Duties: Assist professional staff in various activities of the institution; opportunities to learn about art and museums through practice.

Schedule: Full- or part-time in summer and fall.

Stipend or Pay: Rarely.

Academic Credit Offered: Per student's own arrangements with academic institution.

ELIGIBILITY: Students or non-students with academic backgrounds in art history.

REQUIREMENTS: Availability in Philadelphia.

APPLICATION PROCEDURE: Send résumé and cover letter *to* Business Administrator *by* August for fall semester and April for summer.

CONNIE ROGERS, INC.

152 East 94th Street   **Phone:** 212/410-3492
New York, NY 10128   **FAX:**   N/A

* * *

ORGANIZATION'S ACTIVITIES: Curatorial consultants, putting together art collections for major corporations.

Number of Internships: Flexible; varies with need.

Type: Curatorial assistant.

Function/Duties: Varied and interesting work in art business.

Schedule: Full-time and part-time, flexible term.

Stipend or Pay: No.

Academic Credit Offered: Per student's own arrangement with academic institution.

ELIGIBILITY: College and graduate students.

REQUIREMENTS: Interests, goals, and/or experience relevant to available assignments.

APPLICATION PROCEDURE: Submit résumé *to* Connie Rogers and follow up with a phone call.

SAN DIEGO MUSEUM OF ART

Balboa Park
P.O. Box 2107   **Phone:** 619/232-7931
San Diego, CA 92112-2107   **FAX:**   619/232-9367

* * *

ORGANIZATION'S ACTIVITIES: SDMA is San Diego County's largest visual arts resource with 10,000 members and 300,000 annual visitors. Collections include Italian Renaissance and Spanish Old Masters, American art, 19th-century European painting, Asian art, 20th-century paintings and sculpture, and the Frederick R. Weisman Gallery for California art. Education programs include teacher training, Family Days, a mobile museum (visits schools and neighborhoods), and music and film programs.

Number of Internships: Varies; fairly numerous.

Type: Education, fundraising, curatorial, design/installation, and registrar duties.

Function/Duties: According to intern's skills and interests.

Schedule: Part-time and year-round (3 to 12 months).

Stipend or Pay: No.

Academic Credit Offered: Per intern's arrangement with academic institution.

ELIGIBILITY: Undergraduate and graduate students are encouraged to apply; non-students and career-changers are welcome. *Special Eligibilities:* minorities, women, senior citizens are encouraged; *Plus* internship may lead to full-time employment.

REQUIREMENTS: Majors preferred: Art History, Education, and Museum Administration. Enthusiasm and a great sense of humor are required.

APPLICATION PROCEDURE: Request application and submit full application *to* Barbara Smith.

SAN JOSE MUSEUM OF ART

110 South Market Street
San Jose, CA 95113

Phone: 408/294-2797
FAX: 408/294-2977

* * *

ORGANIZATION'S ACTIVITIES: The San Jose Museum of Art is a lively visual arts center for the entire family. Serving the growing metropolitan community of San Jose and the entire Bay Area, the museum presents contemporary art in an exciting and dynamic environment designed to entertain as well as educate.

Number of Internships: 5–15.

Type: Curatorial, membership, public relations, development, and art school.

Function/Duties: Assist staff of specific departments according to intern's skills and interests. Intern should be familiar with general office procedures.

Schedule: Year-round, seasonal (at least six months), full-time and part-time internships available.

Stipend or Pay: None.

Academic Credit Offered: Per intern's arrangement with academic institution.

ELIGIBILITY: High-school, undergraduate, and graduate students are welcome to apply; open to non-students and career-changers as well.

REQUIREMENTS: Provide a letter of interest, statement of qualifications, and résumé along with an application.

APPLICATION PROCEDURE: Submit full application *to* Christy Adams.

SPOLETO FESTIVAL USA

P.O. Box 15
Charleston, SC 29402

Phone: 803/722-2764
FAX: N/A

* * *

ORGANIZATION'S ACTIVITIES: Nonprofit visual and performing arts organization that presents an internationally renowned summertime festival each year.

Number of Internships: 50.

Type: Administrative and production.

Function/Duties: Assist staff in variety of assignments related to presentation of festival.

Schedule: Full-time, May–June.

Stipend or Pay: May be arranged.

Academic Credit Offered: Per intern's arrangement with academic institution.

ELIGIBILITY: Undergraduate and graduate students are encouraged to apply; non-students and career-changers are considered if qualified.

REQUIREMENTS: Majors preferred: Communications, Theater Arts, Marketing.

APPLICATION PROCEDURE: Send inquiries *to* Internship Coordinator *by* March.

VIRGINIA MUSEUM OF FINE ARTS

2800 Grove Avenue   **Phone:** 804/367-0844
Richmond, VA 23221   **FAX:**   804/367-9393

* * *

ORGANIZATION'S ACTIVITIES: A cultural institution with a national reputation both for its collections and its cultural and community programs.

Number of Internships: 12.

Type: Management.

Function/Duties: Interns placed in one of a dozen management-related offices, to assist and learn from professionals in arts administration, human resources, finance, etc., depending on need and intern's interests.

Schedule: Full-time for 10 weeks in the summer.

Stipend or Pay: No.

Academic Credit Offered: Per student's own arrangements with academic institution.

ELIGIBILITY: Primarily graduate or undergraduate students, but recent graduates also will be considered.

REQUIREMENTS: Individuals with studies or a degree in topics relevant to arts and/or arts management, who are considering careers in art museums.

APPLICATION PROCEDURE: Send inquiries for complete information *to* Internship Coordinator in time to submit résumé, cover letter, references, and writing samples *by* early March.

VIRGINIA MUSEUM OF FINE ARTS (PROGRAM 2)

2800 Grove Avenue   **Phone:** 804/367-0844
Richmond, VA 23221   **FAX:**   804/367-9393

* * *

ORGANIZATION'S ACTIVITIES: A cultural institution with a national reputation both for its collections and its cultural and community programs.

Number of Internships: 1 paid minority internship.

Type: Professional development intern.

Function/Duties: Assist museum administration in developing ways to increase cultural diversity of institution, researching new concepts related to exhibits, and planning and implementing statewide educational programs in the arts.

Schedule: Full-time for one year beginning in September.

Stipend or Pay: $15,000 plus health benefits.

Academic Credit Offered: Per student's arrangement with academic institution.

ELIGIBILITY: A member of an underrepresented minority group who is a recent college graduate, master's degree candidate, or recent masters recipient in arts- or museum-related field.

REQUIREMENTS: Individuals with above qualifications who are interested in pursuing musuem career and who meet criteria of funding organization.

APPLICATION PROCEDURE: Send inquiries for complete information *to* Internship Coordinator in time to submit résumé, cover letter, references, and writing samples *by* February 1.

VIRGINIA MUSEUM OF FINE ARTS (PROGRAM 3)

2800 Grove Avenue　　　　　　　　**Phone:** 804/367-0844
Richmond, VA 23221　　　　　　　　**FAX:**　804/367-9393

* * *

ORGANIZATION'S ACTIVITIES: A cultural institution with a national reputation both for its collections and its cultural and community programs.

Number of Internships: 10.

Type: Curatorial, education, library.

Function/Duties: Interns are placed in one of the museum's exhibition-related offices, to assist and learn from professionals in curating, exhibiting, educating public and children's groups, depending on need and intern's interests.

Schedule: Full-time for 10 weeks in the summer.

Stipend or Pay: No.

Academic Credit Offered: Per student's own arrangements with academic institution.

ELIGIBILITY: Primarily graduate or undergraduate students, but recent graduates will also be considered.

REQUIREMENTS: Individuals with studies or a degree in topics relevant to arts and/or arts management, who are considering careers in art museums.

APPLICATION PROCEDURE: Send inquiries for complete information *to* Internship Coordinator in time to submit résumé, cover letter, references, and writing samples *by* early March.

WADSWORTH ATHENEUM

600 Main Street   **Phone:** 203/278-2670
Hartford, CT 06103   **FAX:**   203/527-0803

*   *   *

ORGANIZATION'S ACTIVITIES: Oldest public art museum in country. Houses a fine arts collection that includes 19th-century American painting; Renaissance and Baroque European painting; European and American decorative arts; the Amistad Foundation collection of African-American art and artifacts; and colonial American furniture, as well as rotating series of major exhibitions and special contemporary art.

Number of Internships: Flexible; varies with need.

Type: Curatorial, education, public relations, library, registrar, development, marketing.

Function/Duties: Assist staff of specific departments, according to intern's skills and interests.

Schedule: Part-time, year-round: 120 hours per semester.

Stipend or Pay: No.

Academic Credit Offered: Per intern's arrangement with academic institution.

ELIGIBILITY: Students in junior or senior year of college. Majors preferred: Art History, History, Art, English, Business, among others. High-school degree and a minimum of two years undergraduate college study in related coursework required; graduate students also accepted. Open to non-students and career-changers as well. *Plus* internship occasionally leads to full-time employment.

REQUIREMENTS: Must submit official academic transcript and two letters of recommendation along with application; personal interviews are also conducted.

APPLICATION PROCEDURE: Request application form; submit full application *to* Associate Curator of Education for Adult Programs. *Deadline:* Fall—July 15; Spring—December 15; Summer—April 15.

WALNUT STREET THEATER

Walnut at 9th Street   **Phone:** 215/574-3550
Philadelphia, PA 19107   **FAX:**   N/A

*   *   *

ORGANIZATION'S ACTIVITIES: A resident theater company that offers a variety of productions year-round and provides training programs for actors and production specialists.

Number of Internships: 12.

Type: Marketing, business, production, stage management.

Function/Duties: Assist in all areas of theater, front- and backstage.

Schedule: Full-time September–May.

Stipend or Pay: Yes.

Academic Credit Offered: Per student's own arrangements with academic institution.

ELIGIBILITY: Students or non-students with background and/or strong interest in theater.

REQUIREMENTS: Availability to meet theater schedules.

APPLICATION PROCEDURE: Send cover letter and résumé *to* Managing Director *by* April 1.

WOLF TRAP FOUNDATION FOR THE PERFORMING ARTS

1624 Trap Road   **Phone:** 703/255-1939
Vienna, VA 22182   **FAX:** N/A

*   *   *

ORGANIZATION'S ACTIVITIES: Major nonprofit theater organization presenting a variety of musical and dramatic productions in a large center near Washington, D.C.

Number of Internships: 30.

Type: Administrative and technical.

Function/Duties: Assist staff in variety of assignments related to presentation of festival.

Schedule: Full-time, May–June; part-time, fall and spring.

Stipend or Pay: May be arranged.

Academic Credit Offered: Per intern's arrangement with academic institution.

ELIGIBILITY: Undergraduate and graduate students are encouraged to apply; non-students and career-changers are considered if qualified.

REQUIREMENTS: Majors preferred: Communications, Theater Arts, Marketing.

APPLICATION PROCEDURE: Send inquiries *to* Internship Coordinator *by* 3 months prior to start date.

YESHIVA UNIVERSITY MUSEUM

2520 Amsterdam Avenue   **Phone:** 212/960-5390
New York, NY 10033   **FAX:** 212/960-5406

*   *   *

ORGANIZATION'S ACTIVITIES: Exhibitions, programs for adults and children, and publications related to Jewish art, history, and culture.

Number of Internships: Varies with availability.

Type: Curatorial.

Function/Duties: Research.

Schedule: Part-time, 4-month minimum.

Stipend or Pay: No.

Academic Credit Offered: Yes.

ELIGIBILITY: Upper-level college students and graduate students. Majors preferred: Art, History, Judaic Studies.

APPLICATION PROCEDURE: Submit résumé *to* Randi Glickberg.

Organizations/Resources for Further Information about Internships in the Arts

AMERICAN ASSOCIATION OF MUSEUMS
1225 I Street NW
Washington, DC 20005
202/289-1818

AMERICAN COUNCIL FOR THE ARTS
1 East 53rd Street
New York, NY 10022
212/223-2787

LEAGUE OF AMERICAN THEATRES AND PRODUCERS
226 West 47th Street
New York, NY 10036
212/764-1122

NATIONAL ENDOWMENT FOR THE ARTS
1100 Pennsylvania Avenue NW
Washington, DC 20506
For formal museum training programs, internships, and apprenticeships, call 202/682-5442. For jazz study apprenticeships for aspiring performers and professionals, call 202/682-5445.

See also pages 181 and 143–144.

INTERNSHIP SOURCES IN BUSINESS

■■■

Notes on Interning in Business:

Often overlooked by potential interns (and other directories), a large and growing number of businesses, industries, and professional firms have established active internship programs. Most interested and interesting are those on the fast track, like *Travel & Hospitality . . . Pharmaceuticals . . . Communications . . . Energy.* In addition to the corporate opportunities here, more are included in other sections, especially in *Communications*, *Environment*, and *Science*.

TIPS: During your internship in business . . . 1. Be businesslike in speech, behavior, and appearance. (That does not mean wearing a shirt and tie or pumps in a setting where even the CEO is in jeans; rather, pick the winners within the corporate culture you find yourself and imitate their costumes and manner.) 2. Adopt a mentor; find someone who will supervise your internship projects and give you feedback and guidance. In a well-structured internship, you may be assigned a mentor. 3. Do all you can to tour, even briefly, all departments of a company. If possible, arrange to intern in every department; if not, become familiar with all of them and do formal or informal "information interviewing" with as many people as possible. That kind of show of interest can create a priceless career network.

> *Glen, having just turned his second internship into a regular job with a small computer-related research company near Washington, D.C., cannot say enough about the "great opportunities possible interning in the private sector." Having gained management skills while interning at a trade association, he also made contacts there that led him to his current position. "There are so many niche industries and companies that no one has ever heard of where there are great jobs—but you'll never know till you try!" How to get the best experience: "Good cover letters and résumés are vital."*

ABBOTT LABORATORIES

1 Abbott Park Road   **Phone:** 708/937-6100
Abbott Park, IL 60064   **FAX:**   708/937-1511

* * *

ORGANIZATION'S ACTIVITIES: A diversified, global health care company with worldwide sales of over $8 billion, primarily in pharmaceuticals, hospital products, and nutritionals, employing some 50,000 in 44 countries.

Number of Internships: 200 or more.

Type: Science, engineering, computer, accounting, business, marketing, human resources.

Function/Duties: In labs, offices, and computer centers, "assigned by manager—meaningful and developmental, not busywork."

Schedule: Full-time, summers at company's Illinois headquarters as well as at other U.S. facilities.

Stipend or Pay: Yes, ranging from $8.35 for undergraduates to $25 an hour for graduate students; *Plus* free housing provided by company.

Academic Credit Offered: No, unless student has made special arrangements with academic institution; *Plus* interns are usually offered career positions.

ELIGIBILITY: Graduate and undergraduate students as well as career-changers with appropriate qualifications are welcome.

REQUIREMENTS: Prefer students with good academic records in the sciences and business.

APPLICATION PROCEDURE: Send résumé, including college GPA and field of interest, *to* College Relations Manager *by* March 31.

AMELIA ISLAND PLANTATION

P.O. Box 3000	**Phone:** 904/261-6161
Amelia Island, FL 32034	**FAX:** 904/277-5950

* * *

ORGANIZATION'S ACTIVITIES: A luxury resort/residential community located on 1250 acres of an island just off Florida's Atlantic coast, featuring beaches, sports, a health center, restaurants, and shops.

Number of Internships: About 20 per season.

Type: Needed in 6 distinct areas, including recreation, special events, horticulture, culinary, health and fitness, and public relations.

Function/Duties: Varies with each assignment.*

Schedule: Spring: February–May; Summer: May–September; Fall: August–December; 12–16 weeks per season depending on academic demands, 40+ hours per week; some evening hours; 1–2 days off per week.

---

*Amelia Island **Culinary Interns** work closely with recognized professionals in all facets of operation, including food preparation and presentation, baking and pastry, banquets, and purchasing. Additional compensation up to $7.50 per hour.

Amelia Island **Promotions Interns** participate in producing publications and other special projects that involve activities in all facets of the operation. Their tour of duty begins with an in-depth orientation and features regular seminars and reviews to assure the training benefits and educational value of the internship.

Stipend or Pay: $1,000 per season.

Academic Credit Offered: Per student's own arrangements with academic institution; *Plus* internships may lead to permanent positions. Aid in locating housing provided.

ELIGIBILITY: Undergraduate and graduate students.

REQUIREMENTS: Full or partial degrees in subjects related to position; "well-organized, flexible, highly motivated and outgoing"; available to work varied schedules.

APPLICATION PROCEDURE: Send résumé and cover letter, and employer and academic references *to* Ms. Amy Wampler *by* 3 months prior to seasonal start dates.

AMERICAN AIRLINES

P.O. Box 619616   **Phone:** 817/963-1234
Dallas, TX 75261   **FAX:**   N/A

* * *

ORGANIZATION'S ACTIVITIES: One of the leading airlines in the United States, expanded internationally; has the world's largest computer reservation system.

Number of Internships: 1 or more.

Type: Corporate communications.

Function/Duties: With corporate communications supporting the company's computer systems including the SABRE technology group, including marketing SABRE computerized reservations throughout the travel industry, the intern's activities encompass a wide scope that also includes assisting with publicity and media relations.

Schedule: 15 to 20 hours per week, year-round availability.

Stipend or Pay: No.

Academic Credit Offered: Per student's own arrangements with academic institution.

ELIGIBILITY: Primarily graduate and undergraduate students, but others may be considered if qualified.

REQUIREMENTS: Excellent communications skills, knowledge of computers.

Amelia Island **Recreation Interns** and **Health and Fitness Center Interns** are directly involved with seasonally appropriate recreation activities, exercises, and events for guests and residents, individually and in groups, and with the management of the recreation facility as a business. The internship includes completion of a special project and regular, formal evaluations throughout the term.

Amelia Island **Special Events Interns** and **Public Relations Interns** participate actively in the varied work of these departments and also participate in Management Training seminars and other workshops, while receiving regular evaluations throughout their internship.

APPLICATION PROCEDURE: Send inquiries *to* Teresa Hanson. *Deadline:* On going.

AMTRAK (NATIONAL RAILROAD PASSENGER CORPORATION)

60 Massachusetts Avenue NE   **Phone:** 202/906-2513
Washington, DC 20002   **FAX:** 202/906-3865

*   *   *

ORGANIZATION'S ACTIVITIES: The U.S. nationwide intercity passenger railroad, carrying some 40 million passengers annually.

Number of Internships: Varies.

Type: Public affairs, special events, and often others.

Function/Duties: Publicity, events planning, public relations, report writing.

Schedule: Full- and/or part-time; summers and school semesters.

Stipend or Pay: Stipend may be offered for summer internships.

Academic Credit Offered: Per student's own arrangements with academic institution; *Plus* 3 free round-trip tickets on AMTRAK. Internships often open elsewhere in company: request information through public affairs office.

ELIGIBILITY: Primarily undergraduate students, but non-students and career-changers also considered.

REQUIREMENTS: Excellent writing, communications, and interpersonal skills, plus some experience on computers.

APPLICATION PROCEDURE: Send inquiries *to* Sue Martin *by* two months prior to start date.

ARTHUR ANDERSEN & CO.

1345 Avenue of the Americas   **Phone:** 212/708-4000
New York, NY 10105   **FAX:** 212/708-3661

*   *   *

ORGANIZATION'S ACTIVITIES: A major national accounting firm, with offices around the country.

Number of Internships: 20+.

Type: Accounting, auditing, tax.

Function/Duties: After participation in training program, work as professionals jointly with full-time staff.

Schedule: Most in summer program; some year-round openings.

Stipend or Pay: Yes, at rate of entry-level employees.

Academic Credit Offered: Per student's own arrangements with academic institution.

ELIGIBILITY: Primarily students at undergraduate and graduate levels, though non-students and career-changers may be considered; *Plus* most interns are offered full-time jobs.

REQUIREMENTS: Good record in related coursework; highly competitive positions requiring intensive interviews.

APPLICATION PROCEDURE: Send cover letter and résumé *to* Michael Denkensohn to arrange for interviews *by* as soon as possible before internship.

ATLANTA GAS LIGHT COMPANY

P.O. Box 4569   **Phone:** 404/584-3780
Atlanta, GA 30302   **FAX:**   404/584-3709

* * *

ORGANIZATION'S ACTIVITIES: Natural gas distribution company with offices throughout Georgia and Chattanooga, Tennessee. Publicly held utility.

Number of Internships: Varies with availability.

Type: Public relations.

Function/Duties: Assist regular staff with writing, press relations, clips, events, etc.

Schedule: Full-time.

Stipend or Pay: Minimum wage.

Academic Credit Offered: Yes.

ELIGIBILITY: College and graduate students. *Preferred major:* Public Relations.

REQUIREMENTS: Excellent communications skills.

APPLICATION PROCEDURE: Send inquiries *to* Human Resources.

BANKAMERICA CORP.

555 California Street   **Phone:** 415/622-3456
San Francisco, CA 94104   **FAX:**   415/624-3107

* * *

ORGANIZATION'S ACTIVITIES: Major national and international banking and finance institution, offering a wide variety of consumer and business services.

Number of Internships: Varies (fairly numerous).

Type: Customer service, management, data processing.

Function/Duties: Varies according to locale and to intern's skills; includes jobs as tellers as well as in administration.

Schedule: Full-time summers, part-time during academic year, at headquarters and at branches and subsidiaries.

Stipend or Pay: Summer positions usually paid.

Academic Credit Offered: Per student's own arrangements with academic institutions; *Plus* internships may lead to career positions.

ELIGIBILITY: Primarily undergraduate and graduate students.

REQUIREMENTS: Studies and/or experience related to assignments; responsible individuals with good grade point averages.

APPLICATION PROCEDURE: Send inquiries *to* Employment Office for application to submit with résumé and cover letter *by* about 2 months prior to availability date.

BANKERS TRUST

280 Park Avenue   **Phone:** 212/250-2500
New York, NY 10017   **FAX:** 212/454-3078

* * *

ORGANIZATION'S ACTIVITIES: A leading financial institution with domestic and international interests.

Number of Internships: Varies; approximately 12.

Type: Corporate finance, real estate, international trade, Latin American investments.

Function/Duties: Assist staff in assigned positions.

Schedule: Mostly summer; some year-round.

Stipend or Pay: Yes.

Academic Credit Offered: Per student's own arrangements with academic institution.

ELIGIBILITY: Graduate and undergraduate students; *Plus* possibility of full-time employment following internship.

REQUIREMENTS: Prefer students in finance-related fields; availability for work in New York City offices.

APPLICATION PROCEDURE: Request application kit *from* Traci Farber *by* at least 3 months prior to internship.

BASF CORPORATION

8 Campus Drive   **Phone:** 201/397-2700
Parsippany, NJ 07054   **FAX:** 201/397-2737

* * *

ORGANIZATION'S ACTIVITIES: Major producer of chemicals used primarily in agriculture, with facilities throughout the country and in locations worldwide.

Number of Internships: About 200.

Type: Research, scientific, technical, sales.

Function/Duties: Participate in significant projects in biological and chemical laboratories; also learn and practice marketing techniques.

Schedule: Full-time, summers, at headquarters and other locations.

Stipend or Pay: Yes.

Academic Credit Offered: Per student's own arrangements with academic institution; *Plus* this is a competitive program and usually leads to career placement.

ELIGIBILITY: Graduate and undergraduate students.

REQUIREMENTS: Prefer students with excellent academic records in the sciences, particularly chemistry and biology.

APPLICATION PROCEDURE: Send résumé, transcript, and cover letter *to* Human Resources Manager *by* March 1 to be considered.

BEACON PRESS

25 Beacon Street   **Phone:** 617/742-2110
Boston, MA 02108-2892   **FAX:** 617/723-3097

*   *   *

ORGANIZATION'S ACTIVITIES: Beacon Press is a small, nonprofit publisher of general and scholarly nonfiction books. The business department oversees all financial matters, such as budgeting, long-range planning, cash flow, subsidiary rights income, and financial reporting. It is also responsible for inventory control, royalty reporting, and financial communications with Farrar, Straus & Giroux, the company that distributes Beacon's books to booksellers. In addition, the business department controls Beacon's on-site fulfillment center, from which review copies and special orders are shipped. In providing support to the business staff, interns have the opportunity to learn about the financial side of the publishing industry.

Number of Internships: Approximately 6.

Type: Business department.

Function/Duties: Varied—mostly clerical.

Schedule: Depends on the season and the intern's schedule, usually 15 hours per week, except during January when 9–5 for at least 3 weeks is expected; 4 terms: fall (September–December); January; spring (February–May); and summer (June-August).

Stipend or Pay: No.

ELIGIBILITY: All students. Career-changers and non-students welcome to apply. This is an equal opportunity/affirmative action employer.

REQUIREMENTS: Live in Boston area, strong interest in book publishing, good writing and clerical skills; prior office experience helpful but not essential.

APPLICATION PROCEDURE: Submit résumé, cover letter, and application form *to* Internship Coordinator.

BOB EVANS FARMS, INC.

3776 South High Street	**Phone:** 614/491-2225
Columbus, OH 43207	**FAX:** 614/492-4949

* * *

ORGANIZATION'S ACTIVITIES: Owner and operator of 280 full-service family restaurants. Produces and distributes fresh food products.

Number of Internships: Varies with availability.

Type: Public relations.

Function/Duties: Writing press releases, internal communications, and brochures; planning special events.

Schedule: Full-time and part-time, term flexible.

Stipend or Pay: Depends on skill level and number of hours.

Academic Credit Offered: Yes.

ELIGIBILITY: College and graduate students; Majors preferred: Public Relations/Communications.

REQUIREMENTS: Must have good written and verbal communications skills; computer experience helpful.

APPLICATION PROCEDURE: Submit résumé and cover letter *to* Tammy Roberts.

BP AMERICA

200 Public Square	**Phone:** 216/586-4141
Cleveland, OH 44114	**FAX:** 216/586-5751

* * *

ORGANIZATION'S ACTIVITIES: U.S. subsidiary of British Petroleum, explorers for and refiners of oil and gas and manufacturers of petroleum-related products; administrative headquarters are in New York City.

Number of Internships: About 60.

Type: Research, technical, management, computer science.

Function/Duties: Work in labs as well as in administrative offices.

Schedule: Full- and/or part-time, summers as well as school semesters; hours flexible.

Stipend or Pay: Most internships are paid.

Academic Credit Offered: Per student's own arrangements with academic institution; *Plus* internships usually lead to regular employment.

ELIGIBILITY: Primarily undergraduate students, but career-changers may be considered.

REQUIREMENTS: Good academic record in sciences and in business-related coursework.

APPLICATION PROCEDURE: Send résumé *to* Recruiting Office in time to arrange for interview *by* 2 months before start date.

BURROUGHS WELLCOME

3030 Cornwallis Road   **Phone:** 919/248-3000
Durham, NC 27705   **FAX:** 919/248-8375

*   *   *

ORGANIZATION'S ACTIVITIES: One of the world's largest pharmaceutical manufacturers, producing both prescriptive and over-the-counter medicines.

Number of Internships: 100-plus.

Type: Research, technical, scientific.

Function/Duties: "Meaningful" professional work on laboratory and other projects.

Schedule: Full-time, summers.

Stipend or Pay: Yes; equivalent to entry-level salaries.

Academic Credit Offered: Per student's own arrangements with academic institution; *Plus* internships often lead to offers of regular employment.

ELIGIBILITY: Graduate and undergraduate students.

REQUIREMENTS: Prefer interns with background and/or coursework in science.

APPLICATION PROCEDURE: Send résumé and cover letter *to* Human Resources Director *by* end of January.

CENTRAL HUDSON GAS & ELECTRIC CORPORATION

284 South Avenue   **Phone:** 914/452-2000
Poughkeepsie, NY 12601   **FAX:** 914/486-5894

*   *   *

ORGANIZATION'S ACTIVITIES: Gas and electric utility serving a 1,200-square-mile area in the Hudson Valley Region. Educational Services' responsibilities include the corporate speakers' bureau, teacher workshops, an educators' newsletter, power plant tours, and the yearly production of a catalog.

Number of Internships: 1.

Type: Community relations–educational services intern.

Function/Duties: The bulk of this internship entails a semester-long project involving the writing and developing of a slide presentation. In its final form, the slide presentation will be used for public appearances by members of Central Hudson's Speakers Bureau. This project involves research, interviewing, writing (including typing), organizational and photography skills. Depending on the intern's progress, a final project— negotiated with the student—will be assigned.

Schedule: Semester-long term.

Stipend or Pay: No.

Academic Credit Offered: Per student's own arrangements with academic institution.

ELIGIBILITY: College juniors and seniors; preferred majors: Communications and English.

REQUIREMENTS: Strong writing skills a must; photography skills a plus. On the day of the interview, the student might be asked to perform an editing activity.

APPLICATION PROCEDURE: Submit résumé and writing samples *to* Meg Kearney, Educational Services Coordinator. *Deadline:* Semester or summer prior to semester student wishes to intern.

CHARLES HOTEL IN HARVARD SQUARE

One Bennett Street   **Phone:**   617/864-1200
Cambridge, MA 02138   **FAX:**   617/661-5053

*   *   *

ORGANIZATION'S ACTIVITIES: The Charles Hotel is an independent luxury hotel in the heart of Harvard Square. It caters to the business and leisure traveler—and is known as Cambridge's hotel of choice for national and international leaders of industry. It features an award-winning jazz club, the Regatta bar, plus a bistro with indoor and outdoor seating.

Number of Internships: 1.

Type: Public relations.

Function/Duties: Assist with phone calls and communications within the hotel departments, maintain press clipping files, research and update editorial calendar lists, assist with special events, conduct hotel mailings and other sales/public relations projects as necessary.

Schedule: Part-time and full-time; flexible term.

Stipend or Pay: No.

Academic Credit Offered: If arranged by intern. *Plus* other types of internships often available elsewhere in hotel management.

ELIGIBILITY: High school graduates, college and graduate students; preferred majors: English, Communications, and Public Relations. Career-changers and non-students welcome to apply.

REQUIREMENTS: Career interest in hospitality; excellent communications skills.

APPLICATION PROCEDURE: Submit letter of introduction and résumé *to* Martha Solwan, Director of Public Relations.

CHARTER ONE FINANCIAL INC.

1215 Superior Avenue	**Phone:**	216/566-5300
Cleveland, OH 44114	**FAX:**	216/566-1465

* * *

ORGANIZATION'S ACTIVITIES: A banking and commercial financial institution.

Number of Internships: 30.

Type: Tellers.

Function/Duties: Work in commercial departments.

Schedule: Full- or part-time for 10 weeks each summer.

Stipend or Pay: Minimum wage.

Academic Credit Offered: Per student's own arrangements with academic institution; *Plus* internship may lead to permanent position.

ELIGIBILITY: Prefer college students.

REQUIREMENTS: Interests, goals, skills, and/or experience relevant to available assignments.

APPLICATION PROCEDURE: Send request for application *to* Human Resources Manager *in time to* arrange for interview in April.

CHESEBROUGH-POND'S, USA

33 Benedict Place	**Phone:**	203/661-2000
Greenwich, CT 06830	**FAX:**	203/625-1602

* * *

ORGANIZATION'S ACTIVITIES: Major international manufacturer of cosmetics and personal care products.

Number of Internships: Varies; fairly numerous.

Type: Management, some technical.

Function/Duties: Varies with assignment, according to intern's skills and interests.

Schedule: Mostly full-time, year-round; in headquarters or in regional offices.

Stipend or Pay: Yes.

Academic Credit Offered: Per student's own arrangements with academic institution, where applicable; *Plus* internship may lead to career position.

ELIGIBILITY: Primarily graduate students.

REQUIREMENTS: Interests, goals, skills, and/or experience relevant to available assignments.

APPLICATION PROCEDURE: Send inquiries *to* Jim Corcoran, Internship Coordinator. *Deadline:* Ongoing.

CONSOLIDATED EDISON

4 Irving Place   **Phone:**   212/460-4600
New York, NY 10003   **FAX:**   212/674-6570

* * *

ORGANIZATION'S ACTIVITIES: Utility company that provides power for New York City and nearby counties.

Number of Internships: Up to 200.

Type: Engineering, computer, business (undergrads); management (recent grads).

Function/Duties: Assist in technical and management departments; post-grad interns rotated through a variety of field assignments.

Schedule: Some summer-only; some year-round.

Stipend or Pay: Yes.

Academic Credit Offered: Per student's own arrangements with academic institution.

ELIGIBILITY: Engineering and business students; non-students also with backgrounds or majors in finance, accounting, and other nontechnical fields; *Plus* internships very competitive, but may lead to full-time employment.

REQUIREMENTS: Completion of junior year or college degree; interview and screening process.

APPLICATION PROCEDURE: Submit résumé and cover letter *to* Vincent Frankel *by* February 28 for summer program and October 31 for graduates' program.

COOPERS & LYBRAND

1251 Avenue of the Americas   **Phone:**   212/536-2000
New York, NY 10020   **FAX:**   212/536-3500

* * *

ORGANIZATION'S ACTIVITIES: A major national accounting firm, with offices throughout the country.

Number of Internships: Several hundred.

Type: Auditing.

Function/Duties: Performing auditing and accounting duties.

Schedule: Full-time, summers.

Stipend or Pay: Equivalent to entry-level salary.

Academic Credit Offered: Per student's own arrangements with academic institution; *Plus* internship usually leads to career position.

ELIGIBILITY: Undergraduate and graduate students.

REQUIREMENTS: Prefer juniors with business majors and first-year MBA students.

APPLICATION PROCEDURE: Send inquiries *to* Internship Coordinator at headquarters *or* at local office *by* early in the school year.

COORS BREWING COMPANY

Twelfth and Ford Streets **Phone:** 303/279-6565
Golden, CO 80401 **FAX:** 303/277-6517

* * *

ORGANIZATION'S ACTIVITIES: National manufacturer of beer (and glass products).

Number of Internships: 60.

Type: Engineering and management.

Function/Duties: Work with Coors engineering and administrative employees and participate in learning programs.

Schedule: Mostly summers, full-time.

Stipend or Pay: Some paid internships.

Academic Credit Offered: Per student's own arrangements with academic institution; *Plus* includes supervised educational programs as well as hands-on experience.

ELIGIBILITY: College students.

REQUIREMENTS: Interests, goals, skills, and/or experience relevant to available assignments.

APPLICATION PROCEDURE: Send inquiries *to* College Recruiting Representative *during* spring before internship.

CURTIS 1000

2100 Riveredge Parkway **Phone:** 404/951-1000
Atlanta, GA 30328 **FAX:** 404/955-0707

* * *

ORGANIZATION'S ACTIVITIES: Curtis 1000 is one of the nation's largest direct-to-business-customer marketers of envelopes and business forms.

Number of Internships: 4.

Type: Advertising, communications.

Function/Duties: Assist local advertising divisions and publicity staff; aid with market research and postal program.

Schedule: Part-time, semester or quarter term.

Stipend or Pay: No.

Academic Credit Offered: Intern must arrange through school.

ELIGIBILITY: College juniors and seniors.

REQUIREMENTS: Majors preferred: Advertising, Communications, or Public Relations.

APPLICATION PROCEDURE: Submit résumé and cover letter *to* Lynn Amaya.

CUSTOM FLOOR BROKERAGE

4 World Trade Center	**Phone:** 212/775-1649
New York, NY 10048	**FAX:** N/A

* * *

ORGANIZATION'S ACTIVITIES: Participating company in Commodities Exchange, trading precious metals.

Number of Internships: Several per season.

Type: Financial trading.

Function/Duties: Oversee clearing of brokers' trades and transactions in gold "pit" of NY Commodities Exchange.

Schedule: Full-time, 3-month minimum.

Stipend or Pay: Not usually.

Academic Credit Offered: Per student's own arrangements with academic institution; *Plus* positions may lead to full-time employment.

ELIGIBILITY: Primarily undergraduate and graduate students.

REQUIREMENTS: "Bright, quick learner, energetic, able to stand on feet all day, not easily frazzled, interest in financial markets."

APPLICATION PROCEDURE: Send inquiries *to* Michael Ferraro. *Deadline:* Ongoing.

DELMARVA POWER

800 King Street	**Phone:** 302/429-3595
Wilmington, DE 19899	**FAX:** 302/429-3665

* * *

ORGANIZATION'S ACTIVITIES: Public utility company covering the eastern Delaware, Maryland, and Virginia area.

Number of Internships: 1.

Type: General corporate, communications.

Functions/Duties: Assist staff members with duties, assigned according to intern's interests where possible.

Schedule: Full-time position during June, July, and August.

Stipend or Pay: $8 to $9 an hour.

Academic Credit Offered: Can be arranged.

ELIGIBILITY: Prefer college juniors; preferred majors: Journalism and Communications.

REQUIREMENTS: Availability to work full-time in Wilmington; excellent communications skills.

APPLICATION PROCEDURE: Request application *from* Human Resources. *Deadline* for completed application: February 1.

DELOITTE & TOUCHE

10 Westport Road
Wilton, CT 06897

Phone: 203/761-3000
FAX: 203/834-2200

* * *

ORGANIZATION'S ACTIVITIES: A major accounting firm with offices around the country.

Number of Internships: 200 or more nationwide.

Type: Accounting.

Function/Duties: Work as auditors, tax accountants, consultants.

Schedule: Full-time summers; part-time year-round.

Stipend or Pay: Yes.

Academic Credit Offered: Per student's own arrangements with academic institution; *Plus* internships usually lead to full-time employment.

ELIGIBILITY: Undergraduate students.

REQUIREMENTS: Prefer junior and senior accounting majors.

APPLICATION PROCEDURE: Send résumé, transcript, and cover letter *to* Recruiting Director at headquarters or at branch offices *by* several months prior to start date.

DUNHILL PERSONNEL SYSTEMS

1000 Woodbury Road
Woodbury, NY 11797

Phone: 516/364-8800
FAX: N/A

* * *

ORGANIZATION'S ACTIVITIES: A leading international multiservice employment organization.

Number of Internships: 1 or more.

Type: Communications.

Function/Duties: Assist corporate communications director with on-going duties and special projects.

Schedule: 10–12 hours per week, year-round.

Stipend or Pay: Small stipend.

Academic Credit Offered: Per student's own arrangements with academic institution.

ELIGIBILITY: Undergraduate students.

REQUIREMENTS: Prefer some background in journalism.

APPLICATION PROCEDURE: Send inquiries *to* Kathy McCollough. *Deadline:* Open.

ENTERPRISE RENT-A-CAR

8850 Ladue Road   **Phone:**   314/863-7000
St. Louis, MO 63124   **FAX:**   314/863-7621

* * *

ORGANIZATION'S ACTIVITIES: Automobile rental and leasing company with over 1,500 offices in the U.S. and Canada.

Number of Internships: Several hundred.

Type: Customer service, administrative.

Function/Duties: Entry-level rental duties and administrative support functions.

Schedule: Part-time, year-round and summer, plus Christmas break.

Stipend or Pay: Yes—varies with assignment.

Academic Credit Offered: If applicable, per student's own arrangements with academic institution; *Plus* internships often lead to career positions.

ELIGIBILITY: College undergraduate students in business or liberal arts majors.

REQUIREMENTS: Must be at least 18 years old, with valid driver's license and good driving record.

APPLICATION PROCEDURE: Send résumés or application forms *to* Group Personnel Services in city where work is desired. *Deadline:* Open.

ERNST & YOUNG

277 Park Avenue   **Phone:**   212/773-3000
New York, NY 10172   **FAX:**   212/773-1996

* * *

ORGANIZATION'S ACTIVITIES: A large national accounting firm, with offices throughout the country.

Number of Internships: 300 or more nationwide.

Type: Auditing.

Function/Duties: Work independently and as assistant in accounting, tax, and management capacities.

Schedule: Full-time in summers; some part-time year-round.

Stipend or Pay: Yes.

Academic Credit Offered: Per student's own arrangements with academic institution; *Plus* positions usually lead to full-time employment.

ELIGIBILITY: Mostly undergraduate and graduate students.

REQUIREMENTS: Prefer business students, particularly accounting majors.

APPLICATION PROCEDURE: Send inquiries *to* Director of Recruiting in headquarters or at local offices *by* 2 months prior to start date.

FEDERAL HOME LOAN MORTGAGE CORP. (FREDDIE MAC)

8200 Jones Branch Drive	**Phone:** N/A
McLean, VA 22102	**FAX:** N/A

* * *

ORGANIZATION'S ACTIVITIES: A stockholder-owned corporation chartered by Congress to create a flow of funds for mortgages, Freddie Mac helps to finance one in eight American homes.

Number of Internships: Varies.

Type: Accounting, computers, MIS, finance, economics, marketing, communications, real estate, library science, human resources.

Function/Duties: Providing assistance to "further the goals and objectives of the corporation."

Schedule: 12-week summer program.

Stipend or Pay: Yes; varies.

Academic Credit Offered: Per student's own arrangements with academic institution.

ELIGIBILITY: Graduate and undergraduate students. *Special Eligibilities:* "Seek diverse areas and backgrounds"; an equal opportunity employer; *Plus* may open way to permanent employment.

REQUIREMENTS: Appropriate major plus availability to work in Washington, D.C., area.

APPLICATION PROCEDURE: Send résumé and cover letter explaining interest in program and goals *to* Human Resources, Dept. IP. *Deadline:* As far in advance as possible before summer period.

FLORIDA DESIGN COMMUNITIES

2020 Clubhouse Drive
Sun City Center, FL 33573

Phone: 813/634-3311
FAX: 813/633-2565

* * *

ORGANIZATION'S ACTIVITIES: One of Florida's largest developers of master-planned communities. In-house corporate marketing/advertising/public relations agency.

Number of Internships: 2 per semester.

Type: Varies.

Function/Duties: Writing, editing, photography, community relations, special events.

Schedule: 16 hours per week, including one 8-hour day for at least 15 weeks.

Stipend or Pay: No.

Academic Credit Offered: No.

ELIGIBILITY: College seniors and graduate students; preferred majors: Communications, Public Relations, English, Advertising, Journalism, and Marketing.

REQUIREMENTS: Interests, goals, and/or experience relevant to available assignments.

APPLICATION PROCEDURE: Call Margie Adams Martin at 813/634-3311.

GENERAL FOODS USA

250 North Street
White Plains, NY 10625

Phone: 914/335-2500
FAX: 914/335-3511

* * *

ORGANIZATION'S ACTIVITIES: Major producer and distributor of food products.

Number of Internships: 75.

Type: Managerial.

Function/Duties: Pursue assignments and special projects in most divisions of headquarters ("not make-work").

Schedule: Mostly full-time, summers.

Stipend or Pay: Yes.

Academic Credit Offered: Per student's own arrangements with academic institution; *Plus* regular seminars with corporate executives.

ELIGIBILITY: Some undergraduate, mostly graduate students.

REQUIREMENTS: Prefer those pursuing business-related courses.

APPLICATION PROCEDURE: Send inquiries *to* Manager of College Relations *by* as early in the school year as possible.

GLAXO, INC.

5 Moore Drive
Research Triangle, NC 27709

Phone: 919/248-2100
FAX: 919/248-2381

* * *

ORGANIZATION'S ACTIVITIES: A manufacturer of prescriptive pharmaceuticals.

Number of Internships: Several hundred.

Type: Scientific, research.

Function/Duties: Perform scientific research in professional laboratories.

Schedule: Full-time, summers.

Stipend or Pay: Yes.

Academic Credit Offered: Per student's own arrangements with academic institution; *Plus* internships often lead to career positions.

ELIGIBILITY: Graduate and undergraduate students.

REQUIREMENTS: Excellent background in science.

APPLICATION PROCEDURE: Send résumé and cover letter *to* Human Resources Director *after* November 1 and *before* March 1.

GREEN CENTURY CAPITAL MANAGEMENT

29 Temple Place
Boston, MA 02111

Phone: 617/482-0800
FAX: N/A

* * *

ORGANIZATION'S ACTIVITIES: An investment advisory company offering environmental mutual funds designed to let investors earn dividends through environmentally sound investments.

Number of Internships: Varies with need.

Type: Marketing, research, analysis.

Function/Duties: Assist senior staff in initiation and followup of new ventures in new field.

Schedule: Fall and spring, minimum of 12 hours per week.

Stipend or Pay: No.

Academic Credit Offered: Per student's own arrangements with academic institution.

ELIGIBILITY: Undergraduate and graduate students; *Plus* internships may lead to full-time employment.

REQUIREMENTS: Availability to work business hours in Boston; background and/or interest in finance and/or environmental issues.

APPLICATION PROCEDURE: Call Adrienne Shishko for details *by* early in semester prior to internship.

THE HOME DEPOT

2727 Paces Ferry Road   **Phone:** 404/433-8211
Atlanta, GA 30339   **FAX:** 404/431-2739

*   *   *

ORGANIZATION'S ACTIVITIES: Nation's largest home center retailer.

Number of Internships: 1 or more at headquarters; more elsewhere.

Type: Communications and marketing.

Function/Duties: Press releases, media relations, events, etc.

Schedule: Part-time, full-time, negotiable term.

Stipend or Pay: Sometimes.

Academic Credit Offered: Yes.

ELIGIBILITY: All students; preferred majors: Public Relations, Journalism, Communications. Non-students and career-changers welcome to apply.

REQUIREMENTS: Interest in retailing preferred; excellent communications skills.

APPLICATION PROCEDURE: Submit résumé and writing samples *to* Valerie Lindsay.

HUE, INC.

358 Fifth Avenue   **Phone:** 212/645-2342
New York, NY 10001   **FAX:** 212/947-7389

*   *   *

ORGANIZATION'S ACTIVITIES: Manufacturer and distributor of women's hosiery, a subsidiary of Leslie Fay Companies.

Number of Internships: 4 at any given time.

Type: Creative services, sales, merchandising, production.

Function/Duties: Learn from and assist staff in area of interest, including hands-on responsibilities as assigned.

Schedule: Full- and/or part-time summers, school semesters, some year-round.

Stipend or Pay: No.

Academic Credit Offered: Per student's own arrangements with academic institution.

ELIGIBILITY: Primarily undergraduate and graduate students.

REQUIREMENTS: Computer skills; self-starting; education and/or experience in area of business or design a plus.

APPLICATION PROCEDURE: Send inquiries *to* Lisa Ferarro. *Deadline:* Ongoing.

ISLAND CREEK CORP.

250 West Main Street
Lexington, KY 40507

Phone: 606/288-3000
FAX: 606/288-3780

* * *

ORGANIZATION'S ACTIVITIES: Energy exploration company, seeking and developing coal, oil, and other fuels within the U.S.

Number of Internships: Varies.

Type: Management training.

Function/Duties: Work in management departments throughout the corporation.

Schedule: Full-time, 9 to 18 months.

Stipend or Pay: Regular salary.

Academic Credit Offered: N/A; *Plus* all paid benefits; leads to career employment.

ELIGIBILITY: Engineering graduates.

REQUIREMENTS: Must meet company criteria for employment; seeking those with degrees in various types of engineering.

APPLICATION PROCEDURE: Send inquiries *to* Human Resources Department. *Deadline:* Ongoing.

HEWLETT-PACKARD

3000 Hanover Street
Palo Alto, CA 94304

Phone: 415/857-1501
FAX: 415/857-5518

* * *

ORGANIZATION'S ACTIVITIES: Manufacturer and distributor of computers, printers, and other high-tech electronic equipment.

Number of Internships: 350.

Type: Technical, managerial, communications, sales.

Function/Duties: Assist regular staff in substantial capacities throughout corporation.

Schedule: Full-time summers (10 weeks) and part-time during school semesters at 60-plus locations around the country.

Stipend or Pay: Yes.

Academic Credit Offered: Per student's own arrangements with academic institution; *Plus* internship often leads to offer of regular employment.

ELIGIBILITY: Some high school, mostly undergraduate and graduate students.

REQUIREMENTS: Interests, goals, skills, and/or experience relevant to available assignments.

APPLICATION PROCEDURE: Send inquiries *to* Human Resources at headquarters office *by* as early in the school year as possible.

JOHN WILEY & SONS

605 Third Avenue   **Phone:**   212/850-6000
New York, NY 10158   **FAX:**   212/850-6088

* * *

ORGANIZATION'S ACTIVITIES: America's "oldest independent publisher," specializing in text, technical, scientific, and business books.

Number of Internships: 10.

Type: Editorial, managerial.

Function/Duties: Learn editing, finance, marketing functions.

Schedule: Summers, full-time.

Stipend or Pay: $250 per week.

Academic Credit Offered: Per student's own arrangements with academic institution.

ELIGIBILITY: Junior and senior students in college preferred; *Plus* possibility of regular employment following internship.

REQUIREMENTS: Availability in New York City during summer; interest in publishing as career.

APPLICATION PROCEDURE: *Contact* Employment Office for details.

K. HOVNANIAN ENTERPRISES, Inc.

10 Highway 35   **Phone:**   908/747-7800
Red Bank, NJ 07701   **FAX:**   N/A

* * *

ORGANIZATION'S ACTIVITIES: Designs, constructs, and markets single-family homes and townhouses in planned residential communities in New Jersey, Pennsylvania, Virginia, North Carolina, and Florida. Also develops and manages income-producing properties.

Number of Internships: 6.

Type: Construction, estimating, land acquisition, finance, human resources, and legal.

Function/Duties: Assist department heads with special projects.

Schedule: Full-time, in land acquisitions, finance, and legal during the summer; fall, spring, and summer for other departments.

Stipend or Pay: $550–$750 per week.

Academic Credit Offered: If arranged by intern.

ELIGIBILITY: Second-year MBA students, MBA in real estate, second year Master of Science students and Human Resources students; preferred majors: Construction Management and Civil Engineering.

REQUIREMENTS: Career interest in development and related matters preferred.

APPLICATION PROCEDURE: Submit cover letter stating area of interest and résumé *to* Sydney Koerner.

KRAFT GENERAL FOODS

555 Waukegan Road
Northfield, IL 60093

Phone: 708/998-2000
FAX: 708/998-2922

* * *

ORGANIZATION'S ACTIVITIES: A major manufacturer and distributor of food products and other consumer goods.

Number of Internships: 300.

Type: Managerial, technical.

Function/Duties: Professional-level work; content varies depending on assignment and intern's background; includes research in KGF food science laboratories.

Schedule: Full-time summers, for the most part, though in some regions part-time year-round positions are available.

Stipend or Pay: Equivalent to entry-level salaries.

Academic Credit Offered: Per student's own arrangements with academic institution; *Plus* internships usually lead to offer of regular positions; interns' learning is monitored through meetings and reports.

ELIGIBILITY: Undergraduate and graduate students. *Special Eligibilities*: Minorities and women especially encouraged to apply.

REQUIREMENTS: Coursework or experience relevant to assignments sought.

APPLICATION PROCEDURE: Send inquiries *to* Manager of Staffing & Organization for submission spring prior to start date.

LEVI STRAUSS AND CO.

1155 Battery Street
San Francisco, CA 94111

Phone: 415/544-6000
FAX: 415/544-3939

* * *

ORGANIZATION'S ACTIVITIES: The century-old manufacturer of blue jeans and other sportswear is focusing on "building a culture where employees have to take responsibility to improve and enhance both the company's output and their own value." The company's mission is to make a profit from quality products using ethical practices in a work environment that is "safe and productive, and characterized by fair treatment, teamwork, open communications, personal accountability, and opportunities for growth and development."

Number of Internships: 20.

Type: Public affairs, marketing, operations, finance.

Function/Duties: Assist and learn from permanent staff throughout organization as assigned according to need and to interns' interests.

Schedule: Flexible, usually summers, from 20 to 40 hours per week.

Stipend or Pay: Yes—up to $15 per hour.

Academic Credit Offered: Per student's own arrangement with academic institution; *Plus* highly competitive positions; can lead to permanent employment.

ELIGIBILITY: Upper-level undergraduate and graduate students.

REQUIREMENTS: Interests, goals, skills, and/or experience relevant to available assignments.

APPLICATION PROCEDURE: Send cover letter and résumé *to* College Intern Program well in advance of availability in order to arrange for interview and further processing.

LITTLE CAESAR'S PIZZA

Fox Office Centre
2211 Woodward Avenue   **Phone:**   313/983-6158
Detroit, MI 48201   **FAX:**   313/983-6197

*   *   *

ORGANIZATION'S ACTIVITIES: Major national food and restaurant business; corporate communications department maintains national media service.

Number of Internships: 4 to 8.

Type: Corporate communications intern.

Function/Duties: Write news releases, assist in coordinating special events, write articles for company's publications, work on community relations projects, compile media list, and conduct media follow-up.

Schedule: Part-time and full-time, 3-month term.

Stipend or Pay: Yes.

Academic Credit Offered: Through intern's school.

ELIGIBILITY: High school, college, and graduate students, preferred majors: Journalism and Communications. Career-changers and non-students welcome to apply.

REQUIREMENTS: Studying a related field, like journalism.

APPLICATION PROCEDURE: Contact Julie Ulle, Media Relations Specialist.

MARTIN MARIETTA ENERGY SYSTEMS

P.O. Box 628   **Phone:**   614/289-2331
Piketon, OH 45661 ·   **FAX:**   614/897-2985

*   *   *

ORGANIZATION'S ACTIVITIES: Exploration and development of fuel resources and other sources of energy.

Number of Internships: Varies, numerous.

Type: Management.

Function/Duties: Program for science and technical students to learn managerial techniques.

Schedule: Summers and/or semesters; on some college campuses and at Oak Ridge National Laboratory in Tennessee.

Stipend or Pay: Some tuition assistance offered.

Academic Credit Offered: Per student's own arrangements with academic institution.

ELIGIBILITY: Undergraduate and graduate students in computer science, physics, engineering, and other technical areas. *Special Eligibilities*: Primarily for minorities, especially African-Americans.

REQUIREMENTS: Faculty recommendations requested.

APPLICATION PROCEDURE: Send inquiries *to* Manager, Education Programs, Oak Ridge (or call 615/576-1065). *Deadline:* Ongoing.

MAUI HOTEL

2365 Kaanapali Parkway   **Phone:**   808/667-2525
Lahaina, Maui, HI 96861   **FAX:**   808/661-5831

*   *   *

ORGANIZATION'S ACTIVITIES: Large beachfront resort with 761 guest rooms, 4 restaurants, 3 lounges. Features include 5 swimming pools, full range of sporting activities, children's day camp, and a $2 million art collection.

Number of Internships: 2 or more.

Type: Public relations.

Function/Duties: Assist with public relations activities: Writing, editing press releases; handling phones and office work.

Schedule: Part-time; 20 hours per week for 3- to 6-month term; specific schedule flexible.

Stipend or Pay: No.

Academic Credit Offered: Yes.

ELIGIBILITY: Students with at least two years of college in various communications majors; non-students and career-changers also welcome; all participants eligible; Public Relations majors preferred.

REQUIREMENTS: Need a commitment of 20 hours per week; interns must provide own housing in Hawaii.

APPLICATION PROCEDURE: Submit résumé, cover letter, and writing samples *to* Julia Gajcak, Public Relations Director, *by* 2 months prior to beginning of internship.

MEADOWLANDS SPORTS COMPLEX

Paterson-Plank Road   **Phone:** 201/460-4043
East Rutherford, NJ 07073   **FAX:** N/A

* * *

ORGANIZATION'S ACTIVITIES: Major sports center, including stadium, arena, and racetrack.

Number of Internships: 1 or more per term.

Type: Media relations.

Function/Duties: Assist in writing releases and other promotional materials; research and distribute background information.

Schedule: Full- or part-time, including evenings, especially in summer.

Stipend or Pay: Stipend unless credit is earned; free parking and supper.

Academic Credit Offered: Per student's own arrangements with academic institution; *Plus* expert supervision to develop writing skills.

ELIGIBILITY: Graduate and undergraduate college students.

REQUIREMENTS: Interests, goals, skills, and/or experience relevant to available assignments.

APPLICATION PROCEDURE: Send inquiries *to:* Ellen Harvey. *Deadline:* Open.

MERRILL LYNCH INC.

225 Liberty Street   **Phone:** 212/449-1000
New York, NY 10080   **FAX:** 212/449-7370

* * *

ORGANIZATION'S ACTIVITIES: A national and international "multifaceted financial institution" with all types of offices in cities and towns around the country.

Number of Internships: Varies with locale; average about 15.

Type: Finance and management.

Function/Duties: Varies with locale; some research and investment-related work, some administrative.

Schedule: Part-time, year-round availability.

Stipend or Pay: Usually not.

Academic Credit Offered: Per student's own arrangements with academic institution; *Plus* internship may lead to career position.

ELIGIBILITY: Primarily undergraduate and graduate students.

REQUIREMENTS: Prefer courses or background in business-related topics.

APPLICATION PROCEDURE: Send inquiries *to* Human Resources Department (or to local offices). *Deadline:* Open.

OPINICUS CORPORATION

28870 US Highway 19N, Suite 4000   **Phone:** 813/799-4558
Clearwater, FL 34621   **FAX:** 813/799-4645

*   *   *

ORGANIZATION'S ACTIVITIES: Engineering firm specializing in the development, application, and integration of simulation software and hardware.

Number of Internships: Varies by project.

Type: Engineering.

Function/Duties: Participate in projects as they are assigned.

Schedule: Part-time, project by project.

Stipend or Pay: No.

Academic Credit Offered: Per student's own arrangements with academic institution; *Plus* participation may lead to ongoing work.

ELIGIBILITY: Engineering students, undergraduate and graduate; non-students with appropriate training.

REQUIREMENTS: Training and/or experience related to assigned projects; prefer computer and aero-engineers.

APPLICATION PROCEDURE: Send cover letter and résumé *to* Jennifer Smith. *Deadline:* Ongoing.

OSCAR MAYER FOODS CORP.

P.O. Box 7188   **Phone:** 608/241-3311
Madison, WI 53707   **FAX:** 608/242-6102

*   *   *

ORGANIZATION'S ACTIVITIES: A major national manufacturer of cured meat and other food products.

Number of Internships: 12.

Type: "Wienermobile" drivers; promotional campaigners and marketers called "Hotdoggers."

Function/Duties: Continuous travel through 10 to 12 states in Oscar Mayer promotional "hot dog" vehicle.

Schedule: 1-year, full-time assignment.

Stipend or Pay: $20,000; *Plus* health benefits, paid vacations, career counseling.

Academic Credit Offered: Per student's own arrangements with academic institution.

ELIGIBILITY: Students, non-students, career-changers with skills or background in dealing with the public.

REQUIREMENTS: Extremely competitive position; needs time, good grades, good humor, and energy.

APPLICATION PROCEDURE: Request application requirements for interview; call for *Deadline* and other details.

THE PEABODY ORLANDO

9801 International Drive   **Phone:**   401/345-4521
Orlando, FL 32819   **FAX:**   401/363-1505

* * *

ORGANIZATION'S ACTIVITIES: Prestigious resort-hotel; "Orlando's only 5-duck resort."

Number of Internships: 4 or more.

Type: Public relations and others.

Function/Duties: Assist local, national, and international media by supplying them with news and background material; also assist with special events and other public relations/marketing services.

Schedule: Part-time, summers and school semesters.

Stipend or Pay: No.

Academic Credit Offered: Per student's own arrangements with academic institution; *Plus* professional supervision to assure optimum learning experience.

ELIGIBILITY: Primarily undergraduate students.

REQUIREMENTS: Interests, goals, skills, and/or experience relevant to available assignments.

APPLICATION PROCEDURE: Send inquiries *to* Sonya Snyder. *Deadline:* Ongoing.

PIER 39 LIMITED PARTNERSHIP

P.O. Box 193730   **Phone:**   415/705-5542
San Francisco, CA 94119-3730   **FAX:**   415/981-8808

* * *

ORGANIZATION'S ACTIVITIES: Opened in 1978, this transformed cargo pier on the San Francisco waterfront has more than 100 specialty shops and two restaurants, making it an outstanding resource for those interested in marketing, tourism, or retail promotion.

Number of Internships: Varies.

Type: Marketing, promotion, tourism, advertising.

Function/Duties: Varies; includes writing, assisting with events, aid in advertising and promotion planning; "specific assignments depend on the needs of the Pier and the abilities of the intern."

Schedule: Part-time (minimum 12 hours per week), year-round; minimum 3-month commitment, with flexible start dates.

Stipend or Pay: No.

Academic Credit Offered: Arranged in conjunction with intern's school.

ELIGIBILITY: Junior- or senior-year college students and graduate students, especially those pursuing a degree in marketing, communications, or related fields; non-students and career-changers also invited to apply. *Special Eligibilities*: Open to all who qualify.

REQUIREMENTS: Availability for personal interview in San Francisco as well as for 2- to 3-day workweek during 2- to 3-month period in the city. Note that parking is free to interns.

APPLICATION PROCEDURE: Request application form and submit it, along with statement of interest and goals as well as letter of recommendation and résumé, *to* Kim Vaughn, PIER 39 Internship Program. *Deadline:* Open.

PROCTER & GAMBLE

P.O. Box 398707   **Phone:**   513/983-1100
Cincinnati, OH 45239   **FAX:**   513/562-4500

* * *

ORGANIZATION'S ACTIVITIES: Leading manufacturer of household chemicals, food products, and other consumer goods.

Number of Internships: Several hundred in various programs.

Type: Science, engineering, management.

Function/Duties: Assist and learn from staff and laboratory scientists in various projects, depending on interest and assignment.

Schedule: Mostly summers, full-time.

Stipend or Pay: Regular salary.

Academic Credit Offered: Per student's own arrangements with academic institution; *Plus* travel expenses reimbursed; internships often lead to career positions.

ELIGIBILITY: Undergraduate and graduate students, especially junior-year undergraduates. *Special Eligibilities*: Some programs designed only for minorities; some for PhD candidates.

REQUIREMENTS: Prefer chemical engineering and other science students.

APPLICATION PROCEDURE: Send inquiries *to* Director of Recruiting *by* March 1.

RANDOM HOUSE PUBLISHING

201 East 50th Street   **Phone:**   212/751-2600
New York, NY 10022   **FAX:**   212/872-8026

* * *

ORGANIZATION'S ACTIVITIES: One of the country's leading trade book publishers.

Number of Internships: 6.

Type: Similar to any entry-level job.

Function/Duties: Assist in every type of department to learn functions; also clerical work.

Schedule: Summer, full-time.

Stipend or Pay: $225 per week.

Academic Credit Offered: Per student's own arrangements with academic institution.

ELIGIBILITY: Undergraduate and graduate students.

REQUIREMENTS: Availability for full-time work in New York City; career interest in publishing a plus.

APPLICATION PROCEDURE: Submit résumé and cover letter; discuss details and arrange for interview *with* Personnel Recruiting *by* as early in the year as possible.

SPACE NEEDLE CORP.

203 Sixth Avenue North   **Phone:**   206/443-9700
Seattle, WA 98109   **FAX:**   206/441-7415

* * *

ORGANIZATION'S ACTIVITIES: Owns and operates the 605-foot tower that symbolizes Seattle and represents the top tourist attraction in the Pacific Northwest. Tower contains one of the busiest restaurants in the U.S. and attracts more than 1.2 million visitors annually.

Number of Internships: Varies.

Type: Public relations and marketing.

Function/Duties: Assist public relations department with marketing and other activities designed to increase Space Needle revenues.

Schedule: "Hours and time of year are flexible and negotiable."

Stipend or Pay: No, but free parking, lunch, other perks.

Academic Credit Offered: Yes; *Plus* internship may lead to career position.

ELIGIBILITY: Some high school seniors, but college undergraduate and graduate students are preferred; career-changers welcome.

REQUIREMENTS: Typing and word processing skills; strong writing and interpersonal skills; must have own transportation.

APPLICATION PROCEDURE: Send résumé and cover letter *to* Mr. R. Hap Hopper, Marketing Coordinator. *Deadline:* Open.

STANLEY WORKS

1000 Stanley Drive   **Phone:**   203/225-5111
New Britain, CT 06050   **FAX:**   203/827-3895

* * *

ORGANIZATION'S ACTIVITIES: A Fortune 500 manufacturer of diverse hardware and household products, including tools and builders supplies.

Number of Internships: Varies.

Type: Management intern program.

Function/Duties: Work and learn in different departments throughout corporation.

Schedule: Full-time, 6 to 12 months.

Stipend or Pay: Regular salary.

Academic Credit Offered: N/A; *Plus* internships lead to career employment.

ELIGIBILITY: College graduates.

REQUIREMENTS: Degrees in engineering, accounting, or marketing preferred.

APPLICATION PROCEDURE: Send inquiries *to* Human Resources Department. *Deadline:* Ongoing.

STORAGETEK

2270 South 88th Street   **Phone:**   303/673-5151
Louisville, CO 80028   **FAX:**   303/673-5019

* * *

ORGANIZATION'S ACTIVITIES: Research, development, and manufacture of high-tech information storage and retrieval equipment.

Number of Internships: 40 or more.

Type: Engineering and management.

Function/Duties: Assist and learn from engineers and administrators in variety of ongoing duties and special projects.

Schedule: Mostly full-time in summers.

Stipend or Pay: Yes.

Academic Credit Offered: Per student's own arrangements with academic institution; *Plus* many internships lead to career positions.

ELIGIBILITY: Primarily upper-level undergraduate and graduate students.

REQUIREMENTS: Studies in engineering or other related subjects.

APPLICATION PROCEDURE: Send inquiries *to* Senior Technical Recruiter. *Deadline:* Ongoing.

3M COMPANY (MINNESOTA MINING & MANUFACTURING)

3M Center
St. Paul, MN 55144

Phone: 612/733-1110
FAX: 612/736-3094

* * *

ORGANIZATION'S ACTIVITIES: Major conglomerate that is an international researcher, manufacturer, and distributor of wide variety of goods.

Number of Internships: 300.

Type: Engineering and technical; some managerial, communications.

Function/Duties: Varies depending on assignment, but work is substantive in structured program.

Schedule: Full-time summers, some part-time during school year, at locations around the country and the world; also sponsors 2-year co-op program for engineering students.

Stipend or Pay: Yes.

Academic Credit Offered: Per student's own arrangements with academic institution; *Plus* employee benefits given; internship usually leads to offer of regular position.

ELIGIBILITY: Graduate and undergraduate students.

REQUIREMENTS: Coursework and career goals relevant to assignments sought.

APPLICATION PROCEDURE: Send inquiries *to* Student Programs Manager *by* as early in the school year as possible.

SCHOLASTIC, INC.

555 Broadway   **Phone:** 212/343-6100
New York, NY 10012   **FAX:** 212/343-6928

*   *   *

ORGANIZATION'S ACTIVITIES: Leading publisher of books, magazines, and other materials for young people and educators.

Number of Internships: Numerous; varies.

Type: Magazine and book editorial and design, business, and production.

Function/Duties: Assist in every aspect of company's activities.

Schedule: 10 weeks in summer, full-time weekdays.

Stipend or Pay: $315 per week.

Academic Credit Offered: Per student's own arrangements with academic institution.

ELIGIBILITY: College students preferred.

REQUIREMENTS: Availability for work in New York City; career interest in publishing.

APPLICATION PROCEDURE: Call for application form; submit *to* Human Resources Department *by* February 28.

SEALASKA CORPORATION

One Sealaska Plaza, Suite 400   **Phone:** 907/586-1512
Juneau, AK 99801   **FAX:** 907/586-9227

*   *   *

ORGANIZATION'S ACTIVITIES: Sealaska Corporation is one of 13 regional corporations created under the Alaska Native Claims Settlement Act enacted into law by Congress in 1971. Currently, the company's primary activities are as a harvester and marketer of timber and as an investment portfolio manager. The company also is actively studying another major asset for development—more than 600,000 acres of subsurface mineral rights.

Type: Engineering, management, accounting, computer technology, communications, law.

Function/Duties: Assist and learn from regular staff and administrators with ongoing duties and special projects related to intern's goals and interests.

Schedule: Full-time, usually 12 weeks during the summer.

Stipend or Pay: Yes, between $10.25 and $11.25 per hour.

Academic Credit Offered: May be arranged.

ELIGIBILITY: Must be at least a sophomore in college.

REQUIREMENTS: Must be enrolled in college on a full-time basis and have at least a 2.5 GPA.

APPLICATION PROCEDURE: Complete an application form and return it to Sealaska with recent college transcripts, a letter of recommendation from the school, a résumé, and a cover letter indicating why you wish to work at Sealaska; additional information may be included. Send *to* Ron Williams, Shareholder Relations Coordinator.

TELEWAY INC.

1600 Stewart Avenue
Westbury, NY 11590

Phone: 516/237-6000
FAX: 516/237-6060

* * *

ORGANIZATION'S ACTIVITIES: Teleway, Inc., is the parent company of 1-800-FLOWERS. Activities include the solicitation and processing of FTD and other wire service orders for floral and other gift products using the toll-free telephone number 1-800-FLOWERS.

Number of Internships: Varies; numerous.

Type: Marketing and public relations campaigns.

Function/Duties: Learn from and assist regular staff with ongoing duties and special projects.

Schedule: Part-time position.

Stipend or Pay: Yes.

Academic Credit Offered: Per student's own arrangement with academic institution.

ELIGIBILITY: High school, college, and graduate students; preferred majors: Marketing and Communications; non-students and career-changers welcome.

REQUIREMENTS: Excellent communication skills; ability to work well with others and with public.

APPLICATION PROCEDURE: Submit cover letter and résumé *to* Tracey Gitters, Communications Manager.

US WEST INC.

7800 East Orchard Road
Englewood, CO 80111

Phone: 303/793-6500
FAX: 303/793-6654

* * *

ORGANIZATION'S ACTIVITIES: A transnational diversified corporation in communications, finance, marketing, and other services.

Number of Internships: 200.

Type: Technical, managerial, communications.

Function/Duties: Primarily engineering and computer-related openings, but also learn from and assist managers and administrators in ongoing duties as well as special projects.

Schedule: Full-time, summers.

Stipend or Pay: Yes.

Academic Credit Offered: Per student's own arrangements with academic institution; *Plus* internships often lead to full-time employment.

ELIGIBILITY: Primarily upper-level undergraduate students.

REQUIREMENTS: Interests, goals, skills, and/or experience relevant to available assignments.

APPLICATION PROCEDURE: Send inquiries *to* Staffing Manager *by* as early in the school year as possible.

WALDENBOOKS HEADQUARTERS

201 High Ridge Road   **Phone:** 203/352-2000
Stamford, CT 06904   **FAX:**   203/352-2191

* * *

ORGANIZATION'S ACTIVITIES: Waldenbooks is a national retailer of books, magazines, and audio books and videos; owns over 1,200 stores nationwide.

Number of Internships: Varies with availability.

Type: Marketing and public relations.

Function/Duties: Writing press releases and advertising copy, proofing copy, handling book donations.

Schedule: 8 hours a week (fall, spring, summer semesters).

Stipend or Pay: No.

Academic Credit Offered: Yes.

ELIGIBILITY: College students; preferred majors: Communications and English.

REQUIREMENTS: Good writing skills, typing; some knowledge of computers is helpful. Student should be within an hour's drive of the company.

APPLICATION PROCEDURE: Submit résumé *to* Susan Arnold.

WALT DISNEY

500 South Buena Vista Street   **Phone:** 818/560-1000
Burbank, CA 91521   **FAX:**   818/560-1930

* * *

ORGANIZATION'S ACTIVITIES: Movie and animation studio; headquarters for film production company.

Number of Internships: Varies.

Type: Animation, film production, finance, marketing.

Function/Duties: Assist staff in creative or managerial areas of interest.

Schedule: Full-time summers.

Stipend or Pay: $200 per week.

Academic Credit Offered: Per student's own arrangements with academic institution.

ELIGIBILITY: Primarily undergraduate and graduate students, as well as recent grads.

REQUIREMENTS: Some experience in area of interest is useful.

APPLICATION PROCEDURE: Send résumé and cover letter *to* Production Administrator *between* January 1 and March 31.

WESTIN HOTELS AND RESORTS

2001 Sixth Avenue   **Phone:** 206/443-5000
13th Floor   **FAX:**   206/443-8997
Seattle, WA 98121

* * *

ORGANIZATION'S ACTIVITIES: Westin Hotels and Resorts is a hotel management company representing over 75 hotels and resorts in 15 countries.

Number of Internships: 3 or more.

Type: Public relations, management.

Function/Duties: Assist public relations manager and other administrators as needed

Schedule: Full-time or part-time, 3-month minimum.

Stipend or Pay: No.

Academic Credit Offered: Yes.

ELIGIBILITY: College and graduate students; preferred majors: Communications and Public Relations. Non-students with prior experience or working knowledge of the field are also welcome to apply.

REQUIREMENTS: All applicants must have knowledge of public relations and sound writing skills.

APPLICATION PROCEDURE: Submit résumé and cover letter *to* Elizabeth Vasey.

WEYERHAUSER COMPANY

33663 Weyerhauser Way   **Phone:** 206/924-2345
Federal Way, WA 98003   **FAX:**   206/924-7407

*   *   *

ORGANIZATION'S ACTIVITIES: Diversified international corporation with interests in land, timber, lumber, paper, packaging, and other enterprises.

Number of Internships: Varies.

Type: Technical and managerial—in 3 formats (see following).

Function/Duties: **Summer interns** work in technical or forestry areas; **manufacturing interns** work in production areas; and **professional interns** work full-time to learn the business.

Schedule: Professional internships are 1- or 2-year assignments; others are part-time and/or summers only.

Stipend or Pay: Regular salary plus benefits.

Academic Credit Offered: Per student's own arrangements with academic institution where applicable; *Plus* internships lead to regular career positions.

ELIGIBILITY: Primarily college students for part-time programs; professional interns must be college graduates.

REQUIREMENTS: Background and/or education related to program of interest is required.

APPLICATION PROCEDURE: Send inquiries *to* Manager of Recruiting. *Deadline:* Varies.

WINDERMERE SERVICES COMPANY

5424 Sand Point Way, NE   **Phone:** 206/527-3801
Seattle, WA 98105   **FAX:**   206/526-7629

*   *   *

ORGANIZATION'S ACTIVITIES: Provides communications, legal, accounting, and other services to real estate offices.

Number of Internships: 1 or more.

Type: Communications.

Function/Duties: Assist in welcoming new sales associates to Windermere Real Estate by writing bios for in-house newsletters and news releases for state-wide media. Assist in general communications projects such as mailing list updates, miscellaneous news release and press kit organization, etc.

Schedule: 12 to 15 hours per week.

Stipend or Pay: Start at $5 per hour.

Academic Credit Offered: Available if arranged by intern.

ELIGIBILITY: College students preferred.

REQUIREMENTS: Macintosh skills necessary.

APPLICATION PROCEDURE: Send résumé and cover letter *to* Suzie Lettunich or Jeanne Grainger.

Organizations/Resources for Further Information about Internships in Business

With most jobs—and internship openings—available in small- to mid-sized companies (which are not likely to list internship opportunities in any directory), those should be among your prime targets. Check out the memberships of trade and professional associations in your desired field, for a start. To conduct a national job search within *small* organizations, the following reference books are worth investigating at your campus or local library:

America's Fastest Growing Employers (1992, Bob Adams), profiles 700 high-growth organizations.

Corporate Technology Directory (Corporate Technology Information Services), lists 35,000 high-tech companies, including 22,000 that employ fewer than 1,000 people each.

You can also contact these small-business organizations:

NFIB NATIONAL FEDERATION OF
  INDEPENDENT BUSINESS
Suite 700
600 Maryland Avenue SW
Washington, DC 20024
202/554-9000

150 West 20th Avenue
San Mateo, CA 94403
415/341-7441

Suite 680
3401 West End Avenue
Nashville, TN 37203
615/297-9955

NATIONAL ASSOCIATION OF PRIVATE
  ENTERPRISE
P.O. Box 470397
Fort Worth, TX 76147
800/223-NAPE

Many directories list companies and their offerings. This one:

The Career Guide
Dun & Bradstreet, Inc.
Three Sylvan Way
Parsippany, NJ 07054

An annual volume available in many libraries, this one includes notations about internships and work-study in its detailed corporate listings.

Here are a few of the thousands of trade and professional associations that can provide information about internship possibilities in your career of choice:

Banking

AMERICAN BANKERS ASSOCIATION
1120 Connecticut Avenue NW
Washington, DC 20036
202/663-5221

Securities

NATIONAL ASSOCIATION OF SECURITIES
   DEALERS
1735 K Street NW
Washington, DC 20006
202/728-8000

PUBLIC SECURITIES ASSOCIATION
40 Broad Street, 12th Floor
New York, NY 10004
212/809-7000

SECURITIES INDUSTRY ASSOCIATION
120 Broadway
New York, NY 10271
212/608-1500

Insurance

ALLIANCE OF AMERICAN INSURERS
1501 Woodfield Road
Schaumburg, IL 60173-4980
708/330-8500

INSURANCE INFORMATION INSTITUTE
110 William Street
New York, NY 10038
212/669-9200

NATIONAL ASSOCIATION OF PROFESSIONAL
   INSURANCE AGENTS
400 North Washington Street
Alexandria, VA 22314
703/836-9340

For a full listing of groups that promote the advancement of one or another area of professional interest, see these annuals in your library:

Encyclopedia of Associations, available from Gale Publications

National Trade & Professional Associations, available from Columbia Books

Or, use your computer to go online with databases that can bring you up to date on opportunities. Two related to business:

DOW JONES & CO., INC.
Route 1 at Ridge Road
South Brunswick, NJ 08852
609/520-4000

Offers a full range of business information from encyclopedias to investment data, business publications, and newspapers.

NEWSNET
945 Haverford Road
Bryn Mawr, PA 19010
800/345-1301 or 215/527-8030

Has an extensive collection of newsletters in all fields, including economics, industry, law, and medicine.

Also see pages 297–298 and 382–386.

Internship Sources in Communications

Notes on Interning in Communications:

The communications fields—encompassing publishing, public relations, advertising, broadcasting, and the news media—are the ones where internships are almost a necessity for career success, so competition for these openings is keen. On the other hand, most organizations within the field have come to rely heavily on interns, with the result that they are eager to attract good ones and often have well-organized internship programs to offer.

TIPS: 1. The public relations/public affairs/corporate communications department of any organization is a great vantage point for a clear view of the whole operation—so even if you do not plan a lifetime of PR, you can learn a lot about a given industry or profession through a stint in this division. 2. This is one field where English majors have career possibilities ... and computer skills are a big plus for landing a communications internship.

> *"It changed my life!" says Ed of his internship in a publicity firm. "It wasn't always glamorous, but provided me with the opportunity to use my theoretical skills, and, moreover, gave me insight into an industry I've thirsted to be a part of for so long. I learned how publicity affects sales. . . . Most important, I was able to solidify what I want to do with my life. . . ."*
>
> *Of her internship in corporate communications, Kristine says, "It was a great learning experience and a way to get my foot in the door. Without this internship I'd be nowhere. I learned how to do business consulting and also learned a lot about the company through working in corporate PR."*

Note that internships in most other sections of this book offer communications positions if you seek a specific focus for your communications skills.

ACCURACY IN MEDIA, Inc.

1275 K Street NW
Suite 1150   **Phone:** 202/371-6710
Washington, DC 20005   **FAX:** 202/371-9054

* * *

ORGANIZATION'S ACTIVITIES: Accuracy in Media is an organization that serves as a consumer advocate for broadcast fairness.

Number of Internships: Flexible; varies with need.

Type: Reporter/writer.

Function/Duties: Assist staff according to intern's skills and interests (i.e., writing and research).

Schedule: Year-round full-time (12 to 16 months).

Stipend or Pay: $125 per week.

Academic Credit Offered: Per intern's arrangement with academic institution; *Plus* internship sometimes leads to full-time employment.

ELIGIBILITY: Students with a high-school education, including students presently attending high school and above, are encouraged to apply; open to non-students and career-changers as well.

REQUIREMENTS: Provide a résumé and writing sample on a current event subject along with an application.

APPLICATION PROCEDURE: Submit full application *to* Donald Irvine. *Deadlines:*Fall—August 15; spring—November 15; summer—March 15.

ACROPOLIS BOOKS

13950 Park Center Road   **Phone:** 703/689-2453
Herndon, VA 22071   **FAX:** 703/709-0942

* * *

ORGANIZATION'S ACTIVITIES: Mid-sized publisher of nonfiction books.

Number of Internships: 3 or more.

Type: Editorial, publicity, marketing.

Function/Duties: Assist in office of choice with substantive efforts involving manuscripts, authors, public relations.

Schedule: Full-time summers and/or part-time semesters.

Stipend or Pay: Yes.

Academic Credit Offered: Per student's own arrangements with academic institution.

ELIGIBILITY: Primarily college students.

REQUIREMENTS: Prefer upper-level undergraduates with relevant majors and/or interests.

APPLICATION PROCEDURE: Send inquiries *to* Personnel Manager. *Deadline:*Varies.

AFRICA REPORT

African-American Institute
833 UN Plaza
New York, NY 10017

Phone: 212/949-5666
FAX: N/A

* * *

ORGANIZATION'S ACTIVITIES: A journal on African and African-American affairs.

Number of Internships: 4.

Type: Research, editorial, clerical, writing.

Function/Duties: Maintaining files, producing books and articles, updating resources.

Schedule: Part-time or full-time, 2 months to 1 year, year-round.

Stipend or Pay: No.

Academic Credit Offered: Per student's own arrangements with academic institution.

ELIGIBILITY: High school through graduate students as well as interested non-students.

REQUIREMENTS: Interests, goals, and/or experience relevant to available assignments.

APPLICATION PROCEDURE: For details, *contact* Research Editor. *Deadline:* Open.

AGORA, INC.

824 East Baltimore Street
Baltimore, MD 21202

Phone: 410/234-0515
FAX: 410/837-1999

* * *

ORGANIZATION'S ACTIVITIES: Direct-mail publisher of travel and financial newsletters and/or books.

Number of Internships: Varies with need.

Type: Editorial interns.

Function/Duties: General research, writing, and other editorial duties.

Schedule: Year-round for about 2 to 6 months.

Stipend or Pay: Daily expenses covered.

Academic Credit Offered: Yes, depending on arrangements with academic institution.

ELIGIBILITY: Students who are at least at junior level of undergraduate studies or recent college graduates; need strong background in English, journalism, and/or liberal arts.

REQUIREMENTS: Great communication skills, research skills, and a basic knowledge of world geography.

APPLICATION PROCEDURE: Submit résumé with cover letter *to* Kathleen Peddicord. *Deadline:* No.

AMNESTY INTERNATIONAL—USA

322 Eighth Avenue   **Phone:** 212/807-8400
New York, NY 10001-1451   **FAX:**   212/627-1451

* * *

ORGANIZATION'S ACTIVITIES: Amnesty International promotes awareness of and adherence to Human Rights as set down in the Universal Declaration of Human Rights. Within the New York office, special projects are handled, proposed local cases are interviewed before going on to the international body; the staff also manages administrative duties for the country.

Number of Internships: Varies with availability and need.

Type: Executive unit—publications, communications.

Function/Duties: Active participation in special projects; aid staff with ongoing assignments.

Schedule: Full-time and part-time; term varies.

Stipend or Pay: Sometimes.

Academic Credit Offered: Must be arranged by intern.

ELIGIBILITY: All students. Career-changers and non-students also welcome to apply.

REQUIREMENTS: Each internship requires distinct abilities and tasks. Most require computer literacy or proven ability to master a computer program efficiently.

APPLICATION PROCEDURE: Call Susan Farley, Internship Coordinator and National Membership Program Assistant, for application form and list of current opportunities. Must send a completed application form, writing sample, résumé, and one letter of recommendation.

ARCHIVE FILMS INC.

530 West 25th Street   **Phone:** 212/620-3955
New York, NY 10001   **FAX:**   212/645-2137

* * *

ORGANIZATION'S ACTIVITIES: A leading international supplier of motion picture stock footage for commercial, broadcast, corporate, educational, and other purposes since 1979.

Number of Internships: 30.

Type: Acquisitions, research, and film sales.

Function/Duties: Assist staff of specific departments according to intern's skills and interests. Intern must have good verbal and communication skills.

Schedule: Year-round, seasonal (6 weeks or 3 months) internships available.

Stipend or Pay: No.

Academic Credit Offered: Per intern's arrangement with academic institution.

ELIGIBILITY: High school seniors, undergraduate, and graduate students are encouraged to apply; preferred majors: Cinema Studies, History, Film; *Plus* internship may lead to employment opportunities.

REQUIREMENTS: Provide a cover letter and résumé along with an application.

APPLICATION PROCEDURE: Submit full application *to* Lisa Sutherland. *Deadline:* No.

THE ARIZONA REPUBLIC

P.O. Box 1950   **Phone:**   602/271-8928
Phoenix, AZ 85001   **FAX:**   602/271-8044

*   *   *

ORGANIZATION'S ACTIVITIES: A daily newspaper containing news, columns, features, and advertising.

Number of Internships: Varies.

Type: News department—photography, editing, reporting.

Function/Duties: Assist in research, reporting, and preparing articles for publication.

Schedule: Full-time in summers.

Stipend or Pay: $391 per week.

Academic Credit Offered: Per student's own arrangements with academic institution.

ELIGIBILITY: Undergraduate students.

REQUIREMENTS: Must have some journalistic credits.

APPLICATION PROCEDURE: Send letter, résumé, professional references, and clips *to* Robert Franken, Assistant Managing Editor *by* December 1.

BEACON PRESS

25 Beacon Street   **Phone:**   617/742-2110
Boston, MA 02108-2892   **FAX:**   617/723-3097

*   *   *

ORGANIZATION'S ACTIVITIES: Beacon Press is a small, nonprofit publisher of general and scholarly nonfiction books. The editorial department is responsible for persuading authors to publish their books with Beacon, and preparing manuscripts for production after contracts have been signed. In addition to working with authors to improve their manuscripts, editors keep on top of developments in various subject areas, develop contacts with agents and promising writers, negotiate contracts, and write jacket and catalog copy for forthcoming books.

Number of Internships: Approximately 6.

Type: Editorial.

Function/Duties: Varied (applying for copyrights and reading and responding to unsolicited manuscripts), mostly clerical.

Schedule: Depends on the season and the intern's schedule, usually 15 hours per week except during January, when 9 to 5 for at least 3 weeks is expected; 4 terms: fall (September–December); January; spring (February–May), and summer (June–August).

Stipend or Pay: No.

Number of Internships: Approximately 6.

Type: Marketing.

Function/Duties: Varied, mostly clerical.

Schedule: Depends on the season and the intern's schedule, usually 15 hours per week except during January, when 9 to 5 for at least 3 weeks is expected; 4 terms: fall (September–December); January; spring (February–May), and summer (June–August).

Stipend or Pay: No.

ELIGIBILITY: All students. Career-changers and non-students welcome to apply; *Plus* Beacon is an equal opportunity/affirmative action employer.

REQUIREMENTS: Live in Boston area, strong interest in book publishing, good writing and clerical skills. Prior office experience helpful but not essential.

Number of Internships: Approximately 6.

Type: Publicity.

Function/Duties: Varied, mostly clerical.

Schedule: Depends on the season and the intern's schedule, usually 15 hours per week except during January, when 9 to 5 for at least 3 weeks is expected; 4 terms: fall (September–December); January; spring (February–May), and Summer (June–August).

Stipend or Pay: No.

ELIGIBILITY: All students. Career-changers and non-students welcome to apply.

APPLICATION PROCEDURE: Submit résumé, cover letter, application form *to* Atissa Banuazizi, Internship Program Coordinator.

THE BLAZE COMPANY

228 Main Street **Phone:** 310/450-6060
Venice, CA 90291 **FAX:** 310/206-3938

* * *

ORGANIZATION'S ACTIVITIES: A full-service public relations agency specializing in a wide variety of West Coast clients.

Number of Internships: 1 or more as needed.

Type: Public relations and marketing.

Function/Duties: Research, writing, media relations.

Schedule: Flexible.

Stipend or Pay: May be arranged.

Academic Credit Offered: Per student's own arrangements with academic institution; *Plus* may lead to advancement within firm.

ELIGIBILITY: College students.

REQUIREMENTS: Public Relations majors preferred; English and Journalism also.

APPLICATION PROCEDURE: Contact Jan Wayne, Executive Administrator *to* arrange for interview. *Deadline:* Ongoing.

BOZELL WORLDWIDE, INC.

625 North Michigan Avenue **Phone:** 312/988-2300
Chicago, IL 60611 **FAX:** 312/988-2194

* * *

ORGANIZATION'S ACTIVITIES: International public relations firm, providing full range of services for wide spectrum of clients.

Number of Internships: Varies.

Type: Public relations.

Function/Duties: Aid staff in consumer and health-care divisions of large PR firm, participating in ongoing duties as well as special projects.

Schedule: Full- and/or part-time, 3 to 6 months, year-round availability.

Stipend or Pay: Yes.

Academic Credit Offered: Per student's own arrangements with academic institution.

ELIGIBILITY: College students or recent graduates.

REQUIREMENTS: "All liberal arts majors are welcome to apply," encourages Bozell.

APPLICATION PROCEDURE: Send cover letter and résumé *to* Internship Coordinator, then follow up with phone call. *Deadline:* Ongoing.

THE BRICKMAN GROUP

304 Park Avenue South
Room 216
New York, NY 10010

Phone: 212/260-5300
FAX: 212/260-5344

* * *

ORGANIZATION'S ACTIVITIES: Public relations, marketing.

Number of Internships: 1.

Type: Writing, clips, media relations.

Function/Duties: Clerical, support.

Schedule: Full-time and part-time.

Stipend or Pay: $5 per hour *or* carfare and lunch.

Academic Credit Offered: If arranged by intern.

ELIGIBILITY: Bright, motivated high-school students, undergraduate and graduate students; preferred majors: English, Political Science, and Journalism.

REQUIREMENTS: Proficiency in IBM PC (Word Perfect 5.1), well organized, good phone manner.

APPLICATION PROCEDURE: Submit résumé *to* R. Brickman.

CBS-TV

51 West 52nd Street
New York, NY 10019

Phone: 212/975-4321
FAX: 212/975-4615

* * *

ORGANIZATION'S ACTIVITIES: Headquarters of international broadcasting network; offices in cities nationwide.

Number of Internships: Varies; fairly numerous.

Type: Research, production.

Function/Duties: Provide support for news staff, aid in production activities.

Schedule: Full-time summers, part-time during school semesters.

Stipend or Pay: No.

Academic Credit Offered: Per student's own arrangements with academic institution.

ELIGIBILITY: Primarily undergraduate students; very competitive.

REQUIREMENTS: Prefer sophomore and junior journalism majors.

APPLICATION PROCEDURE: Send résumé and cover letter *to* Internship Coordinator *by* April 1 at *latest* for summer (earlier is better) and in June for fall.

CABLE NEWS NETWORK (CNN)

100 International Boulevard   **Phone:** 404/827-1500
Atlanta, GA 30303   **FAX:** 404/827-1593

*   *   *

ORGANIZATION'S ACTIVITIES: Headquarters for 24-hour international news cable network; offices in cities nationwide.

Number of Internships: Various; numerous.

Type: News and features.

Function/Duties: Interns *rotate* through editorial and production aspects of news operations and/or assist regular staff on *alternate* duties with specials and feature programs.

Schedule: Varies with student's availability and staff's need.

Stipend or Pay: No.

Academic Credit Offered: Per student's own arrangements with academic institution.

ELIGIBILITY: Undergraduate and graduate students.

REQUIREMENTS: Interests, goals, skills, and/or experience relevant to available assignments.

APPLICATION PROCEDURE: Send inquiries *to* Intern Coordinator *by* as far in advance of availability as possible.

CAIRNS & ASSOCIATES INC.

641 Lexington Avenue   **Phone:** 212/421-9770
New York, NY 10022   **FAX:** 212/421-9799

*   *   *

ORGANIZATION'S ACTIVITIES: A full-service public relations/marketing communications firm representing a broad spectrum of industries; small but rapidly growing.

Number of Internships: Varies.

Type: Public relations.

Function/Duties: Media relations, list maintenance, clipbooks, some writing and research.

Schedule: 15 hours per week, mostly summers.

Stipend or Pay: No.

Academic Credit Offered: Per student's own arrangements with academic institution; *Plus* personalized attention from account teams and regular weekly "PR Skills Workshops" led by staff professionals.

ELIGIBILITY: Primarily college students; some non-students may be considered.

REQUIREMENTS: Interests, goals, and/or experience relevant to available assignments.

APPLICATION PROCEDURE: Send inquiries *to* Karen Ravensbergen *by* early in the academic year.

CALIFORNIA INDEPENDENT PETROLEUM ASSOCIATION

1112 I Street, #350	**Phone:** 916/447-1177
Sacramento, CA 95814	**FAX:** 916/447-1144

* * *

ORGANIZATION'S ACTIVITIES: Six hundred-plus member non-profit trade association representing independent oil and natural gas producers and the companies that service and supply them throughout California.

Number of Internships: Varies with availability.

Type: Publications.

Function/Duties: Dependent on the skills of the individual.

Schedule: Full-time and part-time, open term.

Stipend or Pay: Not usually.

Academic Credit Offered: Must be arranged by intern.

ELIGIBILITY: College and graduate students; preferred major: Liberal Arts.

REQUIREMENTS: Excellent communications skills; some editorial experience useful.

APPLICATION PROCEDURE: Submit résumé and cover letter *to* Dan Kramer.

CAMPBELL COMMUNICATIONS

8530 Holloway Drive, Suite 226	**Phone:** 310/659-5427
Los Angeles, CA 90069-2475	**FAX:** 310/659-6427

* * *

ORGANIZATION'S ACTIVITIES: Public affairs, media relations, marketing and special events for the arts and entertainment fields, cultural festivals, art galleries, motion picture projects, fashion products and consumer goods.

Number of Internships: Varies upon need.

Type: Account executive assistant.

Function/Duties: Assist with public relations and events.

Schedule: Part-time, year-round, with a minimum of 3 months.

Stipend or Pay: Dependent on project funding.

Academic Credit Offered: Yes, if coordinated with academic institution.

ELIGIBILITY: Undergraduate and graduate students.

REQUIREMENTS: Journalism, communications, and arts administration majors a plus; must have a car in Southern California.

APPLICATION PROCEDURE: Mail résumé with cover letter citing goals *to* Carolyn M. Campbell or the Internship Counselor. *Deadline:* Open-ended.

CANAAN PUBLIC RELATIONS

301 East 47th Street, Suite 10M   **Phone:** 212/223-0100
New York, NY 10017   **FAX:** 212/223-3737

* * *

ORGANIZATION'S ACTIVITIES: Public relations for celebrities, restaurants, designers, fashion, beauty, and diverse list of other clients. Interaction with major TV networks and other media to promote clients.

Number of Internships: 2 to 3 per semester.

Type: Administrative duties.

Function/Duties: Assist in pitching, writing, and other related public relations activities.

Schedule: 4–6 months during the spring, summer, or fall semester.

Stipend or Pay: Yes; daily expenses such as food and transportation are paid for.

Academic Credit Offered: Per student's own arrangements with academic institution.

ELIGIBILITY: Students must have undergraduate college degree; non-students and career-changers also welcome.

REQUIREMENTS: Public relations, communications, creative writing, and/or English majors preferred. Must have good verbal and writing skills.

APPLICATION PROCEDURE: Send résumé and writing samples, if available, *to* Mr. Lee Canaan. *Deadline:* No.

CAPITAL CITIES/ABC

77 West 66th Street   **Phone:** 212/456-7777
New York, NY 10023   **FAX:** 212/456-7112

* * *

ORGANIZATION'S ACTIVITIES: Headquarters of international broadcasting network; offices in cities nationwide.

Number of Internships: Varies; fairly numerous.

Type: Research, technical, communications, managerial.

Function/Duties: Aid regular staff, provide support for news staff and others.

Schedule: Full-time summers, part-time during academic year.

Stipend or Pay: No.

Academic Credit Offered: Per student's own arrangements with academic institution.

ELIGIBILITY: Graduate and undergraduate students.

REQUIREMENTS: Must be at least in junior year; prefer majors in fields related to internship; very competitive positions.

APPLICATION PROCEDURE: Send résumé and cover letter requesting type of internship *to* Internship Coordinator *by* April 1 at latest for summer.

CAPLAN/CAPOZZI

938 Penn Avenue, Suite 501
Pittsburgh, PA 15222

Phone: 412/281-3889
FAX: 412/281-3887

* * *

ORGANIZATION'S ACTIVITIES: Creative marketing communications; public relations, advertising, special events planning, promotions.

Number of Internships: Flexible; varies with need.

Type: Public relations/special events intern.

Function/Duties: Assist with writing, planning special events, implementing promotions, etc.

Schedule: Part-time during school hours.

Stipend or Pay: No.

Academic Credit Offered: Per student's own arrangements with academic institution.

ELIGIBILITY: Juniors and seniors in college; preferred majors: Journalism, Marketing, Writing, and English; will consider career-changers.

REQUIREMENTS: Interests, goals, and/or experience relevant to available assignments.

APPLICATION PROCEDURE: Submit cover letter, résumé, 2 writing samples *to* Internship Coordinator. *Deadline:* 2 months before school term begins.

CENTER FOR INVESTIGATIVE REPORTING

568 Howard Street, 5th Floor
San Francisco, CA 94105

Phone: 415/543-1200
FAX: 415/543-8311

* * *

ORGANIZATION'S ACTIVITIES: A private, nonprofit organization that serves as a base and research/resource center for "journalists in pursuit of hidden stories about the individuals and institutions that shape our lives" as well as for teaching investigative skills.

Number of Internships: 12–15.

Type: Research, writing, reporting.

Function/Duties: Assist reporters with research, aid staff with office work while receiving training.

Schedule: 15–20 hours per week, usually for 6 months.

Stipend or Pay: $100 per week.

Academic Credit Offered: Per student's own arrangements with academic institution; *Plus* training from professionals; access to files and library for own stories.

ELIGIBILITY: Consideration given to students, non-students, or career-changers with appropriate qualifications, though publication credits *not* required.

REQUIREMENTS: Availability to work in San Francisco, or, in some cases, in Washington, DC, bureau.

APPLICATION PROCEDURE: Send résumé, cover letter, and writing samples *to* James Curtis *by* December 1 for January–June session; May 1 for June–January.

CHICAGO SUN-TIMES

401 North Wabash Avenue   **Phone:** 312/321-3000
Chicago, IL 60611   **FAX:** 312/321-3084

* * *

ORGANIZATION'S ACTIVITIES: One of the nation's major daily newspapers.

Number of Internships: 8.

Type: Editorial.

Function/Duties: Work with reporters and editors in the newsroom.

Schedule: Full-time, summers (12–13 weeks).

Stipend or Pay: Yes.

Academic Credit Offered: Per student's own arrangements with academic institution; *Plus* internships may lead to regular employment.

ELIGIBILITY: Primarily undergraduate college students.

REQUIREMENTS: Prefer juniors and seniors with journalism training and/or experience.

APPLICATION PROCEDURE: Send résumé, cover letter, and clips *to* the Assistant Editor *by* December 15.

CIGNA COMPANIES

Corporate & Public Affairs Communication
1601 Chestnut Street, 6TLP   **Phone:**   215/761-4756
Philadelphia, PA 19192-2067   **FAX:**   215/761-5632

*   *   *

ORGANIZATION'S ACTIVITIES: Provides communications support to Governmental Affairs unit and CIGNA foundation. Develops internal and external communications efforts.

Number of Internships: 2.

Type: Public affairs–related duties.

Function/Duties: Writing, editing, researching, and assisting in media relations.

Schedule: Year-round, from 6 months to 1 year.

Stipend or Pay: Yes, from $7 to $10 per hour.

Academic Credit Offered: Per student's own arrangements with academic institution.

ELIGIBILITY: Graduate and undergraduate college students.

REQUIREMENTS: Good verbal and written skills.

APPLICATION PROCEDURE: Send a résumé and an availability schedule *to* R. Gerber. *Deadline:* No.

CINCINNATI BALLET

1216 Central Parkway   **Phone:**   513/621-5219
Cincinnati, OH 45210   **FAX:**   513/621-4844

*   *   *

ORGANIZATION'S ACTIVITIES: A classical ballet company giving about 38 local performances a year and about 10 each year in its sister-city, Knoxville. Major staff functions are marketing, fundraising, special events, and development.

Number of Internships: Up to 2.

Type: Public relations.

Function/Duties: Writing, researching, planning promotions and events.

Schedule: Part-time and full-time, year-round; term at least 3 months long.

Stipend or Pay: No.

Academic Credit Offered: Yes.

ELIGIBILITY: College students; preferred majors: Marketing, Public Relations, Development, and Arts Management.

REQUIREMENTS: Availability in Cincinnati and interest in ballet.

APPLICATION PROCEDURE: Submit résumé and cover letter *to* Director of Marketing and Development. *Deadline:* April 1 for summer; August 1 for fall/winter, and November 1 for winter/spring.

CLARKE & COMPANY PUBLIC RELATIONS

535 Boylston Street
Boston, MA 02116

Phone: 617/536-3003
FAX: 617/536-8524

* * *

ORGANIZATION'S ACTIVITIES: Leading New England public relations and crisis communications firm.

Number of Internships: 2 or more.

Type: Public relations.

Function/Duties: Support staff members with research, events, media lists, etc.

Schedule: Summers full-time; school semesters 15 hours per week.

Stipend or Pay: Summer internship paid; school year not.

Academic Credit Offered: Per student's own arrangements with academic institution.

ELIGIBILITY: Junior and senior college students preferred; others considered.

REQUIREMENTS: Communications majors preferred.

APPLICATION PROCEDURE: Send résumé and letter of interest *to* Patricia Pesaturo *by* April 30 for summer; August 15 for fall; November 15 for spring.

CMF & Z PUBLIC RELATIONS

600 East Court Avenue
Des Moines, IA 50306

Phone: 515/246-3500
FAX: 515/246-3512

* * *

ORGANIZATION'S ACTIVITIES: One of nation's larger PR firms; connected with Young & Rubicam Agencies; has offices in Washington, D.C., and elsewhere.

Number of Internships: Varies.

Type: Marketing communications.

Function/Duties: Assist staff in writing, media relations, events, account management.

Schedule: Summers: full-time 3 months; fall and spring: 20 to 35 hours per week for 10 weeks.

Stipend or Pay: Summers, yes; school semesters, no.

Academic Credit Offered: Per student's own arrangements with academic institution; *Plus* "All interns receive individual guidance from an assigned staff professional and participate in an established curriculum."

ELIGIBILITY: Junior and senior college students.

REQUIREMENTS: Good writing skills; study in related majors.

APPLICATION PROCEDURE: Send résumé with writing samples *to* Director of Administration *by* December 31 for spring, March 31 for summer, July 30 for fall.

COLLEGE CONNECTIONS

329 East 82nd Street   **Phone:** 212/734-2190
New York, NY 10028   **FAX:** 212/517-7284

*   *   *

ORGANIZATION'S ACTIVITIES: A public relations and marketing firm founded in 1980. It was one of the first of its kind to serve higher education and remains the only firm in New York City to serve this market exclusively. College Connections clients include a wide variety of public and private colleges and universities, schools, and nonprofit organizations.

Number of Internships: 2 or 3.

Type: Public relations.

Function/Duties: Write pitch letters and news releases; pitch stories to print and broadcast media; word processing; compile and update databases; generate mailing lists and conduct mailings. Interns will work closely with staff in this small firm. There will be many opportunities to learn about the full range of the public relations profession and to gain valuable contacts in the industry.

Schedule: 8–20 hours a week; terms: summer, fall, and spring semesters.

Stipend or Pay: Travel expenses will be paid.

Academic Credit Offered: Per student's own arrangements with academic institution.

ELIGIBILITY: Primarily undergraduate students, though others may be considered.

REQUIREMENTS: Excellent writing skills, self-initiative/a "do-er," creativity, flexibility, and IBM computer skills.

APPLICATION PROCEDURE: Contact Heather Walsh.

THE COLLEGE OF SANTA FE

1600 St. Michael's Drive   **Phone:** 505/473-6011
Santa Fe, NM 87501   **FAX:** 505/473-6127

*   *   *

ORGANIZATION'S ACTIVITIES: Four-year college for arts, film/video, business, and education; enrollment 1,400 students, small classes.

Number of Internships: 2.

Type: Public relations.

Function/Duties: Write press releases and other materials; handle clips, press calls, events, etc.

Schedule: Part-time, term open to negotiation.

Stipend or Pay: No.

Academic Credit Offered: Available on a limited basis.

ELIGIBILITY: College juniors and seniors; preferred majors: Business and Computer Science.

REQUIREMENTS: Hispanics and African-Americans encouraged to apply.

APPLICATION PROCEDURE: Submit résumé and cover letter *to* Janet Wise, Director of Public Relations.

CORPORATION FOR PUBLIC BROADCASTING

901 E Street NW   **Phone:**   202/879-9600
Washington, DC 20004   **FAX:**   202/783-1019

* * *

ORGANIZATION'S ACTIVITIES: Administrative headquarters for public radio and public television nationwide.

Number of Internships: Varies; fairly numerous.

Type: Administrative management, public affairs, finance, fundraising.

Function/Duties: Assist professional staff in offices as suits intern's skills and as needed for ongoing and special projects.

Schedule: Usually full-time in summers and part-time during the academic year.

Stipend or Pay: Honorarium often available.

Academic Credit Offered: Per student's own arrangements with academic institution.

ELIGIBILITY: Primarily graduate and undergraduate students.

REQUIREMENTS: Prefer seniors with relevant experience or interests.

APPLICATION PROCEDURE: Send inquiries *to* Internship Coordinator. *Deadline:* Varies.

CRAIN COMMUNICATIONS

740 North Rush Street   **Phone:**   312/649-5200
Chicago, IL 60611   **FAX:**   312/280-3179

* * *

ORGANIZATION'S ACTIVITIES: Publisher of business and trade magazines in Chicago and elsewhere, including *Advertising Age* and *Crain's New York Business.*

Number of Internships: 10 or more, in headquarters and elsewhere.

Type: Editorial, sales, marketing.

Function/Duties: Assist regular staff in department of choice with on-going duties and special projects.

Schedule: Full-time summers, though schedule may vary in different locales.

Stipend or Pay: Yes.

Academic Credit Offered: Per student's own arrangements with academic institution.

ELIGIBILITY: Primarily undergraduate and some graduate students.

REQUIREMENTS: Interests, goals, skills, and/or experience relevant to available assignments.

APPLICATION PROCEDURE: Send inquiries (including questions about other locales) *to* Personnel Manager *by* as early in the academic year as possible.

CREAMER DICKSON BASFORD

1000 Turks Head Building	**Phone:** 401/456-1664
Providence, RI 02903	**FAX:** 401/456-1538

* * *

ORGANIZATION'S ACTIVITIES: Established marketing communications firm focussing on consumer, high-tech, and business-to-business marketing.

Number of Internships: Varies.

Type: Communications, managerial, research.

Function/Duties: Work as account coordinator, part of account team, doing research, events planning, media relations, etc.

Schedule: Full-time and part-time, summers and school semesters.

Stipend or Pay: No.

Academic Credit Offered: Per student's own arrangements with academic institution.

ELIGIBILITY: Graduate and undergraduate students as well as recent graduates.

REQUIREMENTS: "Solid writing and interpersonal skills."

APPLICATION PROCEDURE: Send inquiries *to* Ellen Miller, Vice President, *by* about 3 months prior to availability.

CURIOUS PICTURES CORP.

632 Broadway   **Phone:** No calls please
New York, NY 10012   **FAX:** 212/677-6114

*   *   *

ORGANIZATION'S ACTIVITIES: Curious Pictures Corporation is a television commercial production company specializing in special effects and animation. Notable past projects include the original MTV station IDs, Bud Bowls I and II, and the first season of *Pee-Wee's Playhouse.* The company runs a full-service studio at 632 Broadway and a sales and administrative office at 23 Watts Street.

Number of Internships: Varies with projects.

Type: Production.

Function/Duties: Assisting producers in preparing and shooting live action and three-dimensional animation projects.

Schedule: At least 10 hours a week for 3 months.

Stipend or Pay: Travel expenses reimbursed.

Academic Credit Offered: Yes.

Type: Art production.

Function/Duties: Assisting producers in two-dimensional animation, ink and paint, and computer graphics.

Schedule: At least 10 hours a week for 3 months.

Stipend or Pay: Travel expenses reimbursed.

Academic Credit Offered: Yes.

Type: Editorial.

Function/Duties: Assisting head of editorial department in dubbing reels, shipping film elements to clients, and logging dailies.

Schedule: At least 10 hours a week for 3 months.

Stipend or Pay: Travel expenses reimbursed.

Academic Credit Offered: Yes.

Type: Sales and marketing.

Function/Duties: Assisting executive producers and sales reps in the presentation and bidding of future projects, editing sales reels, maintaining reel inventory, working with reps in Los Angeles and Chicago, and special events planning.

Schedule: At least 10 hours a week for 3 months.

Stipend or Pay: Travel expenses reimbursed.

Academic Credit Offered: Yes.

ELIGIBILITY: All students; majors preferred: Art and Film. Career-changers and non-students welcome to apply.

REQUIREMENTS: Interests, background, and/or skills relevant to film production business.

APPLICATION PROCEDURE: Submit résumé *to* Susan Squibb at 632 Broadway.

DERA & ASSOCIATES

584 Broadway
Suite 1201   **Phone:** 212/966-4600
New York, NY 10012   **FAX:** 212/966-5763

* * *

ORGANIZATION'S ACTIVITIES: Public relations firm. Coordinates events and publicity for artists/clients, creates and executes press schedules, secures press for artists on tour or surrounding special appearances or recent films/records.

Number of Internships: 2 per term.

Type: Public relations, research, special projects.

Function/Duties: All-inclusive—typing, faxing, telephone, assisting at events.

Schedule: Must be available at least 4 of 5 weekdays, 9:30 A.M. to 6:00 P.M.; should be flexible regarding hours, as events are often in the evenings.

Stipend or Pay: No.

Academic Credit Offered: Yes.

ELIGIBILITY: High-school, college, and graduate students; career-changers and some non-students as well.

REQUIREMENTS: Interests, goals, skills, and/or experience relevant to available assignments, including excellent communications skills.

APPLICATION PROCEDURE: Submit résumé and interview request *to* Laura Perez, Vice President TV and Film, or Elizabeth Freund, Vice President Music.

DORF & STANTON COMMUNICATIONS

111 Fifth Avenue   **Phone:** 212/420-8100
New York, NY 10003   **FAX:** 212/505-1397

* * *

ORGANIZATION'S ACTIVITIES: Public relations and marketing communications firm.

Number of Internships: 3–5 per year.

Type: Assistant to account team.

Function/Duties: Writing, editor follow-up, assistance with special events and other related issues.

Schedule: Full-time during the summer and part-time during the school year.

Stipend or Pay: Yes; minimum wage.

Academic Credit Offered: Per student's own arrangements with academic institution; *Plus* opportunity to sit in on and participate in brainstorming sessions and any staff training and seminars.

ELIGIBILITY: Open to students at college level and graduates.

REQUIREMENTS: Communications and journalism majors preferred.

APPLICATION PROCEDURE: Send cover letter and résumé *to* Mary-Ann Faherty, Office Manager. *Deadline:* 3 months prior to the semester.

FARRAR, STRAUS & GIROUX

19 Union Square West	**Phone:** 212/741-6900
New York, NY 10003	**FAX:** 212/633-9385

* * *

ORGANIZATION'S ACTIVITIES: Book publisher.

Number of Internships: Varies with availability.

Type: Varied.

Function/Duties: Varied.

Schedule: Full-time or part-time, 3 months or one semester.

Stipend or Pay: No.

Academic Credit Offered: Yes.

ELIGIBILITY: All students; career-changers and non-students welcome to apply.

REQUIREMENTS: Interests and/or background related to the book publishing business; interview required.

APPLICATION PROCEDURE: Send inquiries *to* Peggy Miller.

FOREIGN RELATIONS MAGAZINE

COUNCIL ON FOREIGN RELATIONS

58 East 68th Street	**Phone:** 212/734-0400
New York, NY 10021	**FAX:** 212/861-1789

* * *

ORGANIZATION'S ACTIVITIES: A quarterly journal published by the Council on Foreign Relations, a nonpartisan organization whose aim is to increase U.S. awareness of the significance of international issues.

Number of Internships: 2 per year.

Type: Editorial assistant.

Function/Duties: Help with editing and production of magazine.

Schedule: Part-time, throughout winter and throughout summer.

Stipend or Pay: Yes.

Academic Credit Offered: No.

ELIGIBILITY: Graduate students.

REQUIREMENTS: Editorial skills and/or experience; interest and background in foreign affairs.

APPLICATION PROCEDURE: Send résumé, cover letter, and writing samples *to* assistant editor *by* several months prior to internship desired.

FOUNDATION FOR INDEPENDENT VIDEO AND FILM (FIVF)

625 Broadway
Ninth Floor   **Phone:** 212/473-3400
New York, NY 10012   **FAX:** 212/677-8732

*   *   *

ORGANIZATION'S ACTIVITIES: Support of independent film and video makers through programs; publication of *Independent Film and Video Monthly*; festival bureau, publications, activities, seminars, consultations.

Number of Internships: 5.

Type: Clerical.

Function/Duties: Assist staff with ongoing duties and special projects.

Schedule: Part-time.

Stipend or Pay: $100 per month.

Academic Credit Offered: Yes.

ELIGIBILITY: All students; preferred majors: Film and Communications. Non-students and career-changers welcome to apply.

REQUIREMENTS: Education, experience, and/or strong interest in contemporary filmmaking and videography.

APPLICATION PROCEDURE: Submit résumé and cover letter *to* Kathryn Bowser.

FRESH AIR FUND

1040 Avenue of the Americas   **Phone:** 212/221-0900
New York, NY 10018   **FAX:** N/A

*   *   *

ORGANIZATION'S ACTIVITIES: An independent nonprofit agency that has provided free summer vacations to more than 1.6 million disadvantaged New York City children since 1877: in the 1990s, more than 10,000 children go to camps or homes in the country each summer and some 2,000 participate in year-round camping programs.

Number of Internships: 1 or more.

Type: Publicity.

Function/Duties: Participate in all aspects of Fund's publicity campaign and monitor public service ad campaign.

Schedule: 7 to 11 weeks, summers; 35 hours per week.

Stipend or Pay: Approximately $200 per week.

Academic Credit Offered: Per student's own arrangements with academic institution.

ELIGIBILITY: College students.

REQUIREMENTS: "Outgoing, organized, dedicated"; excellent communications and writing skills.

APPLICATION PROCEDURE: Request application *from* Executive Director as early as possible. *Deadline:* February 15.

GALLIER AND WITTENBERG, INC.

2700 Fairmount
Suite 600   **Phone:**   214/880-0010
Dallas, TX 75201   **FAX:**   214/880-0364

* * *

ORGANIZATION'S ACTIVITIES: A full-service agency—marketing, advertising and public relations.

Number of Internships: Varies.

Type: As assigned by individual.

Function/Duties: General office duties—writing, word processing, and photocopying.

Schedule: Part-time, during fall, spring, and summer semesters.

Stipend or Pay: Yes; $4.25 per hour.

Academic Credit Offered: Per student's own arrangements with academic institution.

ELIGIBILITY: College seniors.

REQUIREMENTS: Journalism majors preferred.

APPLICATION PROCEDURE: Send résumé *to* Fran Wittenberg. *Deadline:* Open.

GANNETT COMPANY INC.

1100 Wilson Boulevard   **Phone:**   703/284-6000
Arlington, VA 22234   **FAX:**   703/558-3813

* * *

ORGANIZATION'S ACTIVITIES: Headquarters of publisher of more than 80 daily papers and some 50 weekly and other papers around the country, including the national *USA Today*, which is produced at headquarters office.

Number of Internships: Varies.

Type: Editorial, production, business.

Function/Duties: Assist regular staff as needed.

Schedule: Varies; also needed in subsidiary publications.

Stipend or Pay: Mostly unpaid.

Academic Credit Offered: Per student's own arrangements with academic institution.

ELIGIBILITY: Primarily students, but others with appropriate qualifications may be considered.

REQUIREMENTS: Informal process, with preference for those with journalism and/or business backgrounds.

APPLICATION PROCEDURE: Send inquiries (about headquarters and other papers) *to* Senior Personnel Administrator. *Deadline:* Varies.

GERALDO

555 West 57th Street   **Phone:**   800/426-0679
New York, NY 10019   **FAX:**   212/581-8196

*   *   *

ORGANIZATION'S ACTIVITIES: Syndicated television talk show produced by The Investigative News Group from New York headquarters.

Number of Internships: Varies.

Type: TV production internship.

Function/Duties: Assisting production and support staff with duties, including responding to mail, pre-interviewing guests, handling phone calls, screening tapes, etc.

Schedule: 1 day per week minimum, throughout semester; more days okay, year-round availability.

Stipend or Pay: No.

Academic Credit Offered: Per student's own arrangements with academic institution.

ELIGIBILITY: College students.

REQUIREMENTS: Prefer communications-related majors; intern *must* be earning college credit for internship.

APPLICATION PROCEDURE: Send inquiries *to* Internship Supervisor. *Deadline:* Ongoing.

HEADLINE COMMUNICATIONS

250 West 57th Street
Suite 1723
New York, NY 10107

Phone: 212/757-0521
FAX: 212/262-0261

* * *

ORGANIZATION'S ACTIVITIES: Headline is a public relations firm specializing in the entertainment industry. The company deals extensively with a client base that includes MTV and television personalities, music artists, and movie studios.

Number of Internships: 3.

Type: Account executive assistants.

Function/Duties: Providing assistance in media relations and special event coordination.

Schedule: Full-time and part-time.

Stipend or Pay: No.

Academic Credit Offered: Through intern's school.

ELIGIBILITY: College and graduate students; preferred major: Communications. Non-students and career-changers welcome to apply.

REQUIREMENTS: Motivated, articulate, with a strong interest in gaining valuable experience and contacts on the music, television, and film industries.

APPLICATION PROCEDURE: Submit résumé and cover letter *to* Nathan Nazario.

IMPRESSION IMPACT

113 Hill Street
Concord, MA 01742

Phone: 508/287-0718
FAX: N/A

* * *

ORGANIZATION'S ACTIVITIES: A public relations and marketing firm serving a wide variety of clients with services including media relations, special event planning, publications, etc.

Number of Internships: 1 or more as needed.

Type: Public relations, marketing, writing.

Function/Duties: Write press releases and other material; research and other projects for clients; media relations.

Schedule: 16 hours per week as needed.

Stipend or Pay: No.

Academic Credit Offered: Yes; *Plus*, as a small company with well-structured internship program, it offers varied opportunities and thorough evaluation.

ELIGIBILITY: Undergraduate and graduate students.

REQUIREMENTS: Good communication skills; ability to work independently.

APPLICATION PROCEDURE: Send inquiries *to* Nancy Michaels. *Deadline:* Ongoing.

INFORMATION TECHNOLOGY RESOURCE CENTER

59 East Van Buren   **Phone:** 312/939-8050
Suite 2020   **FAX:** 312/939-8060
Chicago, IL 60605

*   *   *

ORGANIZATION'S ACTIVITIES: The Information Technology Resource Center is a nonprofit organization dedicated to helping other nonprofits in their uses of computers and other technology. Facilities include a classroom, a library, and a 22-workstation computer lab equipped with both Macintosh and IBM-compatible computers. Core programs include basic information about computers, workshops that focus on common computer applications, planning sessions to assist in analyzing computer requirements, making purchase decisions, and troubleshooting. Hands-on training is offered in word processing, spreadsheet, database, desktop publishing, operating systems, and other subjects.

Number of Internships: 1 or more.

Type: Marketing and public relations assistants.

Function/Duties: Aid communications and production specialists with regular functions and special projects.

Schedule: Full-time and part-time, term of at least 3 months.

Stipend or Pay: No.

Academic Credit Offered: Available.

ELIGIBILITY: College and graduate students; preferred majors: Journalism and English. Both career-changers and non-students with at least two years of college are also welcome to apply.

REQUIREMENTS: Capacity to house one or two interns at any time.

APPLICATION PROCEDURE: Submit résumé and letter expressing interest, proposed period, and purpose of internship *to* Information Technology Resource Center.

JACOB'S PILLOW DANCE FESTIVAL

P.O. Box 287   **Phone:** 413/637-1322
Lee, MA 01238   **FAX:** 413/243-4744

*   *   *

ORGANIZATION'S ACTIVITIES: America's oldest dance festival. Presents 10 weeks of dance performances and conducts a professional dance school each summer.

Number of Internships: 3.

Type: Marketing and press.

Function/Duties: Participate in the promotion of the festival and school through the use of house publications, paid advertising, and the press. Working with the Pillow's professional staff, responsibilities will include hosting groups/tours, guiding tours of the festival grounds, on-site displays, advertisement mechanical preparation, information collection and dissemination, various "grass roots" marketing efforts, writing press releases, hosting press visits, arranging interviews, maintenance of press records including clipping books, and working with visiting artists to prepare program materials. Use of word processing and desktop publishing systems. Responsibilities also include weekly shifts in the box office.

Schedule: Seasonal—3 months.

Stipend or Pay: $100 a month.

Academic Credit Offered: Per student's own arrangements with academic institution.

ELIGIBILITY: College and graduate students; *Plus* internship often leads to career position.

REQUIREMENTS: Computer skills and a strong interest in dance are desirable.

APPLICATION PROCEDURE: Submit résumé and cover letter *to* Jackie Thomas. *Deadline:* March 1.

JOHN WILEY & SONS

605 Third Avenue   **Phone:** 212/850-6000
New York, NY 10158   **FAX:** 212/850-6088

*   *   *

ORGANIZATION'S ACTIVITIES: America's "oldest independent publisher," specializing in text, technical, scientific, and business books.

Number of Internships: 10.

Type: Editorial, managerial.

Function/Duties: Learn editing, finance, marketing functions.

Schedule: Summers, full-time.

Stipend or Pay: $250 per week.

Academic Credit Offered: Per student's own arrangements with academic institution.

ELIGIBILITY: Junior and senior college students preferred; *Plus* possibility of regular employment following internship.

REQUIREMENTS: Availability in New York City during summer; interest in publishing as a career.

APPLICATION PROCEDURE: Contact Employment Office for details and deadline.

KCET-TV

4401 Sunset Boulevard   **Phone:** 213/666-6500
Los Angeles, CA 90027   **FAX:** 213/665-6067

* * *

ORGANIZATION'S ACTIVITIES: "Community television of California": the public broadcasting company that covers the Los Angeles metropolitan area, via Channel 28.

Number of Internships: Varies.

Type: Broadcasting, technical, managerial, editorial.

Function/Duties: Assist in every department of station as needed.

Schedule: Varies, according to need and to special projects.

Stipend or Pay: Yes.

Academic Credit Offered: Per student's own arrangements with academic institution.

ELIGIBILITY: Primarily graduate, undergraduate, and technical students though some non-students or career-changers with appropriate qualifications may be considered; *Plus* may lead to regular employment.

REQUIREMENTS: Flexibility in schedule, and interests, goals, skills, and/or experience relevant to available assignments.

APPLICATION PROCEDURE: Send inquiries *to* Human Resources Department. *Deadline:* Open.

KQED RADIO

2601 Mariposa Street   **Phone:** 415/864-2000
San Francisco, CA 94100   **FAX:** 415/553-2241

* * *

ORGANIZATION'S ACTIVITIES: An FM all-news station affiliated with National Public Radio.

Number of Internships: Varies.

Type: Research, public affairs, outreach, public relations.

Function/Duties: Assist producers and other staff members with research, writing, publicity, and other activities.

Schedule: Full- and/or part-time, year-round availability.

Stipend or Pay: No.

Academic Credit Offered: Per student's own arrangements with academic institution.

ELIGIBILITY: Primarily undergraduate and graduate students.

REQUIREMENTS: Candidates need appropriate background or experience related to assignments.

APPLICATION PROCEDURE: Send inquiries *to* Human Resources Director. *Deadline:* Varies.

KVIE-TV

2595 Capitol Oaks Drive   **Phone:**   916/929-5843
Sacramento, CA 95833   **FAX:**   916/929-7215

* * *

ORGANIZATION'S ACTIVITIES: The Public Broadcasting System's TV affiliate for the California capital area.

Number of Internships: 8 or more.

Type: Production, community relations.

Function/Duties: Assist regular staff with ongoing duties and special projects.

Schedule: Year-round, part-time.

Stipend or Pay: No.

Academic Credit Offered: Per student's own arrangements with academic institution; *Plus* internships often lead to regular employment.

ELIGIBILITY: Primarily undergraduate and some graduate students.

REQUIREMENTS: Prefer applicants with interest in TV production or public affairs.

APPLICATION PROCEDURE: Send inquiries *to* Volunteer Coordinator. *Deadline:* Ongoing.

THE KAMBER GROUP

1920 L Street NW   **Phone:**   202/223-8700
Washington, DC 20036   **FAX:**   202/659-5559

* * *

ORGANIZATION'S ACTIVITIES: Seventh largest independently owned communications and public relations firm in the U.S.; largest in D.C.; providing complete communications, marketing, and business services to wide variety of clients in the U.S. and overseas. Other offices in New York City and Los Angeles.

Number of Internships: Varies; fairly numerous.

Type: Public relations.

Function/Duties: Aid staff specialists in media relations, crisis management, video, design, lobbying, advertising, fundraising, and events management.

Schedule: 3 months, mostly full-time, throughout year.

Stipend or Pay: Yes.

Academic Credit Offered: Per student's own arrangements with academic institution; *Plus* special attention to interns' training needs.

ELIGIBILITY: College and graduate students as well as non-students who are recent graduates.

REQUIREMENTS: Interests, goals, and/or experience relevant to available assignments.

APPLICATION PROCEDURE: Send résumés and applications, along with any writing samples, *to* "Intern for All Seasons" program *by* one month prior to internship period desired.

KAREN WEINER ESCALERA ASSOCIATES, INC.

104 Fifth Avenue
Eleventh Floor **Phone:** 212/255-7403
New York, NY 10011-6901 **FAX:** 212/255-7333

* * *

ORGANIZATION'S ACTIVITIES: An international marketing communications and public relations firm.

Number of Internships: 2 or more.

Type: Editorial.

Function/Duties: Writing press releases, preparing press kits, researching media lists, and exploring editorial leads.

Schedule: Varies.

Stipend or Pay: No. Intern is eligible for a bonus at the discretion of the president and contingent upon a performance review by the supervisor; company will pay for transportation.

Academic Credit Offered: Per student's own arrangements with academic institution.

ELIGIBILITY: Students, non-students, and career-changers.

REQUIREMENTS: Word processing experience, especially with WordPerfect, is preferred. Coursework completed in public relations, journalism, advertising, marketing, and communications a plus.

APPLICATION PROCEDURE: Send inquiries *to* Christina Miranda. *Deadline:* Open.

KETCHUM PUBLIC RELATIONS WORLDWIDE

1133 Avenue of the Americas **Phone:** 212/536-8856
New York, NY 10036 **FAX:** 212/869-8027

* * *

ORGANIZATION'S ACTIVITIES: Video/print production, research crisis management and communications, media placements, events planning, publications and design.

Number of Internships: Varies; from 1 to 5 interns for each of 8 offices.

Type: Account responsibilities.

Function/Duties: Assist with public relations activities.

Schedule: Full-time during summers.

Stipend or Pay: $250–$350 per week.

Academic Credit Offered: Will arrange with academic institution.

ELIGIBILITY: College juniors with strong academic background in public relations and/or good communications and writing skills.

REQUIREMENTS: Majors in communications, journalism, and marketing preferred. Must have a GPA of at least 3.0 and be available for 8 to 10 weeks of the summer to work full-time.

APPLICATION PROCEDURE: Send a résumé with a cover letter and samples of writings *to* Sharyn Lerner, Manager of Communications and Training, or to the office of interest *by* March 31.

LAND BETWEEN THE LAKES

Tennessee Valley Authority
100 Van Morgan Drive **Phone:** 502/924-5602
Golden Pond, KY 42211 **FAX:** 502/924-1399

* * *

ORGANIZATION'S ACTIVITIES: LBL is a 170,000-acre national recreation area located in western Kentucky and Tennessee. LBL provides outdoor recreation and environmental education in a managed natural setting which strengthens environmental responsibility among customers and communicates TVA's environmental leadership role.

Number of Internships: 12.

Type: Public relations.

Function/Duties: Varies by position.

Schedule: Full-time, 40 hours per week, summer months, end of May through mid-August.

Stipend: May be arranged.

Academic Credit Offered: Per student's own arrangement with academic institution.

ELIGIBILITY: Students, preferably college juniors and seniors.

REQUIREMENTS: Interests, goals, and/or experience relevant to available assignments.

APPLICATION PROCEDURE: Submit internship application and résumé *to* Jim Carpenter, Administrator, Professional Development.

LEVINE/SCHNEIDER PUBLIC RELATIONS

8730 Sunset Boulevard **Phone:** 310/659-6400
Los Angeles, CA 90069 **FAX:** 310/659-1309

* * *

ORGANIZATION'S ACTIVITIES: One of the four largest entertainment firms in the nation, representing such celebrities as Charlton Heston, Janet Jackson, Tom Petty, and KISS.

Number of Internships: As many as possible: "constantly looking" for good interns.

Type: Public relations, communications, general office work.

Function/Duties: Assist account execs and "participate in all aspects of the public relations process."

Schedule: 15 hours per week for a 3-month period, with very flexible schedule.

Stipend or Pay: No.

Academic Credit Offered: Per student's own arrangement with academic institution.

ELIGIBILITY: Open to students, non-students and career-changers, though most interns are students; *Plus* opportunities for permanent employment may open in firm's offices in Los Angeles, Las Vegas, New York, and London.

REQUIREMENTS: Be hardworking and willing to learn about any and all aspects of the entertainment industry.

APPLICATION PROCEDURE: *Contact* Melissa Spraul, Internship Coordinator, for application and details. *Deadline:* Open.

LIFESTYLE MEDIA RELATIONS REPORTER

2115 Fourth Street	**Phone:** 510/549-4300
Berkeley, CA 94710	**FAX:** 510/549-4331

* * *

ORGANIZATION'S ACTIVITIES: Newsletter published by Infocom Group for distribution to public relations professionals nationwide to keep them aware of how to approach the country's top journalists.

Number of Internships: 4 or more.

Type: Editorial.

Function/Duties: Write and research two columns and contribute to others in the newsletter; interact with media, aid in production.

Schedule: 15 hours per week for 3 months.

Stipend or Pay: Yes.

Academic Credit Offered: Per student's own arrangements with academic institution.

ELIGIBILITY: Primarily graduate and undergraduate students, but others with appropriate qualifications may be considered.

REQUIREMENTS: Excellent phone and communication skills.

APPLICATION PROCEDURE: Send inquiries *to* Editor *by* 2 months prior to period of availability.

LOBSENZ-STEVENS, INC.

460 Park Avenue South　　　　　　　**Phone:** 212/684-6300
New York, NY 10016　　　　　　　　**FAX:** 212/696-4638

＊　＊　＊

ORGANIZATION'S ACTIVITIES: Mid-size public relations/marketing communications agency with business-to-business, pharmaceutical, and lawn, garden, and outdoor power equipment clients. Day-to-day activities include writing, pitching, placing media tours, booklets, trade show representation, etc. Publicity efforts targeted to consumers and retail trade via print and broadcast media.

Number of Internships: Varies with availability.

Type: Public relations.

Function/Duties: Assist and learn from staff on ongoing public relation and marketing duties as well as special projects.

Schedule: Minimum 4 days per week.

Stipend or Pay: $50 a week including transportation.

Academic Credit Offered: Per student's own arrangement with institution.

ELIGIBILITY: College students; preferred majors: Public Relations, Communications, English, and Marketing.

REQUIREMENTS: Looking for bright, energetic, motivated, well-organized self-starters who are clear and concise writers, articulate and have the ability to get along with others.

APPLICATION PROCEDURE: Submit résumé and cover letter *to* Layne Maly.

LOS ANGELES TIMES

Times/Mirror Square　　　　　　　**Phone:** 213/237-5000
Los Angeles, CA 90053　　　　　　**FAX:** 213/237-4712

＊　＊　＊

ORGANIZATION'S ACTIVITIES: Southern California's leading daily newspaper.

Number of Internships: Varies; fairly numerous.

Type: News, sports, layout, business.

Function/Duties: Assist and learn from regular staff in areas of intern's interest.

Schedule: Full-time summers, part-time during academic terms.

Stipend or Pay: Yes.

Academic Credit Offered: Per student's own arrangements with academic institution.

ELIGIBILITY: Undergraduate or graduate students or recent graduates.

REQUIREMENTS: Highly competitive positions; require some background in area of specialty.

APPLICATION PROCEDURE: Send inquiries *to* Human Resources Department. *Deadline:* Varies.

MAGAZINE INTERNSHIP PROGRAM

American Society of Magazine Editors
919 Third Avenue   **Phone:**   212/752-0055
New York, NY 10022   **FAX:**   N/A

*   *   *

ORGANIZATION'S ACTIVITIES: A national editorial organization's program for the placement of students in internship programs in national magazines.

Number of Internships: Approximately 50.

Type: Editorial.

Function/Duties: As assigned by individual magazines—in general, research, writing, administrative.

Schedule: Full-time, summer; in New York City or (occasionally) Washington, D.C.

Stipend or Pay: Yes; also help with finding housing.

Academic Credit Offered: Per student's own arrangements with academic institution; *Plus* carefully structured, widely respected program; includes orientation week.

ELIGIBILITY: College students between the junior and senior year.

REQUIREMENTS: Journalism majors or other majors with journalism experience recommended by college dean or faculty.

APPLICATION PROCEDURE: Send inquiries *to* Marlene Kahan, Executive Director, for forms that must be submitted *by* March 1.

MAIZIE HALE PUBLIC RELATIONS

2964 Peachtree Road NE
Suite 530   **Phone:**   404/261-7080
Atlanta, GA 30305   **FAX:**   404/261-7101

*   *   *

ORGANIZATION'S ACTIVITIES: Public relations agency specializing in retail and hospitality clients and special events.

Number of Internships: 2.

Type: Public relations.

Function/Duties: Assist account executives with client work; intern must be able to communicate effectively, with emphasis on good writing and organizational skills, and detail-oriented.

Schedule: Year-round, seasonal (12 weeks, starting dates determined individually), full-time (40 hours per week) internships available.

Stipend or Pay: $1,000 for the complete assignment.

Academic Credit Offered: Per intern's own arrangements with academic institution.

ELIGIBILITY: Undergraduate students are encouraged to apply; preferred majors: English, Journalism, and Communications.

REQUIREMENTS: Provide cover letter, two writing samples, and a résumé along with an application.

APPLICATION PROCEDURE: Submit full application *to* Maizie Hale, Public Relations. *Deadline:* Open.

MALLORY FACTOR Inc.

275 Seventh Avenue
Nineteenth Floor   **Phone:** 212/242-0000
New York, NY 10001-6788   **FAX:** 212/242-0001

* * *

ORGANIZATION'S ACTIVITIES: Full-service public relations firm.

Number of Internships: 4.

Type: Public relations.

Function/Duties: Assist with all aspects of academic public relations and office duties.

Schedule: Minimum of 2 months.

Stipend or Pay: No.

Academic Credit Offered: Will discuss.

ELIGIBILITY: College and graduate students; preferred majors: Public Relations, Communications, Journalism, and English.

REQUIREMENTS: Good oral and written skills.

APPLICATION PROCEDURE: Submit résumé and cover letter *to* Internship Coordinator.

MARINE WORLD AFRICA USA

Marine World Foundation
Marine World Parkway   **Phone:** 707/644-4000
Vallejo, CA 94589   **FAX:** 707/644-0241

* * *

ORGANIZATION'S ACTIVITIES: A wildlife center that serves as research and exhibition site for marine animals.

Number of Internships: Varies with need.

Type: Public relations.

Function/Duties: Assist in some or all of the following: special and media event coordination, film and video production shoots, still photography shoots, VIP and travel media, tours. Set up PR resource files. Assist in coordination and distribution of press releases. Update media and VIP lists. Organize/maintain press clipping files and videotape library/logs. Special projects as directed.

Schedule: 3 to 5 full days per week for at least 3 months; some weekends may be required but compensatory time is granted.

Stipend or Pay: No.

Academic Credit Offered: Yes.

ELIGIBILITY: Primarily undergraduate students, but others may be considered.

REQUIREMENTS: Able to live and work in Vallejo area; solid writing and proofreading; good organizational and filing skills; precise, detail-oriented work style; accurate typing (45 wpm is fine); Macintosh or "Altos" system computer experience a plus. Must be able to juggle a variety of tasks at one time, liaison effectively with many personalities; flexible; able to "switch gears" at a moment's notice.

APPLICATION PROCEDURE: Make inquiries *to* Media Relations Manager: call 707/644-4000, ext. 227, for details.

MARKETING MIX

12 South Hanley	**Phone:** 314/721-8444
St. Louis, MO 63105	**FAX:** 314/721-6823

* * *

ORGANIZATION'S ACTIVITIES: A full-service marketing firm providing public relations, events, and advertising services to a variety of clients.

Number of Internships: Approximately 8.

Type: Public relations, advertising, marketing, management.

Function/Duties: Assist staffs in different divisions with writing, research, planning, media, and public contact.

Schedule: Full- or part-time, summers and/or school semesters.

Stipend or Pay: No.

Academic Credit Offered: Per student's own arrangements with institution.

ELIGIBILITY: College students, as well as non-students or career-changers who are college graduates.

REQUIREMENTS: Those with good writing skills and some computer and business knowledge seeking hands-on experience in communications.

APPLICATION PROCEDURE: Send inquiries *to* Julie Hausen. *Deadline:* Open.

MENTAL HEALTH INITIATIVES

4545 42nd Street NW	**Phone:** 202/364-7111
Washington, DC 20016	**FAX:** 202/363-3891

* * *

ORGANIZATION'S ACTIVITIES: A not-for-profit organization dedicated to promoting mental health and preventing emotional disorders. For example: preparing a public education campaign on fostering emotional resilience in children.

Number of Internships: Varies; 2 or more.

Type: Public relations intern.

Function/Duties: Assist staff in development and preparation of press releases, media relations, promotional materials, special events.

Schedule: Full- and part-time, summers and school semesters.

Stipend or Pay: No.

Academic Credit Offered: Per student's own arrangements with academic institution.

ELIGIBILITY: Primarily undergraduate or graduate students.

REQUIREMENTS: Prefer psychology or communications majors.

APPLICATION PROCEDURE: Send résumé, cover letter, and writing sample *to* Internship Coordinator *by* 2 to 3 months prior to availability.

MONTEL WILLIAMS SHOW

1500 Broadway	**Phone:** 212/921-9600
New York, NY 10036	**FAX:** 212/302-8025

* * *

ORGANIZATION'S ACTIVITIES: Nationally syndicated television talk show headquartered in New York City.

Number of Internships: Varies.

Type: Production assistance.

Function/Duties: Aid production, communications, technical staff of daily television show.

Schedule: Full- and/or part-time.

Stipend or Pay: No.

Academic Credit Offered: Per student's own arrangements with academic institution.

ELIGIBILITY: Undergraduate and some graduate students.

REQUIREMENTS: Must be full-time student receiving academic credit for internship.

APPLICATION PROCEDURE: Send résumé and cover letter *to* Susan Daniels. *Deadline:* Ongoing.

MULLEN ADVERTISING AND PUBLICATIONS

36 Essex Street   **Phone:** 508/468-1155
Wenham, MA 01984   **FAX:**   508/468-1133

*   *   *

ORGANIZATION'S ACTIVITIES: A full-service agency offering advertising, public relations, design, and research. The company employs over 150 professionals.

Number of Internships: 6–10.

Type: Assistant to executives.

Function/Duties: Assist professionals with duties related to advertising, public relations, and media.

Schedule: Year-round for about 3 to 6 months.

Stipend or Pay: No.

Academic Credit Offered: Per student's own arrangements with academic institution.

ELIGIBILITY: Undergraduate students, non-students, and career-changers.

REQUIREMENTS: If possible some field-based experience or coursework and/or other internship. Preferred majors: Communications, Marketing, Journalism, and English.

APPLICATION PROCEDURE: Send résumé and cover letter with portfolio of work to date *to* staff professional in discipline of interest: Susan Schumacher—Public Relations, Susan Marty—Advertising, R. Buchanan—Media, and B. Clausen—Creative. *Deadline:* prior to beginning of semester.

MUSEUM OF ART, INC.

1 East Las Olas Boulevard   **Phone:** 305/525-5500
Ft. Lauderdale, FL 33301   **FAX:**   305/524-6011

*   *   *

ORGANIZATION'S ACTIVITIES: Art museum designed by Edward Larrabee Barnes, which is the largest repository of William Glackens' work as well as owning the largest collection of CoBrA (post-World War II expressionistic art) in the Americas. Also offers traveling exhibitions such as works from the Metropolitan Museum of Art, photographs of Annie Liebovitz, and sculpture by Willa Shalit.

Number of Internships: Varies according to need.

Type: Public relations assistant.

Function/Duties: Writing, desktop publishing, clerical.

Schedule: Full-time and part-time from September to June.

Stipend or Pay: $6 per hour.

Academic Credit Offered: Per student's own arrangement with academic institution.

ELIGIBILITY: College and graduate students; preferred majors: Journalism or Public Relations.

REQUIREMENTS: Must be good typist; detail-oriented; creativity a plus; deadlines must be met; desktop publishing training a plus.

APPLICATION PROCEDURE: Submit résumé, cover letter, and articles written *to* Cynthia Hancock, Manager of PR/Publications.

NBC-TV

30 Rockefeller Plaza	**Phone:** 212/664-4444
New York, NY 10112	**FAX:** 212/664-5830

* * *

ORGANIZATION'S ACTIVITIES: Headquarters of international broadcasting network; offices in cities nationwide.

Number of Internships: Varies; numerous.

Type: Research, finance, communications, production, sports, publicity.

Function/Duties: Assist staff in department of choice as assigned, in ongoing duties and on projects.

Schedule: Full-time summers; 3 days per week during academic year.

Stipend or Pay: No.

Academic Credit Offered: *Must* be arranged by student with academic institution.

ELIGIBILITY: Graduate and undergraduate students.

REQUIREMENTS: Competition is great for these positions; relevant majors with some experience preferred.

APPLICATION PROCEDURE: Send résumé and cover letter *to* Intern Coordinator *by* mid-April at latest for summer internship.

NATIONAL JOURNALISM CENTER

800 Maryland Avenue NE	**Phone:** 202/544-1333
Washington, DC 20002	**FAX:** 202/544-5368

* * *

ORGANIZATION'S ACTIVITIES: Journalism training program.

Number of Internships: Varies.

Type: Journalism.

Function/Duties: Work with staff on stories.

Schedule: Full-time for 3-month stints.

Stipend or Pay: $100 per week.

Academic Credit Offered: Yes.

ELIGIBILITY: Primarily undergraduate students.

REQUIREMENTS: English majors with some writing experience.

APPLICATION PROCEDURE: Request application form and return with résumé and writing samples *to* Mal Kline or Piper Lowell, editors, *by* 2 weeks before session desired.

NATIONAL PUBLIC RADIO

635 Massachusetts Avenue NW   **Phone:** 202/414-2000
Washington, DC 20036   **FAX:** 202/414-3043

* * *

ORGANIZATION'S ACTIVITIES: Headquarters for national network providing news and other programming to over 400 AM and FM member stations nationwide.

Number of Internships: Varies; fairly numerous.

Type: Research, writing, technical, communications.

Function/Duties: Aid regular staff in production, reporting, publicity, news and information writing and support.

Schedule: Full- and/or part-time, summers, semesters, and year-round.

Stipend or Pay: Some paid internships.

Academic Credit Offered: Per student's own arrangements with academic institution.

ELIGIBILITY: Primarily graduate and undergraduate students.

REQUIREMENTS: Prefer college seniors and graduate students with some experience and/or relevant career goals.

APPLICATION PROCEDURE: Send inquiries *to* Personnel Director. *Deadline:* Depends on time period sought.

NATIONAL WILDLIFE FEDERATION

1400 16th Street NW   **Phone:** 202/797-6800
Washington, DC 20036   **FAX:** 202/797-6646

* * *

ORGANIZATION'S ACTIVITIES: The world's largest nonprofit, non-governmental conservation education organization, sponsoring research, public education, and legislative and legal advocacy among other environmental protection activities.

Number of Internships: 12.

Type: Advocacy journalism.

Function/Duties: Work with *The Leader*, the NWF's monthly national newspaper covering all major resources issues for conservationists.

Schedule: Full-time 6 months (January–June and July–December).

Stipend or Pay: About $300 per week plus some benefits.

Academic Credit Offered: Per student's own arrangements with academic institution.

ELIGIBILITY: Some graduate students; mostly college graduates with degrees and/or experience in environmentally related sciences and social issues. *Special Eligibilities*: A completely equal-opportunity program; women and minorities are encouraged to apply.

REQUIREMENTS: These are highly competitive positions and some related background is a plus; excellent speaking and writing skills required.

APPLICATION PROCEDURE: Send cover letter, résumé, contact information for 3 to 5 academic or professional references, and 4 writing samples *to* Nancy Hwa, Resources Conservation Internship Program, *by* October 2 for January start and *by* April 1 for July start.

NEWS USA

4601-H Eisenhower Avenue		**Phone:**	703/461-8500
Alexandria, VA 22304		**FAX:**	703/461-9507

* * *

ORGANIZATION'S ACTIVITIES: Washington, D.C., area media/public relations firms specializing in writing, editing, and distributing information to print and broadcast media; offices in New York and Los Angeles areas.

Number of Internships: Varies.

Type: Public relations, sales, communications, computers.

Function/Duties: Assist staff with research, surveys, database maintenance, special projects.

Schedule: Full- or part-time, about 3 months.

Stipend or Pay: No.

Academic Credit Offered: Per student's own arrangements with academic institution; *Plus* may lead to career position.

ELIGIBILITY: Consideration given to students, non-students, or career-changers with appropriate qualifications.

REQUIREMENTS: Interests, goals, and/or experience relevant to available assignments; some Macintosh skills preferred.

APPLICATION PROCEDURE: Send résumé *to* Patrick Summers, Director of Administration. *Deadline:* Ongoing.

NEWSWEEK

444 Madison Avenue
New York, NY 10022

Phone: 212/350-4275
FAX: 212/421-4993

* * *

ORGANIZATION'S ACTIVITIES: Weekly newsmagazine with international circulation.

Number of Internships: A dozen or more.

Type: Researcher/fact checker.

Function/Duties: Support, assist, and learn from staff reporters, editors, and production.

Schedule: Full-time, 13 weeks: June, July, and August.

Stipend or Pay: $425; *Plus* Independent work encouraged; bylines possible.

Academic Credit Offered: No.

ELIGIBILITY: College students who have finished their junior years and graduate students. Non-students and career-changers welcome to apply.

REQUIREMENTS: Should have some journalism background and strong reporting skills.

APPLICATION PROCEDURE: Submit cover letter, résumé, and 5 published clips *to* Liz Shofner.

PAM BERG CONSULTANTS, INC.

2709 Brambleton Avenue
Roanoke, VA 24015

Phone: 703/774-1736
FAX: 703/774-8917

* * *

ORGANIZATION'S ACTIVITIES: Public relations and marketing firm providing consulting services to profit and nonprofit businesses.

Number of Internships: 2 or more.

Type: Project assistant.

Function/Duties: Assist with client work—various duties and responsibilities.

Schedule: Part-time, one semester term.

Stipend or Pay: No.

Academic Credit Offered: Yes.

ELIGIBILITY: College juniors and seniors; preferred major: Communications.

REQUIREMENTS: Availability to work in Roanoke; excellent communications skills.

APPLICATION PROCEDURE: Submit résumé and letter, listing classes taken in major *to* Pam Berg Horner, APR.

THE PEABODY ORLANDO

9801 International Drive **Phone:** 407/352-4000
Orlando, FL 32819 **FAX:** 407/351-9177

* * *

ORGANIZATION'S ACTIVITIES: Full-service luxury hotel located in central Florida servicing convention attendees, business travelers, and vacationers. Public relations department handles all promotion/publicity for the award-winning property.

Number of Internships: 2 or more.

Type: Public relations internships.

Function/Duties: Assist public relations staff with releases, brochures, media relations, etc.

Schedule: Full-time and part-time.

Stipend or Pay: No.

Academic Credit Offered: Per student's own arrangements with academic institution.

ELIGIBILITY: College and graduate students; preferred majors: Public Relations, Communications, Journalism/Public Relations mix; possibly high-school students for future college credit approved in advance by institution.

REQUIREMENTS: Availability to work in Orlando; excellent communications skills.

APPLICATION PROCEDURE: Submit introduction letter, college requirements, and writing sample *to* Ms. Sonya Snyder, Director of Public Relations.

PHILADELPHIA INQUIRER

400 North Broad Street **Phone:** 215/854-2000
Philadelphia, PA 19130 **FAX:** 215/854-4794

* * *

ORGANIZATION'S ACTIVITIES: Major daily newspaper.

Number of Internships: Varies.

Type: Journalism.

Function/Duties: Intensive program in one or more of these areas of paper: business, photography, sports, feature writing, medical reporting.

Schedule: 2 years full- or part-time, first year on *Inquirer*; second on another of the chain's papers.

Stipend or Pay: Yes.

Academic Credit Offered: Per student's own arrangements with academic institution.

ELIGIBILITY: Junior and senior college students and graduating seniors heading for graduate school. *Special Eligibilities:* Program for minorities.

REQUIREMENTS: Some newspaper experience required.

APPLICATION PROCEDURE: Send clips, résumé, and cover letter *to* Senior Editor *by* January 1.

PHILLIPS PUBLISHING INTERNATIONAL

7811 Montrose Road	**Phone:** 301/340-2100
Potomac, MD 20854	**FAX:** 301/424-4297

* * *

ORGANIZATION'S ACTIVITIES: The largest newsletter publisher in the U.S. and one of the largest publishers of periodicals, with annual sales of nearly $120 million and an annual list of more than 100 consumer and business publications, produced at headquarters near Washington, D.C., and at over 16 other offices around the nation and the world.

Number of Internships: Varies; usually numerous at various locations.

Type: Editorial, marketing, production, finance, administration.

Function/Duties: Assist and learn from staff members in areas closest to intern's expertise and interest.

Schedule: Usually full-time throughout summer; also some at holiday times.

Stipend or Pay: May be arranged.

Academic Credit Offered: Per student's own arrangements with academic institution.

ELIGIBILITY: Primarily undergraduate and graduate students.

REQUIREMENTS: Coursework and/or experience related to area of intern's choice.

APPLICATION PROCEDURE: Send cover letter and résumé *to* Director of Corporate Resources *by* 3 months prior to start date.

THE PHOENIX GAZETTE

120 East Van Buren	**Phone:** 602/271-8600
Phoenix, AZ 85004	**FAX:** 602/271-8911

* * *

ORGANIZATION'S ACTIVITIES: Daily newspaper containing news, columns, features, and advertising. The news department produces photos and articles for publication.

Number of Internships: 4 per year.

Type: Photographer intern.

Function/Duties: Aid and learn from photo staff.

Schedule: Full-time, 3-month term: June, July, August.

Stipend or Pay: $391 per week.

Academic Credit Offered: Per student's own arrangements with academic institution.

ELIGIBILITY: Prefer at least 2 years of college education; graduating seniors and post-grad students may apply, as may non-students with a college education; preferred major: Photojournalism.

REQUIREMENTS: Standing, walking, some lifting of equipment (30 pounds), good communication skills, driver's license, and reliable transportation; must use color processors.

APPLICATION PROCEDURE: Submit slide portfolio—sports, news, feature—*to* Tim Koors, Director of Photography.

PLANNED TV ARTS

25 West 43rd Street   **Phone:** 212/921-5111
New York, NY 10036   **FAX:**   212/768-1216

* * *

ORGANIZATION'S ACTIVITIES: Independent public relations agency specializing in media placement. Works with local and national broadcast media as well as all print outlets securing interviews for authors and spokespeople.

Number of Internships: 4.

Type: Clerical, booking shows, media placement training, and media research.

Function/Duties: Assist staff of specific departments according to intern's skills and interests.

Schedule: Year-round/seasonal (4 months); full-time and part-time internships available.

Stipend or Pay: No; company reimburses travel expenses.

Academic Credit Offered: Per intern's own arrangements with academic institution.

ELIGIBILITY: Undergraduate and graduate students are encouraged to apply; preferred majors: Communications and Public Relations; *Plus* internship occasionally leads to full-time employment.

REQUIREMENTS: Provide cover letter and résumé along with an application.

APPLICATION PROCEDURE: Submit full application *to* David Hahn.
Deadline: No.

PORTER/NOVELLI

1633 Broadway   **Phone:** 212/315-8000
New York, NY 10019-6785   **FAX:**   212/315-8107

*   *   *

ORGANIZATION'S ACTIVITIES: Public relations firm.

Number of Internships: Flexible; 1–4.

Type: Assistant to account executive.

Function/Duties: Developing and updating media lists, account team support, developing and writing media pitch letters, and other related duties.

Schedule: Full-time, during summer.

Stipend or Pay: $250 per week.

Academic Credit Offered: Per student's own arrangements with academic institution.

ELIGIBILITY: Graduate students and career-changers with undergraduate degrees (must have B.A. or B.S.).

REQUIREMENTS: Specializations in journalism, English, communications, and public relations.

APPLICATION PROCEDURE: Mail résumé and cover letter *to* Deborah Kaufman. *Deadline:* Rolling.

PRICE STERN SLOAN

11150 Olympic Boulevard
Sixth Floor   **Phone:** 310/477-6100
Los Angeles, CA 90064   **FAX:**   310/445-3933

*   *   *

ORGANIZATION'S ACTIVITIES: Book publisher—trade books, children's humor, cookbooks, automotive.

Number of Internships: Varies.

Type: Editorial, design, advertising, publicity.

Function/Duties: Some clerical as well as entry-level work.

Schedule: Part-time and some full-time, flexible term.

Stipend or Pay: No salary, only mileage money.

Academic Credit Offered: No.

ELIGIBILITY: College students, career-changers, and non-students with related experience.

REQUIREMENTS: Relevant interests, skills, and/or background; excellent communications skills.

APPLICATION PROCEDURE: Submit résumé *to* Human Resources.

PRIME TICKET

10000 Santa Monica Boulevard
Los Angeles, CA 90067

Phone: 310/286-3800
FAX: 310/286-3875

* * *

ORGANIZATION'S ACTIVITIES: Cable TV company that operates the nation's largest regional sports network.

Number of Internships: 2.

Type: Communications.

Function/Duties: Assist with public relations and other media functions.

Schedule: Full- or part-time summers, part-time fall and spring semesters (20 hours a week).

Stipend or Pay: No.

Academic Credit Offered: Per student's own arrangements with academic institution.

ELIGIBILITY: Primarily undergraduate and graduate students.

REQUIREMENTS: Excellent communications skills; interest in sports media or cable production.

APPLICATION PROCEDURE: Send inquiries *to* Bryan Bird. *Deadline:* Ongoing.

PUBLIC RELATIONS JOURNAL

33 Irving Place
New York, NY 10003

Phone: 212/995-2230
FAX: 212/995-0757

* * *

ORGANIZATION'S ACTIVITIES: The leading national monthly publication on public relations.

Number of Internships: Varies.

Type: Editorial.

Function/Duties: Participate in "all phases of magazine work," with some telephone and clerical duties.

Schedule: 15 hours per week, 2 months' commitment.

Stipend or Pay: No.

Academic Credit Offered: Per student's own arrangements with academic institution.

ELIGIBILITY: Primarily undergraduate and graduate students; career-changers and others with appropriate qualifications considered.

REQUIREMENTS: Prefer some writing and reporting experience, some public relations background.

APPLICATION PROCEDURE: Send inquiries *to* Senior Editor. *Deadline:* Ongoing.

RANDOM HOUSE PUBLISHING

201 East 50th Street   **Phone:** 212/751-2600
New York, NY 10022   **FAX:**   212/872-8026

*   *   *

ORGANIZATION'S ACTIVITIES: One of the country's leading trade book publishers.

Number of Internships: 6.

Type: Similar to any entry-level job.

Function/Duties: Assist in every type of publishing department to learn functions; also clerical work.

Schedule: Summertime, full-time.

Stipend or Pay: $225 per week.

Academic Credit Offered: Per student's own arrangements with academic institution.

ELIGIBILITY: Undergraduate and graduate students.

REQUIREMENTS: Availability for full-time work in New York City; career interest in publishing a plus.

APPLICATION PROCEDURE: Submit résumé and cover letter; discuss details and arrange for interview *with* Personnel Recruiting *by* as early in the year as possible.

THE REGISTER-GUARD

P.O. Box 10188   **Phone:** 503/485-1234
Eugene, OR 97440   **FAX:**   503/683-7631

*   *   *

ORGANIZATION'S ACTIVITIES: Newspaper.

Number of Internships: 1 or more.

Type: News reporter, photographer.

Function/Duties: Under guidance of staff members, research and cover stories.

Schedule: June through August, full-time; part-time during school semesters.

Stipend or Pay: Varies.

Academic Credit Offered: Available sometimes.

ELIGIBILITY: College and graduate students; preferred major: Journalism.

REQUIREMENTS: Must be available to work irregular hours in Eugene; some journalistic background preferred.

APPLICATION PROCEDURE: Submit letter, résumé, and clips *to* Kay Black. *Deadline:* April 1.

RESNICK COMMUNICATIONS

1529 Walnut Street   **Phone:**   215/977-7383
Philadelphia, PA 19102   **FAX:**   215/977-8920

* * *

ORGANIZATION'S ACTIVITIES: Full-service public relations and marketing communications firm specializing in representing, among others, museums and other cultural groups.

Number of Internships: Varies.

Type: Public relations.

Function/Duties: Assist professional staff in all aspects of media relations, writing, research, and client services.

Schedule: Full-time summers; part-time year-round or per semester.

Stipend or Pay: No.

Academic Credit Offered: Per student's own arrangements with academic institution.

ELIGIBILITY: Consideration given to students, non-students, or career-changers with appropriate qualifications.

REQUIREMENTS: Interests, goals, and/or experience relevant to available assignments.

APPLICATION PROCEDURE: Send inquiries *to* Kelly Anne Burke. *Deadline:* Ongoing.

RUDER FINN

1615 M Street NW   **Phone:**   202/466-7800
Washington, DC 20036   **FAX:**   202/887-0905

* * *

ORGANIZATION'S ACTIVITIES: One of the nation's largest full-service independent public relations firms, with offices in Washington, New York, and elsewhere in the country and around the world.

Number of Internships: Varies.

Type: Executive training program.

Function/Duties: Well-known competitive work-learn program whose participants work full-time at the agency in hands-on assignments and also attend seminars for which homework is assigned.

Schedule: 3 four-month sessions per year are held, in firm's New York and Washington offices only, involving "long hours."

Stipend or Pay: Yes—about $300 per week.

Academic Credit Offered: N/A; *Plus* most program graduates are hired by firm; others "obtain jobs elsewhere without difficulty" because program is "widely respected."

ELIGIBILITY: College graduates with at least a BA; "and many with advanced degrees who are seeking entry in the P.R. field."

REQUIREMENTS: Applicants must pass writing test and interviewing process.

APPLICATION PROCEDURE: Send application forms, writing tests, résumé, writing samples, references, and other materials *to* Executive Training Program. *Deadline:* 2 months prior to start date of each session; call for details.

SAGE MARCOM, INC.

717 Erie Boulevard West **Phone:** 315/478-6612
Syracuse, NY 13204 **FAX:** 315/475-9723

* * *

ORGANIZATION'S ACTIVITIES: Business-to-business marketing communications firm (including advertising, public relations).

Number of Internships: Approximately 3 per semester.

Type: Public relations, trade media advertising, graphic design.

Function/Duties: All-around assistance, limited client contact, writing.

Schedule: Full-time and part-time, minimum 15 hours per week; semester or summer long term.

Stipend or Pay: No.

Academic Credit Offered: Per student's own arrangements with academic institution.

ELIGIBILITY: College students, preferably graduate students; preferred majors: Business, Communications, and Marketing.

REQUIREMENTS: Research and phone work a plus. Must be mature, willing to do "gofer" work to be exposed to agency environment and establish contacts and relationships and gain business-to-business insight.

APPLICATION PROCEDURE: Submit customized cover letter, résumé, and work samples (if applicable) *to* Ms. Robin Farewell. *Deadline:* April for summer, June for fall, and November for winter-spring.

SAMUEL GOLDWYN COMPANY

888 Seventh Avenue
Suite 2901 **Phone:** No calls
New York, NY 10106 **FAX:** 212/307-6051

* * *

ORGANIZATION'S ACTIVITIES: Movie and entertainment producer and distributor.

Number of Internships: Varies; a few per semester.

Type: Publicity.

Function/Duties: Assisting the publicity department in all areas—mass screening mailings, marketing areas to send mass promotional material, promotional ideas for film projects, interacting with media.

Schedule: Part-time during fall and spring, full-time and part-time during summer.

Stipend or Pay: No.

Academic Credit Offered: Yes.

ELIGIBILITY: Undergraduate students; film, communications, or production majors preferred but not necessary.

REQUIREMENTS: Interests, goals, skills, and/or experience relevant to available assignments.

APPLICATION PROCEDURE: Submit résumé *to* Suzanne Dushoff. Application due *by* the last week in August for fall placement, December for the spring, and April for the summer.

SAN FRANCISCO BAY GUARDIAN

520 Hampshire Street   **Phone:**   415/255-3100
San Francisco, CA 94114   **FAX:**   415/241-8037

* * *

ORGANIZATION'S ACTIVITIES: The Bay area's alternative weekly newspaper, covering news, culture, and entertainment.

Number of Internships: 12.

Type: Research, editorial.

Function/Duties: Assist staff with fact-checking, and some reporting and writing.

Schedule: At least 2 days a week each term, year-round.

Stipend or Pay: No.

Academic Credit Offered: Per student's own arrangements with academic institution; *Plus* internships may lead to regular employment.

ELIGIBILITY: Students, non-students, or career-changers welcome to apply. *Special Eligibilities:* People of color and women are given special consideration.

REQUIREMENTS: Highly competitive positions.

APPLICATION PROCEDURE: Send cover letter, résumé, and 3 writing samples *to* Personnel Department *by* April for summer term, August for fall, and December for spring.

SAN FRANCISCO CHRONICLE

901 Mission Street   **Phone:**   415/777-1111
San Francisco, CA 94103   **FAX:**   415/512-8196

* * *

ORGANIZATION'S ACTIVITIES: Leading California daily paper: the largest in the northern part of the state.

Number of Internships: 10.

Type: Reporting, photography, layout.

Function/Duties: Work independently on assignments under guidance of staff professionals.

Schedule: Full-time, summer.

Stipend or Pay: Regular salary.

Academic Credit Offered: Per student's own arrangements with academic institution; *Plus* competition is intense for positions.

ELIGIBILITY: Open to undergraduate and graduate students, but most positions are awarded to graduates, many with advanced degrees.

REQUIREMENTS: Must successfully compete with thousands of other applicants; have some journalistic credits already.

APPLICATION PROCEDURE: Send inquiries IN WRITING ONLY *to* Director of Promotions in time to complete application process *by* November 1.

SAVVY MANAGEMENT PUBLIC RELATIONS, Inc.

80 Fourth Avenue
Suite 800   **Phone:** 212/477-1717
New York, NY 10003   **FAX:** 212/477-1736

*   *   *

ORGANIZATION'S ACTIVITIES: A public relations, marketing, and special events firm.

Number of Internships: Varies with need.

Type: Assistants to account executives.

Function/Duties: Writing press releases and pitch letters, media list research, compiling press kits, event production, and other office functions.

Schedule: Flexible.

Stipend or Pay: Yes; $100 per week.

Academic Credit Offered: As arranged by student with academic institution; *Plus* media placement technique training, written recommendations, and guarantee of references.

ELIGIBILITY: Graduate and undergraduate college students.

REQUIREMENTS: Strong written and verbal skills a plus.

APPLICATION PROCEDURE: Send résumé with cover letter *to* John Johmann. *Deadline:* Open.

SCHOLASTIC, INC.

555 Broadway   **Phone:** 212/343-6100
New York, NY 10012   **FAX:** 212/343-6928

*   *   *

ORGANIZATION'S ACTIVITIES: Leading publisher of books, magazines, and other materials for young people and educators.

Number of Internships: Numerous; varies.

Type: Magazine and book editorial and design.

Function/Duties: Assist in and involvement with every aspect of company's activities.

Schedule: 10 weeks in summer, full-time weekdays.

Stipend or Pay: $315 per week.

Academic Credit Offered: Per student's own arrangements with academic institution.

ELIGIBILITY: College students preferred.

REQUIREMENTS: Availability for work in New York City; career interest in publishing.

APPLICATION PROCEDURE: Call for application form; submit *to* Human Resources Department *by* February 28.

SEATTLE/KING COUNTY NEWS BUREAU

520 Pike Street
Suite 1325   **Phone:** 206/461-5805
Seattle, WA 98101   **FAX:**   206/461-5871

* * *

ORGANIZATION'S ACTIVITIES: Proactive/reactive media relations for Seattle and King County. Work primarily with out-of-state travel media.

Number of Internships: 2 or more.

Type: Media relations assistant.

Function/Duties: Media relations.

Schedule: Part-time and full-time, term September through May.

Stipend or Pay: No.

Academic Credit Offered: Flexible.

ELIGIBILITY: College and graduate students; preferred majors: Public Relations and Communications. Career-changers and non-students welcome to apply.

REQUIREMENTS: Excellent communications skills, self-starter.

APPLICATION PROCEDURE: Submit résumé *to* or *call* David Blandford.

STACK MARKETING COMMUNICATIONS, INC.

425 Madison Avenue   **Phone:** 212/750-3434
New York, NY 10021   **FAX:** N/A

* * *

ORGANIZATION'S ACTIVITIES: Full-service marketing communications firm specializing in corporate sponsorship for sports and special events.

Number of Internships: 1.

Type: Junior account executive.

Function/Duties: Varies with client.

Schedule: Part-time, semester or summer term.

Stipend or Pay: Yes.

Academic Credit Offered: No.

ELIGIBILITY: Junior or senior college students; all graduate students; preferred majors: Journalism and Public Relations.

REQUIREMENTS: Prefer member of PRSSA or SPJ. Assignments are extremely demanding and require attention to deadline and detail.

APPLICATION PROCEDURE: Submit résumé and cover letter *to* Bob Stack.

STERLING HAGER INC.

2 Lewis Street   **Phone:** 617/259-1400
Lincoln, MA 01773   **FAX:** 617/259-1512

* * *

ORGANIZATION'S ACTIVITIES: Full-service public relations firm that provides professional public relations counsel to high-technology companies exclusively.

Number of Internships: Varies.

Type: Editorial, marketing, public relations.

Function/Duties: Assist and learn from professional staff, participating in ongoing functions as well as special projects.

Schedule: Full- and/or part-time, summers and academic semesters.

Stipend or Pay: No.

Academic Credit Offered: Per student's own arrangements with academic institution; *Plus* internships may lead to career positions.

ELIGIBILITY: Primarily undergraduate and graduate students.

REQUIREMENTS: "Willingness to learn and interest in public relations as a career."

APPLICATION PROCEDURE: Send résumé and writing samples *to* Roberta Carlton *by* about 2 months prior to beginning of semester.

TEMERLIN McCLAIN

201 East Carpenter Freeway   **Phone:** 214/556-1100
Dallas/Fort Worth Airport, TX 75261-9200   **FAX:** 214/830-2619

* * *

ORGANIZATION'S ACTIVITIES: Temerlin McClain Public Relations is affiliated with Temerlin McClain, the largest advertising agency in the Southwest. The Public Relations department is composed of 25 employees and has approximately $1.5 million in annual billings, ranking in the top three PR firms in Dallas.

Number of Internships: Flexible; varies with need.

Type: Public relations internships.

Function/Duties: Interns work on a variety of accounts in industries including high technology, health care, transportation, banking, and energy. Exposure to national accounts like American Airlines, Nations Bank, Marriott, Texas Instruments, JCPenney, and Southland Corporation (owner of 7-Eleven).

Schedule: Minimum of 20 hours a week during spring and fall semesters and full-time during the summer.

Stipend or Pay: $5 per hour.

Academic Credit Offered: Per student's own arrangements with academic institution.

ELIGIBILITY: College students, preferably juniors and seniors.

REQUIREMENTS: Work in Dallas office. Must be self-starter, dependable, detail-oriented, good writer, and truly interested in pursing a career in public relations.

APPLICATION PROCEDURE: Send résumé *to* David Nieland, Account Executive, and follow up with a phone call *to* 214/830-2663.

TEXAS ALLIANCE FOR HUMAN NEEDS

2520 Longview
Suite 311
Austin, TX 78705   **Phone:** 512/474-5019
     FAX: N/A

* * *

ORGANIZATION'S ACTIVITIES: "The only independent statewide multi-issue coalition of organizations concerned about low- and moderate-income Texans," serving as a clearinghouse for information, technical assistance, and materials.

Number of Internships: 1.

Type: Archivist and researcher.

Function/Duties: Organize articles gathered from press related to issues supported by TAHN; research information for press.

Schedule: Year-round; 5 to 10 hours minimum per week, plus more during special projects.

Stipend or Pay: No; free housing may be arranged.

Academic Credit Offered: Per student's own arrangements with academic institution.

ELIGIBILITY: Students, non-students, or career-changers.

REQUIREMENTS: Interest in research and issues; good organizational ability.

APPLICATION PROCEDURE: *Contact* Executive Director for details. *Deadline:* Open.

Number of Internships: 1.

Type: Newsletter editor.

Function/Duties: Gather and/or write articles for "TAHN News," manage and supervise production and distribution.

Schedule: Year-round, 1 week per month.

Stipend or Pay: No; free housing may be arranged.

Academic Credit Offered: Per student's own arrangements with academic institution.

ELIGIBILITY: Students, non-students, or career-changers.

REQUIREMENTS: Good writing skills, good organizational ability.

APPLICATION PROCEDURE: *Contact* Executive Director for details. *Deadline:* Open.

Number of Internships: 1.

Type: Legislative reporter.

Function/Duties: Report on state legislative and government activities as they relate to TAHN matters.

Schedule: Minimum 15 hours per week, flexible.

Stipend or Pay: No; free housing may be arranged.

Academic Credit Offered: Per student's own arrangements with academic institution.

ELIGIBILITY: Students, non-students, or career-changers.

REQUIREMENTS: Good writing and communications skills, interest in issues.

APPLICATION PROCEDURE: *Contact* Executive Director for details. *Deadline:* Open.

THOMAS JEFFERSON UNIVERSITY

1015 Chestnut Street	**Phone:**	215/955-6300
Philadelphia, PA 19107	**FAX:**	215/955-5008

* * *

ORGANIZATION'S ACTIVITIES: An educational institution over 150 years old, includes undergraduate and graduate as well as medical divisions.

Number of Internships: Varies.

Type: Media relations.

Function/Duties: Work with public relations specialist to translate and produce articles and other matter that make clear research findings and other technical material.

Schedule: Part-time, summers as well as fall and spring semesters.

Stipend or Pay: No.

Academic Credit Offered: Per student's own arrangements with academic institution; *Plus* reimbursement of commuting costs and meals.

ELIGIBILITY: Primarily graduate and undergraduate students.

REQUIREMENTS: Availability to work in Philadelphia office; good communications skills and interest in technical writing.

APPLICATION PROCEDURE: Send résumé with cover letter and writing sample *to* Carole Gan *by* several months prior to start date.

TRANSLINK COMMUNICATIONS

25 West 43rd Street
Suite 1017   **Phone:** 212/921-5111
New York, NY 10036   **FAX:** 212/382-3341

* * *

ORGANIZATION'S ACTIVITIES: Full-service production company: domestic and international satellite TV tours, B-roll newsfeeds, video news releases, electronic press kits, media training, product launches, teleconferences, press junkets.

Number of Internships: 3 or 4 per year.

Type: Assistant to the director of operations.

Function/Duties: Production assistant.

Schedule: Full-time and part-time, flexible term.

Stipend or Pay: Transportation costs only.

Academic Credit Offered: If arranged by intern.

ELIGIBILITY: High-school, college, and graduate students. Non-students and career-changers welcome.

REQUIREMENTS: Must be detail oriented and computer literate.

APPLICATION PROCEDURE: *Call* company to set up an initial interview. *Deadline:* Open.

WBEZ-FM

103 West Adams
Chicago, IL 60603

Phone: 312/460-9150
FAX: N/A

* * *

ORGANIZATION'S ACTIVITIES: National Public Radio member station for the Chicago area.

Number of Internships: Varies.

Type: Editorial, research, technical.

Function/Duties: Assist staff as needed with ongoing activities and special projects.

Schedule: Full- and/or part-time, year-round availability.

Stipend or Pay: Some paid, some unpaid.

Academic Credit Offered: Per student's own arrangements with academic institution.

ELIGIBILITY: Primarily undergraduate and graduate students.

REQUIREMENTS: Prefer those with career interest in broadcasting and/or public affairs.

APPLICATION PROCEDURE: Send inquiries *to* Programming Coordinator. *Deadline:* Ongoing.

WGN RADIO

435 North Michigan Avenue
Chicago, IL 60611

Phone: 312/222-4700
FAX: 312/222-5165

* * *

ORGANIZATION'S ACTIVITIES: Leading Midwest all-news AM-radio station.

Number of Internships: 16.

Type: News, sports, programming.

Function/Duties: Assist regular staff in significant ways with ongoing operations and special projects.

Schedule: 13 weeks full-time, four times per year.

Stipend or Pay: Yes.

Academic Credit Offered: Per student's own arrangements with academic institution; *Plus* internships often lead to regular employment.

ELIGIBILITY: Primarily undergraduate or graduate students as well as recent graduates.

REQUIREMENTS: Interests, goals, skills, and/or experience relevant to available assignments.

APPLICATION PROCEDURE: Send inquiries *to* Intern Director. *Deadline:* About 2 months prior to start date.

WKXL AM & FM

P.O. Box 875
37 Redington Road   **Phone:**   603/225-5521
Concord, NH 03302-0875   **FAX:**   603/224-6404

*   *   *

ORGANIZATION'S ACTIVITIES: Radio broadcasting—full-service format—emphasis on local and state news and sports; a CBS affiliate.

Number of Internships: 1.

Type: News and/or sales.

Function/Duties: Assist reporters in gathering, writing, editing; assist sales reps with sales and service of accounts.

Schedule: Part-time and full-time, 3- to 6-month term.

Stipend or Pay: No.

Academic Credit Offered: If arranged by intern.

ELIGIBILITY: College students in sophomore through senior years and graduate students; preferred majors: Broadcasting, Journalism, Communications, and Marketing. Career-changers accepted by special arrangement.

REQUIREMENTS: Must have own transportation and living arrangements.

APPLICATION PROCEDURE: Submit résumé and cover letter *to* Richard W. Osborne, President and General Manager.

WMAR-TV

6400 York Road   **Phone:**   410/377-2222
Baltimore, MD 21212   **FAX:**   410/377-0493

*   *   *

ORGANIZATION'S ACTIVITIES: NBC Network affiliate broadcast station.

Number of Internships: Varies.

Type: Journalism, communications, public relations.

Function/Duties: Varies.

Schedule: One semester term.

Stipend or Pay: No.

Academic Credit Offered: Yes.

ELIGIBILITY: College juniors and seniors, graduate students; preferred majors: Journalism, Communications, and Public Relations.

REQUIREMENTS: Interests, goals, skills, and/or background related to broadcast media.

APPLICATION PROCEDURE: Request application and submit *to* Darcel Guy, Director of Public Relations. *Deadline:* One semester prior to desired start date.

WNET-TV

356 West 58th Street
New York, NY 10019

Phone: 212/560-2000
FAX: 212/582-3297

* * *

ORGANIZATION'S ACTIVITIES: The Public Broadcasting System (PBS) station covering the New York City metropolitan area.

Number of Internships: 30.

Type: Production, marketing, fundraising.

Function/Duties: Aid staff in department of choice as assigned, with ongoing duties and with special projects.

Schedule: Minimum 16 hours per week.

Stipend or Pay: Daily-expense stipend is available.

Academic Credit Offered: Per student's own arrangements with academic institution.

ELIGIBILITY: Graduate and undergraduate students.

REQUIREMENTS: Seniors and graduate students with some appropriate experience preferred.

APPLICATION PROCEDURE: Send inquiries *to* Manager for Recruitment and Staffing. *Deadline:* Varies.

WNYC RADIO AND TV

One Centre Street
New York, NY 10007

Phone: 212/669-7800
FAX: 212/669-8986

* * *

ORGANIZATION'S ACTIVITIES: Major Public Broadcasting Station, serving the New York metropolitan area with news, music, cultural affairs, and educational broadcasting daily.

Number of Internships: Varies with need and interest.

Type: Radio and TV programming, station operations, engineering, public relations, radio news.

Function/Duties: Assist staff according to need and intern's interest.

Schedule: Year-round; at least 15 to 20 hours per week, with hours varying by assignment.

Stipend or Pay: No.

Academic Credit Offered: Yes.

ELIGIBILITY: Graduate and undergraduate students, as well as occasional non-students or career-changers.

REQUIREMENTS: Interests, goals, and/or experience relevant to available assignments; interns encouraged to apply for more than one position.

APPLICATION PROCEDURE: Request application, return according to instructions *to* Internship Coordinator. *Deadline:* Ongoing.

WTTW-TV

5400 North St. Louis Avenue   **Phone:** 312/583-5000
Chicago, IL 60625   **FAX:** 312/583-3046

*   *   *

ORGANIZATION'S ACTIVITIES: The Chicago area's Public Broadcasting System affiliate.

Number of Internships: 2.

Type: "Harris Internships."

Function/Duties: These special interns are assigned full-time to one particular production staff under the supervision of that show's executive producer.

Schedule: Full-time, 1 year.

Stipend or Pay: Yes.

Academic Credit Offered: N/A; *Plus*: These are competitive positions.

ELIGIBILITY: College graduates.

REQUIREMENTS: Must be college graduate by the September start date of program; must meet criteria set forth in competition rules.

APPLICATION PROCEDURE: Send inquiries *to* Internship Coordinator in time to complete application process *by* February 28.

WTVS-TV

7441 Second Boulevard   **Phone:** 313/873-7200
Detroit, MI 48202   **FAX:** 313/876-8118

*   *   *

ORGANIZATION'S ACTIVITIES: Detroit's Public Television station.

Number of Internships: About 40 annually.

Type: In 12 areas of station activities, including production, marketing, events.

Function/Duties: Assist and learn from station professionals through participation in activities best suited to intern's skills and interests.

Schedule: Most internship are 20 hours per week, with 3-month minimum commitment.

Stipend or Pay: No.

Academic Credit Offered: Yes.

ELIGIBILITY: Primarily college students, but others considered with appropriate qualifications.

REQUIREMENTS: Interest in broadcasting as a career; some education or background in area of operations selected.

APPLICATION PROCEDURE: Send résumé and cover letter *to* Internship Coordinator, in Human Resources Department. *Deadline:* Ongoing.

THE WASHINGTON POST

1150 15th Street NW	**Phone:** 202/334-6000
Washington, DC 20071-5501	**FAX:** 202/334-1031

* * *

ORGANIZATION'S ACTIVITIES: Newsroom of one of the nation's leading daily newspapers.

Number of Internships: 20.

Type: Editors, copy editors, photographers, graphic artists.

Function/Duties: Aid and learn from professional staff in areas of greatest interest to intern.

Schedule: 12-week term during the summer.

Stipend or Pay: $721 per week.

Academic Credit Offered: Per student's own arrangement with educational institution.

ELIGIBILITY: College juniors and seniors, graduate students.

REQUIREMENTS: Interns must be good writers; previous internships or working at school newspaper; 6 newspaper clips.

APPLICATION PROCEDURE: Send postcard asking for application *to* Summer News Program. *Deadline:* Completed application must be postmarked *by* November 15.

THE WASHINGTON TIMES

3600 New York Avenue NE	**Phone:** 202/636-3200
Washington, DC 20002	**FAX:** 202/269-3419

* * *

ORGANIZATION'S ACTIVITIES: Conservative daily newspaper.

Number of Internships: 10.

Type: Editorial, production, photography.

Function/Duties: Work with regular staff on news features, and other departments of choice at paper.

Schedule: Full-time, 8 weeks in summer.

Stipend or Pay: Yes.

Academic Credit Offered: Per student's own arrangements with academic institution.

ELIGIBILITY: College students.

REQUIREMENTS: Students must be actively involved in their school newspapers.

APPLICATION PROCEDURE: Send inquiries *to* Internship Coordinator in time to complete application process *by* January 31.

WEINGART CENTER ASSOCIATION

566 South San Pedro Street   **Phone:** 213/627-9000
Los Angeles, CA 90013   **FAX:** 213/488-3419

*   *   *

ORGANIZATION'S ACTIVITIES: The Weingart Center is one of the nation's largest complexes providing health and human services for the homeless, widely regarded as a model for innovative partnerships with public and private agencies toward the goal of enabling homeless people to achieve economic and personal self-sufficiency.

Number of Internships: 3 or more.

Type: Public relations.

Function/Duties: Work directly with senior management on media plans, newsletters, press releases, and other materials.

Schedule: Full and/or part-time, summers and/or school semesters.

Stipend or Pay: No.

Academic Credit Offered: Per student's own arrangements with academic institution.

ELIGIBILITY: Consideration given to students, non-students, or career-changers with appropriate qualifications.

REQUIREMENTS: Interests, goals, skills, and/or experience relevant to available assignments.

APPLICATION PROCEDURE: Send inquiries *to* Vice President, Development and Community Affairs. *Deadline:* Ongoing.

WHEELOCK COLLEGE

200 The Riverway   **Phone:** 617/734-5200
Boston, MA 02215   **FAX:** 617/734-7103

*   *   *

ORGANIZATION'S ACTIVITIES: Undergraduate and graduate college whose academic focus is programs in teaching, social work, and child-life education and care.

Number of Internships: Varies.

Type: Writer or photographer.

Function/Duties: Participate in activities of college public relations and publications department.

Schedule: Full- and/or part-time, year-round availability.

Stipend or Pay: No.

Academic Credit Offered: Per student's own arrangements with academic institution.

ELIGIBILITY: Graduate or undergraduate students as well as career-changers.

REQUIREMENTS: Good communications skills, interest in public relations.

APPLICATION PROCEDURE: Send inquiries *to* Ann Comer. *Deadline:* open.

THE WILEY BROOKS COMPANY

603 Stewart Street **Phone:** 206/621-8538
Seattle, WA 98101 **FAX:** 206/623-8612

* * *

ORGANIZATION'S ACTIVITIES: A full-service public relations firm, specializing in crisis communications. Clients include nationally recognized companies. There is a special focus on legal and health care issues.

Number of Internships: Flexible depending on need.

Type: Entry-level professional.

Function/Duties: Perform entry-level duties in public relations, such as support and assistance of staff.

Schedule: Year-round for a 4-month period.

Stipend or Pay: Yes; $6 per hour, with a raise to $7 per hour after probationary period.

Academic Credit Offered: Per student's own arrangements with academic institution.

ELIGIBILITY: Graduate students and college seniors. *Special Eligibilities:* Women and minorities encouraged to apply.

REQUIREMENTS: Familiarity with computers, strong writing and verbal skills; must be self-starter. Preferred majors: Journalism and Public Relations.

APPLICATION PROCEDURE: Send résumé plus 3 writing samples *to* Mark Firmani. *Deadline:* Rolling.

WOODWARD-CLYDE GROUP, INC.

4582 South Ulster Street **Phone:** 303/740-2633
Denver, CO 80237 **FAX:** 303/740-2650

* * *

ORGANIZATION'S ACTIVITIES: Corporate communications department of international engineering firm.

Number of Internships: 1.

Type: Advertising, public relations, or publications/writing.

Function/Duties: Advertising, public relations, work on newsletter.

Schedule: Full-time and part-time, 3- to 6-month term.

Stipend or Pay: No.

Academic Credit Offered: No.

ELIGIBILITY: Undergraduates; preferred majors: Journalism, Public Relations, Advertising; some career-changers accepted.

REQUIREMENTS: Computer skills and excellent communications skills.

APPLICATION PROCEDURE: Submit résumé *to* Anne Bonelli.

WORLD FEDERALIST ASSOCIATION

418 7th Street SE   **Phone:** 202/546-3950
Washington, DC 20001   **FAX:** 202/546-3649

* * *

ORGANIZATION'S ACTIVITIES: The U.S. branch of an international movement seeking to replace global anarchy with a system of limited global governance through formal global cooperation to solve global problems.

Number of Internships: 5 or more.

Type: Communications and publications.

Function/Duties: Aid directors in producing news releases and other materials, in organizing events, and in preparing newsletters.

Schedule: Flexible, about 30 hours per week.

Stipend or Pay: Small stipend for expenses.

Academic Credit Offered: Per student's own arrangements with academic institution.

ELIGIBILITY: Primarily graduate and undergraduate students.

REQUIREMENTS: Strong communications skills and organizational ability, plus commitment "to building a better, more peaceful world."

APPLICATION PROCEDURE: Send résumé and letter of interest *to* Student Programs Director in time to schedule interview and complete applications *by* at least one month prior to start date.

Organizations/Resources for Further Information about Internship Possibilities in Communications

PUBLIC RELATIONS SOCIETY OF AMERICA
33 Irving Place
New York, NY 10003
Phone: 212/995-2230
FAX: 212/995-0757

National association of public relations professionals working in every PR aspect and setting; maintains career bank and internship referral network; the Public Relations Students Society of America (PRSSA) is a rich internship resource for those studying public relations. Contact for information on how to make use of PRSA and PRSSA services.

Or register with:

INTERN PLACEMENT SERVICE
P.O. Box 1287
Maplewood, NJ 07040
Phone: 201/763-9409
FAX: 201/763-4818

IPS selects highly qualified college interns interviewed and screened to meet firms' specific design, marketing, advertising, or public relations needs.

OF FURTHER INTEREST

These associations of professionals in communications fields may offer internships themselves, and they can provide directions toward opportunities among their members.

ACTORS EQUITY ASSOCIATION
165 West 46th Street
New York, NY 10036
212/869-8530

ADVERTISING WOMEN OF NEW YORK
153 East 57th Street
New York, NY 10022
212/593-1950

AMERICAN ADVERTISING FEDERATION
1400 K Street NW
Suite 1000
Washington, DC 20005
202/898-0089

AMERICAN ASSOCIATION OF ADVERTISING
   AGENCIES
666 Third Avenue
New York, NY 10017
212/682-2500

AMERICAN SOCIETY OF COMPOSERS,
   AUTHORS AND PUBLISHERS (ASCAP)
One Lincoln Plaza
New York, NY 10023
212/595-4600

ASSOCIATION OF AMERICAN PUBLISHERS
220 East 23rd Street
New York, NY 10010
212/689-8920

DIRECTORS GUILD OF AMERICA
7920 Sunset Boulevard
Los Angeles, CA 90046
310/289-2000

DOW JONES NEWSPAPER FUND
P.O. Box 300
Princeton, NJ 08543
609/452-2820

THE MAGAZINE PUBLISHERS ASSOCIATION
575 Lexington Avenue
New York, NY 10022
212/752-0055

MOTION PICTURE ASSOCIATION OF
AMERICA
1133 Sixth Avenue
New York, NY 10036
212/840-6161

NATIONAL ASSOCIATION OF
BROADCASTERS
1771 N Street NW
Washington, DC 20036
202/429-5300

PROMOTION MARKETING ASSOCIATION OF
AMERICA, INC.
322 Eighth Avenue
Suite 1201
New York, NY 10001
212/206-1100

THE SCREEN ACTORS GUILD
7065 Hollywood Boulevard
Hollywood, CA 90028
213/465-4600

THE WRITER'S GUILD
555 West 57th Street
New York, NY 10019
212/767-7800

In addition to the specific opportunities listed above, the following professional and trade associations sponsor prestigious and highly competitive internship programs. Contact them directly for details.

INTERNATIONAL RADIO AND TELEVISION SOCIETY (IRTS)
420 Lexington Avenue
New York, NY 10170
Phone: 212/867-6650

An association representing member stations and broadcast organizations nationally and internationally that coordinates an annual Summer Fellowship Program. Through this program, 25 students are selected competitively for placement in New York City communications-related firms. Internships are, in general, unpaid, but transportation and housing stipends are offered, and many placements lead to full-time positions. Upper-level undergraduates with communications backgrounds should contact the IRTS Manager of Programs and Services for application information in time to complete the process by the November prior to placement.

ALLIANCE OF MOTION PICTURE & TELEVISION PRODUCERS
14144 Ventura Boulevard
Sherman Oaks, CA 91423
Phone: 818/995-3600

Association of film and video professionals that manages the industry's competition for the Assistant Directors Training Program. Those selected are assigned to member organizations for a year-plus of work, hands-on training, and seminars. To be eligible for consideration, candidates must be at least 21 years old, have U.S. citizenship or a green card, and either have a college or associates degree or have 2 years' work experience in the film or video industry. Placements are made in the fall, so those interested should contact the Program Administrator as early in the year as possible.

ACADEMY OF TELEVISION ARTS & SCIENCES
5220 Lankership Boulevard
North Hollywood, CA 91601
Phone: 818/754-2800

Through its competitive John H. Mitchell Internship Program, this association of TV professionals places recent college graduates in summer internships with TV production companies. Applicants should send a résumé, cover letter, transcript, 3 letters of recommendation, and an essay on their career goals in the industry to the Director of Educational Programs by January 1.

INTERNSHIP SOURCES IN CULTURE AND EDUCATION

■ ■

Notes on Interning in Culture and Education

Arts administration, sports and event management and marketing, and leisure planning are wide-open career paths—and museums, teams, parks, and other cultural and recreational groups, as listed in this section, especially welcome interns.

TIPS: 1. Considering a career in teaching? Explore it informally in cultural institutions.

2. Love to study history, the arts, science? Here are places to put that pleasure to work.

3. Have management skills, computer skills, other specialties, that you would like to put to new uses? Here is where to investigate some enjoyable new directions.

4. Want to put a professional polish on gardening, music, other arts to turn an avocation into a paid vocation? Try interning here before checking the want ads.

> *With an interest in archeology Lori Gibson landed a "job"*
> *analyzing 12,000-year-old mammoth bones at the*
> *Smithsonian Institution's Museum of Natural History in*
> *Washington, D.C. She did not earn money or academic*
> *credit but still thinks the opportunity was wonderful. "I*
> *was excited to work at the Smithsonian and have a chance*
> *to talk to people there and find out more about museum*
> *and lab work."*

THE ADLER PLANETARIUM

1300 South Lake Shore Drive   **Phone:** 312/322-0304
Chicago, IL 60605   **FAX:**   312/322-2257

*   *   *

ORGANIZATION'S ACTIVITIES: The Adler Planetarium is a world leader in astronomy education that serves nearly 700,000 visitors each year. The facilities include two theaters with state-of-the-art projection systems, three floors of exhibits, a fully automated observatory, and one of the world's largest collections of historical scientific instruments.

Number of Internships: Approximately 6.

Type: Astronomy, education.

Function/Duties: Operate planetarium sky shows and observatory, teach in the Space Explorers programs, TA for college-level astronomy class, answer astronomy-related questions by phone and mail, learn sky-show production techniques, and assist with special projects in the Astronomy Department.

Schedule: Full-time, 13 months—June 1 through June 30 of following year.

Stipend or Pay: $1,100 per month, plus vacation days and medical coverage.

Academic Credit Offered: N/A.

ELIGIBILITY: Intern must have a college degree in astronomy or related field.

REQUIREMENTS: Intern must be able to demonstrate basic astronomical knowledge and desire a career in the planetarium profession. Preference will be given to candidates with previous planetarium or astronomy teaching experience.

APPLICATION PROCEDURE: Submit a résumé, biographical sketch, and 3 references with phone numbers *to* A.S. Whitt, Associate Astronomer. *Deadline:* February 1.

AMERICAN HORTICULTURAL SOCIETY

7921 East Boulevard Drive   **Phone:** 703/765-6032
Alexandria, VA 22308   **FAX:**   703/765-6032

*   *   *

ORGANIZATION'S ACTIVITIES: National gardening and plant society with international reputation, headquartered in historic farm property near Washington, D.C.

Number of Internships: 20 throughout the year.

Type: Horticulture, education.

Function/Duties: Work with plants; work with elementary school groups; provide research and computer skills for national information service.

Schedule: Summers and year-round.

Stipend or Pay: $6 or more per hour.

Academic Credit Offered: Per student's own arrangements with academic institution; *Plus* participation in seminars and field trips throughout region.

ELIGIBILITY: Students, non-students, and career-changers welcome to apply.

REQUIREMENTS: Educational background for some; special interest in horticulture and botany.

APPLICATION PROCEDURE: Send inquiries *to* Education Coordinator in time to apply *by* March for summer programs or 2 months prior to start date in other seasons.

ANASAZI HERITAGE CENTER

U.S. DEPARTMENT OF THE INTERIOR,
Bureau of Land Management
27501 Highway 184   **Phone:** 303/882-4811
Dolores, CO 81323   **FAX:** 303/882-7035

* * *

ORGANIZATION'S ACTIVITIES: A center for the protection, study, and display of the culture and archeology of the Native Americans of the Southwest region.

Number of Internships: 2 to 4.

Type: Curatorial assistant, archeology assistant, visitor services.

Function/Duties: Varies with need.

Schedule: Full-time, 8 weeks in summers.

Stipend or Pay: $40 per week; communal housing provided.

Academic Credit Offered: Per student's own arrangements with academic institution.

ELIGIBILITY: College and graduate students as well as non-students and career-changers; preference given to students and new professionals in the fields of anthropology, archeology, and museum studies.

REQUIREMENTS: Working knowledge of southwestern U.S. prehistory.

APPLICATION PROCEDURE: Send letter of interest and résumé *to* Intern coordinator *by* April 15.

APPLEWOOD

1400 East Kearsley Street   **Phone:** 312/233-3031
Flint, MI 48503   **FAX:** N/A

* * *

ORGANIZATION'S ACTIVITIES: The estate of C. S. Mott, a benefactor of ecological horticulture; developing new plant and pesticide systems; exhibiting plant collections.

Number of Internships: 5.

Type: Horticulture, outside maintenance.

Function/Duties: Aid in greenhouse and gardens development and maintenance, production, design.

Schedule: Full-time summers.

Stipend or Pay: $6 per hour.

Academic Credit Offered: Per student's own arrangements with academic institution; *Plus* housing available on grounds.

ELIGIBILITY: Students, non-students, or career-changers able to do physical work outdoors.

REQUIREMENTS: Interest in botany and gardening.

APPLICATION PROCEDURE: Send inquiries *to* Estate Manager. *Deadine:* April 1.

THE ARTS AND EDUCATION COUNCIL OF GREATER ST. LOUIS

3526 Washington Avenue
St. Louis, MO 63103

Phone: 314/535-3600
FAX: 314/535-3606

* * *

ORGANIZATION'S ACTIVITIES: Fundraising for arts and cultural organizations in the St. Louis bistate area.

Number of Internships: 1 per semester.

Type: Public relations.

Function/Duties: Writing and assisting in special projects.

Schedule: Part-time during the winter, spring, and summer.

Stipend or Pay: No.

Academic Credit Offered: Per student's own arrangements with academic institution.

ELIGIBILITY: All students as well as non-students welcome to apply.

REQUIREMENTS: Interests, goals, skills, and/or experience relevant to available assignments.

APPLICATION PROCEDURE: Submit résumé and cover letter *to* Renee Bazin, Communications Coordinator.

ARTS EXTENSION SERVICE

602 Goodell Building
University of Massachusetts
Amherst, MA 01003

Phone: 413/545-2360
FAX: 413/545-3351

* * *

ORGANIZATION'S ACTIVITIES: AES is a national arts service organization which works to achieve access to and integration of the arts communities through continuing education for artists, arts organizations, and community leaders.

Number of Internships: Varies, approximately 12.

Type: Program and promotion assistants.

Function/Duties: Research related to arts administration.

Schedule: Full-time and part-time, September–May; occasional summer internships; minimum 3-month term.

Stipend or Pay: No.

Academic Credit Offered: Available.

ELIGIBILITY: College and graduate students; non-students and career-changers welcome.

REQUIREMENTS: Interns must work in AES office, a minimum of 12 hours per week depending on the position.

APPLICATION PROCEDURE: Submit letter of inquiry or phone call *to* Pam Korza. *Deadline:* August and November.

ARTS INC.

315 West Ninth Street   **Phone:** 213/627-9276
Los Angeles, CA 90015   **FAX:** N/A

* * *

ORGANIZATION'S ACTIVITIES: A private nonprofit arts-management service involved with community-based and other arts projects.

Number of Internships: 12.

Type: Management, public affairs.

Function/Duties: Aid staff in administrative and publicity duties and special projects.

Schedule: Full-time summers.

Stipend or Pay: $3,000 for 3 months.

Academic Credit Offered: Per student's own arrangements with academic institution.

ELIGIBILITY: Undergraduate students of color.

REQUIREMENTS: Competitive position for minority students with interests in arts management.

APPLICATION PROCEDURE: Request application forms *from* Internship Coordinator *by* early spring.

ATLANTA BOTANICAL GARDEN

Piedmont Park at The Prado   **Phone:** 404/876-5859
Atlanta, GA 77246   **FAX:** 404/876-7472

* * *

ORGANIZATION'S ACTIVITIES: Leading horticultural research & exhibition center.

Number of Internships: 5.

Type: Marketing.

Function/Duties: Draft press releases and media advisories on Garden events and business; send out press materials; make follow-up calls to media; draft thank-you or follow-up letters to media, volunteers, and vendors; track media coverage by monitoring articles written about ABG; assist with photo shoots, both still photography and video; write articles for *Clippings*, the quarterly newsletter; edit copy for newsletter and other materials; update media lists and calendar listings for public relations specialist; assist with media on-site; assist with mailings and faxing; assist PR specialist with day-to-day operations; participate in creative brainstorm session; assist with the design and copywriting for direct-mail invitations and flyers; assist Special Events Coordinator with day-to-day operations; assist with coordination of all Garden events, including weddings, corporate retreats, staff events, etc.; draft follow-up letters; show rental space to client prospects; work on-site with caterers, florists, and other vendors; and draft confirmation letters and other correspondence.

Schedule: 8:30 A.M.–5:00 P.M.; Monday through Friday, 8-to-10-week term, and staff some special events after hours or weekends (approximately 2 to 4 events per internship).

Stipend or Pay: No.

Academic Credit Offered: Per student's own arrangements with academic institution.

ELIGIBILITY: Background preferred: Bachelor's degree (or studying toward degree) in journalism, marketing, English, business, or communications.

REQUIREMENTS: Strong writing skills, computer literacy—word processing, ability to manage and prioritize different tasks, familiarity with the not-for-profit organization, flexibility, eager to learn, organized, good presentation skills, nonsmoker, have high energy.

Number of Internships: 3.

Type: Marketing.

Function/Duties: Assist marketing staff with promotion projects.

Schedule: Full-time, 3-month term.

Stipend or Pay: No.

Academic Credit Offered: Per student's own arrangements with academic institution.

REQUIREMENTS: Interests, goals, skills, and/or experience relevant to available assignments.

APPLICATION PROCEDURE: Submit résumé and cover letter *to* Julie Heron, Marketing Manager. Application due *by* January for the spring, April for the summer, July for the fall, and October for the winter.

BAYARD CUTTING ARBORETUM

P.O. Box 466
Oakdale, NY 11769

Phone: 516/581-1002
FAX: N/A

* * *

ORGANIZATION'S ACTIVITIES: Nationally known horticultural research and exhibition center.

Number of Internships: 2.

Type: Horticulture, landscape architecture.

Function/Duties: Curating, records maintenance, grounds work.

Schedule: Summers, full-time.

Stipend or Pay: $6 per hour.

Academic Credit Offered: Per student's own arrangements with academic institution.

ELIGIBILITY: Undergraduate or graduate students.

REQUIREMENTS: Prefer landscape architecture or horticulture students.

APPLICATION PROCEDURE: Send inquiries *to* Director in time to apply *by* mid-March.

BIRMINGHAM BOTANICAL GARDENS

2612 Lane Park Road
Birmingham, AL 35223

Phone: 205/879-1227
FAX: N/A

* * *

ORGANIZATION'S ACTIVITIES: A 67-acre horticultural research and exhibition center, including a 1/2-acre greenhouse.

Number of Internships: 8.

Type: Gardening, record-keeping.

Function/Duties: Work in library and/or on grounds.

Schedule: Full-time summers; some available year-round.

Stipend or Pay: $7 per hour.

Academic Credit Offered: Per student's own arrangements with academic institution.

ELIGIBILITY: Primarily students at all levels.

REQUIREMENTS: Able to work outdoors, mostly May to September.

APPLICATION PROCEDURE: Send inquiries *to* Director in time to apply *by* March 1 for summer.

BOK TOWER GARDENS

P.O. Box 3810
Lake Wales, FL 33859

Phone: 813/676-1408
FAX: N/A

* * *

ORGANIZATION'S ACTIVITIES: Subtropical year-round horticultural research and exhibition center specializing in developing protections for endangered plant species.

Number of Internships: 4 throughout year.

Type: Gardening, research.

Function/Duties: Gain practical experience in public garden with high maintenance standards and active research program.

Schedule: Full-time for 10 weeks each quarter.

Stipend or Pay: $1,700 per quarter; *Plus* housing provided on estate.

Academic Credit Offered: Per student's own arrangements with academic institution.

ELIGIBILITY: Students, non-students, or career-changers welcome to apply.

REQUIREMENTS: Background, studies, skills, and/or interest in horticulture; ability to do physical work.

APPLICATION PROCEDURE: Send inquiries *to* Internship Coordinator. *Deadline:* Open.

B'NAI B'RITH HILLEL

Jewish Association for College Youth
381 Park Avenue South
Suite 613
New York, NY 10016

Phone: 212/696-1590
FAX: 212/696-0964

* * *

ORGANIZATION'S ACTIVITIES: B'nai B'rith Hillel/JACY provides Jewish cultural, religious, educational, and social activities to students on college campuses in New York City, Long Island, and Westchester.

Number of Internships: 30 placements.

Type: Summer internship program.

Function/Duties: Varies with specific placement.

Schedule: Full-time summer (June–August) only.

Stipend or Pay: $1,200 for 8 weeks.

Academic Credit Offered: Per intern's own arrangements with academic institution.

ELIGIBILITY: Undergraduate students are requested; freshmen, sophomores, and juniors are encouraged to apply.

REQUIREMENTS: Submit application, résumé, and references.

APPLICATION PROCEDURE: Request application and submit full application *to* Wendy Levinson. *Deadline:* Early March.

BOSTON MUSEUM OF SCIENCE

1 Science Park   **Phone:** 617/589-0100
Boston, MA 02114   **FAX:**   617/742-2246

* * *

ORGANIZATION'S ACTIVITIES: A private science and technology museum featuring public exhibits and education programs.

Number of Internships: Varies.

Type: Research, education, data processing, public relations.

Function/Duties: Varies with need, but includes preparation of exhibits and public events as well as scientific and computer-based research.

Schedule: Full- and part-time per semester and year-round.

Stipend or Pay: Some, including year-long fellowship.

Academic Credit Offered: Per student's own arrangements with academic institution; *Plus* internships may lead to career positions.

ELIGIBILITY: Students at all levels; also college graduates for competitive fellowships.

REQUIREMENTS: Preference for those with science and education backgrounds.

APPLICATION PROCEDURE: Send inquiries *to* Employment Recruiter. *Deadline:* Varies depending on start date.

BROOKFIELD ZOO

3400 Golf Road   **Phone:** 708/485-0263
Brookfield, IL 60513   **FAX:**   N/A

* * *

ORGANIZATION'S ACTIVITIES: A major zoological center, with exhibits featuring some 2,500 animals.

Number of Internships: 40.

Type: Zookeeping as well as education, maintenance, and public relations.

Function/Duties: Animal interns aid with care of animals and live exhibits; others work in administrative offices and as tour guides.

Schedule: Full-time in summer and during school semesters, from 6- to 12-week commitment.

Stipend or Pay: No.

Academic Credit Offered: Per student's own arrangements with academic institution.

ELIGIBILITY: Primarily junior and senior college students.

REQUIREMENTS: Relevant career goals, minimum C average.

APPLICATION PROCEDURE: Send application form, transcript, and references *to* Internship Coordinator to arrange for interview. *Deadline:* February 1 for summer openings; 3 months in advance for others.

BROOKINGS INSTITUTION

1775 Massachusetts Avenue NW
Washington, DC 20036

Phone: 202/797-6000
FAX: 202/797-6004

* * *

ORGANIZATION'S ACTIVITIES: A nonpartisan, nonprofit research and educational organization devoted to research on public policy issues.

Number of Internships: Varies; fairly numerous.

Type: Public affairs, research, communications.

Function/Duties: Aid professional staff in gathering information for and producing reports and analyses and public education presentations.

Schedule: Summers, full-time.

Stipend or Pay: Not usually.

Academic Credit Offered: Per student's own arrangements with academic institution; *Plus* attend seminars and conferences.

ELIGIBILITY: Upper-level undergraduate and graduate students.

REQUIREMENTS: Excellent communications skills; courses of study in areas related to Brookings specialties.

APPLICATION PROCEDURE: Send inquiries *to* Public Affairs Office as early in the year as possible for submission of applications *by* March 1.

BROOKLYN BOTANIC GARDEN

1000 Washington Avenue
Brooklyn, NY 11225

Phone: 718/622-4433
FAX: N/A

* * *

ORGANIZATION'S ACTIVITIES: One of the nation's most visible centers for gardening, horticultural research, education, and exhibition.

Number of Internships: 12.

Type: Community horticulture, education, gardening.

Function/Duties: Some interns work in community helping residents develop gardens; others lead tours of gardens and work with school groups; also gardening and grounds maintenance.

Schedule: 1 year for community work, or summers, or 6-month gardening stint March–October.

Stipend or Pay: $5 to $7 per hour.

Academic Credit Offered: Per student's own arrangements with academic institution.

ELIGIBILITY: Students, non-students, or career-changers welcome to apply.

REQUIREMENTS: Background, education, and/or special interest in gardening, plus ability to do outdoor physical work.

APPLICATION PROCEDURE: Send inquiries *to* Personnel Director. *Deadline:* Varies.

CHICAGO BOTANIC GARDEN

P.O. Box 400   **Phone:** 708/835-8300
Glencoe, IL 60022   **FAX:**   708/835-4484

* * *

ORGANIZATION'S ACTIVITIES: Major national center for horticultural research, education, therapy, and exhibition.

Number of Internships: 24.

Type: Gardening, education, therapy, publications.

Function/Duties: Depending on interest and expertise, aid in developing and maintaining garden as well as in developing programs for disabled and other groups; design and production of brochures and press materials.

Schedule: Flexible, 3- to 9-month periods, full- or part-time.

Stipend or Pay: Approximately $6 per hour depending on activity.

Academic Credit Offered: Per student's own arrangements with academic institution; *Plus* participate in field trips, lectures, classes.

ELIGIBILITY: Students, non-students, or career-changers welcome, depending on position sought.

REQUIREMENTS: Background and/or interest in botany, ecology, or conservation as well as appropriate specialty depending on activity.

APPLICATION PROCEDURE: Send inquiries *to* Intern Coordinator. *Deadline:* Varies.

THE CHILDREN'S MUSEUM OF BOSTON

300 Congress Street   **Phone:** 617/426-6500
Boston, MA 02210   **FAX:**   617/426-1944

* * *

ORGANIZATION'S ACTIVITIES: A private, nonprofit museum and education center featuring interactive exhibits and special activities.

Number of Internships: 24.

Type: Museum guides.

Function/Duties: Interpret exhibits for visiting children and adults.

Schedule: Full- and part-time for 5-week sessions during school year and for 3-month summer sessions.

Stipend or Pay: Yes.

Academic Credit Offered: Per student's own arrangements with academic institution.

ELIGIBILITY: Students at all levels; some non-students may be considered.

REQUIREMENTS: Career interest in teaching, science, or the arts preferred.

APPLICATION PROCEDURE: Send inquiries *to* Interpreter Program Coordinator *by* as far ahead of availability as possible.

CHILDREN'S MUSEUM OF INDIANAPOLIS

3000 North Meridian Street　　　　**Phone:** 317/924-5421
Indianapolis, IN 46208　　　　　　**FAX:**　317/921-4019

* * *

ORGANIZATION'S ACTIVITIES: With its mission to enrich the lives of children, the "world's largest museum for children" features 325,000 square feet and 5 stories of hands-on activities, and over 140,000 artifacts in the collection, including the world's largest water clock.

Number of Internships: 7.

Type: Collections, marketing.

Function/Duties: Guide or instruct visiting children in collections, do publicity and/or fundraising in marketing.

Schedule: Full- and/or part-time, year-round availability, flexible hours.

Stipend or Pay: Sometimes.

Academic Credit Offered: Yes.

ELIGIBILITY: Primarily undergraduate and graduate students.

REQUIREMENTS: Interests, goals, skills, and/or experience relevant to available assignments.

APPLICATION PROCEDURE: Send résumé and cover letter *to* Intern Coordinator *by* 6 months prior to start date.

THE CLOISTERS

Fort Tryon Park　　　　　　　　**Phone:** 212/923-3700
New York, NY 10040　　　　　　　**FAX:**　212/795-3640

* * *

ORGANIZATION'S ACTIVITIES: The Education Department at the Cloisters—a reconstructed medieval castle housing Metropolitan Museum of Art collections from the Middle Ages—provides programs and exploration activities to school groups and the public.

Number of Internships: 8.

Type: Educational, curatorial, tours.

Function/Duties: Work with curators and conservators; conduct day camp and other activities, including delivery of a public gallery talk.

Schedule: Full-time; mid-June to mid-August.

Stipend or Pay: $2,000.

Academic Credit Offered: Possibly.

ELIGIBILITY: All undergraduates; preferred major: Humanities. First- and second-year students given special consideration.

REQUIREMENTS: Two academic recommendations; transcript of last 2 years schooling; essay of about 500 words describing why student wishes to be accepted in the program; name, home and school addresses, and telephone numbers; type of degree sought and class year, special honors, work or internship experience (list dates).

APPLICATION PROCEDURE: Submit materials *to* Internship Coordinator *by* early in February. After an initial review, a small group of students will be selected for a required interview at the museum during the month of March.

THE COLLEGE OF SANTA FE

1600 St. Michael's Drive	**Phone:** 505/473-6011
Santa Fe, NM 87501	**FAX:** 505/473-6127

* * *

ORGANIZATION'S ACTIVITIES: Four-year college, arts, film/video, business, education; 1,400 students enrolled, small classes.

Number of Internships: 3 or more.

Type: Accounting, computer systems, data research.

Function/Duties: Assist staff with ongoing duties and special projects.

Schedule: Part-time, term open to negotiation.

Stipend or Pay: No.

Academic Credit Offered: Available on a limited basis.

ELIGIBILITY: College juniors and seniors; preferred majors: Business and Computer Science. *Special Eligibilities:* Hispanics and African-Americans encouraged to apply.

REQUIREMENTS: Skills appropriate to assignment.

APPLICATION PROCEDURE: Submit résumé and cover letter *to* Director of Public Relations.

THE COLONIAL WILLIAMSBURG FOUNDATION

P.O. Box 1776
Williamsburg, VA 23187-1776

Phone: 804/220-7211
FAX: 804/220-7398

* * *

ORGANIZATION'S ACTIVITIES: Established to restore, re-create, preserve, and interpret 18th-century Williamsburg and to teach the history of early America while providing visitors with high-quality hospitality and service.

Number of Internships: Varies; about 3 dozen a year.

Type: Work in any of over a dozen departments at the Foundation, including architectural research, communications, development, costume design, tour presentations, curating, and others.

Function/Duties: Varies with assignment; includes research, program development, and presentation as well as assisting staff members in routine activities as needed.

Schedule: From minimum of 1 month to as long as a year, full-time or part-time, with hours arranged.

Stipend or Pay: None, though grants *occasionally* available for individual departments.

Academic Credit Offered: Per intern's own arrangements with academic institution; supervisors provide detailed evaluation for institution.

ELIGIBILITY: Students at all levels of college or graduate school as well as non-students experienced in the field, career-changers, and those re-entering the work force. *Special Eligibilities* and interests considered when matching intern with activity. *Plus* Foundation's research facilities are available to interns; interns receive passes to entire exhibition and to events; interns programs, activities, and evaluations are carefullyorganized throughout the Foundation.

REQUIREMENTS: Interns must provide own housing, though Foundation provides information on possibilities. Interview may also need to be arranged.

APPLICATION PROCEDURE: Submit letter, résumé, and, where appropriate, recommendation from faculty advisor *to* Peggy McDonald Howells, Manager, Museum Professional Services, *by* 3 to 4 months prior to internship period desired.

COOPER-HEWITT MUSEUM

2 East 91st Street
New York, NY 10128

Phone: 212/860-6868
FAX: 212/860-6909

* * *

ORGANIZATION'S ACTIVITIES: The National Museum of Design, under the auspices of the Smithsonian Institution, features public exhibits and research collections covering all aspects of architecture and design.

Number of Internships: 2 special fellowships and number of student internships.

Type: Research, program planning, exhibit design.

Function/Duties: Assist staff in administrative assignments and special projects.

Schedule: Full- and/or part-time; summers as well as year-round.

Stipend or Pay: Kreuger summer research interns receive $2,500; Christie's Fellowship holders receive $15,000 per year; others are unpaid.

Academic Credit Offered: Per student's own arrangements with academic institution; *Plus* internships may lead to career positions.

ELIGIBILITY: Primarily college and graduate students.

REQUIREMENTS: Background and/or interest in art history, museum management, or related fields.

APPLICATION PROCEDURE: Send inquiries *to* Internship Coordinator *by* March.

DAHLEM ENVIRONMENTAL EDUCATION CENTER

7117 South Jackson Road   **Phone:** 517/782-3453
Jackson, MI 49201   **FAX:** N/A

*   *   *

ORGANIZATION'S ACTIVITIES: Serves as a major field-trip site for schools (approximately 400 per year); offers weekend public programming and special events; maintains a comprehensive bluebird recovery project, and has a visitor/exhibit area and a 300-acre site with 5 miles of trails.

Number of Internships: 6.

Type: Environmental day camp counselor.

Function/Duties: Select and implement environmental education activities for 5- to 12-year-old children enrolled in weeklong day-camp sessions (groups of 12); prepare, inventory, and care for camp equipment and materials; co-plan and facilitate programs.

Schedule: Residential full-time summers.

Stipend or Pay: Free on-site housing and a weekly stipend of $200.

Academic Credit Offered: Available if arranged by intern.

ELIGIBILITY: College juniors and seniors, as well as graduate students. Non-students with college-level training and career-changers also welcome to apply.

REQUIREMENTS: Experience working with children, preferably in an outdoor educational setting; background in natural and/or environmental sciences; responsible, flexible, innovative personality with a friendly teaching style.

APPLICATION PROCEDURE: Send a résumé and a cover letter with application form *to* Diane Valen, Program Coordinator.

DALLAS ARBORETUM

8617 Garland Road **Phone:** 214/327-8263
Dallas, TX 75218 **FAX:** 214/324-9801

* * *

ORGANIZATION'S ACTIVITIES: Leading center for horticultural and botanical research, education, and exhibitions.

Number of Internships: 88.

Type: Tour guide, education, landscape maintenance.

Function/Duties: Lead education groups, aid with special projects, grounds maintenance.

Schedule: 6 months—January–June and July–December, or summer, or 1 full year.

Stipend or Pay: $6 per hour; $12,000 for the full-year internship.

Academic Credit Offered: Per student's own arrangements with academic institution.

ELIGIBILITY: Students, non-students, or career-changers welcome to apply.

REQUIREMENTS: Interests, background, or studies in horticulture; ability to work outdoors and deal with public.

APPLICATION PROCEDURE: Send inquiries *to* Director of Horticulture in time to apply *by* 2 months prior to start date.

DALLAS ZOOLOGICAL SOCIETY

621 East Clarendon Drive **Phone:** 214/942-1183
Dallas, TX 75203 **FAX:** 214/670-6717

* * *

ORGANIZATION'S ACTIVITIES: The Dallas Zoo is dedicated to increasing knowledge and inspiring individual involvement in the conservation of wildlife and the environment.

Number of Internships: Flexible; varies with need.

Type: Special events assistant.

Function/Duties: Plan and implement public events.

Schedule: Seasonal (April–September); part-time internship available. Weekend availability is a must.

Stipend or Pay: No.

Academic Credit Offered: Per student's own arrangements with academic institution.

ELIGIBILITY: Undergraduate students are encouraged to apply; open to career-changers. *Special Eligibilities:* Commitment to diversity.

REQUIREMENTS: Provide a cover letter and résumé, along with an application.

APPLICATION PROCEDURE: Submit full application *to* Dawn McDonough.

DENVER ZOOLOGICAL FOUNDATION

825 East Speer Boulevard   **Phone:** 303/722-1110
Denver, CO 80218   **FAX:**   303/722-0551

* * *

ORGANIZATION'S ACTIVITIES: Runs the Denver Zoo.

Number of Internships: 1.

Type: Collections keeper, education specialist.

Function/Duties: Handle and care for (small) live animals and artifacts for use in education demonstrations with visiting children; also, prepare materials for and lead classes and demonstrations for children.

Schedule: Full-time, 3 to 5 months, depending on availability.

Stipend or Pay: Yes.

Academic Credit Offered: Per student's own arrangements with academic institution.

ELIGIBILITY: Undergraduate students.

REQUIREMENTS: "Self-starters" who enjoy animals (including reptiles).

APPLICATION PROCEDURE: Request application *from* Karin Hostetter, Education Department, to submit *by* 1 month prior to start date.

GREATER PITTSBURGH CONVENTION & VISITORS BUREAU

Four Gateway Center
Suite 514   **Phone:** 412/281-7711
Pittsburgh, PA 15222   **FAX:**   412/664-5512

* * *

ORGANIZATION'S ACTIVITIES: Official tourist promotion agency for Allegheny County. Primary functions include convention and group tour marketing.

Number of Internships: 12.

Type: Communications, tourism, conventions sales, membership.

Function/Duties: Varies per department; for example, communications involves writing media releases, public service announcements, calendar of events, stories, etc.

Schedule: Full-time and part-time, term varies with department.

Stipend or Pay: Varies.

Academic Credit Offered: Varies by department.

ELIGIBILITY: High-school, college, and graduate students; preferred majors: Communications, English, Journalism, Marketing, Tour and Travel. Both non-students and career-changers with appropriate backgrounds are welcome to apply.

REQUIREMENTS: Varies by department; business students preferred.

APPLICATION PROCEDURE: Send résumé, cover letter, and writing samples for communications internships *to* Marla Meyer.

HOLDEN ARBORETUM

9500 Sperry Road   **Phone:** 216/256-1110
Mentor, OH 44060   **FAX:**   216/256-1655

* * *

ORGANIZATION'S ACTIVITIES: Leading educational, research, and exhibition center for horticulture, landscaping, and botany.

Number of Internships: 10 at any given time.

Type: Horticulture, education, gardening, conservation, therapy.

Function/Duties: Assist staff and learn specialty of choice.

Schedule: 3 to 12 months, depending on activity sought.

Stipend or Pay: $5+ per hour.

Academic Credit Offered: Per student's own arrangements with academic institution; *Plus* housing available with pool and recreational facilities; regular educational sessions offered; opportunities for field trips in U.S. and Canada.

ELIGIBILITY: Primarily students or recent graduates in relevant fields.

REQUIREMENTS: Background in subjects related to activity; interns expected to complete term project or paper.

APPLICATION PROCEDURE: Send inquiries *to* Intern Coordinator for details on applying and *deadlines* for various positions.

INDIANAPOLIS ZOO

1200 West Washington Street   **Phone:** 317/630-2041
Indianapolis, IN 46222   **FAX:**   317/630-5114

* * *

ORGANIZATION'S ACTIVITIES: Wildlife protection institution, center for environmental education and cultural activities for children and families.

Number of Internships: 3.

Type: Animal care.

Function/Duties: Work under supervision of expert keepers. Work with animals in these biomes: desert, plains, encounters, forests, waters, and with marine animals.

Schedule: 40 hours per week.

Stipend or Pay: No.

Academic Credit Offered: Yes.

ELIGIBILITY: College students.

Number of Internships: 2.

Type: Marketing and development.

Function/Duties: Gain experience in promoting activities and exhibits to corporate sponsors and the general public. The goal of this department is to provide a strong link between the Indianapolis Zoo and the community. Interns will assist in the following areas: publicity, membership, special events, group sales, public relations and fundraising.

Schedule: Minimum of 20 hours per week.

Stipend or Pay: No.

Academic Credit Offered: Yes.

REQUIREMENTS: Interests, goals, skills, and/or experience relevant to available assignments. On-site interview required.

APPLICATION PROCEDURE: Submit résumé, 2 letters of recommendation, a copy of current grade transcript, a letter of interest, and application form *to* Volunteer Coordinator. Call for deadline and details.

INTERLOCHEN CENTER FOR THE ARTS

P.O. Box 199   **Phone:** 616/276-7200
Interlochen, MI 49643   **FAX:** 616/276-6321

*   *   *

ORGANIZATION'S ACTIVITIES: Center for the study and performance of music by students (mostly young) and master-teachers from around the country and the world.

Number of Internships: Varies with need and interest.

Type: Communications and public relations.

Function/Duties: Work with staff to support communication and public relations needs.

Schedule: Full-time; September–December, January–May, June–August.

Stipend or Pay: Yes; plus room and board.

Academic Credit Offered: Available.

ELIGIBILITY: College and graduate students; preferred majors: Journalism, Public Relations, and Communications. Some career-changers and non-students accepted.

REQUIREMENTS: Good organizational skills and ability to work independently.

APPLICATION PROCEDURE: Submit cover letter, résumé, and writing samples *to* Clay Cronin, Human Resources.

JEWISH CHAUTAUQUA SOCIETY

838 Fifth Avenue   **Phone:** 212/570-0707
New York, NY 10021   **FAX:** 212/570-0960

* * *

ORGANIZATION'S ACTIVITIES: The oldest and largest interfaith educational program sponsored by the Jewish Reform movement. With goals of promoting interreligious understanding and educating non-Jews about Jewish history, culture, and tradition, the JCS, in today's multicultural environment, is launching initiatives to reach new audiences.

Number of Internships: Varies according to project and location.

Type: Wide variety, in communications, programs, public relations.

Function/Duties: Assist staff in New York office; also opportunities available in campus and community activities around country.

Schedule: Flexible.

Stipend or Pay: Possible.

Academic Credit Offered: Per student's own arrangements with academic institution.

ELIGIBILITY: Students at all levels, as well as non-students and career-changers. *Special Eligibilities:* Knowledge of and interest in religious activities and Jewish culture a plus.

REQUIREMENTS: Vary by location and project.

APPLICATION PROCEDURE: Submit résumé or desired work description *to* Bradley Frome at New York office. *Deadline:* No.

KOHL CHILDREN'S MUSEUM

165 Green Bay Road   **Phone:** 708/256-6056
Wilmette, IL 60091   **FAX:** 708/256-2921

* * *

ORGANIZATION'S ACTIVITIES: A nonprofit cultural institution that annually provides over 200,000 children, their families, and teachers with a wide array of creative, hands-on exhibits, educational programs, and community outreach programs, including a teaching academy.

Number of Internships: 10.

Type: Exhibit interpreter, exhibit developer, education, marketing, communications.

Function/Duties: Plan and prepare exhibits and/or lead groups through exhibits, interact with children and other visitors, plan and participate in special events.

Schedule: Full-time and part-time (15 hours per week minimum) year-round, for 15-week minimum term.

Stipend or Pay: No.

Academic Credit Offered: Per student's own arrangements with academic institution; *Plus* Museum also offers Kohl International Teaching Awards internship, for education students through teaching academy.

ELIGIBILITY: College and graduate students as well as non-students and career-changers.

REQUIREMENTS: Varies by department, but interest in education and museum work important.

APPLICATION PROCEDURE: Send résumé and cover letter stating career goals *to* Christy Rocca, Director of Volunteer and Intern Services. *Deadline:* Depends on start date.

LAND BETWEEN THE LAKES

100 Van Morgan Drive   **Phone:** 502/924-5602
Golden Pond, KY 42211   **FAX:**   502/924-1399

* * *

ORGANIZATION'S ACTIVITIES: LBL is a 170,000-acre national recreation area located in western Kentucky and Tennessee. Operated by the Tennessee Valley Authority, LBL provides outdoor recreation and environmental education in a managed natural setting which strengthens environmental responsibility among customers and communicates the TVA's environmental leadership role.

Number of Internships: 12.

Type: Recreation.

Function/Duties: Varies by position.

Schedule: Full-time, 40 hours per week, summer months from end of May through mid-August.

Academic Credit Offered: Per student's own arrangements with academic institution.

ELIGIBILITY: Students, preferably college juniors and seniors. Applicants for apprenticeships ($150 per week plus housing) must not be enrolled in school and must have a college degree.

REQUIREMENTS: Interests, goals, and/or experience relevant to available assignments.

APPLICATION PROCEDURE: Submit internship application and résumé *to* Jim Carpenter, Administrator, Professional Development.

LONGWOOD GARDENS

P.O. Box 501   **Phone:** 215/388-6741
Kennett Square, PA 19348   **FAX:** 215/388-2908

*   *   *

ORGANIZATION'S ACTIVITIES: Internationally known center for gardening, for horticulture education—and for performing arts offered on the grounds of large estate.

Number of Internships: 22.

Type: Horticulture, performing arts, education.

Function/Duties: Varies depending on interests and skills of intern; includes gardening, groundskeeping, education, curating, and performing.

Schedule: Full-time for 3- to 12-month periods.

Stipend or Pay: $800 per month.

Academic Credit Offered: Per student's own arrangements with academic institution; *Plus* free housing.

ELIGIBILITY: College students or recent graduates. *Special Eligibilities:* Accommodations for those with disabilities.

REQUIREMENTS: Prefer majors related to activity; require driver's license (unless prevented by disability).

APPLICATION PROCEDURE: Send inquiries *to* Student Programs Coordinator in time to apply *by* 2 months prior to start date.

THE MARITIME CENTER AT NORWALK

10 North Water Street   **Phone:** 203/852-0700
Norwalk, CT 06854   **FAX:** 203/838-5416

*   *   *

ORGANIZATION'S ACTIVITIES: The Maritime Center (TMC) is a $30 million nonprofit facility consisting of 20 aquarium displays, a Maritime History Hall, a rotating exhibit gallery, and an IMAX theater. TMC's mission is to educate visitors about the maritime ecosystems of Long Island Sound and the rich nautical history of New England. TMC offers educational programs for students levels K–12, as well as for the general public. Topics can include the natural history of Long Island Sound, current environmental issues, and assorted nautical themes. Internships take place within the facility or at the Norwalk Harbor.

Number of Internships: Flexible; varies with need.

Type: Education internships.

Function/Duties: Assist with school and after-school programs, summer and weekend programs, development of independent projects to enhance current education curriculum.

Schedule: No limited length.

Stipend or Pay: No.

Academic Credit Offered: Per student's own arrangements with academic institution.

ELIGIBILITY: Anyone age 16 and up.

REQUIREMENTS: Internship is ideal for those students with a strong commitment to education and teaching. Students will learn effective methods of teaching while enhancing their knowledge of marine life and the human impact on these organisms.

Number of Internships: Flexible; varies with need.

Type: Natural history interpreter.

Function/Duties: Assist general public in explaining the living collection, including fishes and harbor seals; increasing awareness about the sea's fragile environment; interpreting exhibits on boatbuilding and New England maritime and natural history; interpreting special temporary exhibits.

Schedule: No limited length.

Stipend or Pay: No.

Academic Credit Offered: Per student's own arrangements with academic institution.

Number of Internships: Flexible; varies with need.

Type: Exhibit creation.

Function/Duties: Assist with fabrication and installation of new exhibits, updating current exhibits, researching background information for exhibits, cataloging artifacts.

Schedule: No limited time.

Stipend or Pay: No.

Academic Credit Offered: Per student's own arrangements with academic institution.

ELIGIBILITY: Anyone age 16 and up.

REQUIREMENTS: Internship is ideal for those students who possess artistic and creative talents or who work well with their hands. The student will experience how exhibits are planned and created, assist in exhibit fabrication, and contribute to exhibit maintenance. The research of background information for new exhibits and assistance with cataloging artifacts will be ideal for a student whose interests include history, library science, and/or scientific research. This student will enhance reference and information retrieval skills, while learning about varied topics in nautical history, natural history, and marine science.

APPLICATION PROCEDURE: *Contact* Jack Schneider for details.

MISSOURI BOTANICAL GARDEN

P.O. Box 229   **Phone:** 314/577-5142
St. Louis, MO 63166   **FAX:**   314/577-9598

* * *

ORGANIZATION'S ACTIVITIES: Internationally acclaimed botanical garden and research center.

Number of Internships: 2 or more.

Type: Interns will work in the public relations office in such activities as publicity, special events, and writing assignments.

Function/Duties: Writing, editing, events.

Schedule: Full-time and part-time; seasonal: June through August, 3-month minimum.

Stipend or Pay: No.

Academic Credit Offered: Through intern's school.

ELIGIBILITY: College juniors and seniors; preferred major: Journalism.

REQUIREMENTS: Word processing skills.

APPLICATION PROCEDURE: Submit résumé and cover letter *to* Douglas Arnold. *Deadline:* February 1.

THE NATIONAL LEARNING CENTER

800 Third Street NE   **Phone:** 202/675-4180
Washington, DC 20002   **FAX:**   202/675-4140

* * *

ORGANIZATION'S ACTIVITIES: A multifaceted organization that researches and develops educational programs as the umbrella organization for a Model Early Learning Center, an Options School, a Media Arts Center, and a Future Center offering community access to computer technology.

Number of Internships: Varies; numerous.

Type: Public relations, education, design, computer specialist.

Function/Duties: Assist staff in every area of program, according to skills and interests.

Schedule: Flexible.

Stipend or Pay: No.

Academic Credit Offered: Per student's own arrangements with academic institution; *Plus* particular attention given to interests and needs of interns in planning assignments.

ELIGIBILITY: Students at all levels as well as non-students and career-changers are welcome.

REQUIREMENTS: Depends upon activity desired; individual internship advisers consult on optimum approach.

APPLICATION PROCEDURE: Call for information and to request application *from* Volunteer Center in time to apply *by* 4 to 6 weeks before start date.

NEW YORK OPEN CENTER

83 Spring Street   **Phone:** 212/219-2527
New York, NY 10012   **FAX:**   N/A

* * *

ORGANIZATION'S ACTIVITIES: A nonprofit holistic learning center providing courses, workshops, and programs in spiritual development, nutrition, health, exercise, and other aspects of personal development.

Number of Internships: Varies.

Type: Administration, registration, public relations, data processing, publications.

Function/Duties: Assist staff with running of center and with special projects.

Schedule: 10 to 16 hours per week, usually for a 6-month period.

Stipend or Pay: No.

Academic Credit Offered: Per student's own arrangements with academic institution; *Plus* interns may attend classes free and get first priority in assignments to classes.

ELIGIBILITY: Students at all levels as well as non-students and career-changers welcome to apply.

REQUIREMENTS: Interests, goals, skills, and/or experience relevant to available assignments.

APPLICATION PROCEDURE: Send inquiries *to* Volunteer/Intern Coordinator. *Deadline:* Ongoing.

92ND STREET Y

1395 Lexington Avenue   **Phone:** 212/415-5452
New York, NY 10128   **FAX:**   212/410-1254

* * *

ORGANIZATION'S ACTIVITIES: The 92nd Street Y is one of America's and Manhattan's oldest cultural and community centers offering a diversity of programs as reflected in its 6 program "centers"— The Tisch Center for the Arts (which includes the Unterberg Poetry Center), Center for Adult Life and Learning, Center for Youth and Family, the School for the Arts, a Center for Health, Fitness and Sports, and the Bronfman Center for Jewish Life.

Number of Internships: 3 to 4 per year.

Type: Marketing and public relations.

Function/Duties: Assist in press and marketing functions, event coordination, and editorial duties.

Schedule: Full- and/or part-time; per semester all year.

Stipend or Pay: $75 and up per week.

Academic Credit Offered: Yes.

APPLICATION PROCEDURE: Send inquiries *to* Public Relations Director.

NORTHWEST FOLKLIFE

505 Harrison Street   **Phone:** 206/684-7300
Seattle, WA 98109   **FAX:**   206/684-7190

* * *

ORGANIZATION'S ACTIVITIES: A nonprofit arts organization dedicated to preserving and promoting ethnic and traditional arts of the highest standards through an annual festival and other smaller events.

Number of Internships: Flexible; varies with need.

Type: Public relations, research, editing, and administration.

Function/Duties: Assist staff of specific departments according to intern's skills and interests.

Schedule: Seasonal internships available.

Stipend or Pay: Varies by internship.

Academic Credit Offered: Per intern's own arrangements with academic institution.

ELIGIBILITY: Undergraduate (seniors only) and graduate students are encouraged to apply; open to career-changers and non-students as well; *Plus* internship may lead to employment opportunities.

REQUIREMENTS: Request application procedures by letter.

APPLICATION PROCEDURE: Submit application *to* Ms. Tiffany Taylor. *Deadline:* Open.

OKLAHOMA CITY ZOOLOGICAL PARK

2101 NE 50th Street   **Phone:** 405/424-3344
Oklahoma City, OK 73111   **FAX:**   405/424-3349

* * *

ORGANIZATION'S ACTIVITIES: Public zoo and wildlife center.

Number of Internships: 1 or more.

Type: Public relations.

Function/Duties: Assist with marketing, publicity, and outreach activities, including writing, arranging events, and producing and distributing special materials.

Schedule: 12 hours per week year-round.

Stipend or Pay: No.

Academic Credit Offered: Per student's own arrangements with academic institution; *Plus* other internships often available in other zoo departments.

ELIGIBILITY: Students and non-students with training, interest, and/or background in public relations–related skills.

REQUIREMENTS: Good communications skills and willingness to learn.

APPLICATION PROCEDURE: Send inquiries *to* Tara Henson. *Deadline:* Open.

OPRYLAND USA

2802 Opryland Drive   **Phone:** 615/871-6650
Nashville, TN 37075   **FAX:**   615/871-7785

* * *

ORGANIZATION'S ACTIVITIES: The public relations department is responsible for media and community relations for Opryland USA, a diverse entertainment and hospitality resort.

Number of Internships: 3.

Type: Public relations.

Function/Duties: Media and community relations.

Schedule: Full-time in June, July, and August for 3 interns; part-time work for 1 intern September–May.

Stipend or Pay: Yes.

Academic Credit Offered: Available.

ELIGIBILITY: All students; preferred majors: Public Relations, Journalism, and Communications. Non-students with college degrees also welcome to apply.

REQUIREMENTS: Background, interest, goals, and/or skills related to assignments.

APPLICATION PROCEDURE: Submit résumé and work samples *to* Opryland Personnel Department.

OREGON COAST AQUARIUM

2820 SE Ferry Slip Road   **Phone:** 503/867-3474
Newport, OR 97365   **FAX:** 503/867-6846

*   *   *

ORGANIZATION'S ACTIVITIES: Center for study and public education on northwest marine life.

Number of Internships: Flexible; varies with need.

Type: Exhibit aide.

Function/Duties: Aid the exhibit coordinator in the creation and production of new exhibits; help maintain existing exhibits; painting, woodworking, artwork, and photo mounting, etc.

Schedule: 20 hours per week for 8 to 10 weeks during spring, summer, fall, and winter terms.

Stipend or Pay: $5 per hour.

Academic Credit Offered: Available.

ELIGIBILITY: Consideration given to students, non-students, or career-changers with appropriate qualifications.

REQUIREMENTS: Must have familiarity with hand tools and portable power tools and ability to work alone with little supervision. Art background preferred.

APPLICATION PROCEDURE: Submit résumé and cover letter *to* Exhibits Coordinator.

Number of Internships: Flexible; varies with need.

Type: Interpreter/volunteer coordinator aide.

Function/Duties: Serving as guide ("interpreter") for the public at Oregon Coast Aquarium and assist volunteer coordinator with volunteer scheduling, volunteer communication, compilation, and analysis of volunteer data, etc.

Schedule: 15 to 20 hours per week for 8 to 10 weeks during spring, summer, fall, and winter terms.

Stipend or Pay: $5 per hour.

Academic Credit Offered: Available.

ELIGIBILITY: Consideration give to students, non-students, or career-changers with appropriate qualifications.

REQUIREMENTS: Must have strong communication skills, interest in natural sciences, organizational skills, interest in volunteer program management in a not-for-profit organization, and word processing skills.

Number of Internships: Flexible; varies with need.

Type: Aquarium education intern.

Function/Duties: Assist aquarium educators in the organization and presentation of classroom and auditorium programs, help children with classroom activities, assist in set-up and take-down of program, help keep classroom clean and orderly, continually monitor children for acceptable and safe behaviors, etc.

Schedule: 15 to 20 hours a week for 8 to 10 weeks during spring, summer, fall, and winter terms.

Stipend or Pay: $5 per hour or academic credit available.

ELIGIBILITY: Consideration given to students, non-students, or career-changers with appropriate qualifications.

REQUIREMENTS: Must have strong communication skills, experience working with children, kindergarten through grade 8, and interest in teaching marine studies in an aquarium setting.

APPLICATION PROCEDURE: Submit résumé and cover letter *to* Volunteer Coordinator.

PENNSBURY MANOR

400 Pennsbury Memorial Road   **Phone:** 215/946-0400
Morrisville, PA 19067   **FAX:**   N/A

* * *

ORGANIZATION'S ACTIVITIES: Reconstructed 17th-century home of William Penn of Pennsylvania, along the Delaware River.

Number of Internships: Varies.

Type: Research, education, horticulture.

Function/Duties: Help to maintain old home and grounds; give guided tours; do historical research.

Schedule: Full- and/or part-time, mostly summers.

Stipend or Pay: Yes.

Academic Credit Offered: Per student's own arrangements with academic institution.

ELIGIBILITY: Consideration given to students, non-students, or career-changers with appropriate qualifications.

REQUIREMENTS: Interests, goals, skills, and/or experience relevant to available assignments.

APPLICATION PROCEDURE: Send inquiries *to* Internship Coordinator by November.

PENNSYLVANIA DUTCH CONVENTION & VISITORS BUREAU

501 Greenfield Road
Lancaster, PA 17601

Phone: 717/299-8901
FAX: 717/299-0470

* * *

ORGANIZATION'S ACTIVITIES: Destination marketing organization for Lancaster County, Pennsylvania Dutch County.

Number of Internships: 1.

Type: Marketing/public relations intern.

Function/Duties: Surveying, assisting with writing, data entry, research, assist with advertising placement and trading.

Schedule: Part-time.

Stipend or Pay: Yes.

Academic Credit Offered: Yes.

ELIGIBILITY: College students; preferred majors: Business and Communications. Career-changers may be accepted.

REQUIREMENTS: Excellent oral and written communication skills. Ability to work independently.

APPLICATION PROCEDURE: Submit résumé and explanation of where and how intern will live during internship *to* Stephanie A. Shertzer, Vice President and Director of Marketing.

PHILADELPHIA ACADEMY OF NATURAL SCIENCES

1900 Ben Franklin Parkway
Philadelphia, PA 19103

Phone: 215/299-1050
FAX: N/A

* * *

ORGANIZATION'S ACTIVITIES: A major natural history museum offering exhibitions as well as providing a research library and laboratories.

Number of Internships: 4 per semester.

Type: Education, research, public affairs, communications.

Function/Duties: Assist staff in various departments of the museum and work directly with public.

Schedule: Part-time during spring and fall semesters.

Stipend or Pay: No.

Academic Credit Offered: Per student's own arrangements with academic institution.

ELIGIBILITY: College and graduate students.

REQUIREMENTS: Interests, goals, skills, and/or experience relevant to available assignments.

APPLICATION PROCEDURE: Send inquiries *to* Education Director for application *by* August for fall and *by* November for spring.

RAND CORPORATION

Box 2138   **Phone:** 310/393-0411
Santa Monica, CA 90407   **FAX:**   310/393-4818

* * *

ORGANIZATION'S ACTIVITIES: Private nonprofit research institution whose activities focus on reports and analysis of issues related to national security and social welfare.

Number of Internships: Varies.

Type: Graduate student interns.

Function/Duties: Assist in and learn about research, analysis, and reports-writing on project basis.

Schedule: Full-time summers, in California and Washington, D.C.

Stipend or Pay: Yes.

Academic Credit Offered: Per student's own arrangements with academic institution.

ELIGIBILITY: Graduate students.

REQUIREMENTS: Must have completed at least one year of graduate studies toward a Ph.D. in a wide variety of disciplines.

APPLICATION PROCEDURE: Send inquiries *to* Personnel Director in time to complete application *by* February 1.

SMITHSONIAN INSTITUTION

1000 Jefferson Drive SW   **Phone:** 202/357-2700
Washington, DC 20560   **FAX:**   202/786-2515

* * *

ORGANIZATION'S ACTIVITIES: With its mission to promote research and public education in the arts, sciences, and history, this public agency connected to the federal government manages a variety of galleries and museums, including the National Gallery of Art, the Air and Space Museum, and others in Washington, D.C., as well as the Cooper-Hewitt Museum in New York City.

Number of Internships: 600 or more.

Type: Wide variety, including education, research, publications, curatorial, public affairs.

Function/Duties: Many professional-level; varies according to assignment and intern's interests.

Schedule: Full- and/or part-time, summers, semesters, and year-round.

Stipend or Pay: Yes.

Academic Credit Offered: Per student's own arrangements with academic institution; *Plus* health and other benefits during employment.

ELIGIBILITY: Consideration given to students, non-students, or career-changers with appropriate qualifications.

REQUIREMENTS: Vary depending on specific opening; see *Internships & Fellowships* booklet available from Smithsonian.

APPLICATION PROCEDURE: Request application details *from* Internship Services Coordinator. *Deadline:* February 15 for summer, June 15 for fall, and October 15 for spring.

SMITHSONIAN INSTITUTION, HORTICULTURAL SERVICES

Arts & Industries Building
Room 2282 **Phone:** 202/357-1926
Washington, DC 20560 **FAX:** N/A

* * *

ORGANIZATION'S ACTIVITIES: Nation's major public cultural institution requires plants, landscaping, grounds maintenance.

Number of Internships: 24.

Type: Greenhouse, grounds work, administration.

Function/Duties: Aid and learn from staff in developing and designing plantings and landscapes in and around Institution's facilities.

Schedule: Full-time, 10-week minimum.

Stipend or Pay: $200 per week.

Academic Credit Offered: Per student's own arrangements with academic institution.

ELIGIBILITY: Students, non-students, or career-changers welcome to apply.

REQUIREMENTS: Ability to do physical work, often outside.

APPLICATION PROCEDURE: Send inquiries *to* Horticultural Services Director *by* 3 months prior to start date.

SOUTH STREET SEAPORT MUSEUM

207 Front Street **Phone:** 212/669-9400
New York, NY 10038 **FAX:** 212/732-5168

* * *

ORGANIZATION'S ACTIVITIES: A cultural and historical center for the preservation, study, and exhibition of ships, maritime establishments, and other historic sites and artifacts related to New York's history as a maritime center.

Number of Internships: Varies by season, need, and assignment.

Type: Archeology, curatorial, exhibition design, research, education, tour guides, retail shops.

Function/Duties: Learn from and assist regular staff as assigned according to interest and skill.

Schedule: Full- and/or part-time, year-round availabilities; minimum seasonal commitment preferred.

Stipend or Pay: No.

Academic Credit Offered: May be arranged per student's agreement with academic institution.

REQUIREMENTS: Interest, background, skills, and/or experience in internship specialty requested.

APPLICATION PROCEDURE: For information and to schedule an appointment for interview (required), *call* Patricia Sands, Director of Volunteer Programs, at 212/669-9445. *Deadline:* Ongoing.

THOMAS JEFFERSON UNIVERSITY

1015 Chestnut Street   **Phone:** 215/955-6300
Philadelphia, PA 19107   **FAX:** 215/955-5008

* * *

ORGANIZATION'S ACTIVITIES: An educational and scientific institution over 150 years old, including a Medical College, Hospital, and College of Allied Health Services, as well as undergraduate and graduate divisions.

Number of Internships: Varies.

Type: Medical writing.

Function/Duties: Work with media relations specialist to translate basic research findings (primarily in molecular biology techniques) into lay language and to write articles on medical research topics.

Schedule: Part-time, summers as well as fall and spring semesters.

Stipend or Pay: No.

Academic Credit Offered: Per student's own arrangements with academic institution; *Plus* reimbursement of commuting costs and meals.

ELIGIBILITY: Primarily graduate and undergraduate students.

REQUIREMENTS: An interest in writing about science, good communications skills; prefer those with life-science background or knowledge.

APPLICATION PROCEDURE: Send résumé with cover letter and writing sample *to* Carole Gan *by* several months prior to start date.

UNITED STATES INSTITUTE FOR THEATER TECHNOLOGY

10 West 19th Street
Suite 502
New York, NY 10011

Phone: 212/924-9088
FAX: 212/924-9343

* * *

ORGANIZATION'S ACTIVITIES: Individuals, colleges, organizations producing theatrical groups, manufacturers, and students in the U.S. and Canada interested in the advancement of theater technique and technology. Conducts research and investigations. Sponsors competitions. Presents awards.

Number of Internships: Flexible; varies with need.

Type: Administrative.

Function/Duties: Data entry, list tracking, mailing, editing.

Schedule: Part-time; term can coincide with school term.

Stipend or Pay: Round-trip subway transportation and lunch up to $5 a day.

Academic Credit: Per student's own arrangements with academic institution.

ELIGIBILITY: College juniors and seniors, graduate students and non-students with appropriate background.

REQUIREMENTS: Candidate should be intelligent, friendly, eager, and reliable, with computer knowledge and experience. Interview required.

APPLICATION PROCEDURE: Submit cover letter and résumé *to* Internship Coordinator.

U.S. NATIONAL ARBORETUM

3501 New York Avenue NE
Washington, DC 20002

Phone: 202/475-4865
FAX: N/A

* * *

ORGANIZATION'S ACTIVITIES: Nation's public center for horticultural research collections; specialty gardens include National Herb Garden, Native Plants, Asian collections.

Number of Internships: 3.

Type: Horticulture.

Function/Duties: Wide range of activities in curating and gardening.

Schedule: 1, for full year; others, 3 to 6 months.

Stipend or Pay: $18,000 plus benefits for full year internship; shorter term interns paid $8 per hour.

Academic Credit Offered: N/A.

ELIGIBILITY: College graduates with interest in horticulture.

REQUIREMENTS: College degree in plant-related fields.

APPLICATION PROCEDURE: Send inquiries *to* Curator *by* as far in advance of start date as possible.

WINTERTHUR MUSEUM AND GARDENS

Winterthur, DE 19735   **Phone:** 302/888-4830

                                       FAX: N/A

* * *

ORGANIZATION'S ACTIVITIES: "The finest naturalistic display gardens in the United States," sited on grounds of historic estate.

Number of Internships: 7 or more.

Type: Horticulture.

Function/Duties: Work and learn in all aspects of horticultural practices, including nursery production.

Schedule: Full-time summers, plus some year-round.

Stipend or Pay: $6 per hour.

Academic Credit Offered: Per student's own arrangements with academic institution.

ELIGIBILITY: Students, non-students, or career-changers welcome to apply.

REQUIREMENTS: "A unique opportunity for a beginning horticulturist or landscape architect."

APPLICATION PROCEDURE: Send inquiries *to* Employment Manager in time to apply *by* 3 months prior to start date.

YESHIVA UNIVERSITY MUSEUM

2520 Amsterdam Avenue   **Phone:** 212/960-5390

New York, NY 10033   **FAX:**   212/960-5406

* * *

ORGANIZATION'S ACTIVITIES: Exhibitions, programs for adults and children, and publications related to Jewish art, history, and culture.

Number of Internships: Varies; fairly numerous.

Type: Curatorial.

Function/Duties: Research schedule—part-time, 4-month minimum.

Stipend or Pay: No.

Academic Credit Offered: Available.

ELIGIBILITY: Upper-level college students and graduate students; preferred majors: Art, History, Judaic Studies.

APPLICATION PROCEDURE: Submit résumé *to* Randi Glickberg.

Number of Internships: Varies according to availability.

Type: Education.

Function/Duties: Tours, workshops.

Schedule: Full-time and part-time.

Stipend or Pay: Yes.

ELIGIBILITY: Upper-level college students and graduate students; preferred majors: Art, History, Judaic Studies.

REQUIREMENTS: Interests, goals, background, and/or skills related to internship requested.

APPLICATION PROCEDURE: Submit résumé *to* Randi Glickberg.

Organizations/Resources for Further Information about Internships in Culture and Education

AMERICAN ASSOCIATION OF BOTANICAL GARDENS AND ARBORETA
786 Church Road
Wayne, PA 19087
Phone: 215/688-1120

AMERICAN ASSOCIATION OF MUSEUMS
1225 I Street NW
Washington, DC 20005
Phone: 202/289-1818

ARTS & BUSINESS COUNCIL
25 West 45th Street
New York, NY 10019
Phone: 212/819-9287

NATIONAL ENDOWMENT FOR THE HUMANITIES
Washington, DC 20506
Phone: 202/786-0284

Also see: Resources for *Arts*, *Science*, and the *Environment*.

INTERNSHIP SOURCES IN ENVIRONMENTAL ORGANIZATIONS

■■

Notes on Environmental Interning:

Protecting every aspect of the environment is not only socially popular, but is also a very hot career path. As a result, environmental internships are both valuable and widely available in a broad spectrum of settings, as described here.

TIPS: If you have any environmental interest or experience, present it as a plus *wherever* you seek an internship—including corporations. All aspects of business and government are getting "green" these days, and environmental expertise is in great demand. Note that *environment* is the focus of entries in sections covering international, social service, cultural, and business internship opportunities.

> *Jason was able to combine his international curiosity with his concern for the environment, by bringing his biology studies and his language abilities to bear on a community problem in a South American village where he found a placement through the Overseas Development Network. "I learned how it all came together," he says, "...the economy, the society, the land." He went from there to graduate business school, where he hopes to learn how to do the same kind of work on a larger scale.*

AMERICAN COUNCIL FOR AN ENERGY EFFICIENT ECONOMY

1001 Connecticut Avenue NW   **Phone:** 202/429-8873
Washington, DC 20036   **FAX:**   N/A

* * *

ORGANIZATION'S ACTIVITIES: Nonprofit research and advocacy organization that promotes greater energy efficiency among consumers and businesses.

Number of Internships: 4 or more.

Type: Support and administration.

Function/Duties: Aid in research projects and office work.

Schedule: Part-time, year-round.

Stipend or Pay: Stipend may be arranged.

Academic Credit Offered: Per student's own arrangements with academic institution.

ELIGIBILITY: Primarily undergraduate and graduate students.

REQUIREMENTS: Interest in environmental issues.

APPLICATION PROCEDURE: Send inquiries *to* Publications Director. *Deadline:* Ongoing.

AMERICAN RIVERS

801 Pennsylvania Avenue SE
Washington, DC 20003

Phone: 202/547-6900
FAX: N/A

* * *

ORGANIZATION'S ACTIVITIES: The nation's principal river-saving organization, dedicated to preserving and restoring America's river systems.

Number of Internships: Varies.

Type: Research, marketing, administrative.

Function/Duties: Aid staff in developing information on projects and on fundraising.

Schedule: Full-time summer, spring, and fall; minimum 2- to 3-month commitment.

Stipend or Pay: No.

Academic Credit Offered: Per student's own arrangements with academic institution.

ELIGIBILITY: College students and non-students or career-changers who are college graduates.

REQUIREMENTS: Self-starter with excellent research and writing skills.

APPLICATION PROCEDURE: Send inquiries *to* Corporate Marketing Coordinator *by* 2 months prior to start date desired.

AUDUBON NATURALIST SOCIETY

8940 Jones Mill Road
Chevy Chase, MD 20815

Phone: 301/652-9188
FAX: 301/951-7179

* * *

ORGANIZATION'S ACTIVITIES: ANS seeks to increase environmental awareness and understanding for people of all ages and to encourage conservation action on the local level. Independent of any national group, and serving the Washington, D.C., metropolitan area.

Number of Internships: 5 to 6.

Type: Environmental education.

Function/Duties: Research and educational assistance in regional conservation centers.

Stipend or Pay: $1,200 per internship.

Schedule: Prefer full-time summers; part-time during school year possible.

Academic Credit Offered: Per student's own arrangements with academic institution.

ELIGIBILITY: College juniors and seniors, graduate students; preferred majors: Education and Natural Sciences. High-school students accepted as volunteers only. Non-students and career-changers welcome to apply.

REQUIREMENTS: Interests, goals, skills, and/or background related to ANS activities and purposes.

APPLICATION PROCEDURE: Submit cover letter, résumé, and 2 letters of recommendation *to* Karyn Molines.

CARRYING CAPACITY NETWORK

| 1325 G Street NW | **Phone:** 202/879-3044 |
| Washington, DC 20005 | **FAX:** N/A |

* * *

ORGANIZATION'S ACTIVITIES: A clearinghouse and catalyst for information exchange among environmental organizations around the country, focusing on issues of sustainable development and related topics.

Number of Internships: Varies.

Type: Research, data processing, communications, media relations.

Function/Duties: Assist staff with gathering information and conveying it to media, public, and environmental groups.

Schedule: Full- and/or part-time, year-round; minimum 3-month commitment.

Stipend or Pay: Can be arranged.

Academic Credit Offered: Per student's own arrangements with academic institution.

ELIGIBILITY: Graduate and undergraduate students as well as non-students with degrees.

REQUIREMENTS: Commitment to environmental goals; enthusiasm; good writing and computer skills.

APPLICATION PROCEDURE: Send inquiries *to* Internship Coordinator. *Deadline:* Ongoing.

CITIZENS FOR A BETTER ENVIRONMENT

122 Lincoln Boulevard
Venice, CA 90291

Phone: 310/450-5192
FAX: N/A

* * *

ORGANIZATION'S ACTIVITIES: California nonprofit organization dedicated to reducing toxic pollution in urban areas.

Number of Internships: Varies; fairly numerous.

Type: Research, activist, writing.

Function/Duties: Aid with factual research on issues, with surveys and legislative monitoring, with grassroots organizing, and with writing reports and other materials.

Schedule: Full- and/or part-time, year-round.

Stipend or Pay: No.

Academic Credit Offered: Per student's own arrangements with academic institution.

ELIGIBILITY: Primarily undergraduate and graduate students, but non-students and career-changers also considered.

REQUIREMENTS: Interest and experience in related topics; Macintosh computer skills.

APPLICATION PROCEDURE: Send résumé and cover letter *to* Program Director. *Deadline:* Ongoing.

CONCERN

1794 Columbia Road NW
Washington, DC 20009

Phone: 202/328-8160
FAX: N/A

* * *

ORGANIZATION'S ACTIVITIES: A nonprofit organization dedicated to providing environmental information to individuals, community groups, government officials, educators, and others.

Number of Internships: Varies.

Type: Research, writing, community development.

Function/Duties: Assist with research, writing, and production of publications, and presentation of reports and programs.

Schedule: 20 hours per week, year-round.

Stipend or Pay: $75 per week.

Academic Credit Offered: Per student's own arrangements with academic institution.

ELIGIBILITY: Consideration given to students, non-students, or career-changers with appropriate qualifications.

REQUIREMENTS: Knowledge of environmental issues, strong research and communications skills.

APPLICATION PROCEDURE: Send inquiries *to* Darragh Lewis. *Deadline:* Ongoing.

DAHLEM ENVIRONMENTAL EDUCATION CENTER

7117 South Jackson Road
Jackson, MI 49201

Phone: 517/782-3453
FAX: NA

* * *

ORGANIZATION'S ACTIVITIES: Serves as a major field-trip site for schools (approximately 400 per year); offers weekend public programming and special events; maintains a comprehensive bluebird recovery project, and has a visitor/exhibit area and a 300-acre site with 5 miles of trails.

Number of Internships: Varies.

Type: Naturalist intern.

Function/Duties: Organizing, conducting, and evaluating school and youth group field experiences utilizing the Center's award-winning curriculum. Additional projects may include programming for special events, animal care, exhibit design and construction, writing news releases, assisting in the visitor center and gift shop, leading public programs, and/or preparing educational materials.

Schedule: Full-time; year-round; prefer 3-month term.

Stipend or Pay: Free on-site housing and a weekly stipend of $150.

Academic Credit Offered: Available if arranged by intern.

ELIGIBILITY: College juniors and seniors as well as graduate students. Non-students with college-level training and career-changers also welcome to apply.

REQUIREMENTS: Applicants should have a good background in either natural history or environmental education. Outdoor teaching experience and/or relevant course work are desirable. Interns need to be enthusiastic, creative, and flexible with a friendly teaching style.

Type: Wildlife biologist/naturalists.

Function/Duties: Coordinate community-oriented restoration program for the eastern bluebird. Monitor and keep accurate records for 400 nestboxes. Provide on-site supervision and assistance to volunteers and property owners involved in the project. Generate a better understanding of and support for the bluebird project through presentations to community organizations and youth groups.

Schedule: Full-time, year-round; prefer 3-month stay.

Stipend or Pay: Free on-site housing and a weekly stipend of $100 to $150 (depending on experience).

Academic Credit Offered: Available if arranged by intern.

ELIGIBILITY: College juniors and seniors as well as graduate students. Non-students with college-level training and career-changers also welcome to apply.

REQUIREMENTS: Applicants must have formal training in wildlife management, biology, natural history interpretation, or a related field. Experience working with children in an educational setting is desirable. Should be a good communicator who enjoys working with the public. Must have dependable transportation. Will be required to use personal vehicle on the job.

APPLICATION PROCEDURE: Send a résumé and a cover letter requesting an application form *to* Diane Valen, Program Coordinator.

EARTHWATCH

680 Auburn Street   **Phone:** 617/926-8200
Watertown, MA 02272   **FAX:**   617/926-8532

* * *

ORGANIZATION'S ACTIVITIES: Coalition of scientists and laypeople collaborating on projects to improve the quality of life on the earth. Massachusetts headquarters supports research projects by providing interns to assist scientists.

Number of Internships: Hundreds annually.

Type: Research, environmental, administrative.

Function/Duties: Varies with project—most interns aid scientists in many sites and settings; assistance is also needed in headquarters office.

Schedule: Varies with assignment.

Stipend or Pay: Sometimes may be arranged.

Academic Credit Offered: Per student's own arrangements with academic institution.

ELIGIBILITY: Primarily graduate and undergraduate students, but non-students and career-changers may also be considered.

REQUIREMENTS: Interest in environmentally related issues; details vary with assignment.

APPLICATION PROCEDURE: Send inquiries *to* Personnel Director. *Deadline:* Ongoing.

ENVIRONMENTAL DEFENSE FUND

257 Park Avenue South   **Phone:** 212/505-2100
New York, NY 10010   **FAX:**   212/505-2375

* * *

ORGANIZATION'S ACTIVITIES: Nonprofit national public interest organization of lawyers, scientists, economists, and others dedicated to the enhancement of public health and environmental quality.

Number of Internships: Varies; numerous.

Type: Research, editorial, educational, other.

Function/Duties: Varies depending on locale; regional branches offer fieldwork as well as surveys and other projects; administrative duties and publications assistance available in headquarters and other offices.

Schedule: Full- and/or part-time, year-round.

Stipend or Pay: Not usually.

Academic Credit Offered: Per student's own arrangements with academic institution.

ELIGIBILITY: Primarily graduate and undergraduate students, but qualified non-students and career-changers also may be considered.

REQUIREMENTS: Interests, goals, skills, and/or experience relevant to available assignments.

APPLICATION PROCEDURE: Send inquiries *to* Internship Manager. *Deadline:* Ongoing.

ENVIRONMENTAL INVESTIGATIONS

1911 Meredith Drive	**Phone:** 919/544-7500
Durham, NC 27713	**FAX:** N/A

* * *

ORGANIZATION'S ACTIVITIES: Private company that acts as consultants on environmental hazards for manufacturers, investors, and law firms.

Number of Internships: 5 or more.

Type: Research and technical.

Function/Duties: Work with professional staff in field investigations of potential environmental hazards.

Schedule: Full- and/or part-time, summers and school semesters.

Stipend or Pay: No.

Academic Credit Offered: Per student's own arrangements with academic institution.

ELIGIBILITY: Primarily undergraduate students, though others with appropriate skills and experience considered.

REQUIREMENTS: Prefer those with science and/or environmental experience.

APPLICATION PROCEDURE: Send inquiries *to* President's Office. *Deadline:* Ongoing.

FARM SANCTUARY

Box 150
Watkins Glen, NY 14891

Phone: 607/583-2225
FAX: N/A

* * *

ORGANIZATION'S ACTIVITIES: Rural center for vegetarians concerned with animal rights.

Number of Internships: Varies.

Type: Farm and office work.

Function/Duties: Help maintain farm and help with office work related to activism for animal rights.

Schedule: Full-time, residential; 1-month minimum.

Stipend or Pay: $30 per week.

Academic Credit Offered: Per student's own arrangements with academic institution; *Plus* housing and food provided.

ELIGIBILITY: Students as well as non-students and career-changers.

REQUIREMENTS: Commitment to vegetarian and vegan practice; ability to perform physical labor.

APPLICATION PROCEDURE: Send inquiries *to* Holly McNulty. *Deadline:* Open.

FRIENDS OF THE EARTH

218 D Street SE
Washington, DC 20003

Phone: 202/544-2600
FAX: 202/543-4710

* * *

ORGANIZATION'S ACTIVITIES: An independent, global environmental advocacy organization that works at local, national, and international levels to protect the earth's environment as well as human diversity.

Number of Internships: Varies.

Type: Research, writing, administrative.

Function/Duties: Work with staff at professional level on a wide variety of projects—research, education, public affairs, organizing, etc.—in areas assigned according to intern's interests.

Schedule: Full- and/or part-time, year-round.

Stipend or Pay: No; commuting costs reimbursed.

Academic Credit Offered: Per student's own arrangements with academic institution.

ELIGIBILITY: Consideration given to students, non-students, and career-changers with appropriate qualifications. *Special Eligibilities:* people of color are especially encouraged to apply.

REQUIREMENTS: Energetic, committed to goals and activities of organization; studies and/or experience in environmental law, social issues, journalism, the sciences; strong writing, word processing, and communications skills.

APPLICATION PROCEDURE: Send inquiries *to* Internship Coordinator. *Deadline:* Ongoing.

GLOBAL ENVIRONMENTAL ISSUES PROGRAM

1000 Pope Road **Phone:** 808/956-8191
Honolulu, HI 96822 **FAX:** 808/956-5286

* * *

ORGANIZATION'S ACTIVITIES: University-based studies of ozone depletion, climatic changes, etc.

Number of Internships: Varies.

Type: Research, reports-writing.

Function/Duties: Participate with professionals in studies of environment and surveys on people's attitudes toward environmental hazards.

Schedule: Flexible.

Stipend or Pay: No.

Academic Credit Offered: Per student's own arrangements with academic institution.

ELIGIBILITY: Primarily graduate and undergraduate students.

REQUIREMENTS: Strong writing and communication skills.

APPLICATION PROCEDURE: Send inquiries *to* Dr. Bruce Miller. *Deadline:* Open.

INDIANAPOLIS ZOO

1200 West Washington Street **Phone:** 317/630-2041
Indianapolis, IN 46222 **FAX:** 317/630-5114

* * *

ORGANIZATION'S ACTIVITIES: Wildlife protection institution, center for environmental education for children and families.

Number of Internships: Varies.

Type: Environmental education.

Function/Duties: Opportunity to enhance public appreciation and understanding of natural world. Professional educators offer support and guidance to interns as they work with the zoo visitors program, school programs, subscription programs, volunteer programs, and library programs.

Schedule: Minimum of 20 hours per week.

Stipend or Pay: No.

Academic Credit Offered: Per student's own arrangements with academic institution.

ELIGIBILITY: College students.

REQUIREMENTS: Interest, skills, and experience in the environment and in dealing with children.

APPLICATION PROCEDURE: Submit résumé, 2 letters of recommendation, a copy of current grade transcript, cover letter, and application form. Cover letter should answer the following questions: Why are you interested in an internship at the Indianapolis Zoo? What would you like to gain from an internship? What internship opportunities interest you most? Where did you hear about the internship program? All application materials should be sent as a packet *to* Mary Kay Hood, Volunteer Coordinator. You will be contacted about an interview upon receipt of all materials.

IZAAK WALTON LEAGUE OF AMERICA

1401 Wilson Boulevard   **Phone:** 703/528-1818
Arlington, VA 22209   **FAX:**   703/528-1836

*   *   *

ORGANIZATION'S ACTIVITIES: A national environmental protection organization that coordinates the local activities of chapters.

Number of Internships: Varies.

Type: Research, editorial.

Function/Duties: Varies depending on location; in general help with background for special projects, help produce and write newsletter and issues paper.

Schedule: Full- and/or part-time, either at national office or at local chapters.

Stipend or Pay: No.

Academic Credit Offered: Per student's own arrangements with academic institution.

ELIGIBILITY: Primarily undergraduate students.

REQUIREMENTS: Interests, goals, skills, and/or experience relevant to available assignments.

APPLICATION PROCEDURE: Send inquiries *to* Program Director.
Deadline: Ongoing.

THE LAND AGRICULTURAL PROGRAM

EPCOT Center Science & Technology Group
P.O. Box 10,000   **Phone:** 407/560-7450
Lake Buena Vista, FL 32830   **FAX:**   407/560-7227

*   *   *

ORGANIZATION'S ACTIVITIES: The Land showcases agricultural technologies in one-acre greenhouses at EPCOT Center, demonstrating new and developing processes and techniques.

Number of Internships: Varies; Approximately 36.

Type: Technical and scientific; agricultural engineering; aquaculture; entomology; horticulture; plant nutrition; plant tissue culture; marine life; plant pathology.

Function/Duties: Research; participate in demonstration projects; maintenance; tour guidance.

Schedule: 6-month residential program (December–June and June–January).

Stipend or Pay: $315 per week minimum. *Plus* relocation allowance; housing available.

Academic Credit Offered: Per intern's arrangement with own academic institution; *Plus* weekly seminars with scientific professionals.

ELIGIBILITY: Undergraduate, graduate, and post-doctoral students in all fields mentioned above, as well as non-students on sabbatical or experienced in appropriate fields.

REQUIREMENTS: Minimum of junior year in college; relevant career goals and/or experience; personal interview (may be conducted on college campus).

APPLICATION PROCEDURE: Send résumé, transcript, 3 recommendations, and cover letter *to* Intern Recruiting Coordinator *by* 9 months prior to starting date in order to be considered.

LOST VALLEY EDUCATIONAL CENTER

818 Lost Valley Lane   **Phone:** 503/937-3351
Dexter, OR 97431   **FAX:**   N/A

* * *

ORGANIZATION'S ACTIVITIES: Residential sustainable living community practicing organic gardening, land stewardship, and permaculture.

Number of Internships: Varies.

Type: Agroecology.

Function/Duties: Work and learn sustainable living techniques within a community setting.

Schedule: Residential 40-hour week for 1 month or for 7 months.

Stipend or Pay: No; lodging and food provided.

Academic Credit Offered: Per student's own arrangements with academic institution.

ELIGIBILITY: Consideration given to students, non-students, or career-changers with appropriate qualifications.

REQUIREMENTS: Compatible interests, goals, skills, and/or experience; environmental and agricultural skills preferred.

APPLICATION PROCEDURE: Send inquiries *to* Vicci Carroccio. *Deadline:* Open.

MERCK FOREST AND FARMLAND CENTER

Box 86   **Phone:** 802/394-7836
Rupert, VT 05768   **FAX:**   N/A

* * *

ORGANIZATION'S ACTIVITIES: Development and operations in forestry and small-scale farming.

Number of Internships: Varies.

Type: Education, farming, forestry.

Function/Duties: Plan and implement projects in conjunction with center's staff.

Schedule: Full-time, residential; year-round and/or seasonal.

Stipend or Pay: $55 per week; *Plus* housing and food provided.

Academic Credit Offered: Per student's own arrangements with academic institution.

ELIGIBILITY: Students, non-students, or career-changers welcome to apply.

REQUIREMENTS: Natural-science background with interest in conservation and environmental education.

APPLICATION PROCEDURE: Send résumé, letter of interest, and 3 references *to* Executive Director. *Deadline:* Ongoing.

MOTER MARINE LABORATORY

1600 Thompson Parkway   **Phone:** 813/388-4441
Sarasota, FL 34236   **FAX:**   813/388-4312

* * *

ORGANIZATION'S ACTIVITIES: An independent, nonprofit organization dedicated to excellence in marine and environmental research and education.

Number of Internships: Varies; about 12.

Type: Research, technical, education, public affairs.

Function/Duties: Assist in laboratories with biomedical, chemical, environmental and other research; or in education programs; or in public relations projects.

Schedule: Full-time 8 to 16 weeks.

Stipend or Pay: No.

Academic Credit Offered: Per student's own arrangements with academic institution; *Plus* opportunities for independent research.

ELIGIBILITY: Graduate and undergraduate students.

REQUIREMENTS: Prefer background and/or experience in related areas of study.

APPLICATION PROCEDURE: Send inquiries *to* Internship Coordinator *by* 2 months prior to start date.

NATIONAL AUDUBON SOCIETY

700 Broadway   **Phone:** 212/979-3000
New York, NY 10003   **FAX:** 212/353-0508

* * *

ORGANIZATION'S ACTIVITIES: National nonprofit organization with the purpose of wildlife preservation through education and information programs on a large and small scale.

Number of Internships: Varies; fairly numerous.

Type: Varies widely depending on locale.

Function/Duties: Interns used in locally sponsored outdoor education programs; publications assistance in headquarters and wide variety in between.

Schedule: Varies widely—contact national office (above) for referral to regions and activities of interest.

Stipend or Pay: Some.

Academic Credit Offered: Per student's own arrangements with academic institution.

ELIGIBILITY: Consideration given to students, non-students, or career-changers with appropriate qualifications.

REQUIREMENTS: Interests, goals, skills, and/or experience relevant to available assignments.

APPLICATION PROCEDURE: Send inquiries *to* Education Coordinator. *Deadline:* Ongoing.

NATIONAL INSTITUTE OF ENVIRONMENTAL HEALTH SCIENCE

Box 12333   **Phone:** 919/541-3206
Research Triangle Park, NC 27709   **FAX:** N/A

* * *

ORGANIZATION'S ACTIVITIES: Federal government–supported research organization that engages in its own biomedical research and sponsors that of other organizations.

Number of Internships: 150.

Type: Research, scientific.

Function/Duties: Support scientists and participate in laboratory research in genetics and other research.

Schedule: Mostly full-time in summers; some during school semesters.

Stipend or Pay: No.

Academic Credit Offered: Per student's own arrangements with academic institution.

ELIGIBILITY: Graduate and undergraduate students.

REQUIREMENTS: Chemistry, premed, and biology students preferred.

APPLICATION PROCEDURE: Send résumé and cover letter *to* Scientific Director *by* April 15 for summer, July 15 for fall, and September 15 for spring.

NATIONAL RENEWABLE ENERGY LABORATORY

1617 Cole Boulevard   **Phone:** 303/231-1455
Golden, CO 80401   **FAX:** N/A

* * *

ORGANIZATION'S ACTIVITIES: Research organization seeking to enhance development of solar and other renewable fuels.

Number of Internships: 50.

Type: Research, scientific.

Function/Duties: Participate in laboratory research in topics including engineering and biotechnology.

Schedule: Full-time summers.

Stipend or Pay: Yes.

Academic Credit Offered: Per student's own arrangements with academic institution.

ELIGIBILITY: Primarily undergraduate and graduate students, but qualified non-students or career-changers may be considered.

REQUIREMENTS: Background and education in sciences preferred.

APPLICATION PROCEDURE: Send résumé and cover letter *to* Intern Director by early in spring prior to start date.

NATIONAL WILDLIFE FEDERATION

1400 16th Street NW   **Phone:** 202/797-6800
Washington, DC 20036   **FAX:** 202/797-6646

* * *

ORGANIZATION'S ACTIVITIES: The world's largest nonprofit, nongovernmental conservation education organization, sponsoring research, public education, and legislative and legal advocacy among other environmental protection activities.

Number of Internships: 12.

Type: Resources Conservation: Biodiversity, environmental quality, international, corporate.

Function/Duties: Participate as a member of multidisciplinary team dealing with scientific, legal, and legislative aspects of a specific problem; independent research.

Schedule: Full-time 6 months (January–June and July–December).

Stipend or Pay: About $300 per week; *Plus* some benefits.

Academic Credit Offered: Per student's own arrangements with academic institution.

ELIGIBILITY: Some graduate students; otherwise, college graduates with degrees and/or experience in environmentally related sciences and social issues. *Special Eligibilities:* equal-opportunity program; women and minorities are encouraged to apply.

REQUIREMENTS: These are highly competitive positions, and some related background is a plus; excellent speaking and writing skills required.

APPLICATION PROCEDURE: Send cover letter, résumé, contact information for 3 to 5 academic or professional references, and a 2- to 4-page sample of nonacademic professional writing *to* Nancy Hwa, Resources Conservation Internship Program, *by* October 2 for January and *by* April 1 for July.

NATURALISTS AT LARGE

Box 3517   **Phone:** 805/642-2692
Ventura, CA 93006   **FAX:**   N/A

* * *

ORGANIZATION'S ACTIVITIES: Wilderness travel specialists, organizing tours and expeditions that focus on natural history.

Number of Internships: Varies.

Type: Teachers, guides.

Function/Duties: Depending on program, organize groups and group activities; lead hikes and tours.

Schedule: Short-term, residential; seasonal and/or year-round.

Stipend or Pay: $250 to $450 per program; *Plus* lodging and food provided.

Academic Credit Offered: Per student's own arrangements with academic institution.

ELIGIBILITY: Consideration given to students, non-students, or career-changers with appropriate qualifications.

REQUIREMENTS: Outdoor skills, camping experience, and group supervision experience required.

APPLICATION PROCEDURE: Send résumé and cover letter *to* Charles Slosberg. *Deadline:* Ongoing.

NATURE CONSERVANCY

1815 North Lynn Street	**Phone:** 703/841-5300
Arlington, VA 22209	**FAX:** 703/841-1283

*   *   *

ORGANIZATION'S ACTIVITIES: An international membership organization dedicated to protecting the earth's "rare species and natural communities."

Number of Internships: Varies nationwide.

Type: Research, communications, outdoors, editorial.

Function/Duties: Varies with project and locale—some fieldwork, some administrative.

Schedule: Full- and/or part-time, summers and/or school semesters; contact national office for referral to appropriate regional activities.

Stipend or Pay: Some paid.

Academic Credit Offered: Per student's own arrangements with academic institution.

ELIGIBILITY: Primarily graduate and undergraduate students, but qualified non-students and career-changers also considered.

REQUIREMENTS: Interests, goals, skills, and/or experience relevant to available assignments.

APPLICATION PROCEDURE: Send inquiries *to* Internship Coordinator. *Deadline:* Ongoing.

PEACE VALLEY NATURE CENTER

170 Chapman Road	**Phone:** 215/345-7860
Doylestown, PA 18901	**FAX:** N/A

*   *   *

ORGANIZATION'S ACTIVITIES: Environmental education center for school groups and other members of the public.

Number of Internships: Varies.

Type: Naturalist, educator.

Function/Duties: Teach hands-on environmental education program, help produce newsletter.

Schedule: Full time, 10 to 12 weeks.

Stipend or Pay: $650; *Plus* housing provided.

Academic Credit Offered: Per student's own arrangements with academic institution.

ELIGIBILITY: Primarily undergraduate and graduate students, but others considered.

REQUIREMENTS: Interest in teaching and in environmental studies.

APPLICATION PROCEDURE: Send résumé, cover letter, and 3 references *to* Assistant Naturalist *by* 2 months prior to start date.

PLANET DRUM FOUNDATION

P.O. Box 31251   **Phone:** 415/285-6556
San Francisco, CA 94131   **FAX:**   N/A

*   *   *

ORGANIZATION'S ACTIVITIES: A nonprofit educational and research organization promoting the concept of "bioregionalism" as an environmentally sound approach to ecology and development.

Number of Internships: Dozens.

Type: Research, editorial, communications.

Function/Duties: Aid in special projects as well as on publications and in community development programs.

Schedule: Part-time, flexible; year-round.

Stipend or Pay: No.

Academic Credit Offered: Yes.

ELIGIBILITY: Primarily graduate and undergraduate students but qualified non-students and career-changers also considered.

REQUIREMENTS: Interests, goals, skills, and/or experience relevant to available assignments.

APPLICATION PROCEDURE: Send inquiries *to* Office Manager. *Deadline:* Ongoing.

RENEW AMERICA

1400 16th Street NW   **Phone:** 202/232-2252
Washington, DC 20036   **FAX:**   202/232-2617

*   *   *

ORGANIZATION'S ACTIVITIES: The nation's leading source for environmental solutions, which identifies, verifies, and promotes environmental initiatives developed by individuals, community groups, nonprofit organizations, businesses, and public agencies.

Number of Internships: Varies.

Type: Public affairs, research, administrative.

Function/Duties: Assist staff with ongoing functions, with publication of "The Environmental Success Index," and with annual conference and major awards event.

Schedule: Full- and/or part-time; summers or school semesters.

Stipend or Pay: No.

Academic Credit Offered: Per student's own arrangements with academic institution.

ELIGIBILITY: Consideration given to students, non-students, or career-changers with appropriate qualifications.

REQUIREMENTS: Prefer interest in and/or experience with environmental issues.

APPLICATION PROCEDURE: Send inquiries *to* Intern Coordinator *by* 2 months before start date.

SIERRA CLUB

730 Polk Street	**Phone:** 415/776-2211
San Francisco, CA 94109	**FAX:** 415/776-0350

* * *

ORGANIZATION'S ACTIVITIES: National membership conservation organization dedicated to preserving wilderness areas through education, legislation, and litigation.

Number of Internships: Varies; approximately 12.

Type: Research, fundraising, editorial, public relations.

Function/Duties: Aid headquarters staff with research, publications, and membership development.

Schedule: Part-time, year-round.

Stipend or Pay: No.

Academic Credit Offered: Per student's own arrangements with academic institution.

ELIGIBILITY: Primarily graduate and undergraduate students.

REQUIREMENTS: Excellent communications skills; previous related experience in conservation movement a plus.

APPLICATION PROCEDURE: Send cover letter, résumé, and writing sample *to* Intern Coordinator *by* 2 to 3 months prior to start date desired.

SOCIETY OF AMERICAN FORESTERS

5400 Grosvenor Lane	**Phone:** 301/897-8720
Bethesda, MD 20814	**FAX:** 301/897-3690

* * *

ORGANIZATION'S ACTIVITIES: Educational and advocacy group promoting environmentally sound natural resource development.

Number of Internships: 1 or more per term.

Type: Resource policy intern.

Function/Duties: Assist director of resource policy, preparing reports and monitoring legislation.

Schedule: Full-time summers, plus fall, and spring semesters.

Stipend or Pay: $500 to $1,000 per month, depending on qualifications.

Academic Credit Offered: Per student's own arrangements with academic institution.

ELIGIBILITY: Graduate or upper-level undergraduate students in accredited forestry program or in public policy studies.

REQUIREMENTS: Excellent communication skills; members of Society preferred.

APPLICATION PROCEDURE: Send résumé, transcript, writing sample, references, and term desired *to* Resource Policy Director *by* 3 months prior to start date.

STUDENT CONSERVATION ASSOCIATION

Box 550	**Phone:** 603/543-1700
Charlestown, NH 03603	**FAX:** N/A

* * *

ORGANIZATION'S ACTIVITIES: Coordinates environmental education programs for high school and other students; provides information for older students on environmental projects worldwide. Centers in over 35 states.

Number of Internships: Varies.

Type: Resource assistants.

Function/Duties: Providing counseling, recreation, education, and other services for students participating in programs and for other visitors, as well as support services for resource staffs in centers.

Schedule: Full-time, summers.

Stipend or Pay: Maintenance stipend.

Academic Credit Offered: Per student's own arrangements with academic institution; *Plus* career services available.

ELIGIBILITY: Consideration given to students, non-students, or career-changers with appropriate qualifications.

REQUIREMENTS: Interests, goals, skills, and/or experience relevant to available assignments.

APPLICATION PROCEDURE: Send inquiries *to* Public Relations Director *by* 2 months prior to start date.

TENNESSEE VALLEY AUTHORITY'S LAND BETWEEN THE LAKES

100 Van Morgan Drive
Golden Pond, KY 42211

Phone: 502/924-5602
FAX: 502/924-1399

* * *

ORGANIZATION'S ACTIVITIES: LBL is a 170,000-acre national recreation area located in western Kentucky and Tennessee. LBL provides outdoor recreation and environmental education in a managed natural setting that strengthens environmental responsibility among customers and communicates TVA's environmental leadership role.

Number of Internships: 12.

Type: Environmental education.

Function/Duties: Varies by position.

Schedule: Full-time, 40 hours per week, summer months (end of May through mid-August).

Stipend or Pay: Stipends available.

Academic Credit Offered: Per student's own arrangements with academic institution.

ELIGIBILITY: Students, preferably college juniors and seniors. Applicants for apprenticeships ($150 per week plus housing) must not be enrolled in school and must have a college degree.

REQUIREMENTS: Interests, goals, and/or experience relevant to available assignments.

Number of Internships: 12.

Type: Resource management.

Function/Duties: Varies by position.

Schedule: Full-time, 40 hours per week, summer months (end of May through mid-August).

Stipend or Pay: Stipends available.

Academic Credit Offered: Per student's own arrangements with academic institution.

ELIGIBILITY: Students, preferably college juniors and seniors. Applicants for apprenticeships ($150 per week plus housing) must not be enrolled in school and must have a college degree.

REQUIREMENTS: Interests, goals, and/or experience relevant to available assignments.

APPLICATION PROCEDURE: Submit internship application and résumé *to* Jim Carpenter, Administrator, Professional Development.

WILDLIFE HABITAT ENHANCEMENT COUNCIL

1010 Wayne Avenue
Silver Spring, MD 20910

Phone: 301/588-8994
FAX: N/A

* * *

ORGANIZATION'S ACTIVITIES: A nonprofit organization designed to help corporations improve their lands for the benefit of wildlife.

Number of Internships: 1 or more.

Type: Research, writing.

Function/Duties: Background research, production of reports for staff and clients.

Schedule: Full-time, 6 months.

Stipend or Pay: Yes.

Academic Credit Offered: Per student's own arrangements with academic institution.

ELIGIBILITY: Consideration given to students, non-students, or career-changers with appropriate qualifications.

REQUIREMENTS: College graduate or undergraduate in biology or related area; excellent writing skills; computer skills.

APPLICATION PROCEDURE: Send inquiries *to* Director of Field Programs. *Deadline:* Ongoing.

THE WILDLIFE SOCIETY

5410 Grosvenor Lane
Bethesda, MD 20814

Phone: N/A
FAX: N/A

* * *

ORGANIZATION'S ACTIVITIES: Research and advocacy organization dedicated to environmental protection and wildlife management.

Number of Internships: Varies.

Type: Research, editorial.

Function/Duties: Gather background material and write reports and publications, monitor legislation.

Schedule: Full-time, 6-month commitment; flexible starts.

Stipend or Pay: $500 bimonthly.

Academic Credit Offered: Per student's own arrangements with academic institution.

ELIGIBILITY: Graduate and undergraduate students as well as non-students or career-changers with appropriate qualifications.

REQUIREMENTS: Ability to do research and write well; background in wildlife biology and knowledge of federal government preferred.

APPLICATION PROCEDURE: Send résumé, transcript, 3 references, and 2 writing samples *to* Intern Program *by* 2 months prior to start date.

WOMEN'S HUMANE SOCIETY

3025 West Clearfield Street   **Phone:** 215/225-4500
Philadelphia, PA 19132   **FAX:**   215/226-1250

* * *

ORGANIZATION'S ACTIVITIES: For nearly 125 years, the Society has been dedicated to protecting hurt, sick, or unwanted animals through shelters and, more recently, through education and legislation designed to prevent cruelty to animals.

Number of Internships: Varies.

Type: Research, education, communications.

Function/Duties: Assist staff in preparing reports, monitoring legislation, and producing variety of publications and articles.

Schedule: Flexible, full and/or part-time, summers and/or semesters.

Stipend or Pay: No.

Academic Credit Offered: Per student's own arrangements with academic institution.

ELIGIBILITY: Consideration given to students, non-students, or career-changers with appropriate qualifications.

REQUIREMENTS: Interests, goals, skills, and/or experience relevant to available assignments.

APPLICATION PROCEDURE: Send inquires *to* Intern/Volunteer Coordinator. *Deadline:* Ongoing.

WORLD RESOURCE INSTITUTE

1709 New York Avenue NW   **Phone:** N/A
Washington, DC 20006   **FAX:**   N/A

* * *

ORGANIZATION'S ACTIVITIES: An international nonprofit organization providing environmental support to governments and private organizations in developing countries.

Number of Internships: Varies.

Type: Community development, scientific, technical.

Function/Duties: Work with local communities to develop and maintain sustainable natural resources; also support services in office.

Schedule: Varies according to project.

Stipend or Pay: Maintenance as necessary.

Academic Credit Offered: Per student's own arrangements with academic institution.

ELIGIBILITY: College graduates, and/or graduate students.

REQUIREMENTS: Prefer academic work and/or experience in environmental studies; some experience in field; availability to travel if necessary.

APPLICATION PROCEDURE: Write letter of interest and résumé *to* Internship Coordinator. *Deadline:* Ongoing.

WORLD WILDLIFE FUND

1225 24th Street NW	**Phone:** 202/293-4800
Washington, DC 20037	**FAX:** 202/293-2911

* * *

ORGANIZATION'S ACTIVITIES: The largest private organization working worldwide to protect endangered wildlife and wildlands. Working in the U.S. and in more than 70 other countries to promote sustainable development and reduce pollution, the Fund is the U.S. affiliate of the international WWF.

Number of Internships: Varies.

Type: Research, technical, managerial, communications.

Function/Duties: Vary according to intern's skills and organization's needs; includes monitoring regional conditions, studying laws and practices, and assisting in such areas as public affairs and fundraising.

Schedule: Mostly full-time, summers.

Stipend or Pay: Some paid, some unpaid positions.

Academic Credit Offered: Per student's own arrangements with academic institution.

ELIGIBILITY: Primarily undergraduate and graduate students, though others with appropriate experience may be considered.

REQUIREMENTS: Academic background or experience in science and other specialties related to environmental protection; excellent communications skills and some computer experience.

APPLICATION PROCEDURE: Send cover letter, résumé, contact information for 3 references, and a writing sample *to* Human Resources Department *by* mid-April.

Organizations/Resources for Further Information about Internships in Environmental Organizations

CRITICAL MASS ENERGY PROJECT OF PUBLIC CITIZEN
215 Pennsylvania Avenue SE
Washington, DC 20003
Phone: 202/546-4996

Works to oppose nuclear power and promote safe energy.

ENVIRONMENTAL ACTION
Center for Science in the Public Interest
1875 Connecticut Avenue NW
Room 300
Washington, DC 20004
Phone: 202/332-9110

Information from national consumer organization.

STUDENT CONSERVATION ASSOCIATION (SCA)
Box 550
Charlestown, NH 03603
Phone: 603/543-1700

In addition to the internship opportunities it offers itself (see p. 200), the SCA serves as a clearinghouse of information and placements in environmental projects worldwide.

INTERNSHIP SOURCES IN GOVERNMENT

Notes on Interning in Government:

Federal, state, and local governments all provide well-structured internship opportunities that offer readily accepted academic credits and résumé additions of value in many different careers.

However, while economic constraints and budget cutbacks have increased the number of internship opportunities in nonprofit organizations and even in corporations, the opposite is true for government administrative units— shrinking budgets and employee layoffs mean that governments: (1) must consider interns a luxury in an era when longtime paid employees are losing jobs and (2) cannot spend training funds on intern programs when the number of unemployed in need of training is high. But as these listings show, the opportunities are there if you know where and how to look.

TIPS: In addition to the specifics here, think also of finding your own openings, especially on the state, local, or legislative levels. As a resident of your locality, or a constituent of your legislator, you are more likely to win the competition for limited openings than are those from outside your state or region.

1. Many states have programs for special-needs groups, such as young people, the disabled, or recently laid off. These may be worth checking out (see page 00 for contacts). 2. Uncle Sam has employment info outposts throughout the land, and many federal agencies—Agriculture and Park Service especially—have regionally centered activities. 3. Contact regional offices, too—Pages 233–237 guide you through the government maze.

Is it worth it? Definitely. Governmental internships tend to be well organized, and to offer a wide variety of opportunities. 4. Most federal opportunities require the completion of a standard form: you may want to fill some out in bulk prior to any sweep of federal agencies. Many also require passing a standard, professional-level exam, so it is important to check with the federal Office of Personnel Management (OPM) branch near you well ahead of time.

Noni Ellison is gaining experience by working 20 hours a week at the U.S. Department of Justice. "Based on what I've seen, I'd like not only to earn my law degree, but go on to become a criminal investigator," she says.

"It's not only a way to gain work experience, but to get your foot in the door so that you have a solid job opportunity when you graduate," says Stan Becton, an accounting major and a co-op student with the General Services Administration.

Also see federal programs under *Science.*

AGRICULTURE, U.S. DEPARTMENT OF

14th Street and Independence Avenue SW **Phone:** 202/720-2791
Washington, DC 20250 **FAX:** 202/720-5043

* * *

ORGANIZATION'S ACTIVITIES: Large executive agency performing wide scope of functions, including farm subsidies, food inspection, conservation, and education.

Number of Internships: 2,500 nationwide.

Type: Special student programs as well as individual internships in areas including agronomy, engineering, forestry, computers, and management.

Function/Duties: Assist staff in assignments relevant to intern's studies.

Schedule: Part- and/or full-time; summers and/or year-round, in D.C. headquarters as well as locations around country.

Stipend or Pay: Some paid at government salary rates; many unpaid.

Academic Credit Offered: Per student's own arrangements with academic institution.

ELIGIBILITY: Graduate and undergraduate students; *Plus* many internship openings lead to permanent positions.

REQUIREMENTS: Interests, goals, and/or experience relevant to available assignments.

APPLICATION PROCEDURE: Send inquiries *to* Personnel Division. *Deadline:* Ongoing; varies with type of internship.

AMERICAN LEGISLATIVE EXCHANGE COUNCIL

214 Massachusetts Avenue NE **Phone:** 202/547-4646
Washington, DC 20002 **FAX:** 202/393-0898

* * *

ORGANIZATION'S ACTIVITIES: Organization of conservative elected representatives at various legislative levels nationwide.

Number of Internships: 8.

Type: Research, events organization, editorial, fundraising.

Function/Duties: Gather and prepare information on issues of importance to members; assist in arranging conferences, raising money, running office.

Schedule: Summers or school semesters, mostly full-time but flexible.

Stipend or Pay: Yes.

Academic Credit Offered: Per student's own arrangements with academic institution.

ELIGIBILITY: Primarily graduate and undergraduate students, but recent grads or others with appropriate qualifications also considered.

REQUIREMENTS: Excellent communications skills, plus appropriate interests, goals, and/or experience.

APPLICATION PROCEDURE: Send inquiries *to* Internship Coordinator *by* several months prior to availability date.

ARMY CORPS OF ENGINEERS

US Department of the Army	**Phone:** 703/697-8986
Washington, DC 20314	**FAX:** 703/697-3366

* * *

ORGANIZATION'S ACTIVITIES: The largest engineering and construction organization in the world, responsible for improving and maintaining transportation routes, infrastructure, dams and beaches, and NASA facilities, among many others.

Number of Internships: Varies; numerous.

Type: Engineering.

Function/Duties: Hands-on experience combined with seminars to enhance knowledge and skills and engineering and other civil works expertise.

Schedule: 11 to 18 months.

Stipend or Pay: Yes.

Academic Credit Offered: N/A.

ELIGIBILITY: College graduates; *Plus* internship leads to career in Corps if desired.

REQUIREMENTS: Scientific, technical, and/or engineering degrees preferred.

APPLICATION PROCEDURE: Send inquiries *to* Chief of Engineers. *Deadline:* Ongoing.

CALIFORNIA GOVERNOR'S OFFICE INTERNSHIP PROGRAM

Governor's Office	**Phone:** 916/445-4861
Sacramento, CA 95814	**FAX:** N/A

* * *

ORGANIZATION'S ACTIVITIES: The state executive office gener-ates a wide variety of activities, from administrative and legislative to research and child-development projects.

Number of Internships: Varies; approximately 18.

Type: Management, communications, lobbying, research, public affairs, information technology, finance.

Function/Duties: "First-hand involvement" in any or all of the office's 18 areas of activity.

Schedule: Minimum of 20 hours per week for 10 to 12 weeks during each quarter of the year.

Stipend or Pay: No.

Academic Credit Offered: Per student's own arrangements with aca-demic institution.

ELIGIBILITY: Graduate and undergraduate students. *Special Eligibilities:* Likely for California residents.

REQUIREMENTS: Must be available to work in Sacramento and dem-onstrate interest and some appropriate experience.

APPLICATION PROCEDURE: Request application form and submit with résumé and transcript *to* Intern Coordinator *by* several months in advance of January, March, May, or September start of term.

CALIFORNIA STATE LEGISLATIVE FELLOWSHIPS

Legislative Office Building
1020 N Street
Sacramento, CA 95814

Phone: 916/326-9900
FAX: N/A

* * *

ORGANIZATION'S ACTIVITIES: Legislative working/learning intern-ships in the State Senate and State Assembly.

Number of Internships: 18 in Senate, varies in Assembly.

Type: Legislative and constituent-assistance work in committees and in legislators' offices.

Function/Duties: Perform as professional staff.

Schedule: 11 months, October–August, full-time.

Stipend or Pay: Full monthly salary plus health benefits.

Academic Credit Offered: Yes.

ELIGIBILITY: Graduate students or non-students and career-changers. *Special Eligibilities:* Californians or students in California institutions have priority, though not exclusively; *Plus* fellowships often lead to full-time employment.

REQUIREMENTS: Bachelor's degree in any field; highly competitive program.

APPLICATION PROCEDURE: Request application forms in January; return *to* Fellowship Program *by* March 1.

CENTRAL INTELLIGENCE AGENCY

Employment Center
P.O. Box 1255   **Phone:**   703/482-1100
Pittsburgh, PA 15230   **FAX:**   N/A

* * *

ORGANIZATION'S ACTIVITIES: The federal government agency assigned to "collect, analyze, and disseminate foreign intelligence and to coordinate the intelligence efforts of the U.S. government." *All participants in CIA programs must be at least 18 years of age, maintain a minimum 2.75 average, be highly motivated and be able to meet strict medical and security standards, including a polygraph exam and background investigation.*

Number of Internships: Varies.

Type: Undergraduate scholar program.

Function/Duties: Maintain full-time college status; work each summer on assignments in Washington, D.C., area facility.

Schedule: Full-time work in summers; work for agency after graduation.

Stipend or Pay: Yearly competitive salary.

Academic Credit Offered: N/A.

ELIGIBILITY: High-school students headed for college. *Special Eligibilities:* Program is primarily for minorities and those with disabilities who need financial assistance for tuition; *Plus* financial assistance for tuition, fees, books, and supplies; pay increased according to level of education; transportation and housing costs reimbursed during active internship.

REQUIREMENTS: Those above, plus "student scholars must agree to continue employment with the Agency after college graduation for a period one and one-half times the length of their college training."

APPLICATION PROCEDURE: Request application and file with employment center no later than end of first year of high school.

Type: Undergraduate student trainees (co-op) program.

Function/Duties: Work as assigned in D.C.-area facility.

Schedule: Work full-time in alternating terms with college coursework.

Stipend or Pay: Competitive salary; pay increased according to level of education; transportation and housing costs reimbursed during active internship.

Academic Credit Offered: N/A.

ELIGIBILITY: Undergraduate students; *Plus* good chance of full-time employment upon graduation.

REQUIREMENTS: Those above, plus students are required to work at least 3 terms (alternating with study-semesters) prior to graduation.

APPLICATION PROCEDURE: Request application and file with employment center 6 to 9 months prior to availability.

Type: Minority undergraduate studies program.

Function/Duties: Practical assignments in agency departments.

Schedule: Full-time, summers.

Stipend or Pay: Competitive salary.

Academic Credit Offered: Per student's own arrangements with academic institution.

ELIGIBILITY: Undergraduate students. *Special Eligibilities:* Minorities and students with disabilities. *Plus* good chance of full-time employment upon graduation; transportation and housing costs reimbursed.

REQUIREMENTS: See above.

APPLICATION PROCEDURE: Request application and file with employment center by September 30 before summer availability.

CHAMBER OF COMMERCE OF THE UNITED STATES

1615 H Street NW
Washington, DC 20062

Phone: 202/659-6000
FAX: 202/463-5836

* * *

ORGANIZATION'S ACTIVITIES: The world's largest federation of local, state, and business chambers of commerce and trade and professional associations.

Number of Internships: Varies.

Type: Research, writing.

Function/Duties: Assist professional staff in projects analyzing U.S. international trade, and writing reports and grants.

Schedule: Flexible, year-round availability.

Stipend or Pay: Most unpaid.

Academic Credit Offered: Per student's own arrangements with academic institution.

ELIGIBILITY: Primarily undergraduate and graduate students; some recent grads.

REQUIREMENTS: Background in economics, international relations helpful; Spanish fluency required for some openings.

APPLICATION PROCEDURE: Send inquiries *to* Internship Coordinator. *Deadline:* Ongoing.

CITY OF CINCINNATI

Board of Park Commissioners
950 Eden Park Drive
Cincinnati, OH 45202

Phone: 513/352-3000
FAX: N/A

* * *

ORGANIZATION'S ACTIVITIES: Managing the city's public recreation and parks facilities.

Number of Internships: Varies.

Type: Communications, events, community service management.

Function/Duties: Assist with publications, events planning, production and distribution of press releases.

Schedule: Part-time, year-round; flexible hours.

Stipend or Pay: No.

Academic Credit Offered: Per student's own arrangements with academic institution.

ELIGIBILITY: Graduate and undergraduate students.

REQUIREMENTS: Prefer communications major. Must be able to work independently.

APPLICATION PROCEDURE: Send résumé and writing sample *to* Community Services Manager. *Deadline:* Ongoing.

CONGRESSIONAL BUDGET OFFICE

493 Ford House Office Building
Second and D Streets SW
Washington, DC 20515

Phone: 202/226-2621
FAX: N/A

* * *

ORGANIZATION'S ACTIVITIES: Responsible for advising and informing Congress on budgetary matters.

Number of Internships: 20.

Type: Research, accounting, report-writing.

Function/Duties: Assist analysts and other staff members with research projects.

Schedule: Summertime, full-time.

Stipend or Pay: Yes.

Academic Credit Offered: Per student's own arrangements with academic institution.

ELIGIBILITY: Undergraduate and graduate students as well as some non-students with appropriate skills.

REQUIREMENTS: Availability for work in Washington, D.C.; relevant majors preferred.

APPLICATION PROCEDURE: Request applications in January and submit *to* Internships Office *by* mid-March.

CONNECTICUT STATE JUDICIAL BRANCH

2275 Silas Deane Highway   **Phone:** 203/563-5797
Rocky Hill, CT 06067   **FAX:** 203/721-9474

*   *   *

ORGANIZATION'S ACTIVITIES: The office of the Chief Court Administrator is responsible for managing case flow, office administration, research, budget, etc., for a state system of 22 courts.

Number of Internships: Varies; fairly numerous.

Type: Judicial interns.

Function/Duties: Varies with assignment, according to interests and skills of intern; includes probation supervision, work with youth, interviewing, fieldwork, counseling, etc.

Schedule: Full-time per semester (summer, fall, winter).

Stipend or Pay: No, but reimbursement for expenses.

Academic Credit Offered: Per student's own arrangements with academic institution.

ELIGIBILITY: Undergraduate, graduate, law, and paralegal students.

REQUIREMENTS: Good communication skills, mature attitude, interest in criminal justice system.

APPLICATION PROCEDURE: Send inquiries *to* Supervisor, Intern Services *by* several months prior to availability.

COMMERCE, U.S. DEPARTMENT OF

14th and Constitution Avenue NW   **Phone:** 202/377-3301
Washington, DC 20230   **FAX:** N/A

*   *   *

ORGANIZATION'S ACTIVITIES: Functions include the international Trade Administration, responsible for U.S. foreign trade activities, promoting exports and consulting on policy.

Number of Internships: A few.

Type: Technical, administrative, clerical.

Function/Duties: Assist staff as needed.

Schedule: Summers, full-time.

Stipend or Pay: May be arranged.

Academic Credit Offered: Per student's own arrangements with academic institution.

ELIGIBILITY: Undergraduate and graduate students.

REQUIREMENTS: Highly competitive positions located in Washington, D.C.; must be currently enrolled in educational program and have 3.0 average, preferably in economics, political science, business, or international relations.

APPLICATION PROCEDURE: Call for application and submit *to* Office of Personnel *by* as early in the year as possible.

DEMOCRATIC NATIONAL COMMITTEE

430 South Capitol Street SE   **Phone:** 202/863-8000
Washington, DC 20003   **FAX:**   202/863-8081

* * *

ORGANIZATION'S ACTIVITIES: Administrative arm of the Democratic Party, serving to provide information and support to Democratic candidates in local, state, and federal elections.

Number of Internships: Numerous.

Type: Research, media relations, fund-raising, administration.

Function/Duties: Perform significant duties in assisting staff on ongoing as well as project basis.

Schedule: Flexible, year-round.

Stipend or Pay: No.

Academic Credit Offered: Per student's own arrangements with academic institution.

ELIGIBILITY: Primarily graduate and undergraduate students but also recent grads and other qualified non-students.

REQUIREMENTS: Interests, goals, and/or experience appropriate to organization.

APPLICATION PROCEDURE: Send inquiries *to* Internship Coordinator. *Deadline:* Ongoing.

ENERGY, U.S. DEPARTMENT OF

1000 Independence Avenue SW   **Phone:** 202/586-5000
Washington, DC 20585   **FAX:**   202/586-4073

* * *

ORGANIZATION'S ACTIVITIES: Federal agency assigned to coordination of development and oversight of U.S. energy resources and output.

Number of Internships: Varies; numerous.

Type: Engineering, technical, social sciences, business.

Function/Duties: Varies with assignment.

Schedule: Summer and co-op programs; also full-time programs for grad students and recent grads.

Stipend or Pay: Entry-level salaries as well as benefits.

Academic Credit Offered: Per student's own arrangements with academic institution for co-op and summer programs.

ELIGIBILITY: Graduate and undergraduate students as well as non-students who are recent grads with appropriate qualifications; *Plus* internships often lead to career positions.

REQUIREMENTS: Good grade average plus goals and interests appropriate to careers with this agency.

APPLICATION PROCEDURE: Send inquiries *to* National MIDP Coordinator in time to apply *by* at least 4 months prior to start date.

GEORGIA HOUSING & FINANCE AUTHORITY

60 Executive Park South, NE
Suite 250
Atlanta, GA 30329-2229

Phone: 404/679-4840
FAX: 404/679-4837

* * *

ORGANIZATION'S ACTIVITIES: GHFA is Georgia's public corporation for housing and economic development financing. It administers programs to improve affordable housing opportunities and business growth.

Number of Internships: 1.

Type: Public relations, publications, photography.

Function/Duties: Writing, graphic design.

Schedule: Full-time and part-time, 6-week term during April, May, and June.

Stipend or Pay: $5 per hour.

Academic Credit Offered: Per student's own arrangements with academic institution.

ELIGIBILITY: College seniors, graduate students; preferred majors: English and Graphic Arts. Career-changers and non-students welcome.

REQUIREMENTS: Interests, goals, and/or experience relevant to available assignments.

APPLICATION PROCEDURE: Submit résumé and cover letter *to* Mary Emily Johnson.

HENRICO COUNTY, VIRGINIA

Volunteers Office
P.O. Box 27032
Richmond, VA 23273

Phone: 804/672-5231
FAX: 804/672-5287

* * *

ORGANIZATION'S ACTIVITIES: County surrounding Richmond, Virginia's state capital, performs varied government activities.

Number of Internships: Varies.

Type: Social services, recreation, planning, judicial, management, etc.

Function/Duties: Assist permanent staff in regular work and/or special projects.

Schedule: Usually 3-month periods, part-time; year-round availability.

Stipend or Pay: Usually no.

Academic Credit Offered: Per student's own arrangements with academic institution.

ELIGIBILITY: Prefer junior and senior undergraduate students, but all are considered.

REQUIREMENTS: Specifics of internship need to be approved by department and by academic institution.

APPLICATION PROCEDURE: Send request for details and application forms *to* Director of Volunteer Services *by* 3 months prior to availability date.

HOUSING AND URBAN DEVELOPMENT, U.S. DEPARTMENT OF

451 7th Street SW
Washington, DC 20410

Phone: 202/708-0980
FAX: 202/708-0299

* * *

ORGANIZATION'S ACTIVITIES: The federal agency assigned to provide for and supervise the sound development of the nation's communities and urban areas, primarily through coordination of federal activities that affect civic development. Also supervises provision of housing assistance for U.S. citizens.

Number of Internships: Varies; fairly numerous.

Type: Urban interns.

Function/Duties: Varies with assignments, rotated according to need and expertise.

Schedule: Full-time 1 year, in D.C. location or regional offices.

Stipend or Pay: Regular entry-level salary plus benefits.

Academic Credit Offered: N/A.

ELIGIBILITY: College graduates with appropriate qualifications; *Plus* internships often lead to career positions.

REQUIREMENTS: Meet minimum requirements for regular employment; plus goals and interests appropriate to careers with this agency.

APPLICATION PROCEDURE: Send inquiries *to* Personnel Department *by* several months prior to availability.

ILLINOIS, STATE OF

Office of the Governor
State House
Springfield, IL 62706

Phone: 217/782-8639
FAX: N/A

* * *

ORGANIZATION'S ACTIVITIES: Dunn Fellowships.

Number of Internships: Varies.

Type: Governmental management.

Function/Duties: Assist regular staff in offices and projects assigned.

Schedule: Summer full-time.

Stipend or Pay: Varies.

Academic Credit Offered: Per student's own arrangements with academic institution.

ELIGIBILITY: College students from any state in union.

REQUIREMENTS: Good GPAs and interest in public administration.

APPLICATION PROCEDURE: *Contact* governor's office for details and application.

INTERIOR, U.S. DEPT. OF

Bureau of Land Management
Anasazi Heritage Center
27501 Highway 184
Dolores, CO 81323

Phone: 303/882-4811
FAX: 303/882-7035

* * *

ORGANIZATION'S ACTIVITIES: A center for the protection, study, and display of the culture and archeology of the Native Americans of the Southwest region.

Number of Internships: 2–4.

Type: Curatorial assistant, archeology assistant, visitor services.

Function/Duties: Varies with need.

Schedule: Full-time, 8 weeks in summers.

Stipend or Pay: $40 per week; communal housing provided.

Academic Credit Offered: Per student's own arrangements with academic institution.

ELIGIBILITY: College and graduate students as well as non-students and career-changers; preference given to students and new professionals in the fields of anthropology, archeology, and museum studies.

REQUIREMENTS: Working knowledge of southwestern U.S. prehistory.

APPLICATION PROCEDURE: Send letter of interest and résumé *to* Intern Coordinator *by* April 15.

INTERNATIONAL DEVELOPMENT, U.S. AGENCY FOR

320 21st Street NW   **Phone:** 202/663-1451
Washington, DC 20523   **FAX:**   N/A

* * *

ORGANIZATION'S ACTIVITIES: A.I.D. manages U.S. foreign aid to developing countries in Africa, Asia, Latin America, and the Middle East.

Number of Internships: Limited number.

Type: Agriculture, business administration, international relations, public health, finance.

Function/Duties: Varies with assignment and intern's interest, mostly administrative assistance, some clerical.

Schedule: Mostly full-time during summers; other times arranged.

Stipend or Pay: No.

Academic Credit Offered: Per student's own arrangements with academic institution.

ELIGIBILITY: Undergraduate and graduate students.

REQUIREMENTS: Interests, goals, and/or experience relevant to available assignments.

APPLICATION PROCEDURE: Request appropriate form and details *from* Student Program Coordinator *by* early in school year.

IOWA, STATE OF

Internship Development Program
East 14th and Grand Avenue   **Phone:** 515/281-6480
Des Moines, IA 50319   **FAX:**   515/242-6450

* * *

ORGANIZATION'S ACTIVITIES: Governmental administration in more than 30 departments.

Number of Internships: Varies; numerous.

Type: Specially developed work/learn projects.

Function/Duties: Assist in offices that match intern's interests.

Schedule: Year-round, full- and part-time.

Stipend or Pay: Both paid and unpaid available.

Academic Credit Offered: Per student's own arrangements with academic institution.

ELIGIBILITY: College students (both in Iowa and out-of-state institutions). *Special Eligibilities:* Some programs designed for minority-group members and women; *Plus* internships often lead to eligibility for permanent positions.

REQUIREMENTS: Must be enrolled in degree-granting college program.

APPLICATION PROCEDURE: Request application form *from* Internship Program Coordinator. *Deadline:* Ongoing.

LIBRARY OF CONGRESS OF THE UNITED STATES

James Madison Memorial Building
101 Independence Avenue SE
Washington, DC 20540

Phone: 202/707-8803
FAX: 202/287-5844

* * *

ORGANIZATION'S ACTIVITIES: America's National Library, repository of all works published in the U.S. and center of information-resource networks.

Number of Internships: Varies.

Type: Junior Fellowships and other internships as needed.

Function/Duties: Research, reference, administrative assistance work in most of Library's divisions, including special collections and management.

Schedule: Mostly in summer; others can be arranged.

Stipend or Pay: Yes, for Junior Fellows; others unpaid.

Academic Credit Offered: Per student's own arrangements with academic institution.

ELIGIBILITY: Graduate and undergraduate students; *Plus* often an avenue to full-time employment.

REQUIREMENTS: Interests, goals, and/or experience relevant to available assignments.

APPLICATION PROCEDURE: Request forms and details *from* Recruitment Office. *Deadline:* Open.

The Library's Congressional Research Service provides information to members of Congress through research in the nation's leading reference collection.

Number of Internships: Limited.

Type: Research, reference.

Function/Duties: Provide variety of support services for staff responding to congressional requests for information.

Schedule: Year-round, full- or part-time.

Stipend or Pay: No.

Academic Credit Offered: Per student's own arrangements with academic institution.

ELIGIBILITY: Undergraduate and graduate students.

REQUIREMENTS: Minimum sophomore level, with written approval from academic institution.

APPLICATION PROCEDURE: Send letter of interest with résumé *to* Administrative Officer. *Deadline:* Open.

NATIONAL SECURITY AGENCY

9800 Savage Road   **Phone:** 301/688-7111
Fort George Meade, MD 20755   **FAX:**   N/A

* * *

ORGANIZATION'S ACTIVITIES: An agency of the U.S. Department of Defense charged with the coordination of intelligence regarding both domestic and international security challenges.

Number of Internships: Numerous.

Type: Science and technical.

Function/Duties: Entry-level assignments for training in computer sciences, signals research, and other technical fields.

Schedule: Varies; some full-time after college; others, summers and in co-op program during academic year.

Stipend or Pay: Entry-level salary as well as benefits.

Academic Credit Offered: Per student's own arrangements with academic institution for summer or co-op programs; *Plus* internships often lead to career positions.

ELIGIBILITY: College students or recent grads.

REQUIREMENTS: Students with 3.0 averages or degrees in the physical sciences; must be U.S. citizen and pass in-depth security clearance.

APPLICATION PROCEDURE: Send inquiries *to* Department M322 (AAP) *by* at least 6 months prior to availability date.

NORTH CAROLINA, STATE OF

Department of Administration
121 West Jones Street
Raleigh, NC 27603

Phone: 919/733-1110
FAX: N/A

* * *

ORGANIZATION'S ACTIVITIES: Youth Advocacy internships.

Number of Internships: Several hundred.

Type: Variety of assignments in every state department and agency and many federal offices located in the state.

Function/Duties: Assignments designed to introduce students to full range of functions of government.

Schedule: Full-time during the summer.

Stipend or Pay: Approximately $200 per week.

Academic Credit Offered: Per student's own arrangements with academic institution.

ELIGIBILITY: College students and non-students who have completed two years of college; *Plus* participation in seminars on governmental activities.

REQUIREMENTS: Minimum 2 years of college completed with a C+ average or better.

APPLICATION PROCEDURE: Request application and submit with letter of interest and academic transcript *to* Youth Advocacy Office *by* end of January.

NORTH DAKOTA, STATE OF

Central Personnel Division
600 East Boulevard Avenue
Bismarck, ND 58505

Phone: 701/224-3290
FAX: N/A

* * *

ORGANIZATION'S ACTIVITIES: Individual state agencies have variety of internships performing government's administrative functions.

Number of Internships: Varies.

Type: Clerical, administrative, other.

Function/Duties: As assigned by full-time staff to meet office needs and intern's interests.

Schedule: Year-round and/or summers; part-time and/or full-time.

Stipend or Pay: Some paid.

Academic Credit Offered: Per student's own arrangements with academic institution.

ELIGIBILITY: Consideration given to students, non-students, or career-changers with appropriate qualifications.

REQUIREMENTS: Interests, goals, and/or experience relevant to available assignments.

APPLICATION PROCEDURE: *Contact* Central Personnel Office for details on applying to individual agencies.

OHIO, STATE OF

Governor's Office
77 South High Street
Columbus, OH 43266

Phone: 614/466-3555
FAX: 614/466-9354

* * *

ORGANIZATION'S ACTIVITIES: Governor's Honor Program.

Number of Internships: 36.

Type: Competitive program for placement in administrative agencies throughout state government.

Function/Duties: Assist permanent staff in regular work and/or special projects. *Plus* weekly seminars with government administrators as part of learning experience.

Schedule: Summers, full-time.

Stipend or Pay: About $250 per week.

Academic Credit Offered: Per student's own arrangements with academic institution.

ELIGIBILITY: Junior and senior undergraduate students attending Ohio colleges.

REQUIREMENTS: Grade averages, personal and academic recommendations, and essays demonstrating excellence combine for evaluation in this competitive program.

APPLICATION PROCEDURE: Send request for details and application forms *to* Director of Volunteer Initiatives *by* as early in the school year as possible.

PENNSYLVANIA, COMMONWEALTH OF

State Employment Division
Room 110, Finance Building
Harrisburg, PA 17120

Phone: 717/787-5703
FAX: N/A

* * *

ORGANIZATION'S ACTIVITIES: Manages welfare, safety, health, and all other aspects of state administration.

Number of Internships: Varies; numerous.

Type: Service, technical, clerical; special management programs.

Function/Duties: Assist administrators and/or substitute for temporarily absent workers.

Schedule: Temporary part-time workers year-round; Government Services Intern: summers; some during school semesters.

Stipend or Pay: Yes—entry-level equivalents.

Academic Credit Offered: Per student's own arrangements with academic institution.

ELIGIBILITY: High-school, college, graduate students; some non-students and career-changers. *Special Eligibilities:* Equal opportunity employer.

REQUIREMENTS: Must meet state's qualifications for non-civil service employees.

APPLICATION PROCEDURE: Request application form *from* State Employment office; submit as instructed. *Deadline:* Ongoing.

PRESIDENTIAL MANAGEMENT INTERN PROGRAM

U.S. Office of Personnel Management
1900 E Street NE
Washington, DC 20415

Phone: 202/606-2424
FAX: N/A

* * *

ORGANIZATION'S ACTIVITIES: The prestigious Presidential Management Intern (PMI) Program is a career-development program that places qualified applicants with recent graduate degrees and a strong interest in public management into professional-level positions at virtually every federal agency. Placement service provided through headquarters and through regional Office of Personnel Management centers.

Number of Internships: Several hundred.

Type: Management in all areas: human resources, finance, communications, etc.

Function/Duties: Assist civil service staff and participate in projects as assigned.

Schedule: A 2-year program of full-time year-round work; *Plus* regular program of seminars and other developmental programs.

Stipend or Pay: Pay and benefits as for regular federal employees in GS grades 9–12.

Academic Credit Offered: Per student's own arrangements with academic institution.

ELIGIBILITY: Students and non-students with recent postgraduate degrees.

REQUIREMENTS: You must apply for this 2-year program during the academic year in which you will graduate and be nominated by your school.

APPLICATION PROCEDURE: For information contact the dean of your graduate school, your career services department, or the Federal Job

Information Center. Submit a completed application packet, which is available each year in September, per instructions in the packet.

REPUBLICAN NATIONAL COMMITTEE

310 First Street SE **Phone:** 202/863-8500
Washington, DC 20003 **FAX:** 202/863-8820

* * *

ORGANIZATION'S ACTIVITIES: Administrative arm of the Republican Party, serving to provide information and support to Republican candidates in local, state, and federal elections.

Number of Internships: Numerous.

Type: Research, media relations, fundraising, administration.

Function/Duties: Perform significant duties in assisting staff on ongoing as well as project basis.

Schedule: Flexible, year-round.

Stipend or Pay: Most unpaid, but summer program offers paid internships on competitive basis.

Academic Credit Offered: Per student's own arrangements with academic institution.

ELIGIBILITY: Primarily graduate and undergraduate students but also recent grads and other qualified non-students.

REQUIREMENTS: Interests, goals, and/or experience appropriate to organization.

APPLICATION PROCEDURE: Send inquiries *to* Director of Personnel *by* January 31 for summer program; other deadlines ongoing.

STATE, U.S. DEPARTMENT OF

Recruitment Division
Box 12209, Rosslyn Station **Phone:** 703/875-7242
Arlington, VA 22209 **FAX:** 703/875-1027

* * *

ORGANIZATION'S ACTIVITIES: Responsible for managing the nation's foreign affairs.

Number of Internships: Numerous.

Type: Openings available in most of the department's divisions, including the bureaus of African Affairs, Consular Affairs, East Asian Affairs, European and Canadian Affairs, Inter-American Affairs, Near Eastern Affairs, and the offices of Personnel, Law, and Public Affairs.

Function/Duties: Assigned as entry-level professionals, performing research, communications, and similar functions.

Schedule: Year-round as well as summer-only, full- and part-time.

Stipend or Pay: Some unpaid; others receive standard government compensation.

Academic Credit Offered: Per student's own arrangements with academic institution.

ELIGIBILITY: Graduate and undergraduate students, preferably studying political science, international relations, or appropriate languages; *Plus* internship often leads to regular employment.

REQUIREMENTS: Must be currently enrolled in academic study, on at least a half-time basis.

APPLICATION PROCEDURE: Send inquiries *to* Intern Coordinator in time to apply *by* at least 6 months prior to availability.

TENNESSEE VALLEY AUTHORITY'S LAND BETWEEN THE LAKES

100 Van Morgan Drive   **Phone:** 502/924-5602
Golden Pond, KY 42211   **FAX:**   502/924-1399

* * *

ORGANIZATION'S ACTIVITIES: LBL is a 170,000-acre national recreation area located in western Kentucky and Tennessee. LBL provides outdoor recreation and environmental education in a managed natural setting, which strengthens environmental responsibility among customers and communicates the TVA's environmental leadership role.

Number of Internships: 12.

Type: Recreation, education, resource management, public affairs.

Function/Duties: Varies by position.

Schedule: Full-time, 40 hours per week, summer months (end of May through mid-August).

Stipend or Pay: $150 per week plus housing.

Academic Credit Offered: Per student's own arrangements with academic institution.

ELIGIBILITY: Students, preferably college juniors and seniors. Applicants for apprenticeships must not be enrolled in school and must have a college degree.

REQUIREMENTS: Interests, goals, and/or experience relevant to available assignments.

APPLICATION PROCEDURE: Submit internship application and résumé *to* Jim Carpenter, Administrator, Professional Development.

TECHNOLOGY ASSESSMENT, U.S. OFFICE OF

600 Pennsylvania Avenue SE   **Phone:** 202/228-6150
Washington, DC 20003   **FAX:**   N/A

* * *

ORGANIZATION'S ACTIVITIES: Nonpartisan agency responsible for advising and informing the Congress on science and technology policy and issues.

Number of Internships: Varies; as needed.

Type: Research and communications.

Function/Duties: Varies according to project.

Schedule: Flexible, year-round; full- and/or part-time as needed.

Stipend or Pay: In some cases.

Academic Credit Offered: Per student's own arrangements with academic institution.

ELIGIBILITY: Undergraduate and graduate students, as well as non-students and career-changers in some cases.

REQUIREMENTS: Interests, goals, and/or experience relevant to available assignments.

APPLICATION PROCEDURE: Send résumé with cover letter describing goals and availability *to* Personnel Office. *Deadline:* Open.

VIRGINIA OFFICE OF VOLUNTEERISM

720 East Broad Street   **Phone:**   804/662-1950
Richmond, VA 23219   **FAX:**   804/662-1999

* * *

ORGANIZATION'S ACTIVITIES: Provides training, technical assistance, and information to leaders of volunteer programs throughout the state.

Number of Internships: 1 or 2.

Type: General assistants.

Function/Duties: Aid in conducting workshops, planning conferences, publishing newsletter, research, advocacy activities.

Schedule: Full-time or part-time, year-round or seasonal; flexible term and hours.

Stipend or Pay: No.

Academic Credit Offered: Can be arranged.

ELIGIBILITY: Students at all levels, non-students, career-changers. *Special Eligibilities:* Majors or experience in public administration, political science, community development, or social work especially useful. *Plus* contacts and clearinghouse for volunteerism and nonprofit work throughout the state.

REQUIREMENTS: None except proximity to Richmond office.

APPLICATION PROCEDURE: Write letter of interest with résumé *to* Director. *Deadline:* Open.

TREASURY, U.S. DEPARTMENT OF

15th and Pennsylvania Avenue NW
Washington, DC 20220

Phone: 202/566-5411
FAX: 202/566-8066

* * *

ORGANIZATION'S ACTIVITIES: Advises Congress and the executive branch on financial policy; manages and supervises domestic and international monetary matters.

Number of Internships: Varies.

Type: Financial management service, multilateral development banks office; other staffs, including administrative and information technologies.

Function/Duties: Research, communications, other activities depending on assignment.

Schedule: Year-round, part- and full-time.

Stipend or Pay: Some stipends arranged.

Academic Credit Offered: Per student's own arrangements with academic institution.

ELIGIBILITY: Undergraduate and graduate students.

REQUIREMENTS: Availability to work in Washington, D.C.; prefer economics, computer, and/or international relations majors.

APPLICATION PROCEDURE: Send inquiries *to* Internship Coordinator. *Deadline:* Open.

INTERNAL REVENUE SERVICE

1111 Constitution Avenue NW
Washington, DC 20224

Phone: 202/566-4743
FAX: 202/566-6105

* * *

A division within the Treasury Department, offering a variety of internships, including 30-day stints for undergraduates, which offer hands-on experience with real IRS matters.

WASHINGTON STATE GOVERNOR'S INTERNSHIP PROGRAM

600 South Franklin, Box 47561
Olympia, WA 98507

Phone: 206/753-3208
FAX: N/A

* * *

ORGANIZATION'S ACTIVITIES: The state of Washington's Executive Fellowships are offered as needed throughout the agencies of state government primarily to involve graduate students and others in processes of government, especially in research and development of innovative projects.

Number of Internships: Varies; numerous.

Type: Managerial, technical, marketing, environmental.

Function/Duties: Varies by assignment; examples: development of database for state's forest products office; research in drinking water safety; marketing of new rural health program.

Schedule: Year-round, ongoing programs; each lasts one or two years; schedule can be arranged to accommodate studies.

Stipend or Pay: Per regular state rates; usually about $2,000 per month.

Academic Credit Offered: Per student's own arrangements with academic institution.

ELIGIBILITY: Graduate students in appropriate fields. *Special Eligibilities:* Permanent Washington State employees with appropriate authorization; *Plus* internship programs provide full government benefits.

REQUIREMENTS: Must have at least one year of graduate study and be currently enrolled in accredited program; all work is in Washington State.

APPLICATION PROCEDURE: Request official application form and submit it with cover letter, résumé, transcripts, and letters of recommendation *to* Internship Program Manager. *Deadline:* As determined for each program.

WISCONSIN, STATE OF

Department of Employee Relations
101 East Wilson Street   **Phone:**   608/266-3357
Madison, WI 53709   **FAX:**   N/A

* * *

ORGANIZATION'S ACTIVITIES: Provides governmental services.

Number of Internships: Varies.

Type: Summer Affirmative Action Intern Program.

Function/Duties: Varies by assignment, for learning government management.

Schedule: Summers, full-time.

Stipend or Pay: Yes.

Academic Credit Offered: Per student's own arrangements with academic institution.

ELIGIBILITY: College students who are members of minority groups.

REQUIREMENTS: Meet qualifications for minority participation.

APPLICATION PROCEDURE: Request application *from* Division of Affirmative Action *by* as early as possible in school year.

WILDWOOD (NEW JERSEY) DEPARTMENT OF TOURISM

Schellenger Avenue and Boardwalk **Phone:** 609/522-1407
Wildwood, NJ 08260 **FAX:** 609/729-2234

* * *

ORGANIZATION'S ACTIVITIES: Plan, coordinate, and design programs to attract visitors to the Wildwood resort area.

Number of Internships: Varies.

Type: Marketing and public relations.

Function/Duties: Assist in coordination of events, production of publications, other public relations activities.

Schedule: Part-time during summer (May–September).

Stipend or Pay: Yes—minimum wage.

Academic Credit Offered: Per student's arrangements with academic institution.

ELIGIBILITY: Graduate and undergraduate students; career-changers. *Special Eligibilities:* Women especially encouraged; *Plus* position may lead to permanent employment.

REQUIREMENTS: Prefer communications/public relations majors and/or experience.

APPLICATION PROCEDURE: Submit résumé with academic and employment history *to* Tourism Department *by* April.

Organizations/Resources for Further Information about Internships in Government

Alternate Approaches To Government Placements

CONGRESS

Although the best way to get internships with legislators (local, state, or national) is to go directly to *your* representative, there are other ways to approach this rich source of experience and contacts. The following organizations can be useful:

CONGRESSIONAL MANAGEMENT FOUNDATION
513 Capital Court NW
Suite 100
Washington, DC 20002
Phone: 202/546-0100
FAX: 202/547-0936

Helps members of Congress and their staffs better to manage their workloads; can make internship connections.

DEMOCRATIC STUDY GROUP
Job Referral Service
House Post Office
House Annex 2 #219
Third and D Streets SW
Washington, DC 20515
Phone: 202/225-5858

Can serve as clearinghouse for internship and job openings depending on situation; call for details.

For nonpartisan referral services, contact:

CONGRESSIONAL PLACEMENT OFFICE
Ford House Office Building
Room H2-219
Second and D Streets SW
Washington, DC 20515
Phone: 202/226-6731

SENATE PLACEMENT OFFICE
Hart Senate Building
Room 142-B
Washington, DC 20510
Phone: 202/224-9167

These offices are the official job referral services for "the Hill," and they *can* forward résumés of internship candidates, so it's a good idea to get your file into their files.

The most effective route to a Capitol Hill internship, however, is straight through your representative—especially one whose political party you share. Though you can call cold through the Capitol switchboard (202/224-3121), you would do much better to get all the relevant information from the representative's local state or district office.

Other Government Possibilities

The federal government offers a variety of special student employment programs to high school, undergraduate, and graduate students who are at least 16 years of age and are U.S. citizens.

FEDERAL COOPERATIVE EDUCATION PROGRAM

High school, undergraduate, graduate, vocational, and community college students enrolled at least part-time can work a parallel or alternate work/study schedule in the field of their interest. Benefits include salary, annual leave, sick leave, health and life insurance, and retirement plans. Often a "co-op" position can be converted into a permanent position upon graduation.

SUMMER EMPLOYMENT PROGRAM

Summer employees are hired to fill a variety of positions from office support to professional, between May 13 and September 30 every year. Summer employees earn salaries based on their education and experience. Vacancies are advertised annually in the Summer Job Opportunities Announcement No. 414, available the last week of December at the Federal Job Information Center nearest you.

STAY-IN-SCHOOL PROGRAM

This program provides an opportunity for full-time high school, vocational, community college, or undergraduate students to work in order to resume or continue their education. Students work a maximum of 20 hours per week during school and full-time while on school breaks. The local State Employment Service Office must certify that students meet the financial-need criteria. Benefits include salary, annual leave, and sick leave. Agencies recruit candidates directly from schools and local State Employment Service Offices.

SUMMER AIDE

Through this program, the federal government employs economically disadvantaged youths who earn the federal minimum wage. The local State Employment Service Office must certify that candidates meet the financial-need criteria.

STUDENT VOLUNTEER SERVICE

High school, undergraduate, graduate, or vocational students who are enrolled at least part-time can gain experience through this "internship" opportunity in a field related to their academic/career interest. In many cases, you can earn academic credit for your internship. Students interested in placement with a particular government agency should contact that agency's personnel offices directly to inquire about opportunities.

FEDERAL JUNIOR FELLOWSHIPS

This career-related work/study program helps to expose high school seniors, who have a strong academic record and are planning to attend a higher education program, to public service careers. Benefits include salary, annual leave, sick leave, health and life insurance, and retirement plans. Students must be nominated during their senior year by their school.

FURTHER PROGRAMS

In addition, the following formally organized groups can also provide opportunities similar to internships for those willing to make the commitments required.

Job Corps. Formed during the "war on poverty" of the 1960s, the Job Corps is still going strong, though its programs are geared primarily to low-income young people who lack basic skills. For details, call 202/245-7000.

The Peace Corps. The early nineties saw a renewal of interest in the Peace Corps due to a combination of high unemployment rates, heightened idealism, and the opening of new frontiers for service in Asia and Eastern Europe. The Peace Corps asks that you bring some skills with you and pass a qualifying training program. Other than that, there are no age or other restrictions, and you can gain training, education, and experience in valuable international skills while being paid (a little) and seeing the world at Uncle Sam's expense. In return, you agree to spend at least two years of your life on a foreign, usually primitive, post. For details, call 202/606-3886.

Teach America. This corps, established in 1991, is a federally funded project that sends teachers into education-poor urban neighborhoods and rural districts. Most who join this corps of teachers are recent college grads—but not all. No teaching experience or education is required: just an interest and enough aptitude to make it through a training period. As a teacher, you are assigned to a district and a job—and some of those assignments can be rugged. But it is a way to get teaching credentials for free if you are willing to commit to a two-year stint. For details, contact 202/401-3000.

The National Health Service Corps. The National Health Service Corps sends health professionals into needy areas of the country, providing them with support and training. For those who qualify, the corps pays medical or nursing school tuition in return for a commitment to serve as assigned for an additional two years. For details, contact the Public Health Service, Department of Health and Human Services, at 301/443-2900.

FEDERAL AGENCY PROGRAMS

In addition to the above-mentioned programs, many federal agencies offer what they call "management trainee programs," hiring entry-level candidates in professional and administrative occupations for one- to three-year full-time work in rotational or career development positions. Contact agencies of interest directly for these jobs, which carry standard pay and benefits but are usually not protected by civil service personnel safeguards.

Federal Job Information Centers. The Office of Personnel Management maintains Federal Job Information Centers in several major metropolitan areas across the country to provide local job information. They are listed under "U.S. Government" in the white pages of metropolitan area phone directories. In addition, federal employment opportunities, including short-term and temporary jobs, are posted in State Job Service (State Employment Security) offices and on an interactive software system called FOCIS.

Contact:
CAREER ENTRY GROUP
U.S. Office of Personnel Management
1900 E Street NW
Washington, DC 20415
Phone: 202/606-1212

Office of Personnel Management Federal Job Information/Testing Offices around the country. Call for the one nearest the location where you would like to work for information on job opportunities in that area and the forms needed to apply.

For general information, call 202/245-6000. Or to apply agency-by-agency, here is a list:

U.S. DEPARTMENT OF AGRICULTURE
14th Street and Independence
   Avenue SW
Washington, DC 20250
202/447-2791

U.S. DEPARTMENT OF COMMERCE
14th Street and Constitution
   Avenue NW
Washington, DC 20230
202/377-4807

U.S. DEPARTMENT OF DEFENSE
Chief, Staffing and Support
   Programs
Directorate for Personnel and
   Security
Washington Headquarters Services,
   Room 3E843
The Pentagon
Washington, DC 20301
202/695-4436

U.S. DEPARTMENT OF EDUCATION
400 Maryland Avenue SW
Washington, DC 20202
202/245-8366

U.S. Department of Energy
Forrestal Building
1000 Independence Avenue SW
Washington, DC 20585
202/252-8731

U.S. Fish and Wildlife Service
Department of the Interior
Washington, DC 20240
202/343-5634

U.S. Department of Health and
Human Services
200 Independence Avenue SW
Washington, DC 20201
202/472-6631

U.S. Department of Housing and
Urban Development
451 Seventh Street SW
Washington, DC 20410
202/755-5500

U.S. Department of Interior
18th and C Streets NW
Washington, DC 20240
202/343-5065

U.S. Department of Justice
Constitution Avenue and Tenth
Street NW
Washington, DC 20530
202/633-2007

U.S. Department of Labor
200 Constitution Avenue NW
Washington, DC 20210
202/523-6255

Office of Personnel Management
1900 E Street NW
Washington, DC 20415
202/606-2424

U.S. Postal Service
Headquarters Personnel Division
475 L'Enfant Plaza
Washington, DC 20260
202/245-4263

U.S. Secret Service
1800 G Street NW
Washington, DC 20223
202/535-5708

U.S. Department of Transportation
400 Seventh Street SW
Washington, DC 20590
202/426-4000

Or:

Central Employment Training Office
Office of Personnel and Training
U.S. Department of Transportation
400 Seventh Street SW
Washington, DC 20590
202/426-2550

U.S. Department of the Treasury
15th Street and Pennsylvania
Avenue NW
Washington, DC 20220
202/566-5061

Veterans Administration
810 Vermont Avenue
Washington, DC 20420
202/233-2741

U.S. Government Departments
(Military)
Department of the Air Force
Civilian Personnel Office
1947 AS/DMPKS Pentagon
Washington, DC 20330
202/545-6700

Department of the Army
Personnel and Employment Service
The Pentagon
Washington, DC 20310
202/697-0335

Department of the Navy
Navy Civilian Personnel Command
801 North Randolph Street
Arlington, VA 22203
202/696-4450

COMMANDANT OF THE MARINE CORPS
Code (MPC-30)
Headquarters, U.S. Marine Corps
Washington, DC 20380
202/694-2500

DRUG ENFORCEMENT ADMINISTRATION
1405 I Street NW
Washington, DC 20537
202/633-1034

ENVIRONMENTAL PROTECTION AGENCY
401 M Street SW
Washington, DC 20460
202/382-2973

EQUAL EMPLOYMENT OPPORTUNITY
  COMMISSION
2401 E Street NW
Washington, DC 20507
202/634-6922

FEDERAL AVIATION ADMINISTRATION
800 Independence Avenue SW
Washington, DC 20590
202/426-3383

FEDERAL COMMUNICATIONS COMMISSION
1919 M Street NW
Washington, DC 20554
202/632-7260

FEDERAL HOME LOAN BANK BOARD
1700 G Street NW
Washington, DC 20552
202/377-6000

FEDERAL MARITIME COMMISSION
1100 L Street NW
Washington, DC 20573
202/523-5707

FEDERAL RESERVE SYSTEM
Board of Governors of the Federal
  Reserve System
20th Street and Constitution
  Avenue NW
Washington, DC 20551
202/452-3204

FEDERAL TRADE COMMISSION
Pennsylvania Avenue at Sixth
  Street NW
Washington, DC 20580
202/326-2222

FOOD AND DRUG ADMINISTRATION
5600 Fishers Lane
Rockville, MD 20857
301/443-3220

GENERAL SERVICES ADMINISTRATION
General Services Building
18th and F Streets NW
Washington, DC 20505
202/566-0085

GOVERNMENT PRINTING OFFICE
North Capitol and H Streets NW
Washington, DC 20402
202/275-2051

NATIONAL INSTITUTES OF HEALTH
Division of Personnel Management
Bethesda, MD 20892
301/496-4197

OFFICE OF TECHNOLOGY ASSESSMENT
600 Pennsylvania Avenue SE
Washington, DC 20510

SECURITIES AND EXCHANGE COMMISSION
450 Fifth Street NW
Room IC45
Washington, DC 20405
202/272-2550

SELECTIVE SERVICE SYSTEM
National Headquarters
Washington, DC 20435
202/724-0424

SENATE OFFICE BUILDING
First Street and Constitution
  Avenue
Washington, DC 20515
202/224-3121

SMALL BUSINESS ADMINISTRATION
Imperial Building
1441 L Street NW
Washington, DC 20416
202/653-6832

SMITHSONIAN INSTITUTION
1000 Jefferson Drive SW
Washington, DC 20560
202/357-2465

SOCIAL SECURITY ADMINISTRATION
6401 Security Boulevard
Baltimore, MD 21235
301/594-3060

U.S. ARMS CONTROL AND DISARMAMENT
AGENCY
320 21st Street NW
Washington, DC 20451
202/632-2034

Other Resources Providing Information or Networking for Government Internship Opportunities

Government Associations

AMERICAN FEDERATION OF
GOVERNMENT EMPLOYEES
1325 Massachusetts Avenue NW
Washington, DC 20005
202/737-8700

AMERICAN FEDERATION OF STATE,
COUNTY, AND MUNICIPAL EMPLOYEES
1625 L Street NW
Washington, DC 20005
202/452-4800

AMERICAN PUBLIC WORKS ASSOCIATION
1313 East 60th Street
Chicago, IL 60637
312/667-2200

AMERICAN SOCIETY FOR PUBLIC
ADMINISTRATION
1120 G Street NW
Suite 500
Washington, DC 20005
202/393-7878

CIVIL SERVICE EMPLOYEES ASSOCIATION
143 Washington Avenue
Albany, NY 12210
518/434-0191

FEDERAL EXECUTIVE AND PROFESSIONAL
ASSOCIATION
15535 New Hampshire Avenue
Silver Spring, MD 20904
301/384-2616

INTERNATIONAL CITY MANAGEMENT
ASSOCIATION
1120 G Street NW
Washington, DC 20005
202/626-4600

INTERNATIONAL INSTITUTE OF MUNICIPAL
CLERKS
160 North Altadena Drive
Pasadena, CA 91107
818/795-6153

NATIONAL ASSOCIATION OF COUNTY
TRAINING AND EMPLOYMENT
PROFESSIONALS
440 First Street NW
Washington, DC 20001
202/393-6226

NATIONAL ASSOCIATION OF GOVERNMENT
EMPLOYEES
1313 L Street NW
Washington, DC 20005
202/371-6644

NATIONAL FEDERATION OF FEDERAL
EMPLOYEES
1016 16th Street NW
Washington, DC 20005
202/862-4400

PUBLICATIONS: DIRECTORIES OF GOVERNMENT INFORMATION

AN INSIDER'S GUIDE TO FINDING A
JOB IN CONGRESS
Congressional Management
Foundation
333 Pennsylvania Avenue SE
Washington, DC 20003

CONGRESSIONAL DIRECTORY
U.S. Government Printing Office
Washington, DC 20402
202/783-3238

CONGRESSIONAL STAFF DIRECTORY
P.O. Box 62
Mount Vernon, VA 22121
703/765-3400

CONGRESSIONAL YELLOW BOOK
DIRECTORY
Washington Monitor, Inc.
National Press Building
1301 Pennsylvania Avenue NW
Washington, DC 20045
202/347-7757

FEDERAL CAREER DIRECTORY
U.S. Government Printing Office
Washington, DC 20402
202/783-3238

FEDERAL CAREER OPPORTUNITIES
Federal Research Service, Inc.
370 West Maple Avenue
Vienna, VA 22180
703/281-0200

FEDERAL JOBS DIGEST
325 Pennsylvania Avenue SE
Washington, DC 20003
202/762-5111

FEDERAL YELLOW BOOK DIRECTORY
Washington Monitor, Inc.
National Press Building
1301 Pennsylvania Avenue NW
Washington, DC 20045
202/347-7757

MOODY'S MUNICIPAL AND GOVERNMENT
MANUAL
Moody's Investors Service
99 Church Street
New York, NY 10007
212/553-0300

U.S. GOVERNMENT MANUAL
U.S. Government Printing Office
Washington, DC 20402
202/783-3293

WASHINGTON INFORMATION DIRECTORY
Congressional Quarterly, Inc.
1414 22nd Street NW
Washington, DC 20037
202/887-8500

INTERNSHIP SOURCES IN HEALTH CARE

■■■

Notes on Interning in Health Care:

With demands for expertise in health-related and health-care management dramatically increasing, a *non*professional with health-care or health care–management experience gains great competitive advantage. Whether you are interested in improving public health, or are beginning to consider a health-related career, the possibilities here can provide firsthand experience.

TIPS: Take your management skills or other training into this area for a move into high-demand health-related fields, or if you are a health professional looking toward a new direction, take your health-related credentials to organizations like these, where you can learn new skills for a new career.

> *Before her internship, recent graduate Christine was unsure what type of career she wanted in the mental health field. As a psychology major she became interested in working with emotionally disturbed children. Christine served as an intern at a nursery for children from dysfunctional families. After three months of working with the children, Christine decided this was her calling.*

Also see entries in *International, Science,* and *Social Services* sections.

ACTION AIDS
1216 Arch Street
Philadelphia, PA 19107

Phone: 215/981-0088
FAX: N/A

* * *

ORGANIZATION'S ACTIVITIES: Publicly funded organization providing social services and other support for people with AIDS and those close to them.

Number of Internships: 6.

Type: Counseling.

Function/Duties: Work in clinics providing social services as well as medical support.

Schedule: Full- and/or part-time summers and semesters.

Stipend or Pay: No, though grants are available.

Academic Credit Offered: Per student's own arrangements with academic institution.

ELIGIBILITY: Upper-level undergraduate, and graduate students.

REQUIREMENTS: Studies in social work and nursing preferred.

APPLICATION PROCEDURE: Send résumé and cover letter *to* Internship Coordinator in spring for summer positions, and in summer for year-round positions.

AIDS PROJECT LOS ANGELES

6721 Romaine Street   **Phone:** 213/962-1600
Los Angeles, CA 90038   **FAX:**   N/A

* * *

ORGANIZATION'S ACTIVITIES: Nonprofit community-based organization whose purpose is to enhance the quality of life of people with AIDS and those close to them through human services, education, and advocacy.

Number of Internships: Varies.

Type: Social service.

Function/Duties: Aid in providing counseling and support services to clients as well as some community organization and public advocacy.

Schedule: 1-year commitment, minimum 5 hours per week.

Stipend or Pay: Expenses may be covered.

Academic Credit Offered: Per student's own arrangements with academic institution.

ELIGIBILITY: Graduate students or recent grads.

REQUIREMENTS: Prefer those sharing interests or goals, either working toward or in receipt of an advanced degree in related social service area.

APPLICATION PROCEDURE: Send inquiries *to* Internship Coordinator. *Deadline:* Ongoing.

AIDS SUPPORT GROUP

P.O. Box 2322   **Phone:** 804/979-7714
Charlottesville, VA 22902   **FAX:**   N/A

* * *

ORGANIZATION'S ACTIVITIES: A private, nonprofit coalition of individuals, social service agencies, businesses, religious organizations, and professionals responding to HIV/AIDS in the Charlottesville area through workshops, training programs, support groups, residential support, and other services for people with AIDS and for the community at large.

Number of Internships: 12 or more.

Type: Case management.

Function/Duties: Assist individuals with AIDS and their families in direct provision of service and in obtaining other services; also, management in residence for people with AIDS.

Schedule: Varies; flexible.

Stipend or Pay: No.

Academic Credit Offered: Per student's own arrangements with academic institution; *Plus* some training available.

ELIGIBILITY: Graduate students or non-students and career-changers with appropriate education and/or experience.

REQUIREMENTS: Social service training and/or experience.

APPLICATION PROCEDURE: Send inquiries *to* Emily Dreyfus, Director. *Deadline:* Ongoing.

Number of Internships: 6 or more.

Type: Fundraising, administrative, nonprofit management.

Function/Duties: Assist staff and volunteers in coordinating activities of organization.

Schedule: Varies; flexible.

Stipend or Pay: No.

Academic Credit Offered: Per student's own arrangements with academic institution.

ELIGIBILITY: Undergraduate or graduate students as well as qualified non-students and career-changers.

REQUIREMENTS: Interests, goals, skills, and/or experience relevant to available assignments.

APPLICATION PROCEDURE: Send inquiries *to* Emily Dreyfus, Director. *Deadline:* Ongoing.

THE ALLIANCE: A COMMUNITY HEALTHCARE PARTNERSHIP

3033 East First Avenue   **Phone:**   303/333-6767
Denver, CO 80206   **FAX:**   303/322-3830

* * *

ORGANIZATION'S ACTIVITIES: A member-owned managed health care cooperative that serves as a forum where health care purchasers, providers, and consumers can work together to enhance the availability of quality health care services at a reasonable cost.

Number of Internships: 2 or more.

Type: Finance and accounting.

Function/Duties: Aid accounting director and staff with computer support, research, purchasing, and other activities.

Schedule: Full- and/or part-time, year-round availability.

Stipend or Pay: Yes.

Academic Credit Offered: Per student's own arrangements with academic institution.

ELIGIBILITY: Qualified students or career-changers considered.

REQUIREMENTS: Prefer computer knowledge and background in accounting.

APPLICATION PROCEDURE: Send résumé *to* Cristina Davis. *Deadline:* Open.

AMERICAN CANCER SOCIETY

1599 Clifton Road NE
Atlanta, GA 30329

Phone: 404/302-3333
FAX: 404/325-0230

* * *

ORGANIZATION'S ACTIVITIES: National nonprofit organization whose goal is to "prevent cancer and to reduce its effects" through education, fundraising, advocacy, support of research, and other activities; regional and local offices throughout U.S.

Number of Internships: Varies; numerous around country.

Type: Administrative, educational, promotional, other.

Function/Duties: Varies, depending on need and locale.

Schedule: Full- and/or part-time, seasonal and/or year-round, at headquarters office as well as at centers around U.S.

Stipend or Pay: Not usually.

Academic Credit Offered: Per student's own arrangements with academic institution.

ELIGIBILITY: Students, non-students, or career-changers with appropriate qualifications.

REQUIREMENTS: Interests, goals, skills, and/or experience relevant to available assignments.

APPLICATION PROCEDURE: Send inquiries *to* Volunteer/Interns Coordinator for information about work in headquarters or for contacts elsewhere. *Deadline:* Ongoing.

AMERICAN INSTITUTE OF ULTRASOUND IN MEDICINE

14750 Sweitzer Lane   **Phone:** 301/498-5906
Laurel, MD 20707   **FAX:** 301/498-4450

* * *

ORGANIZATION'S ACTIVITIES: A multidisciplinary medical association representing a membership of 11,000 physicians, veterinarians, engineers, and other scientists involved with diagnostic ultrasound.

Number of Internships: 1 or more.

Type: Publications, research.

Function/Duties: Aid in production of books, brochures, and other publications; research and monitor legislative activities related to the health field.

Schedule: Full-time and/or part-time, summers, school semesters, year-round.

Stipend or Pay: Will cover commuting costs to office.

Academic Credit Offered: Per student's own arrangements with academic institution; *Plus* choice of learning opportunities; no clerical work.

ELIGIBILITY: Undergraduate or graduate students as well as college graduates in the process of seeking paying work in the field.

REQUIREMENTS: Interests, goals, skills, and/or experience relevant to available assignments.

APPLICATION PROCEDURE: Send inquiries *to* Kathleen M. Wilson. *Deadline:* Ongoing.

AMERICAN NATIONAL RED CROSS

431 18th Street NW   **Phone:** 202/737-8300
Washington, DC 20006   **FAX:** 202/639-3711

* * *

ORGANIZATION'S ACTIVITIES: U.S. arm of international relief agency providing disaster relief as well as social services, international exchange programs, local and regional educational programs for all ages, as well as supervision of donated blood supply and other health-related services; regional and local offices throughout U.S.

Number of Internships: Numerous.

Type: Varies widely depending on assignment, interest, and locale.

Function/Duties: Varies by assignment.

Schedule: Full- and/or part-time, year-round availabilities, openings at local offices around country.

Stipend or Pay: Some paid internships.

Academic Credit Offered: Per student's own arrangements with academic institution.

ELIGIBILITY: Primarily undergraduate students, though others will be considered.

REQUIREMENTS: Good writing and research skills, plus interests, goals, and/or experience relevant to available assignments.

APPLICATION PROCEDURE: Send inquiries *to* Internship Coordinator. *Deadline:* Open.

AMERICAN SOCIETY OF HOSPITAL PHARMACISTS

7272 Wisconsin Avenue
Bethesda, MD 20814

Phone: 301/657-3000
FAX: 301/652-8278

* * *

ORGANIZATION'S ACTIVITIES: National professional society of pharmacists employed by hospitals and related institutions, providing educational, professional, and career-related services from its headquarters and through groups in each state; maintains library and expertise in 30 areas of practice.

Number of Internships: Varies.

Type: Executive residency program.

Function/Duties: Assist and learn association management and administrative practice.

Schedule: Full-time, 1 year (July–July).

Stipend or Pay: Yes.

Academic Credit Offered: Per student's own arrangements with academic institution, if applicable.

ELIGIBILITY: College graduates with health-related backgrounds.

REQUIREMENTS: Availability for full-time work near Washington, D.C.

APPLICATION PROCEDURE: Send inquiries *to* Senior Vice President in time to apply *by* February 1.

Number of Internships: 1—The George P. Provost Editorial Internship.

Type: Pharmaceutical journalism.

Function/Duties: First months in training and orientation rotation through 9 publications activities, followed by an assignment to a specific area chosen by the intern and the chairman of the committee.

Schedule: July 1 through December 31; training, 1,000 hours over at least 25 weeks.

Stipend or Pay: Yes, plus insurance benefits, social security.

Academic Credit Offered: Per student's own arrangement with academic institution.

ELIGIBILITY: Pharmacists; competitive position.

REQUIREMENTS: The applicant shall be a pharmacist who has graduated from a school of pharmacy, shown demonstrated interest in editing and writing, acceptable English language skills, and who is recommended by his/her present or former employer(s) or preceptor(s) and/or his/her college faculty or dean.

APPLICATION PROCEDURE: Contact Provost Internship Chairperson for details.

AMERICAN SUBACUTE CARE ASSOCIATION

P.O. Box 545939   **Phone:** 305/864-0396
Surfside, FL 33154   **FAX:** 305/868-0905

*   *   *

ORGANIZATION'S ACTIVITIES: A nonprofit trade association, representing the providers of the new "subacute care" specialty—institutions and practitioners who provide medical-related service at a level between that of hospitals, nursing homes, and at-home services.

Number of Internships: Varies; up to 6 at a time.

Type: Communications, fundraising, editorial, management.

Function/Duties: Assist and learn from staff members responsible for publications, membership services, direct mail, and events planning.

Schedule: Flexible; program is new and staff is willing to adapt to intern's needs.

Stipend or Pay: $350 offered, and expense reimbursement provided.

Academic Credit Offered: Per student's own arrangements with academic institution; *Plus* may lead to staff or regular freelance position.

ELIGIBILITY: Students, non-students, or career-changers.

REQUIREMENTS: Availability to work in Florida location; interest in health-care issues and related matters preferred.

APPLICATION PROCEDURE: Contact Mike Freedman for application details. *Deadline:* Ongoing.

BLUE CROSS AND BLUE SHIELD OF KENTUCKY

9901 Linn Station Road   **Phone:** 502/423-2110
Louisville, KY 40223   **FAX:** 502/329-5511

*   *   *

ORGANIZATION'S ACTIVITIES: Health insurance company.

Number of Internships: 4 or more.

Type: Accounting and information technology.

Function/Duties: Assist and learn from staff accountants and computer professionals.

Schedule: Part-time.

Stipend or Pay: Range from $6 to $9.50 per hour.

Academic Credit Offered: As arranged by intern.

ELIGIBILITY: College students; preferred majors: Accounting and Computer Science.

REQUIREMENTS: Skills related to assignments available.

APPLICATION PROCEDURE: Submit résumé *to* Associate Resources Group. *Deadline:* Beginning of each college semester (late August or late December).

CATHOLIC PSYCHOLOGICAL SERVICES

1400 West 9th Street **Phone:** 213/251-3569
Los Angeles, CA 90015 **FAX:** 213/380-4603

* * *

ORGANIZATION'S ACTIVITIES: Deliver psychological services to individuals (adults and children), couples, families, and groups; make psychological assessments.

Number of Internships: Flexible; varies with need.

Type: Professional interns (LCSW, MFCC, or psychologist).

Function/Duties: Psychotherapist.

Schedule: Full-time and part-time, 1-year contract.

Stipend or Pay: No.

Academic Credit Offered: Yes.

ELIGIBILITY: Graduate students in psychology-social work—Masters and Doctoral pre- and post-degree. *Special Eligibilities:* Bilingual, bi-cultural, ethnic diversities a plus.

REQUIREMENTS: Must be currently enrolled in graduate course leading to licensure as an MFCC, LCSW, or psychologist, or a graduate working in licensure hours.

APPLICATION PROCEDURE: Submit résumé *to* Dr. Beverly B. Frank, Clinical Program Director. *Deadlines:* May 15, August 15, December 15.

CRAWFORD LONG HOSPITAL

550 Peachtree Street NE **Phone:** 404/686-4411
Atlanta, GA 30365 **FAX:** 404/686-5902

* * *

ORGANIZATION'S ACTIVITIES: A 583-bed university-based hospital.

Number of Internships: Varies; several per academic quarter.

Type: Communications.

Function/Duties: Writing and production of publications; journalistic interviewing; special event coordination.

Schedule: Full- and part-time, year-round.

Stipend or Pay: No.

Academic Credit Offered: Per student's own arrangements with academic institution; *Plus* career-networking through intern "alumni."

ELIGIBILITY: Primarily undergraduate and graduate students; also recent graduates.

REQUIREMENTS: Education and/or experience in journalism, communications, or marketing.

APPLICATION PROCEDURE: Send résumé, references, and 2 writing samples *to* Publications Coordinator *by* about 2 months prior to start date.

CROHN'S AND COLITIS FOUNDATION OF AMERICA

386 Park Avenue South   **Phone:** 212/685-3440
New York, NY 10016   **FAX:**   212/779-4098

* * *

ORGANIZATION'S ACTIVITIES: A nonprofit organization dedicated to finding the cause of and cure for Crohn's disease and ulcerative colitis, two chronic intestinal illnesses that affect some 2 million Americans; 72 chapters throughout U.S.

Number of Internships: 72 (in chapters).

Type: Communications, events organizing.

Function/Duties: Aid with chapter newsletters, photography, events planning.

Schedule: Part-time, year-round availability.

Stipend or Pay: No.

Academic Credit Offered: Per student's own arrangements with academic institution.

ELIGIBILITY: Upper-level college students as well as non-students and career-changers.

REQUIREMENTS: Preferred majors: Journalism, Communications, and Marketing.

APPLICATION PROCEDURE: Send inquiries *to* Judy Welage. *Deadline:* Ongoing.

DESERT REHAB SERVICES INC.

7885 Annandale Avenue   **Phone:** 619/329-2924
Desert Hot Springs, CA 92240   **FAX:**   619/329-0169

* * *

ORGANIZATION'S ACTIVITIES: Concentration on drug addiction and alcoholism residential treatment programs.

Number of Internships: Flexible; varies with need.

Type: Professional counseling.

Function/Duties: Provide services and training.

Schedule: Internship is full-time or part-time, year-round.

Stipend or Pay: No.

Academic Credit Offered: No.

ELIGIBILITY: Undergraduate and graduate students with counseling backgrounds and experience. Chemical-dependency experience is a plus. Non-students and career-changers are encouraged to apply.

REQUIREMENTS: Inquire by telephone or mail for application procedures.

APPLICATION PROCEDURE: Submit full application *to* Mike Sterkel. *Deadline:* No.

EMORY UNIVERSITY SYSTEM OF HEALTH CARE

1365 Clifton Road, NE   **Phone:**   404/248-7700
Atlanta, GA 30322   **FAX:**   404/248-7789

* * *

ORGANIZATION'S ACTIVITIES: A major provider of health care, through two hospitals, a clinic, and a medical school.

Number of Internships: 2.

Type: Editorial.

Function/Duties: Work with editors, designers, photographers, etc., in producing a wide variety of publications from ads to slick magazines.

Schedule: Full-time, each academic quarter.

Stipend or Pay: One receives $1,000 per quarter; one is unpaid.

Academic Credit Offered: Per student's own arrangements with academic institution.

ELIGIBILITY: Primarily graduate and undergraduate students, though qualified others may be considered.

REQUIREMENTS: Editorial skills and computer skills.

APPLICATION PROCEDURE: Send inquiries *to* Dot Sparer. *Deadline:* Ongoing.

WILLIAM J. GOULD ASSOCIATES INC.

Gould Farm   **Phone:**   413/528-1804
Monterey, MA 01245   **FAX:**   413/528-5051

* * *

ORGANIZATION'S ACTIVITIES: A residential treatment program for the mentally ill that focuses on work and community living on a working farm.

Number of Internships: Varies.

Type: Work leader.

Function/Duties: Varies, depending on team assignment—clinical, kitchen, garden, farm, or activities.

Schedule: Residential full-time; minimum 6-month commitment (prefer 1 year).

Stipend or Pay: Yes; stipend plus room and board.

Academic Credit Offered: Per student's own arrangements with academic institution; *Plus* internships occasionally lead to regular positions.

ELIGIBILITY: Graduate and undergraduate students as well as non-students and career-changers. *Special Eligibilities:* All of all backgrounds are encouraged to apply.

REQUIREMENTS: Human service background perhaps a plus, but not required; rather great interpersonal skills and common sense; mature, stable, and able to lead a group and do some physical labor.

APPLICATION PROCEDURE: Send résumé with cover letter *to* Staff Development Office. *Deadline:* Ongoing.

GREATER BALTIMORE MEDICAL CENTER

6701 North Charles Street   **Phone:** 410/828-2132
Baltimore, MD 21204   **FAX:** 410/828-3024

*   *   *

ORGANIZATION'S ACTIVITIES: Nonprofit 372-bed community hospital performing over 25,000 surgeries annually; specialized programs such as in-vitro fertilization, Cancer Center, EENT, Women's Health, Center for Aging.

Number of Internships: 2 or more.

Type: Public relations and communications.

Function/Duties: Assist with events and publications.

Schedule: Part-time, year-round, 3-to-4-month term.

Stipend or Pay: School course registration fee.

Academic Credit Offered: Available.

ELIGIBILITY: College and graduate students; career-changers and non-students also welcome.

REQUIREMENTS: Intern must be outgoing and active. Skills required: some writing, phone, and organization; physically fit to help set up display, distribute literature, pick up materials.

APPLICATION PROCEDURE: Submit résumé and writing sample *to* Vivienne Stearns-Elliott, Director, Community and Media Relations. *Deadline:* 3 to 4 weeks before internship.

HOSPICE OF LINCOLNLAND

Lincolnland Home Care Foundation, Inc.
Lincolnland Visiting Nurse Association Inc.
75 Professional Plaza
Mattoon, IL 61938

Phone: 217/234-4044
FAX: 217/345-3261

* * *

ORGANIZATION'S ACTIVITIES: Hospice of Lincolnland is a program of home care and support for those with life-threatening diseases. Services include home visits, extended hours of care, nursing home, respite care, in-patient hospital care, medical supplies, equipment, medicines, and other incidental needs as appropriate for the patient/family.

Number of Internships: 6 or more.

Type: Management, clerical, medical.

Function/Duties: Assist staff with ongoing duties or special projects; participate in home visits.

Schedule: Full-time and part-time, usually semester-long term.

Stipend or Pay: No.

Academic Credit Offered: Usually.

ELIGIBILITY: College students.

REQUIREMENTS: Preferred majors: Medical, Secretarial, and Health Studies.

APPLICATION PROCEDURE: Submit résumé *to* Teresa Gritti, Human Resource Manager, Lincolnland Home Care Foundation, Inc.

INSTITUTE FOR MENTAL HEALTH INITIATIVES

4545 42nd Street NW
Washington, DC 20016

Phone: 202/364-7111
FAX: 202/363-3891

* * *

ORGANIZATION'S ACTIVITIES: A not-for-profit organization dedicated to promoting mental health and preventing emotional disorders; for example, a public education campaign on fostering emotional resilience in children.

Number of Internships: Varies; 2 or more.

Type: Mental health intern.

Function/Duties: Assist staff in a variety of special assignments, including issues research, coordinating workshops and seminars, contributing to quarterly publications.

Schedule: Full- and part-time, summers and school semesters.

Stipend or Pay: No.

Academic Credit Offered: Per student's own arrangements with academic institution.

ELIGIBILITY: Primarily undergraduate or graduate students.

REQUIREMENTS: Preferred majors: Psychology or Communications.

APPLICATION PROCEDURE: Send résumé, cover letter, and writing sample *to* Internship Coordinator *by* 2 to 3 months prior to availability.

INSTITUTE FOR VICTIMS OF TRAUMA

6801 Market Square Drive	**Phone:** 703/847-8456
McLean, VA 22101	**FAX:** 703/847-0470

* * *

ORGANIZATION'S ACTIVITIES: Professionals engaged in studying and providing services, on an individual and community-wide basis, to people affected by terrorism, accidents, disasters, and other traumas, including post-traumatic stress and its effects on family and friends.

Number of Internships: Varies.

Type: Research, communications, administrative.

Function/Duties: Aid professional staff in providing information and support as needed; help maintain library, run referral service and speakers bureau.

Schedule: Flexible.

Stipend or Pay: Not usually.

Academic Credit Offered: Per student's own arrangements with academic institution.

ELIGIBILITY: Primarily graduate and undergraduate students.

REQUIREMENTS: Interests, goals, skills, and/or experience relevant to available assignments.

APPLICATION PROCEDURE: Send inquiries *to* Executive Director. *Deadline:* Ongoing.

LEUKEMIA SOCIETY OF AMERICA

600 Third Avenue	**Phone:** 212/573-8484
New York, NY 10016	**FAX:** 212/856-9686

* * *

ORGANIZATION'S ACTIVITIES: A national voluntary nonprofit organization dedicated solely to seeking the causes and eventual cure of leukemia and its related diseases, supporting research, patient aid, public and professional education, and community service programs.

Number of Internships: 1 or more.

Type: Communications.

Function/Duties: Aid staff with public relations activities, writing for publications, aiding local chapters with special events.

Schedule: Part-time, per school semesters.

Stipend or Pay: No.

Academic Credit Offered: Per student's own arrangements with academic institution.

ELIGIBILITY: College students.

REQUIREMENTS: Strong written and oral communications skills, interest in organization.

APPLICATION PROCEDURE: Send résumé and cover letter *to* Scott Lerman. *Deadline:* Open.

MARCH OF DIMES

Birth Defects Foundation
1275 Mamaroneck Avenue
White Plains, NY 10605

Phone: 914/428-7100
FAX: 914/428-8203

* * *

ORGANIZATION'S ACTIVITIES: The mission of the March of Dimes is to improve the health of babies by preventing birth defects and infant mortality. They carry out their mission through the campaign for healthier babies, which funds programs of research, community services, education, and advocacy.

Number of Internships: Flexible; varies with need.

Type: Communications, writing, editing, and doing mailings.

Function/Duties: Assist staff of specific departments according to intern's skills and interests; would prefer interns with an interest in non-profit work or in a specific area (i.e., communications, writing, training, etc.).

Schedule: Part-time (4 hours per day); year-round internships available.

Stipend or Pay: Lunch plus travel expenses.

Academic Credit Offered: Per intern's own arrangements with academic institution; *Plus* internship may possibly lead to full-time employment.

ELIGIBILITY: Students in high school and above are encouraged to apply. Open to non-students and career-changers. Priority is intern's motivation, willingness to work, and applicable skills. *Special Eligibilities:* Minorities, women, senior citizens, etc., are encouraged to apply.

REQUIREMENTS: Must provide cover letter explaining type of skills and a résumé along with an application.

APPLICATION PROCEDURE: Submit full application *to* Susan Rhone. *Deadline:* Open.

MEDICAL CARE DEVELOPMENT, INC.

11 Parkwood Drive   **Phone:** 207/622-7566
Augusta, ME 04330   **FAX:** N/A

* * *

ORGANIZATION'S ACTIVITIES: A private nonprofit organization that teaches public health practices to people in rural African villages and conducts seminars for government officials in the development of medical facilities.

Number of Internships: Varies.

Type: Public health research and community development.

Function/Duties: Work directly with client population or assist professionals in education and development projects.

Schedule: Varies, depending on position.

Stipend or Pay: Stipends may be available.

Academic Credit Offered: Per student's own arrangements with academic institution.

ELIGIBILITY: Graduate and undergraduate students as well as qualified non-students or career-changers.

REQUIREMENTS: Some experience relevant to the position.

APPLICATION PROCEDURE: Send inquiries *to* Dr. John A. La Casse. *Deadline:* Ongoing.

MULTIFAITH AIDS PROJECT OF SEATTLE

1729 Harvard Avenue   **Phone:** 206/324-1520
Seattle, WA 98122   **FAX:** N/A

* * *

ORGANIZATION'S ACTIVITIES: An interfaith nonprofit organization that assists in meeting the spiritual and emotional needs of people living with HIV/AIDS.

Number of Internships: Varies.

Type: Education, community development, social service.

Function/Duties: Assignments vary depending on intern's skills and interests; include assisting with publications and outreach and with special events and direct client services.

Schedule: Full- and/or part-time, year-round availability.

Stipend or Pay: No.

Academic Credit Offered: Per student's own arrangements with academic institution.

ELIGIBILITY: Consideration given to students, non-students, or career-changers with appropriate qualifications.

REQUIREMENTS: Interests, goals, skills, and/or experience relevant to available assignments.

APPLICATION PROCEDURE: Send inquiries *to* Project Administrator. *Deadline:* ongoing.

NATIONAL CITIZENS' COALITION FOR NURSING HOME REFORM

1224 M Street NW
Suite 301
Washington, DC 20005

Phone: 202/393-2018
FAX: 202/393-4122

* * *

ORGANIZATION'S ACTIVITIES: Grassroots citizen coalition to advocate in behalf of the residents of nursing home and board-and-care facilities; 300 member groups across nation provide ombudsman services, legal assistance, monitor quality of care, guide regulatory efforts.

Number of Internships: 1 or more.

Type: Public policy research and advocacy on long-term care.

Function/Duties: Special projects as environment dictates.

Schedule: Part-time and full-time.

Stipend or Pay: Sometimes.

Academic Credit Offered: If arranged by intern.

ELIGIBILITY: Some high-school students, college, and graduate students; preferred majors: Health Administration, Medical, Law, Sociology, and Psychology. Non-students and career-changers welcome to apply. *Special Eligibilities:* Actively seek special populations.

REQUIREMENTS: Perfect place for self-starters, persons comfortable with creative confrontation and dedicated to improving health care.

APPLICATION PROCEDURE: *Write or call* Jacqueline Kuenig.

NATIONAL INSTITUTES OF HEALTH

9000 Rockville Pike
Bethesda, MD 20892

Phone: 301/496-4461
FAX: 301/496-0017

* * *

ORGANIZATION'S ACTIVITIES: Federal government's leading medical research, medical education, and public health development agency.

Number of Internships: Numerous.

Type: Management internship opportunities.

Function/Duties: Varies with assignment; both administrative and technical.

Schedule: Full-time, 1-year.

Stipend or Pay: Yes—at federal government rates.

Academic Credit Offered: Only per student's own arrangements with academic institution if applicable; *Plus* federal government benefits followed by opportunities for regular employment at NIH.

ELIGIBILITY: Graduate students or recent college graduates.

REQUIREMENTS: Meet federal government qualifications.

APPLICATION PROCEDURE: Send inquiries *to* Personnel Office. *Deadline:* Ongoing.

SCRIPPSHEALTH (PUBLIC RELATIONS)

P.O. Box 28　　　　　　　　　　　　**Phone:**　619/457-6954
La Jolla, CA 92093　　　　　　　　**FAX:**　　619/457-3067

* * *

ORGANIZATION'S ACTIVITIES: San Diego's leading health-care system, a health maintenance operation connected with Scripps Memorial Hospital.

Number of Internships: Several each term.

Type: Public relations.

Function/Duties: Work with professionals on marketing, publications, media relations, and other public relations specialties.

Schedule: 16 to 20 hours per week, summers, and spring and fall semesters.

Stipend or Pay: Yes.

Academic Credit Offered: Per student's own arrangements with academic institution.

ELIGIBILITY: Graduate and undergraduate students.

REQUIREMENTS: Excellent communications skills; interest or experience in health care.

APPLICATION PROCEDURE: Send inquiries *to* Leslie Mogul *by* several months prior to availability.

SCRIPPSHEALTH

P.O. Box 28　　　　　　　　　　　　**Phone:**　619/554-8400
La Jolla, CA 92093　　　　　　　　**FAX:**　　619/457-6122

* * *

ORGANIZATION'S ACTIVITIES: San Diego's leading health-care system, a health maintenance operation connected with Scripps Memorial Hospital.

Number of Internships: Varies; fairly numerous.

Type: Administrative, educational, community service.

Function/Duties: Varies with assignment; most nonmedical departments offer some internship possibilities.

Schedule: Full- and/or part-time, summers, and spring and fall semesters.

Stipend or Pay: Some.

Academic Credit Offered: Per student's own arrangements with academic institution.

ELIGIBILITY: Graduate and undergraduate students.

REQUIREMENTS: Excellent communications skills, interest or experience in health care.

APPLICATION PROCEDURE: Send inquiries *to* Human Resources Department *by* several months prior to availability.

TEXAS MEDICAL ASSOCIATION

401 West 15th Street   **Phone:** 512/370-1388
Austin, TX 78701-1634   **FAX:**   512/370-1634

* * *

ORGANIZATION'S ACTIVITIES: TMA represents 83 percent of all Texas physicians and 96 percent of the state's medical students; TMA advocates on their behalf and on behalf of their patients—via legislators, regulation, and the courts—with the goal of improving the health of all Texans.

Number of Internships: 2.

Type: Radio recording studio technician/writer.

Function/Duties: Operate recording studio and assist in writing radio program.

Schedule: Part-time, year-round.

Stipend or Pay: $1,800—subject to change.

Academic Credit Offered: Available if arranged by intern.

ELIGIBILITY: All students; preferred majors: Radio, Television, and Film. Both career-changers and non-students with a strong background in radio also welcome to apply.

REQUIREMENTS: Training and/or provable experience in radio.

APPLICATION PROCEDURE: Submit cover letter and résumé *to* Yasemin Hadley Florey, Communications Manager, Speech and Electronic Media Office.

TOXIC SUBSTANCES AND DISEASE REGISTRY, U.S. AGENCY FOR

1600 Clifton Road
Atlanta, GA 30333

Phone: 404/639-3311
FAX: 404/639-0744

* * *

ORGANIZATION'S ACTIVITIES: Researches, monitors, and classifies toxic substances and other public health hazards.

Number of Internships: Varies.

Type: Research, communications.

Function/Duties: Participate in laboratory and other research projects in biology, toxicology, etc., working with professionals in the field.

Schedule: 10 weeks to 12 months, full- or part-time.

Stipend or Pay: $1,500 to $2,200 per month, depending on work and educational level.

Academic Credit Offered: Per student's own arrangements with academic institution, if applicable; *Plus* travel reimbursement and some tuition.

ELIGIBILITY: Students seeking bachelor's or master's degrees.

REQUIREMENTS: Studies in life sciences, pharmacology, toxicology, environmental science, public health preferred.

APPLICATION PROCEDURE: Send inquiries *to* Linda McCamant. *Deadline:* Ongoing.

VIRGINIA MASON MEDICAL CENTER

1100 Ninth Avenue
P.O. Box 900
Seattle, WA 98111-0900

Phone: 206/583-6090
FAX: 206/223-6706

* * *

ORGANIZATION'S ACTIVITIES: VMMC is a private, nonprofit medical facility that includes a 336-bed hospital, a downtown clinic, 10 satellite facilities, and a research center. It is the largest private group practice in the Northwest and the seventeenth largest in the country. The medical center employs 4,000 people.

Number of Internships: Flexible; varies with need.

Type: Public relations.

Function/Duties: Offers opportunities in a variety of areas, including media relations, employee communications, patient and employee publications, special events, organization and implementation; computer knowledge is helpful and basic writing experience is required.

Schedule: Year-round full-time and part-time internships offered; must serve a minimum of 3 months.

Stipend or Pay: Able to offer a rent break to interns who would like to live in one of the downtown Seattle apartments owned by the medical center during their internship.

Academic Credit Offered: Per intern's own arrangements with academic institution.

ELIGIBILITY: Undergraduate (juniors and seniors) and graduate students; preferred majors: Journalism, Communications, and Public Relations. Non-students and career-changers with related experience are welcome to apply.

REQUIREMENTS: Must provide a résumé and 3 writing samples, along with an application.

APPLICATION PROCEDURE: Submit full application *to* Jennifer Phillips. *Deadline:* May 15 and November 15.

WORLD HEALTH ORGANIZATION

2 UN Plaza
New York, NY 10017

Phone: 212/963-4388
FAX: 212/223-2920

* * *

ORGANIZATION'S ACTIVITIES: United Nations agency responsible for public health enhancement and education throughout developing countries in world; headquarters in Geneva, Switzerland.

Number of Internships: Varies; numerous.

Type: Administrative, educational, research.

Function/Duties: Primarily opportunities in headquarters offices at Geneva or New York City (many other technical and social internships available through agencies working with WHO; ask for lists).

Schedule: Full-time, 6 to 12 weeks.

Stipend or Pay: No.

Academic Credit Offered: Per student's own arrangements with academic institution.

ELIGIBILITY: Graduate or undergraduate students.

REQUIREMENTS: Prefer those enrolled in health-related course of study.

APPLICATION PROCEDURE: Send inquiries *to* Division of Personnel in time to apply *by* 3 months prior to start date.

Organizations/Resources for Further Information about Internships in Health

You need not be a health professional to get health-care experience. Explore the advice and facilities that these organizations have to offer.

THE NATIONAL HEALTH COUNCIL
The National Health Council, Inc.
1730 M Street NW
Suite 500
Washington, DC 20036
202/785-3910

A private, nonprofit umbrella association of 125 of America's most respected health organizations. These include 40 of the nation's leading voluntary health agencies, such as the American Cancer Society, the American Heart Association, and the National Easter Seal Society. A good resource for information about health-related associations sponsoring internships; publishes "200 Ways to Put Your Talent to Work in the Health Field"—an excellent directory to health-care organizations and activities.

NATIONAL COUNCIL OF STATE BOARDS OF NURSING
676 North Saint Clair Street
Suite 550
Chicago, IL 60611-2921
312/787-6555

AMERICAN PHARMACEUTICAL ASSOCIATION
2215 Constitution Avenue NW
Washington, DC 20037
202/628-4410

AMERICAN HOSPITAL ASSOCIATION
840 North Lake Shore Drive
Chicago, IL 60611
312/280-6000

PUBLICATION

DIRECTORY OF U.S.-BASED AGENCIES INVOLVED IN INTERNATIONAL
    HEALTH ASSISTANCE
National Council for International Health
1701 K Street NW
Suite 600
Washington, DC 20036
202/833-5900.

Contains information on more than 700 agencies in the private sector (both profit and nonprofit) with health, nutrition, and population programs in developing countries.

INTERNSHIP SOURCES IN INTERNATIONAL ORGANIZATIONS

■ ■

Notes On International Interning:

International Studies is a booming academic area in today's fast-changing world—and international anything is a vital résumé plus for today's and tomorrow's global economy. In this section you will find U.S. opportunities with internationally focused organizations, as well as overseas internships. You have a huge range of opportunities, depending on your goals and interests, and any of them will add that magic word *international* to your résumé.

TIPS: 1. You will notice that international opportunities include high-level, high-finance institutions, as well as small-scale, grassroots groups—you hardly need a degree in international relations to take advantage of today's global focus.

2. Your religious organization is likely to have international programs for which members of your faith are more readily accepted; investigate these opportunities, too.

> *To IAESTE trainee Francis, "From a cultural point of view it is much more interesting than just coming in as a tourist and visiting....It is not the same thing; you come here and you live with people, and you realize that there are cultural differences.*
>
> *"Doing an internship abroad is a great opportunity for everybody. When you come back home, I think you have a much more open mind....While you're abroad, you realize that you are an immigrant, and maybe that changes the way you look at immigrants when you go back home."*
>
> *Francis, who eventually wants to work on an international level, is a firm believer in the benefits for U.S. employers participating in international exchanges.*

Also see *Social Service* and *Public Affairs* entries, which also include some internationally focused programs.

ACCION INTERNACIONAL/AITEC

130 Prospect Street   **Phone:** 617/492-4930
Cambridge, MA 02139   **FAX:**   N/A

* * *

ORGANIZATION'S ACTIVITIES: Dedicated to rural and small-business development toward economic self-sufficiency in poor communities throughout Latin America.

Number of Internships: Varies according to special projects.

Type: Research, administrative.

Function/Duties: Assist special-projects staff with research and with office duties.

Schedule: Openings available year-round, depending on projects.

Stipend or Pay: No.

Academic Credit Offered: Through student's academic institution.

ELIGIBILITY: College or graduate students; non-students and career-changers with college degrees and interest in the Americas are welcome to apply; *Plus* internship may lead to full employment.

REQUIREMENTS: Available to work in Cambridge office during business hours; possible need to work out of the country.

APPLICATION PROCEDURE: For application and details, *contact* Sheryl Klein, Communications Specialist. *Deadline:* Open.

AFS INTERNATIONAL INTERCULTURAL PROGRAMS

313 East 43d Street   **Phone:** 212/949-4242
New York, NY 10017   **FAX:**   212/949-9379

* * *

ORGANIZATION'S ACTIVITIES: The American Field Service, as AFS, is a nonprofit organization that sponsors educational and cultural exchange programs among some 50 countries.

Number of Internships: 8 or more.

Type: Research, administration, public relations, finance.

Function/Duties: Aid regular staff with administration of international programs, and provide assistance on special projects.

Schedule: Full-time summers, part-time fall and spring semesters.

Stipend or Pay: No.

Academic Credit Offered: Per student's own arrangements with academic institution.

ELIGIBILITY: College students or recent graduates.

REQUIREMENTS: Minimum C+ average.

APPLICATION PROCEDURE: Send inquiries *to* Personnel Office. *Deadline:* Ongoing.

AGENCY FOR INTERNATIONAL DEVELOPMENT

320 21st Street NW   **Phone:** 202/663-1451
Washington, DC 20523   **FAX:**   N/A

*   *   *

ORGANIZATION'S ACTIVITIES: A.I.D. manages U.S. foreign aid to developing countries in Africa, Asia, Latin America, and the Middle East.

Number of Internships: Limited number.

Type: Agriculture, business administration, international relations, public health, finance.

Function/Duties: Varies with assignment and intern's interest; mostly administrative assistance, some clerical.

Schedule: Mostly full-time during summer; other times arranged.

Stipend or Pay: No.

Academic Credit Offered: Per student's own arrangements with academic institution.

ELIGIBILITY: Undergraduate and graduate students.

REQUIREMENTS: Interests, goals, and/or experience relevant to available assignments.

APPLICATION PROCEDURE: Request appropriate form and details *from* Student Program Coordinator *by* early in school year.

AMERICAN FRIENDS SERVICE COMMITTEE

1501 Cherry Street   **Phone:** 215/241-7000
Philadelphia, PA 19102   **FAX:**   215/864-0104

*   *   *

ORGANIZATION'S ACTIVITIES: Promotes international conciliation, peace, justice, and equality domestically and internationally under auspices of the Society of Friends (Quakers) through projects administered from headquarters offices and in international centers; 9 regional offices and one in Washington, D.C.

Number of Internships: Varies.

Type: Research, analysis, administrative, communications.

Function/Duties: Office work, outreach; assist as needed with projects.

Schedule: Full-time, year-round, or as needed per projects.

Stipend or Pay: Subsistence grants available; *Plus* health insurance and other benefits may be available.

Academic Credit Offered: Per student's own arrangements with academic institution.

ELIGIBILITY: Students, non-students, and career-changers all welcome.

REQUIREMENTS: "An understanding of Quaker values" and some experience with advocacy work is preferred.

Type: Specialists in all social services for community development and health projects.

Function/Duties: To aid staff and service providers in centers in Asia, the Middle East, and elsewhere.

Schedule: Full-time residential overseas.

Stipend or Pay: No, but maintenance provided and savings plan offered.

Academic Credit Offered: Per student's own arrangements with academic institution.

ELIGIBILITY: Graduate and undergraduate students, non-students, and career-changers. *Special Eligibilities:* Equal opportunity employer, but special skills preferred.

REQUIREMENTS: Depending on locale and project, age minimums may be required and relevant training and/or experience preferred.

APPLICATION PROCEDURE: *Contact* main office for availabilities there and in regional offices.

AGRICULTURE, U.S. DEPARTMENT OF— OFFICE OF INTERNATIONAL COOPERATION AND DEVELOPMENT (OICD)

14th Street and Independence Avenue SW
Room 3101
Washington, DC 20250

Phone: 202/690-2796
FAX: 202/720-6103

* * *

ORGANIZATION'S ACTIVITIES: Designs, implements, and evaluates agriculture, rural development, health, and education programs in developing nations on every continent.

Number of Internships: Varies; numerous.

Type: Agriculture, health care, education, business.

Function/Duties: Assist in both administrative planning and operation and in hands-on projects as needed.

Schedule: Both short- and long-term, depending on project and intern's availability.

Stipend or Pay: Usually.

Academic Credit Offered: Where relevant.

ELIGIBILITY: Consideration given to students, non-students, or career-changers with appropriate qualifications; *Plus* internships often lead to career positions.

REQUIREMENTS: Interests, goals, and/or experience relevant to available assignments.

APPLICATION PROCEDURE: Send letter *to* Internship Coordinator. *Deadline:* Ongoing.

AMERICAN INSTITUTE FOR FOREIGN STUDY

102 Greenwich Avenue   **Phone:** 203/869-9090 or 800/727-AIFS
Greenwich, CT 06830   **FAX:**   203/869-9615

* * *

ORGANIZATION'S ACTIVITIES: An international college program that offers its enrollees a wide variety of internship opportunities in various European countries.

Number of Internships: Several thousand (as many as are students requesting).

Type: Depending on student's major—in business, social services, arts, and communications.

Function/Duties: Varies according to sponsor's need and intern's interests.

Schedule: 6-week programs at ends of fall and spring semester; longer programs during summers.

Stipend or Pay: Possibly.

Academic Credit Offered: Yes.

ELIGIBILITY: Students enrolled in AIFS courses or special summer program; *Plus* transportation and special training available.

REQUIREMENTS: Must be at least 17 years old; AIFS enrollee or other college with minimum 2.5 GPA.

APPLICATION PROCEDURE: *Contact* AIFS for application; submit with essay, transcript, and academic references *to* Admissions Office *by* May 15 for fall semester, October 15 for spring semester, and March 15 for summer.

AMERICAN SECURITY COUNCIL

Washington Communications Center   **Phone:** 703/547-1750
Boston, VA 22713   **FAX:**   703/547-9737

* * *

ORGANIZATION'S ACTIVITIES: A private, nonprofit research and education organization that focuses on issues of national security and international relations.

Number of Internships: 12 per year.

Type: Research, writing, educational assisting.

Function/Duties: Work on reports and events.

Schedule: Part- or full-time for 4 months during spring, summer, and fall quarters.

Stipend or Pay: No.

Academic Credit Offered: Per student's own arrangements with academic institution; *Plus* participation in weekly briefings and discussions with staff members on foreign policy issues.

ELIGIBILITY: College and graduate students.

REQUIREMENTS: Availability to work in Washington, D.C., suburb; interest in career in international relations.

APPLICATION PROCEDURE: *Contact* Executive Director for application and details. *Deadline:* Open.

AMERICAN SLAVIC STUDENT INTERNSHIP SERVICE (AND TRAINING CORP.) (A.S.S.I.S.T.)

1841 Broadway	
Suite 607	**Phone:** 212/262-3862
New York, NY 10023	**FAX:** 212/262-3865

* * *

ORGANIZATION'S ACTIVITIES: Placement of intern in many fields including education, business, publishing, media, tourism, and sports in Russia. Organization of international transportation and accommodations.

Number of Internships: 50.

Type: Various fields.

Function/Duties: Range from teaching English to consulting on privatization.

Schedule: Full-time and part-time, one month to two years.

Stipend or Pay: 20,000 to 150,000 rubles per month.

Academic Credit Offered: If applicable.

ELIGIBILITY: Undergraduate and graduate students; preferred majors: Business and Russian; non-students and career-changers welcome.

REQUIREMENTS: Knowledge of Russian language is desirable. There is a program fee ranging from $1,500 (for 1 month) to $4,500 (for 2 years), which covers international transportation, accommodations, placement, transfers to residence, visa fees, and in-country service.

APPLICATION PROCEDURE: Request application and submit *to* Lisa Wolfe.

AMIGOS DE LAS AMERICAS

5618 Star Lane	**Phone:** 713/782-5290
Houston, TX 77057	**FAX:** N/A

* * *

ORGANIZATION'S ACTIVITIES: Private, nonprofit organization that works for community health education in Latin America while providing leadership development training for young people and fostering intercultural understanding.

Number of Internships: Varies by needs.

Type: Educational, social-service, health-care-related.

Function/Duties: Participate in community development and health education projects (medical training *not* required).

Schedule: Overseas programs for 4 to 6 weeks in the summer; 3- to 6-month programs year-round.

Stipend or Pay: No.

Academic Credit Offered: Per student's own arrangement with academic institution.

ELIGIBILITY: High-school and college students as well as non-students—mostly recent graduates, but career-changers are welcome to apply. *Special Eligibilities:* Community and health experience not required, but is a plus in applicants.

REQUIREMENTS: Minimum age of 16; basic skills in speaking and reading Spanish.

APPLICATION PROCEDURE: Request application form; return with résumé and cover letter *to* Internship Coordinator *by* 3 months prior to desired internship period.

AMNESTY INTERNATIONAL USA

322 Eighth Avenue
New York, NY 10001

Phone: 212/807-8400
FAX: 212/627-1451

* * *

ORGANIZATION'S ACTIVITIES: A worldwide nonpartisan human rights organization working for the protection and release of political prisoners.

Number of Internships: Varies; numerous.

Type: Research, communications, development, finance.

Function/Duties: Interns work with regular staff in all areas of organization according to interests and needs.

Schedule: Full- and/or part-time, minimum 1 semester; in headquarters or D.C. and half a dozen regional offices.

Stipend or Pay: May be arranged.

Academic Credit Offered: Per student's own arrangements with academic institution.

ELIGIBILITY: Consideration given to students, non-students, or career-changers with appropriate qualifications.

REQUIREMENTS: Interests, goals, and/or experience relevant to available assignments.

APPLICATION PROCEDURE: Send application, résumé, and cover letter *to* Intern Coordinator. *Deadline:* Ongoing.

AMERICAS SOCIETY

680 Park Avenue   **Phone:** 212/249-8950
New York, NY 10021   **FAX:**   N/A

* * *

ORGANIZATION'S ACTIVITIES: Private nonprofit organization for the promotion of economic, political, and cultural understanding within Latin America, the Caribbean, and Canada.

Number of Internships: 5.

Type: Public relations, clerical, writing.

Function/Duties: Assist with media relations, events organization, office tasks, research, reports.

Schedule: Full- or part-time in fall, spring, and summer semesters.

Stipend or Pay: No.

Academic Credit Offered: Yes.

ELIGIBILITY: Undergraduate and graduate students; *Plus* internships often lead to permanent employment.

REQUIREMENTS: Studies in international relations or courses related to Latin America; proficiency in Spanish or Portuguese.

APPLICATION PROCEDURE: Request details *from* Office of Joint Programmes *by* several months prior to internship availability.

ASSOCIATE IN RURAL DEVELOPMENT

110 Main Street   **Phone:** 802/658-3890
Burlington, VT 05402   **FAX:**   N/A

* * *

ORGANIZATION'S ACTIVITIES: International private research and consulting company that provides education and training in agriculture, small business, environmental protection, and other developmental skills, primarily through coordination of short- and long-term consultants worldwide.

Number of Internships: As many as needed, depending on number of projects.

Type: Community development, education, outdoor.

Function/Duties: According to work of project consultant to whom intern is assigned.

Schedule: 1-, 3-, or 6-month assignments or even longer, depending on project.

Stipend or Pay: Yes; varies with assignment.

Academic Credit Offered: Per student's own arrangements with academic institution.

ELIGIBILITY: College graduates, with some master's credits preferred but not required; career-changers accepted with some expertise in projects' subjects.

REQUIREMENTS: Interest in subject area and strong communications skills; ability in language of assigned country a plus.

APPLICATION PROCEDURE: Send résumé and cover letter *to* Internship Coordinator. *Deadline:* Open.

ASSOCIATION FOR INTERNATIONAL PRACTICAL TRAINING (AIPT)

10 Corporate Center
10400 Little Patuxent Parkway   **Phone:**   410/997-2200
Columbia, MD 21044   **FAX:**   410/992-3924

* * *

ORGANIZATION'S ACTIVITIES: A private, nonprofit educational exchange organization that facilitates exchanges between the U.S. and other countries of qualified workers in hospitality, tourism, and a wide variety of other industries.

Number of Internships: About 500 for Americans overseas.

Type: Managerial, professional, technical.

Function/Duties: Varies with assignment, with country, and with organization offering specific internship.

Schedule: Full-time, 6 to 18 months, depending on assignment.

Stipend or Pay: Varies with assignment.

Academic Credit Offered: Per student's own arrangements with academic institution in student-exchange programs.

ELIGIBILITY: Graduate and undergraduate students in student-exchange program; non-students and career-changers in other aspects of program; *Plus* intern programs are formally established and well structured for both work and learning.

REQUIREMENTS: 18 to 35 years of age; college degree or equivalent experience; usually requires skills in language of employing country.

APPLICATION PROCEDURE: *Contact* AIPT for details, forms, and deadline.

BEIJING-WASHINGTON, INC.

4340 East-West Highway   **Phone:**   301/656-4801
Bethesda, MD 20814   **FAX:**   N/A

* * *

ORGANIZATION'S ACTIVITIES: A trade-consulting firm representing three dozen U.S. and European companies doing business in China, especially in the manufacture and sale of electronic equipment.

Number of Internships: Varies with need.

Type: Administrative, clerical, data processing, research, communications.

Function/Duties: Assist regular staff with ongoing activities in public relations, marketing, events coordination, and project planning.

Schedule: About 15 hours per week year-round.

Stipend or Pay: No.

Academic Credit Offered: Per student's own arrangements with academic institution.

ELIGIBILITY: Consideration given to students, non-students, or career-changers with appropriate qualifications; *Plus* internships may develop into regular employment.

REQUIREMENTS: Fluency in Mandarin Chinese preferred; computer skills and excellent writing skills needed.

APPLICATION PROCEDURE: Send résumé and cover letter *to* President's Office *by* several months prior to availability dates.

BORDERLINKS

924 North 6th Avenue   **Phone:** 602/628-8263
Tucson, AZ 85705   **FAX:** N/A

* * *

ORGANIZATION'S ACTIVITIES: Provides experiential, crosscultural learning opportunities along the U.S./Mexico border and in Central America.

Number of Internships: Varies.

Type: Tutoring, community organization.

Function/Duties: Crosscultural learning; tutoring and community assistance.

Schedule: 6 weeks in summer.

Stipend or Pay: No—and fee is required that covers local living expenses, but scholarships are available.

Academic Credit Offered: Per student's own arrangements with academic institution.

ELIGIBILITY: High-school students and other young adults.

REQUIREMENTS: Relevant interests, goals, and/or experience; able to spend 6 weeks outside country; Spanish-language skills helpful.

APPLICATION PROCEDURE: Request application and submit *to* Summer Intern Program *by* March 15.

ROBERT BOSCH FOUNDATION OF STUTTGART, GERMANY

c/o CDS International Inc.
425 Park Avenue
New York, NY 10022

Phone: 212/760-1400
FAX: N/A

* * *

ORGANIZATION'S ACTIVITIES: Sponsors American professionals in high-level projects in German government and private industry.

Number of Internships: 15.

Type: Journalism, law, economics, business administration.

Function/Duties: Work with German professionals on variety of projects.

Schedule: 9 months each year (May–September).

Stipend or Pay: Yes.

Academic Credit Offered: No.

ELIGIBILITY: Working professionals with appropriate graduate degrees or professional experience; *Plus* language training offered; travel provided.

REQUIREMENTS: Highly competitive program; also, must be able to communicate in German by start of program.

APPLICATION PROCEDURE: Request details *from* Internship Coordinator as soon as possible before availability period.

BREAD FOR THE WORLD

802 Rhode Island Avenue NE
Washington, DC 20018

Phone: 202/269-0200
FAX: 202/529-8546

* * *

ORGANIZATION'S ACTIVITIES: A nonprofit religious organization devoted to education, development, and activism in the cause of hunger-relief and related economic and political issues.

Number of Internships: Numerous; varies with projects.

Type: Communications, research, fundraising.

Function/Duties: Report writing; research, presentation; assist marketing, fundraising, and other staffs.

Schedule: Available to work in Washington, D.C., and regional U.S. field offices; minimum 3-month stint preferred.

Stipend or Pay: May be arranged.

Academic Credit Offered: Per student's own arrangements with academic institution.

ELIGIBILITY: Some graduate students; otherwise non-students, career-changers, and others with degrees and background in economics, political science, international studies.

REQUIREMENTS: Must have commitment to Christian faith.

APPLICATION PROCEDURE: *Contact* Personnel Director for internship application; year-round openings. *Deadline:* Open.

C.A.R.E.

660 First Avenue   **Phone:** 212/686-3110
New York, NY 10016   **FAX:**   212/696-4005

* * *

ORGANIZATION'S ACTIVITIES: A private, nonprofit international organization dedicated to the development of self-sufficiency in underdeveloped countries around the world through promotion of self-help economic, social, agriculture, and engineering projects.

Number of Internships: Numerous; varies by project.

Type: Technical in field; nontechnical, clerical, and managerial in NYC office.

Function/Duties: Assist paid specialists on a project basis.

Schedule: Part-time work available in New York year-round; field projects require travel and longer-term commitment.

Stipend or Pay: May be arranged.

Academic Credit Offered: Per student's own arrangements with academic institution.

ELIGIBILITY: Students in New York office; recent grads and non-students or career-changers with appropriate expertise needed in field projects.

REQUIREMENTS: Availability to work in locale required; specialists preferred but not required.

APPLICATION PROCEDURE: *Contact* Ellen Lieber for application forms and procedure. *Deadline:* Open.

CENTRAL INTELLIGENCE AGENCY

Employment Center
P.O. Box 1255   **Phone:** 703/482-1100
Pittsburgh, PA 15230   **FAX:**   N/A

* * *

ORGANIZATION'S ACTIVITIES: The federal government agency assigned to "collect, analyze, and disseminate foreign intelligence and to coordinate the intelligence efforts of the U.S. government." All participants in CIA programs must be at least 18 years of age, maintain a minimum 2.75 average, be highly motivated, and be able to meet strict medical and security standards, including a polygraph exam and background investigation.

Number of Internships: Varies.

Type: Undergraduate scholar program.

Function/Duties: Maintain full-time college status; work each summer on assignments in Washington, D.C., area facility.

Schedule: Full-time work in summers; work for agency after graduation.

Stipend or Pay: Yearly competitive salary.

Academic Credit Offered: N/A.

ELIGIBILITY: High-school students headed for college. *Special Eligibilities:* Program is primarily for minorities and those with disabilities who need financial assistance for tuition; *Plus* financial assistance for tuition, fees, books, and supplies; pay increased according to level of education; transportation and housing costs reimbursed during active internship.

REQUIREMENTS: Those above, plus "student scholars must agree to continue employment with the Agency after college graduation for a period one and one-half times the length of their college training."

APPLICATION PROCEDURE: Request application and file with employment center no later than end of first year of high school.

Type: Undergraduate student trainees (co-op) program.

Function/Duties: Work as assigned in D.C.-area facility.

Schedule: Work full-time in alternating terms with college coursework.

Stipend or Pay: Competitive salary; pay increased according to level of education; transportation and housing costs reimbursed during active internship.

Academic Credit Offered: N/A.

ELIGIBILITY: Undergraduate students; *Plus* good chance of full-time employment upon graduation.

REQUIREMENTS: Those above, plus students are required to work at least 3 terms (alternating with study-semesters) prior to graduation.

APPLICATION PROCEDURE: Request application and file with employment center 6 to 9 months prior to availability.

Type: Minority undergraduate studies program.

Function/Duties: Practical assignments in Agency departments.

Schedule: Full-time, summers.

Stipend or Pay: Competitive salary.

Academic Credit Offered: Per student's own arrangements with academic institution.

ELIGIBILITY: Undergraduate students. *Special Eligibilities:* Minorities and students with disabilities; *Plus* good chance of full-time employment upon graduation; transportation and housing costs reimbursed.

REQUIREMENTS: See above.

APPLICATION PROCEDURE: Request application and file with employment center by September 30 before summer availability.

CHOL-CHOL FOUNDATION FOR HUMAN DEVELOPMENT

3421 M Street NW	**Phone:**	703/525-8844
Washington, DC 20007	**FAX:**	N/A

* * *

ORGANIZATION'S ACTIVITIES: A private nonprofit agricultural organization that sends teams of agricultural experts to Chile, Nigeria, and Argentina to teach small farmers new production techniques.

Number of Internships: Varies by project.

Type: Agricultural.

Function/Duties: Travel and teach in rural areas.

Schedule: Commitment to length of assigned project required.

Stipend or Pay: Room and board.

Academic Credit Offered: Per student's own arrangements with academic institution.

ELIGIBILITY: Students, non-students, and career-changers: Anyone with interest and experience in subject.

REQUIREMENTS: Intelligence, stamina, and willingness to endure hardships.

APPLICATION PROCEDURE: Send letter and résumé *to* Intern Coordinator. *Deadline:* Open.

CONCERN/AMERICA

P.O. Box 1790	**Phone:**	714/953-8575
Santa Ana, CA 92702	**FAX:**	N/A

* * *

ORGANIZATION'S ACTIVITIES: A nonprofit development and relief agency working in Bangladesh, Central America, and Northern Africa on health, economic, and building projects.

Number of Internships: Varies by demand.

Type: Medical, farming, construction, nutrition.

Function/Duties: Treat problems and assist residents in developing solutions.

Schedule: Minimum 1-year placement; year-round openings.

Stipend or Pay: Room, board, transportation, insurance, and small monthly stipend plus matching repatriation fund established in U.S.

Academic Credit Offered: Per student's own arrangements with academic institution.

ELIGIBILITY: Graduate students, non-students, and career-changers: Anyone with appropriate college degree and skills.

REQUIREMENTS: Must be at least 21 years of age with degree in agriculture, engineering, medicine, public health, or nutrition; Spanish language ability required for Latin American placements.

APPLICATION PROCEDURE: *Contact* Volunteer Coordinator for application form and details. *Deadline:* Open.

COMMERCE, U.S. DEPARTMENT OF

14th and Constitution Avenue NW　　**Phone:**　202/377-3301
Washington, DC 20230　　　　　　　　**FAX:**　　N/A

* * *

ORGANIZATION'S ACTIVITIES: Functions include the International Trade Administration, responsible for U.S. foreign trade activities, promoting exports, and consulting on policy.

Number of Internships: A few.

Type: Technical, administrative, clerical.

Function/Duties: Assist staff as needed.

Schedule: Summers, full-time.

Stipend or Pay: May be arranged.

Academic Credit Offered: Per student's own arrangements with academic institution.

ELIGIBILITY: Undergraduate and graduate students.

REQUIREMENTS: Highly competitive positions located in Washington, D.C.; must be currently enrolled in educational program and have 3.0 GPA, preferably in economics, political science, business, or international relations.

APPLICATION PROCEDURE: Call for application and submit *to* Office of Personnel *by* as early in the year as possible.

COOPERATIVE HOUSE FOUNDATION

P.O. Box 91-280　　　　　　　　　　　**Phone:**　301/587-4700
Washington, DC 20090　　　　　　　　**FAX:**　　N/A

* * *

ORGANIZATION'S ACTIVITIES: Private nonprofit group working to aid families worldwide in improving housing and communities.

Number of Internships: Numerous; varies with projects.

Type: Technical for field work; various managerial for office.

Function/Duties: Aid in field projects; or aid headquarters staff with computer, library, fundraising, other work.

Schedule: Part-time work-week available in office; project-term commitment for field work.

Stipend or Pay: Room and board in field; other arrangements may be possible.

Academic Credit Offered: Per student's own arrangements with academic institution.

ELIGIBILITY: Students, non-students and/or career-changers.

REQUIREMENTS: Language skills and technical specialties a plus; schedule availability a must.

APPLICATION PROCEDURE: *Contact* Intern Coordinator for forms, details. *Deadline:* Open.

COUNCIL ON FOREIGN RELATIONS

58 East 68th Street	**Phone:** 212/734-0400
New York, NY 10021	**FAX:** 212/861-1789

*   *   *

ORGANIZATION'S ACTIVITIES: Nonpartisan organization whose aim is to increase U.S. awareness of significance of international issues; publishes *Foreign Affairs* magazine.

Number of Internships: Varies; approximately 12, including International Affairs Fellowships.

Type: Administrative, clerical, research.

Function/Duties: Assist regular staff on office functions and on research projects.

Schedule: 12 to 25 hours per week, year-round.

Stipend or Pay: Some.

Academic Credit Offered: Per student's own arrangements with academic institution.

ELIGIBILITY: Undergraduate and graduate students; post-doctoral students for Fellowships.

REQUIREMENTS: Interest and background in international relations; Availability to work in New York office.

APPLICATION PROCEDURE: Send cover letter and résumé *to* Assistant Director. *Deadline:* Ongoing.

DEVELOPMENT PLANNING RESEARCH ASSOCIATES, INC.

200 Research Drive	**Phone:** 213/539-3565
Manhattan, KS 66502	**FAX:** N/A

*   *   *

ORGANIZATION'S ACTIVITIES: A private international corporation for agricultural and natural resource research and management under contract with variety of public and private agencies.

Number of Internships: Extensive; varies.

Type: Researchers, analysts, writers.

Function/Duties: Perform research, analysis, report writing.

Schedule: Full-time, though usually on project basis.

Stipend or Pay: Can be arranged.

Academic Credit Offered: Per student's own arrangements with academic institution.

ELIGIBILITY: Some graduate students; non-students or career-changers accepted with appropriate skills; *Plus* possibility for regular employment.

REQUIREMENTS: Independent, innovative, skilled researchers; available for full-time work plus travel.

APPLICATION PROCEDURE: *Contact* Dr. Donald Wissman for application and details. *Deadline:* Open.

EXPORT-IMPORT BANK OF THE U.S.

811 Vermont Avenue NW **Phone:** 202/566-2117
Washington, DC 20571 **FAX:** 202/566-7524

* * *

ORGANIZATION'S ACTIVITIES: A federal government organization that supports the competitiveness of U.S. companies' involvements in overseas markets.

Number of Internships: Varies with need and availability.

Type: Accounting, administration, finance, research, information technology.

Function/Duties: Participate in regular functions of office; assist in special projects.

Schedule: Full-time summers; part-time other semesters.

Stipend or Pay: No.

Academic Credit Offered: Per student's own arrangements with academic institution.

ELIGIBILITY: Graduate and undergraduate students with relevant majors.

REQUIREMENTS: Interests, goals, and/or experience relevant to available assignments.

APPLICATION PROCEDURE: Send application and academic transfer *to* Office of Human Resources *by* several months prior to availability.

THE FOUNDATION FOR A CIVIL SOCIETY

1270 Avenue of the Americas
Suite 609
New York, NY 10020

Phone: 212/332-2895
FAX: 212/332-2890

* * *

ORGANIZATION'S ACTIVITIES: The foundation was established in January 1990 to serve as a networking center to facilitate and support projects that encourage the development of democracy and civil society in the Czech Republic and Slovakia. With the support of foundations, corporations and individuals, the Charter 77 Foundation–New York has rapidly mobilized both human and financial resources to address identified needs in the Czech and Slovak Republics. Currently, the Foundation operates projects of assistance in the governmental, educational, and cultural sectors of Czech and Slovak society.

Number of Internships: Flexible; varies with need.

Type: Program intern.

Function/Duties: Assist with clerical and administrative duties.

Schedule: Part-time and year-round; 15 to 20 hours per week.

Stipend or Pay: $7.50 per hour.

Academic Credit Offered: Per student's own arrangements with academic institution.

ELIGIBILITY: Students in undergraduate studies are preferred; preferred major: Slavic Studies. Graduate students are welcome to apply.

REQUIREMENTS: Must submit a cover letter and résumé, along with an application.

APPLICATION PROCEDURE: Request application and submit full application *to* Eric Nonacs, Program Officer. *Deadline:* Ongoing.

GLOBAL EXCHANGE

2017 Mission Street
San Francisco, CA 94110

Phone: 415/255-7296
FAX: 415/255-7498

* * *

ORGANIZATION'S ACTIVITIES: A nonprofit educational, research, and action center aimed at better understanding between U.S. and Third World countries through tours, exchanges, publications, etc.; a sponsor of internship programs, it needs interns itself.

Number of Internships: Varies with availability.

Type: Research, editorial, communications, clerical.

Function/Duties: Assist staff members with operations and special projects.

Schedule: 8 to 15 hours per week (or more) for at least 1 month; year-round during business hours.

Stipend or Pay: No.

Academic Credit Offered: Per student's own arrangements with academic institution.

ELIGIBILITY: Students, non-students, and career-changers all welcome to apply.

REQUIREMENTS: Creativity and self-motivation, plus availability to work in San Francisco.

APPLICATION PROCEDURE: Request application form and return *to* Administrative Director. *Deadline:* At least 1 month before internship period desired.

HOSTELLING INTERNATIONAL—AMERICAN YOUTH HOSTELS

Greater Boston Council
1020 Commonwealth Avenue   **Phone:**   617/731-6692
Boston, MA 02215   **FAX:**   617/734-7614

* * *

ORGANIZATION'S ACTIVITIES: A nonprofit organization that promotes international understanding through educational programming, organized trips, and overnight hostel stays. Connected to an international network, the Boston center provides international information and access, while supporting a network of New England hostels.

Number of Internships: 12 to 18 per year.

Type: Fundraising, recruitment, real estate development, education curriculum development, marketing, publications.

Function/Duties: Work directly with staff on projects assigned according to intern's skills and interests.

Schedule: Minimum of 12 hours per week for full-semester commitment.

Stipend or Pay: Free 1-year membership in hostelling organization; housing available in Boston hostel.

Academic Credit Offered: In most cases.

ELIGIBILITY: Junior and senior-year undergraduate students; graduate students welcome as well.

REQUIREMENTS: Affinity with purposes of organization; excellent communications skills; ability to work independently; experience and/or coursework in areas related to assignments desired.

APPLICATION PROCEDURE: Write *to* Student Internship Program Director for application details. *Deadline:* Ongoing.

INSTITUTE OF INTERNATIONAL EDUCATION (IIE)

PO Box 3087   **Phone:**   210/211-0042
Laredo, TX 78044   **FAX:**   N/A

* * *

ORGANIZATION'S ACTIVITIES: A division of the U.S. Information Service, which provides overseas information about American educational opportunities.

Number of Internships: Varies with assignment and locale.

Type: Educational counseling programs.

Function/Duties: Advise Latin American students at IIE Mexico City location on educational opportunities in the U.S.; assist with research and other projects.

Schedule: About 2 months full-time throughout the year in Mexico City.

Stipend or Pay: $500; aid with housing.

Academic Credit Offered: Per student's own arrangements with academic institution.

ELIGIBILITY: Students, and non-students, with at least 2 years of college.

REQUIREMENTS: Good communication skills in Spanish and in English, plus knowledge of Mexican history and culture.

APPLICATION PROCEDURE: Send application, transcript, résumé, and letters of recommendation *to* Educational Counselling Center *by* 3 months prior to availability.

Number of Internships: Varies with assignment and locale.

Type: International visitors programs.

Function/Duties: Guide visiting faculty and students through parts of their stay in the U.S.; prepare information to facilitate their activities; perform organizational activities related to these projects.

Schedule: Full- and/or part-time during spring, fall, summer semesters; in Washington and/or New York office.

Stipend or Pay: No.

Academic Credit Offered: Per student's own arrangements with academic institution.

ELIGIBILITY: Consideration given to students, non-students, or career-changers with appropriate qualifications.

REQUIREMENTS: Interests, goals, and/or experience relevant to available assignments.

APPLICATION PROCEDURE: Send inquiries *to* Internship Coordinator *by* 3 months prior to availability.

INTERNATIONAL DEVELOPMENT ASSOCIATION

1818 H Street NW	**Phone:** 202/477-1234
Washington, DC 20433	**FAX:** 202/477-6391

* * *

ORGANIZATION'S ACTIVITIES: An affiliate of the World Bank, a UN-related agency, the IDA provides funds for special projects in poorer nations.

Number of Internships: Varies; numerous.

Type: Research, finance, statistics, data processing.

Function/Duties: Assist staff in regular functions and on special projects.

Schedule: Full-time, summers.

Stipend or Pay: Yes.

Academic Credit Offered: Per student's own arrangements with academic institution.

ELIGIBILITY: Undergraduate or graduate students in relevant areas of study; as well as non-students with related experience who plan to return to school.

REQUIREMENTS: Computer skills; Spanish or French skills a plus.

APPLICATION PROCEDURE: Submit resume *to* Summer Employment Program *by* end of February.

THE INTERNATIONAL FINANCE CORPORATION

1818 H Street NW
Washington, DC 20433

Phone: 202/477-1234
FAX: 202/477-6391

* * *

ORGANIZATION'S ACTIVITIES: An affiliate of the World Bank, a UN-related agency, the IFC encourages the growth of the private sector in developing countries.

Number of Internships: Varies; numerous.

Type: Research, finance, statistics, data processing.

Function/Duties: Assist staff in regular functions and on special projects.

Schedule: Full-time, summers.

Stipend or Pay: Yes.

Academic Credit Offered: Per student's own arrangements with academic institution.

ELIGIBILITY: Undergraduate or graduate students in relevant areas of study; as well as non-students with related experience who plan to return to school.

REQUIREMENTS: Computer skills; Spanish or French skills a plus.

APPLICATION PROCEDURE: Submit resume *to* Summer Employment Program *by* end of February.

INTERNATIONAL LABOR ORGANIZATION

220 East 42nd Street
New York, NY 10017

Phone: 212/697-0150
FAX: 212/883-0844

* * *

ORGANIZATION'S ACTIVITIES: A UN agency concerned with collaboration among governments, workers, and employers to resolve work-related matters worldwide. Headquartered in Geneva, Switzerland, the ILO has offices worldwide, including a major center in Washington, D.C.

Number of Internships: Varies; numerous.

Type: Research, communications, translations, writing, administration.

Function/Duties: Assist regular staff with publications, reports, research, data processing, staffing.

Schedule: Minimum of 15 hours per week, year-round.

Stipend or Pay: No, but some reimbursements arranged.

Academic Credit Offered: Per student's own arrangements with academic institution.

ELIGIBILITY: Undergraduate and graduate students with relevant majors, *Plus* increases chances for regular employment.

REQUIREMENTS: Related interests and goals; language skills a plus.

APPLICATION PROCEDURE: Send inquiries *to* Intern Coordinator. *Deadline:* Open.

INTERNATIONAL MONETARY FUND

700 19th Street NW
Washington, DC 20431

Phone: 202/623-7000
FAX: 202/623-4661

* * *

ORGANIZATION'S ACTIVITIES: A UN agency funded by member nations to aid in maintaining members' financial balance situations.

Number of Internships: Varies with need.

Type: Research.

Function/Duties: Aid in research and other projects.

Schedule: 10 to 13 weeks, mostly summers.

Stipend or Pay: Yes.

Academic Credit Offered: Yes.

ELIGIBILITY: Graduate students, *Plus* interns may become candidates for career positions.

REQUIREMENTS: Strong academic record with advanced studies in economics; excellent skills in English.

APPLICATION PROCEDURE: Send inquiries *to* Personnel Officer *by* early in the academic year.

INTERNATIONAL TRADE ADMINISTRATION

14th Street and Constitution Avenue NW   **Phone:** 212/566-2748
Washington, DC 20230   **FAX:**   N/A

* * *

ORGANIZATION'S ACTIVITIES: A division of the U.S. Department of Commerce that provides information and advice to American business and government on international finance and investing; regional offices.

Number of Internships: Varies; numerous.

Type: Research, analysis, communications, administration.

Function/Duties: Assist staff in headquarters and in regional offices with regular functions and special projects.

Schedule: Flexible, depending on need and location: full- and/or part-time; summers and/or year-round.

Stipend or Pay: Some paid.

Academic Credit Offered: Per student's own arrangements with academic institution.

ELIGIBILITY: Undergraduate and graduate students in related majors.

REQUIREMENTS: Interests, goals, and/or experience relevant to available assignments.

APPLICATION PROCEDURE: Send inquiries *to* Personnel Office *by* several months prior to availability, including request for regional location.

INTERNATIONAL VOLUNTARY SERVICES, INC.

1424 16th Street NW
Suite 603
Washington, DC 20036   **Phone:** 202/387-5533
                                   FAX: 202/387-4234

* * *

ORGANIZATION'S ACTIVITIES: Founded in 1953, IVS is a private nonprofit development agency that sends volunteers skilled in a variety of technical areas to work with host organizations in developing countries. IVS programs are designed to promote and sustain self-development throughout Asia and Latin America. The Washington office is concerned with administration and fundraising.

Number of Internships: 1.

Type: AIDS prevention program intern.

Function/Duties: Work with the AIDS prevention programs in Thailand, Viet Nam, Bangladesh, Cambodia, and in the U.S.-based clearinghouse project. The intern is expected to assist in coordinating the AIDS clearinghouse (gathering articles, data on the international AIDS epidemic for dissemination to an international network of partner agencies, writing summary letters on the latest social-psychological literature on HIV-prevention, etc.). The project intern will also assist in fundraising efforts (appeal letters, full proposals to foundations, etc.). Computer proficiency is required.

Schedule: Intern is expected to work at least 2 full days per week, one of which must be either Saturday or Friday; seasonal internships begin September 1, February 1, and June 1.

Stipend or Pay: None.

Academic Credit Offered: Per intern's own arrangement with academic institution.

ELIGIBILITY: Undergraduate and graduate students interested in AIDS crisis and international development are encouraged to apply. *Plus* internship may lead to employment opportunities.

REQUIREMENTS: Must submit a cover letter, résumé, and references.

Number of Internships: Numerous; varies with projects.

Type: Agricultural, public health, business management.

Function/Duties: Assist residents with establishment and maintenance of own small-scale self-support projects.

Schedule: Must serve 2 to 3 years in country.

Stipend or Pay: Room, board, travel costs.

Academic Credit Offered: Per student's own arrangements with academic institution.

ELIGIBILITY: Graduate students, non-students, and career-changers— anyone with appropriate college degree and experience.

REQUIREMENTS: College degree and 2 years' experience in technical field offered.

Number of Internships: 1.

Type: Andes program intern.

Function/Duties: The Andes program intern will work directly with the program administrator, who serves as the field volunteers' link to Washington, keeping track of field activities and helping to coordinate between the field and the Washington office. Duties will include assisting in office administrative related work; interpreting/translating (from Spanish to English) and/or summarizing incoming reports for use by all IVS staff; working with the fundraising office to identify foundations, develop proposals for funding projects and writing proposals to these funders; preparing draft reports on each of the Andes projects, including the agroforestry work with the Shuar peoples in Ecuador, the Women's Health Project in the Chota Afro-Ecuadorean community, the Livestock Improvement in Ecuador, Women's Agriculture in Ecuador, the Handcrafts Project in the Bolivian Altiplano, etc. Good command of the Spanish language is a must! Computer proficiency is necessary.

Schedule: Seasonal internships begin September 1, February 1, and June 1.

Stipend or Pay: None.

Academic Credit Offered: Per intern's own arrangements with academic institution.

ELIGIBILITY: Undergraduate and graduate students interested in Latin America and international development.

APPLICATION PROCEDURE: *Contact* Volunteer Coordinator for details and application for year-round openings. *Deadline:* Open.

INTERNATIONAL WORKCAMPS

Council on International Educational Exchange
205 East 42nd Street   **Phone:** 212/661-1414
New York, NY 10017   **FAX:** 212/972-2321

* * *

ORGANIZATION'S ACTIVITIES: Promotes international understanding and environmental improvements through organizing volunteer work projects in camps around the world.

Number of Internships: Thousands of opportunities.

Type: Manual labor, building, farming.

Function/Duties: Participate in cooperative activities that vary with projects.

Schedule: Usually 2- to 4-week sessions, late June through early September.

Stipend or Pay: No—*and* placement fees are charged; but room and board provided.

Academic Credit Offered: Per student's own arrangements with academic institution.

ELIGIBILITY: Students, non-students, and career-changers are welcome to apply.

REQUIREMENTS: Must be 18 or over; no special skills needed, but some projects require language ability.

APPLICATION PROCEDURE: Request information detailing placements and costs and submit application form *to* CIEE *by* 4 to 6 weeks prior to workcamp starting date desired.

LOS NIÑOS

1330 Continental Street   **Phone:** 619/661-6912
San Ysidro, CA 92073   **FAX:** N/A

* * *

ORGANIZATION'S ACTIVITIES: A nonprofit community development organization devoted to improving the lives of Mexican children in towns and rural areas on the Mexican/U.S. border.

Number of Internships: Several hundred.

Type: Administrative, educational, publications.

Function/Duties: Teaching, economic development, hands-on work projects in the field; public affairs and administrative in the office.

Schedule: Long-term program: minimum of 1 year; short-term and summer, several weeks to several months.

Stipend or Pay: Maintenance expenses for long-term program.

Academic Credit Offered: Per student's own arrangements with academic institution.

ELIGIBILITY: Students, non-students, and career-changers are welcome.

REQUIREMENTS: Interests, goals, and/or experience relevant to available assignments; Spanish language ability necessary.

APPLICATION PROCEDURE: Send inquiries *to* Intern Coordinator. *Deadline:* Ongoing.

MENNONITE CENTRAL COMMITTEE

21 South 12th Street   **Phone:** 717/859-1151
Akron, PA 17501   **FAX:** N/A

* * *

ORGANIZATION'S ACTIVITIES: Sponsors social service projects overseas and in the U.S.

Number of Internships: About 500 overseas.

Type: Youth programs and worker-service projects offering training and crosscultural learning during service in Third World countries.

Function/Duties: Community organization, construction, education, support; specific assignments depend on intern's interests and skills and on community needs.

Schedule: 6 months to 2 years, depending on program.

Stipend or Pay: Room, board, and expenses paid.

Academic Credit Offered: Per student's own arrangements with academic institution.

ELIGIBILITY: Students, non-students, career-changers, and workers with any kind of special skills.

REQUIREMENTS: Active members of a Christian church (not necessarily Mennonite) committed to a nonviolent and peacemaking life style.

APPLICATION PROCEDURE: Apply *to* Personnel Department *by* about 6 months in advance of internship availability.

ORGANIZATION OF AMERICAN STATES (OAS)

1889 F Street NW   **Phone:** 202/458-6046
Washington, DC 20006   **FAX:** N/A

* * *

ORGANIZATION'S ACTIVITIES: International body whose mission is promotion of peace and economic stability among the nations of the Americas.

Number of Internships: Varies with need.

Type: Research, writing, administration.

Function/Duties: Assist regular staff with assignments and special projects.

Schedule: Full-time summers and full- and part-time during other school semesters.

Stipend or Pay: No.

Academic Credit Offered: Per student's own arrangements with academic institution.

ELIGIBILITY: Undergraduate and graduate students. *Special Eligibilities:* National of any OAS member state.

REQUIREMENTS: Meet nationality requirements, and have working knowledge of French and/or Portuguese, as well as good skills in English and Spanish.

APPLICATION PROCEDURE: Submit application form, letters of reference, and résumé *to* Internship Coordinator *by* June 15 for fall, November 15 for winter/spring, and March 15 for summer.

OVERSEAS PRIVATE INVESTMENT CORPORATION

1615 M Street NW
Washington, DC 20527

Phone: 202/475-7010
FAX: 202/331-4234

* * *

ORGANIZATION'S ACTIVITIES: U.S. government agency responsible for promoting American investing in developing nations.

Number of Internships: Varies.

Type: Finance, marketing, international relations, research.

Function/Duties: Research and significant assistance to professional staff on regular activities as well as special projects.

Schedule: Full- and part-time, year-round.

Stipend or Pay: No.

Academic Credit Offered: Per student's own arrangements with academic institution.

ELIGIBILITY: Graduate and undergraduate students.

REQUIREMENTS: U.S. citizenship; studying relevant majors.

APPLICATION PROCEDURE: Send résumé and transcript with cover letter *to* Internship Coordinator. *Deadline:* Open.

PACIFIC INTERNATIONAL EXCHANGE

4225 Executive Square
Suite 1190
La Jolla, CA 92037

Phone: 619/597-1043
FAX: 619/597-0817

* * *

ORGANIZATION'S ACTIVITIES: Nonprofit exchange program for high-school students.

Number of Internships: Varies with need.

Type: Office assistant.

Function/Duties: Making copies, mailing packages, etc.

Schedule: Part-time.

Stipend or Pay: No.

Academic Credit Offered: Per student's own arrangement with academic institution.

ELIGIBILITY: All students; preferred majors: International Affairs and Guidance. Non-students welcome to apply.

APPLICATION PROCEDURE: *Send* letter with name, phone number, and reason interested *to* Trinan Verwys, Information Distribution Manager.

PEOPLE TO PEOPLE, INTERNATIONAL

501 East Armour Boulevard
Kansas City, MO 64109

Phone: 816/531-4701
FAX: 816/561-7502

* * *

ORGANIZATION'S ACTIVITIES: The promotion of international understanding and friendship through educational and cultural activities involving the direct exchange of ideas and experiences among peoples of different countries and diverse cultures.

Number of Internships: Varies with placement; numerous.

Type: Overseas internship.

Function/Duties: Each internship is tailormade for the individual seeking more in-depth exposure to a particular culture and employment situation.

Schedule: 8-week term during the spring, summer, or fall.

Stipend or Pay: No.

Academic Credit Offered: 6 hours.

ELIGIBILITY: College juniors and seniors, graduate students. Non-students and career-changers are welcome to apply.

REQUIREMENTS: Must be in good health.

APPLICATION PROCEDURE: Request application and submit résumé, cover letter, transcript, and application *to* Dr. Alan M. Warne.

QUAKER UNITED NATIONS OFFICE

13 Avenue du Mervelet
CH-1209 Genéve 1209   **Phone:** (22)-733-3397
Switzerland   **FAX:**   N/A
or
777 United Nations Plaza   **Phone:** 212/682-2745
New York, NY 10017   **FAX:**   N/A

* * *

ORGANIZATION'S ACTIVITIES: Promote peace-and-justice goals and values of Society of Friends (Quakers) in UN activities and agencies.

Number of Internships: Varies.

Type: Research, advocacy, communications.

Function/Duties: Assist with ongoing functions and special projects.

Schedule: 6- to 12-month commitments, full- or part-time.

Stipend or Pay: Subsistence grants may be arranged.

Academic Credit Offered: Per student's own arrangements with academic institution.

ELIGIBILITY: Students, non-students, or career-changers are all welcome; an equal-opportunity organization.

REQUIREMENTS: Interests, goals, and/or experience relevant to available assignments; French-language skill useful in Swiss office.

APPLICATION PROCEDURE: Send résumé with cover letter *to* Joel McClennan in Switzerland or Barbara Elfrandt in New York *by* several months prior to internship desired.

RADIO FREE EUROPE/RADIO LIBERTY

1201 Connecticut Avenue NW   **Phone:** 202/457-6900
Washington, DC 20036   **FAX:**   202/457-6974

* * *

ORGANIZATION'S ACTIVITIES: An independent broadcasting corporation with the mission of encouraging communication throughout Europe by providing information on international news and issues.

Number of Internships: Varies depending on need.

Type: Research, engineering.

Function/Duties: Research interns assist writers and broadcasters; engineers learn and assist in broadcast techniques.

Schedule: 2 to 3 months in the summer in European locations.

Stipend or Pay: Maintenance stipend, plus living accommodations and round-trip air fare.

Academic Credit Offered: Per student's own arrangements with academic institution.

ELIGIBILITY: Graduate and some undergraduate students.

REQUIREMENTS: Skills in appropriate foreign language; engineering studies or experience.

APPLICATION PROCEDURE: Request details and application form *from* Summer Internship Program *by* as early in the school year as possible.

SANEFREEZE

777 UN Plaza	**Phone:**	212/949-7033
New York, NY 10017	**FAX:**	N/A
or		
1819 H Street NW	**Phone:**	202/862-9740
Washington, DC 20006	**FAX:**	202/862-9762

* * *

ORGANIZATION'S ACTIVITIES: Private nonprofit membership group dedicated to world peace.

Number of Internships: Varies; numerous.

Type: Public affairs, education, communications.

Function/Duties: Tour guides, events with foreign visitors, communications with other peace groups; clerical. NYC office focuses on UN and members, D.C. group focuses on national activities and missions centered there.

Schedule: According to intern's needs.

Stipend or Pay: No.

Academic Credit Offered: Per student's own arrangements with academic institution.

ELIGIBILITY: Students, non-students, and career-changers: "Anyone from high school to the elderly."

REQUIREMENTS: Interests, goals, and/or experience relevant to available assignments.

APPLICATION PROCEDURE: *Contact* appropriate office. *Deadline:* No.

STATE, U.S. DEPARTMENT OF

Recruitment Division		
Box 12209, Rosslyn Station	**Phone:**	703/875-7242
Arlington, VA 22209	**FAX:**	703/875-1027

* * *

ORGANIZATION'S ACTIVITIES: Responsible for managing the nation's foreign affairs.

Number of Internships: Numerous.

Type: Openings available in most of the department's divisions, including the bureaus of African Affairs, Consular Affairs, East Asian Affairs, European and Canadian Affairs, Inter-American Affairs, Near Eastern Affairs, and the offices of Personnel, Law, and Public Affairs.

Function/Duties: Assigned as entry-level professionals, performing research, communications, and similar functions.

Schedule: Year-round as well as summer-only, full- and part-time.

Stipend or Pay: Some unpaid; others receive standard government compensation.

Academic Credit Offered: Per student's own arrangements with academic institution.

ELIGIBILITY: Graduate and undergraduate students, preferably those studying political science, international relations, or appropriate languages; *Plus* internship often leads to regular employment.

REQUIREMENTS: Must be currently enrolled in academic study, on at least a half-time basis.

APPLICATION PROCEDURE: Send inquiries *to* Intern Coordinator in time to apply *by* at least 6 months prior to availability.

TREASURY, U.S. DEPARTMENT OF

15th and Pennsylvania Avenue NW	**Phone:** 202/566-5411
Washington, DC 20220	**FAX:** 202/566-8066

* * *

ORGANIZATION'S ACTIVITIES: Advises Congress and the Executive branch on financial policy; manages and supervises domestic and international monetary matters.

Number of Internships: Varies.

Type: Financial management service, Multilateral Development Banks office; other staffs, including administrative and information technologies.

Function/Duties: Research, communications, other activities depending on assignment.

Schedule: Year-round, part- and full-time.

Stipend or Pay: Some stipends arranged.

Academic Credit Offered: Per student's own arrangements with academic institution.

ELIGIBILITY: Undergraduate and graduate students.

REQUIREMENTS: Availability to work in Washington, D.C.; preferred majors: Economics, Computer Science, and/or International Relations.

APPLICATION PROCEDURE: Send inquiries *to* Internship Coordinator. *Deadline:* Open.

TECHNOSERVE

49 Day Street
South Norwalk, CT 06854

Phone: 203/852-0377
FAX: N/A

* * *

ORGANIZATION'S ACTIVITIES: A private nonprofit organization providing technical and managerial assistance to help developing countries build community-based enterprises.

Number of Internships: Varies, depending on need.

Type: Business, management, engineering, finance, agricultural science.

Function/Duties: Work with local nationals and organizations to develop projects to meet specific needs.

Schedule: Term according to project length, up to 1 or 2 years or more; residential full-time through field offices in Africa and Latin America.

Stipend or Pay: Maintenance.

Academic Credit Offered: Per student's own arrangements with academic institution where relevant.

ELIGIBILITY: Non-students, including career-changers, with college and graduate degrees in appropriate subjects.

REQUIREMENTS: Experience and/or education relevant to goals; foreign language ability.

APPLICATION PROCEDURE: Send inquiries *to* Internship Coordinator. *Deadline:* Ongoing.

UNITED NATIONS ASSOCIATION OF THE USA (UNAUSA)

485 Fifth Avenue
New York, NY 10017

Phone: 212/697-3232
FAX: 212/682-9185

* * *

ORGANIZATION'S ACTIVITIES: Private nonprofit organization dedicated to enhancing the effectiveness of the United Nations and of the U.S. role in the organization.

Number of Internships: Varies; numerous.

Type: Research, publications, communications.

Function/Duties: Highly substantive activities, including writing, research, and events organizing at New York, Washington, and regional offices.

Schedule: Full- and/or part-time, during school semesters and in summer.

Stipend or Pay: No.

Academic Credit Offered: Yes.

ELIGIBILITY: Graduate and undergraduate students.

REQUIREMENTS: Writing ability, plus interests, goals, and/or experience relevant to available assignments.

APPLICATION PROCEDURE: Send cover letter, résumé, and writing samples *to* Director of Field Administration *by* several months prior to internship availability.

UNITED NATIONS CHILDREN'S EMERGENCY FUND (UNICEF)

3 UN Plaza   **Phone:** 212/362-7000
New York, NY 10017   **FAX:** N/A

* * *

ORGANIZATION'S ACTIVITIES: UN relief and development agency that focuses on international community welfare and health-enhancement projects.

Number of Internships: Varies.

Type: Research, analysis, communications, education.

Function/Duties: Assist staff with ongoing development projects and special research.

Schedule: Flexible; in New York office and occasionally elsewhere.

Stipend or Pay: Expenses reimbursement as needed.

Academic Credit Offered: Per student's own arrangements with academic institution.

ELIGIBILITY: Graduate students in relevant areas of study; *Plus* increases chances for regular employment.

REQUIREMENTS: Interests, goals, and/or experience relevant to available assignments.

APPLICATION PROCEDURE: Send inquiries *to* Internship Coordinator. *Deadline:* Open.

THE UNITED NATIONS INSTITUTE FOR TRAINING AND RESEARCH

801 UN Plaza   **Phone:** 212/963-8622
New York, NY 10017   **FAX:** N/A

* * *

ORGANIZATION'S ACTIVITIES: A UN office that trains diplomats.

Number of Internships: Varies as needed.

Type: Research.

Function/Duties: Aid in research and other projects as needed.

Schedule: Flexible; varies with need.

Stipend or Pay: No.

Academic Credit Offered: Per student's own arrangements with academic institution.

ELIGIBILITY: Undergraduate and graduate students as well as non-students and career-changers; *Plus* increases chances for regular employment.

REQUIREMENTS: Language ability a plus; availability for work in New York office.

APPLICATION PROCEDURE: Send résumé and letter of interest *to* Director of Training. *Deadline:* Open.

UNITED NATIONS VOLUNTEERS PROGRAMME

1990 K Street NW	**Phone:** 202/606-3370
Washington, DC 20526	**FAX:** 202/606-3108

* * *

ORGANIZATION'S ACTIVITIES: International long-term development projects as well as short-term disaster-relief activities, under UN auspices, administered through U.S. Peace Corps.

Number of Internships: Hundreds.

Type: Community organization, technical, health, economic development assistance.

Function/Duties: Work in field projects (or emergency relief) as assigned around the world.

Schedule: 2-year residential commitment (shorter for emergency volunteers).

Stipend or Pay: Room and board, plus minimal stipends.

Academic Credit Offered: Unusual, and only per student's own arrangements with academic institution.

ELIGIBILITY: Although students and young adults are accepted, most in this program are older, non-students and career-changers. Retirees and women especially encouraged to apply; *Plus* training is provided.

REQUIREMENTS: Relevant education and/or experience preferred; for disaster-relief volunteers, 2 years' experience required.

APPLICATION PROCEDURE: Request information and details *from* UN Volunteer Director. *Deadline:* Ongoing.

US COMMITTEE FOR UNICEF

331 East 38th Street	**Phone:** 212/686-5522
New York, NY 10016	**FAX:** N/A

* * *

ORGANIZATION'S ACTIVITIES: A private nonprofit organization dedicated to the support of the United Nations International Children's Fund.

Number of Internships: Varies; some in NY office, some regional.

Type: Administrative, communications, development.

Function/Duties: Assist staff as needed with ongoing operations and special projects.

Schedule: Full- and/or part-time; seasonal and/or year-round.

Stipend or Pay: No.

Academic Credit Offered: Yes.

ELIGIBILITY: Consideration given to students, non-students, or career-changers with appropriate qualifications.

REQUIREMENTS: Interests, goals, and/or experience relevant to available assignments.

APPLICATION PROCEDURE: Request details and application form *from* Intern Coordinator. *Deadline:* Open.

U.S.—ASIA INSTITUTE

232 East Capitol Street NE   **Phone:**   202/544-3181
Washington DC 20003   **FAX:**   N/A

*   *   *

ORGANIZATION'S ACTIVITIES: Nonprofit organization of Americans of Asian descent as well as individuals and companies with an interest in US-Asia trade and cooperation.

Number of Internships: Varies (competitive).

Type: Chan Future Leader Award.

Function/Duties: Participate actively in various activities of the Institute, including research, events, and legislative activities.

Schedule: Varies with assignment and semester.

Stipend or Pay: Yes.

Academic Credit Offered: Per student's own arrangements with academic institution.

ELIGIBILITY: Competition among Asian-American college students for internship positions.

REQUIREMENTS: Winners of competition.

APPLICATION PROCEDURE: Send inquiries *to* Internship Coordinator *by* as early in the school year as possible.

U.S. SERVAS, INC.

11 John Street
Suite 407   **Phone:**   212/267-0292
New York, NY 10038   **FAX:**   212/267-0292

*   *   *

ORGANIZATION'S ACTIVITIES: Servas is an international cooperative system of hosts and travelers established to help build world peace, good will, and cultural understanding by providing opportunities for deeper, more personal contacts among people of diverse cultures and backgrounds. Visitors are invited to share life in the home and in the community.

Number of Internships: Flexible; varies with need.

Type: Varies.

Function/Duties: Assignments as needed. Provide office support according to intern's skills and interests; computer, typing, communication, and writing skills are preferred. One full-time and 2 part-time internships will be available. Seasonal: Fall, spring, summer.

Stipend or Pay: No.

Academic Credit Offered: Per intern's own arrangements with academic institution.

ELIGIBILITY: Students in high school and above with majors in International Relations, Business Administration, and Communications are encouraged to apply. Open to non-students and career-changers as well. *Special Eligibilities:* Equal-opportunity employer—people of color, senior citizens, and women are encouraged to apply.

REQUIREMENTS: Must provide a résumé along with an application.

APPLICATION PROCEDURE: Submit full application *to* Nellie Herman, Administrator. *Deadline:* Open.

VISIONS IN ACTION

3637 Fulton Street NW **Phone:** 202/963-1234
Washington, DC 20007 **FAX:** N/A

* * *

ORGANIZATION'S ACTIVITIES: Urban development internship programs in Africa.

Number of Internships: Varies; numerous.

Type: Project management, education, community organization, health care.

Function/Duties: Varies with project and with skills of intern.

Schedule: Full-time residential; 6-month programs in various countries in Africa.

Stipend or Pay: No—*and* fairly high expense fee is required.

Academic Credit Offered: Per student's own arrangements with academic institution.

ELIGIBILITY: Junior or senior college students or non-student career-changers with equivalent experience; *Plus* 1-month training program is included.

REQUIREMENTS: Must have skills in demand by assignment and be able to afford or pay fee.

APPLICATION PROCEDURE: Request application form.

VOICE OF AMERICA

330 Independence Avenue SW   **Phone:** 202/619-3117
Washington, DC 20547   **FAX:** N/A

*   *   *

ORGANIZATION'S ACTIVITIES: A U.S. government broadcast information service.

Number of Internships: Varies; numerous.

Type: Journalism, communications, linguistics, broadcast engineering.

Function/Duties: Assignments throughout organization, including reporting, writing, translating, production.

Schedule: Part-time, year-round.

Stipend or Pay: No.

Academic Credit Offered: Yes.

ELIGIBILITY: Students of any kind; *Plus* may lead to regular employment.

REQUIREMENTS: Enrollment at least part-time in any accredited educational institution.

APPLICATION PROCEDURE: Request application form and details *from* Office of Personnel. *Deadline:* Ongoing.

WASHINGTON CENTER FOR INTERNSHIPS AND ACADEMIC SEMINARS

514 10th Street NW   **Phone:** 202/624-8030
Washington, DC 20004   **FAX:** N/A

*   *   *

ORGANIZATION'S ACTIVITIES: Sponsors internship programs in Washington-based organizations as well as academic seminars for students and faculty on globally related topics.

Number of Internships: Varies.

Type: Communications, research, development.

Function/Duties: Office work, reports, fundraising, events coordination.

Schedule: Full-time during fall, spring, or summer semester.

Stipend or Pay: No; housing available.

Academic Credit Offered: Yes.

ELIGIBILITY: Undergraduate and graduate students in any major; *Plus* weekly seminars with special speakers, as well as social events.

REQUIREMENTS: B+ average in any major.

APPLICATION PROCEDURE: Request details and information *from* Director of Institutional Relations. *Deadline:* Open.

THE WORLD BANK

1818 H Street NW   **Phone:**   202/477-1234
Washington, DC 20433   **FAX:**   202/477-6391

* * *

ORGANIZATION'S ACTIVITIES: A UN-related agency that provides or arranges for loans and technical assistance to developing nations for economic development projects.

Number of Internships: Varies; numerous.

Type: Research, finance, statistics, data processing.

Function/Duties: Assist staff in regular functions and on special projects.

Schedule: Full-time, summers.

Stipend or Pay: Yes.

Academic Credit Offered: Per student's own arrangements with academic institution.

ELIGIBILITY: Graduate students in relevant areas of study.

REQUIREMENTS: Computer skills, proficiency in at least one foreign language.

APPLICATION PROCEDURE: Submit résumé *to* Summer Employment Program *by* end of February.

WORLD FEDERALIST ASSOCIATION

418 7th Street SE   **Phone:**   202/546-3950
Washington, DC 20001   **FAX:**   202/546-3649

* * *

ORGANIZATION'S ACTIVITIES: The U.S. branch of an international movement seeking to replace global anarchy with a system of limited global governance through formal global cooperation to solve global problems.

Number of Internships: 5 or more.

Type: Research, lobbying, and administration.

Function/Duties: Aid directors in researching background of issues, preparing legislative efforts, and coordinating membership and activities of office and local chapters.

Schedule: Flexible, about 30 hours per week.

Stipend or Pay: Small stipend for expenses.

Academic Credit Offered: Per student's own arrangements with academic institution.

ELIGIBILITY: Primarily graduate and undergraduate students.

REQUIREMENTS: Strong communications skills and organizational ability, plus commitment "to building a better, more peaceful world."

APPLICATION PROCEDURE: Send résumé and letter of interest *to* Student Programs Director in time to schedule interview and complete applications *by* at least 1 month prior to start date.

WORLDTEACH

One Eliot Street   **Phone:** 617/495-5527
Cambridge, MA 02318   **FAX:** N/A

*   *   *

ORGANIZATION'S ACTIVITIES: An activity of the Harvard Institute for International Development, WorldTeach sends volunteer teachers to developing countries around the world.

Number of Internships: Approximately 12.

Type: Administrative and planning, in headquarters office.

Function/Duties: Aid staff in coordinating activities of organization; may develop into teaching and social service work.

Schedule: Full-time in summers; part-time during school semesters.

Stipend or Pay: $100 per week during summer; $50 per week during school semesters.

Academic Credit Offered: Per student's own arrangements with academic institution.

ELIGIBILITY: Consideration given to students, non-students, or career-changers with appropriate qualifications.

REQUIREMENTS: Interests, goals, and/or experience relevant to available assignments.

APPLICATION PROCEDURE: Send résumé, references, and cover letter *to* Office Manager *by* several months prior to availability.

Organizations/Resources for Further Information about Internships in International Organizations

THE COUNCIL ON INTERNATIONAL EDUCATIONAL EXCHANGE (CIEE)
205 East 42nd Street   Phone: 212/661-1414
New York, NY 10017   FAX: N/A

A private nonprofit membership organization with offices throughout the U.S., Europe, and Asia, was founded in 1947 to help reestablish student exchange after the Second World War. Over the years, CIEE's mandate has broadened dramatically, and today CIEE assumes responsibility for developing and administering programs of international educational exchange throughout the world, coordinating work-abroad programs and international workcamps, and facilitating inexpensive international travel for students, teachers, and other budget travelers.

It also publishes directories and other materials of value to anyone considering traveling, working, or interning abroad.

INTERNATIONAL ASSOCIATION FOR THE EXCHANGE OF STUDENTS FOR
    TECHNICAL EXPERIENCE (IAESTE)
Administered by AIPT
10 Corporate Center
10400 Little Patuxent Parkway   Phone: 410/997-3068
Columbia, MD 21044   FAX: 410/992-3924

Coordinates on-the-job training programs in over 50 countries to offer practical training in scientific and technical fields to juniors, seniors, and graduate students in any accredited U.S. college or university studying engineering, computer science, math sciences, architecture, or agriculture.

In general, placements last 3 to 12 months, with salary and a maintenance allowance paid for living expenses. Fluency in a foreign language may be required in some cases. Applications accepted year-round, but must be received 4 months prior to internship period desired. Call or write for details.

INTERNATIONAL ASSOCIATION OF STUDENTS IN ECONOMICS AND COMMERCE
    (AISEC)
841 Broadway   Phone: 212/979-7400
New York, NY 10003   FAX: N/A

A worldwide students' organization offering programs in 70 countries that allow undergraduate and graduate students to participate in a wide variety of management and other activities in commercial projects around the world, paid and unpaid, from 6 weeks to 18 months.

Open *only* to students of academic institutions that are members of AISEC; contact your college activities office or AISEC for details.

NATIONAL COUNCIL FOR WORLD AFFAIRS ORGANIZATIONS
1726 M Street NW
Suite 800   Phone: 202/785-4703
Washington, DC 20036 FAX: 202/833-2369

An umbrella-organization of international groups focused on social service and public affairs; can serve as a clearinghouse for information on global organizations that sponsor internships.

OVERSEAS DEVELOPMENT NETWORK (ODN)
2141 Mission Street   Phone: 415/255-7296
San Francisco, CA 94110   FAX: N/A

Coordinates internship placements in community-based organizations sponsoring educational, environmental, and economic development and other socially responsible projects around the world. Also sponsors "Global Exchange" for those interested in Third World development work through international social-justice agencies. Projects in general are unpaid, but are open to all. Contact organization for lists of participating groups.

PARTNERSHIP FOR SERVICE LEARNING
815 2nd Avenue   Phone: 212/986-0989
New York, NY 10017   FAX: N/A

A coalition of university and service organizations that offers and serves as a clearinghouse for programs of study and intercultural experience combined with community service in Third World countries, available to high-school seniors, college students, and recent grads as well as working professionals in a variety of placements throughout the year.

THE UNITED NATIONS
Internship Programs
2 UN Plaza   Phone: 212/963-1234
New York, NY 10017   FAX: N/A

Listing available of internship opportunities within a connected network with the UN and its agencies around the world.

PUBLICATIONS

The ODN Development Opportunities Catalog lists employment and internship opportunities with United States-based international development organizations. Updated and revised second edition. Students: $7; individuals: $10; institutions: $15.

The Peace Corps and More, subtitled "114 Ways to Work, Study, and Travel in the Third World," contains over 100 suggestions of organizations that allow you to gain Third World experience while promoting the ideals of social justice and sustainable development.

Both published by Overseas Development Network, 333 Valencia St., San Francisco, CA 94103, phone: 415/431-4204.

Directory of International Internships is a regularly updated guide to global opportunities, primarily for students, available for about $20 from the Office of Overseas Study, 108 International Center, Michigan State University, East Lansing, MI 48824; 517/353-8920.

INTERNSHIP SOURCES IN PUBLIC AFFAIRS AND NONPARTISAN POLITICS

■■■■■■■■■■■■■■■■■■■■■■■■■■■■■■■■■■■■

Notes on Interning in Public Affairs and Nonpartisan Politics:

In addition to traditional opportunities in partisan politics, interns are in increasing demand today by *non*partisan public interest and political action groups. Interns find these a satisfying way to give service to causes they believe in—as well as to build a portfolio for political and public service careers, where experience usually carries greater weight than education.

TIP: These are definitely not "just jobs"; find causes you really care about if you want to have a successful and enjoyable experience.

> *When interning in public interest jobs, Cathy learned firsthand, "You can get involved from the bottom up and see what's efficient and what's not, instead of approaching everything from above, through bureaucracies that just don't work."*

Also see entries under *Government, International,* and *Social Service.*

AMERICAN CIVIL LIBERTIES UNION

132 West 43rd Street   **Phone:** 212/944-9800
New York, NY 10036   **FAX:**   212/730-4652

* * *

ORGANIZATION'S ACTIVITIES: A nonpartisan nonprofit organization, with regional and local offices around the U.S., whose mission is the preservation of the Constitution and the Bill of Rights.

Number of Internships: Varies; numerous around country.

Type: Research, writing, advocacy.

Function/Duties: Gather and present background on issues and on specific cases; assist in grassroots organizing and legislative monitoring.

Schedule: Full- and/or part-time; year-round availability—depending on assignment and locale.

Stipend or Pay: Usually none.

Academic Credit Offered: Per student's own arrangements with academic institution.

ELIGIBILITY: Primarily undergraduate, graduate, and law-school students.

REQUIREMENTS: Excellent writing skills and commitment to importance of constitutional rights.

APPLICATION PROCEDURE: Send résumé and cover letter *to* Internship Coordinator at national headquarters or nearby regional offices. *Deadline:* Ongoing.

AMERICAN SECURITY COUNCIL

Washington Communications Center   **Phone:**   703/547-1750
Boston, VA 22713   **FAX:**   703/547-9737

* * *

ORGANIZATION'S ACTIVITIES: A private nonprofit research and education organization that focuses on issues of national security and international relations.

Number of Internships: 12 per year.

Type: Research, writing, educational assisting.

Function/Duties: Work on reports and events.

Schedule: Part- or full-time, for 4 months during spring, summer, and fall quarters.

Stipend or Pay: No.

Academic Credit Offered: Per student's own arrangements with academic institution.

ELIGIBILITY: College and graduate students; *Plus* participation in weekly briefings and discussions with staff members on foreign policy issues.

REQUIREMENTS: Availability to work in Washington, D.C., suburb; interest in career in international relations.

APPLICATION PROCEDURE: Contact Executive Director for application and details. *Deadline:* Open.

AMNESTY INTERNATIONAL

322 Eighth Avenue	**Phone:**	212/807-8400
New York, NY 10001-1451	**FAX:**	212/627-1451

* * *

ORGANIZATION'S ACTIVITIES: Amnesty International promotes awareness of and adherence to human rights as set down in the Universal Declaration of Human Rights within the New York office, which is Amnesty International's regional office for work on the death penalty. Proposed cases are interviewed before going on to the international body. All administrative duties are handled here for the country.

Number of Internships: Varies.

Type: Casework.

Function/Duties: Assist staff in ongoing duties as well as special research and communications projects.

Schedule: Full-time and part-time, term varies.

Stipend or Pay: Sometimes.

Academic Credit Offered: Must be arranged by intern.

ELIGIBILITY: All students; career-changers and non-students also welcome to apply.

REQUIREMENTS: Each internship requires distinct abilities and tasks; most require computer literacy or proven ability to master a computer program efficiently.

APPLICATION PROCEDURE: *Call* Susan Farley, Internship Coordinator and National Membership Program Assistant, for application form and list of current opportunities. Must send completed application form, writing sample, résumé and one letter of recommendation.

THE ASSOCIATION OF THE BAR OF THE CITY OF NEW YORK

42 West 44th Street	**Phone:**	212/382-6770
New York, NY 10036-6690	**Fax:**	212/768-8116

* * *

ORGANIZATION'S ACTIVITIES: An independent association of over 19,000 lawyers that addresses a broad range of local, national, and international public policy issues, and conducts public service and community outreach activities throughout New York City.

Number of Internship Openings: Up to 5.

Type: Assisting the legislative program and participating in public service and community outreach activities.

Function/Duties: Research, administrative, and assistance at legal clinics.

Schedule: Part-time and full-time year-round; term of internship ranges from 2 months to 1 year.

Stipend or Pay: None.

Academic Credit Offered: Per intern's own arrangements with academic institution.

ELIGIBILITY: Students in high school, college, or graduate school are welcome; open to non-students and career-changers as well.

REQUIREMENTS: Applicant must possess strong written and oral communication skills.

APPLICATION PROCEDURE: Request application by writing *to* Robin Kreitner, Director of Personnel. *Deadline:* Varies.

BETTER GOVERNMENT ASSOCIATION

230 North Michigan Avenue	**Phone:** 312/641-1181
Chicago, IL 60601	**FAX:** N/A

* * *

ORGANIZATION'S ACTIVITIES: Membership organization dedicated to overseeing government's handling of tax dollars and public policy decisions.

Number of Internships: Varies.

Type: Research, law, reporting.

Function/Duties: Provide background material to staff and to media in projects involving investigations of public service.

Schedule: Full- and/or part-time year-round.

Stipend or Pay: Not usually.

Academic Credit Offered: Per student's own arrangements with academic institution.

ELIGIBILITY: Primarily undergraduate and graduate students.

REQUIREMENTS: Prefer journalism or law students with public policy interests.

APPLICATION PROCEDURE: Send inquiries *to* Internship Coordinator. *Deadline:* Ongoing.

BROOKINGS INSTITUTION

1775 Massachusetts Avenue NW	**Phone:** 202/797-6000
Washington, DC 20036	**FAX:** 202/797-6004

* * *

ORGANIZATION'S ACTIVITIES: A nonpartisan, nonprofit research and educational organization devoted to research on public policy issues.

Number of Internships: Varies, fairly numerous.

Type: Public affairs, research, communications.

Function/Duties: Aid professional staff in gathering information for and producing reports and analyses and public education presentations.

Schedule: Summers, full-time.

Stipend or Pay: Not usually.

Academic Credit Offered: Per student's own arrangements with academic institution; *Plus* attend seminars and conferences.

ELIGIBILITY: Upper-level undergraduate and graduate students.

REQUIREMENTS: Excellent communications skills; courses of study in areas related to Brookings specialties.

APPLICATION PROCEDURE: Send inquiries *to* Public Affairs Office as early in the year as possible for submission of applications *by* March 1.

CALIFORNIA FIRST AMENDMENT COALITION

| 2218 Homewood Way | **Phone:** | 916/485-2819 |
| Carmichael, CA 95608 | **FAX:** | 916/485-3442 |

* * *

ORGANIZATION'S ACTIVITIES: Public information, education, and assistance concerning rights to open government, freedom of information, freedom of speech, and freedom of press.

Number of Internships: Vary with need; fairly numerous.

Type: Management.

Function/Duties: Volunteer supervision, clerical assistance, nonprofit accounting, conference planning, publication editing, computer consulting (Macintosh), legal research and writing, fundraising, teacher training (social studies), graphic design, and member relations.

Schedule: Part-time; longer term preferred.

Stipend or Pay: No.

Academic Credit Offered: Available if arranged by intern.

ELIGIBILITY: College and graduate students; career-changers and non-students welcome to apply.

REQUIREMENTS: Highly responsible positions for skilled and experienced volunteers.

APPLICATION PROCEDURE: Submit application request *to* Mark Needham, Department VO.

CHALLENGE INTERNATIONAL

| 1204 Ina Lane | **Phone:** | 703/821-3385 |
| McLean, VA 22102 | **FAX:** | N/A |

* * *

ORGANIZATION'S ACTIVITIES: Program to serve the disabled community by promoting positive images in the media and elsewhere, including placement of people with disabilities into media positions.

Number of Internships: Varies.

Type: Media.

Function/Duties: Varies depending on placement.

Schedule: Varies.

Stipend or Pay: May cover expenses.

Academic Credit Offered: Per student's own arrangements with academic institution.

ELIGIBILITY: Students, non-students, or career-changers with disabilities.

REQUIREMENTS: Disability combined with appropriate skills.

APPLICATION PROCEDURE: Send inquiries *to* Executive Director. *Deadline:* Ongoing.

CITIZEN ACTION FUND INC.

1406 West 6th Street
Cleveland, OH 44113

Phone: 216/861-5200
FAX: 216/694-6904

* * *

ORGANIZATION'S ACTIVITIES: A national organization composed of state-based groups working on social justice and environmental issues.

Number of Internships: Varies; numerous.

Type: Fundraising, research, education.

Function/Duties: Aid staff members in headquarters and state offices with development, public programs, legislative activities.

Schedule: Usually full-time, year-round; flexible hours.

Stipend or Pay: Yes.

Academic Credit Offered: Per student's own arrangements with academic institution.

ELIGIBILITY: Primarily graduate and undergraduate students, but non-students and career-changers also considered.

REQUIREMENTS: Prefer those with interest in public affairs and with good communications skills.

APPLICATION PROCEDURE: Send inquiries *to* Director of Volunteers. *Deadline:* Ongoing.

CITIZEN'S COMMITTEE FOR NEW YORK CITY INC.

305 Seventh Avenue
15th Floor   **Phone:** 212/989-0983
New York, NY 10001   **FAX:** 212/989-0983

* * *

ORGANIZATION'S ACTIVITIES: Private nonprofit organization working to develop ways of improving city services and enhancing life in New York.

Number of Internships: 3.

Type: Staff assistants.

Function/Duties: Assist staff of specific departments according to intern's skills and interests; intern should have experience working with youth and/or providing technical assistance and doing problem analysis, surveys, and reports.

Schedule: Year-round/seasonal; full-time and part-time internships are available.

Stipend or Pay: No.

Academic Credit Offered: Per student's own arrangements with own academic institution.

ELIGIBILITY: Undergraduate and graduate students are encouraged to apply; preferred majors: Urban Studies, Sociology, and Criminal Justice. Open to non-students and career-changers as well.

REQUIREMENTS: Applicant must provide a letter of interest along with an application.

APPLICATION PROCEDURE: Submit full application *to* Valerie Oliver-Durrah. *Deadline:* Open.

COMMON CAUSE

2030 M Street NW   **Phone:** 202/833-1200
Washington, DC 20036   **FAX:** 202/659-3716

* * *

ORGANIZATION'S ACTIVITIES: National nonprofit nonpartisan citizen's lobby organization dedicated to making national, state, and local governments more accountable to constituents.

Number of Internships: Varies.

Type: Research, education, communications.

Function/Duties: Varies depending on locale and on needs.

Schedule: Mostly part-time; national office can provide referrals to appropriate regional activities as necessary.

Stipend or Pay: Not usually.

Academic Credit Offered: Per student's own arrangements with academic institution.

ELIGIBILITY: Primarily graduate and undergraduate students but qualified non-students and career-changers also considered.

REQUIREMENTS: Interests, goals, skills, and/or experience relevant to available assignments.

APPLICATION PROCEDURE: Send inquiries *to* Internship Coordinator, *by* July 24 for fall semester, January 1 for spring semester, and April 1 for summer semester.

COUNCIL FOR A LIVABLE WORLD

110 Maryland Avenue NE   **Phone:** 202/543-4100
Washington, DC 20002   **FAX:** 202/543-6297

*   *   *

ORGANIZATION'S ACTIVITIES: Research and writing on arms control issues to reduce the military budget.

Number of Internships: 2 or more.

Type: Research, writing, administrative.

Function/Duties: Intern will have the opportunity to work in the arms control community and attend hearings; office support is also expected.

Schedule: Full-time and part-time, 3- to 4-month term.

Stipend or Pay: May be arranged.

Academic Credit Offered: Yes.

ELIGIBILITY: College students.

REQUIREMENTS: Applicant should have an interest in politics.

APPLICATION PROCEDURE: Submit résumé, cover letter, and writing sample *to* Ingrid Honaker.

FELLOWSHIP OF RECONCILIATION

Box 271   **Phone:** 914/358-4601
Nyack, NY 10960   **FAX:** N/A

*   *   *

ORGANIZATION'S ACTIVITIES: An interfaith pacifist organization founded in 1915 concerned with domestic and international peace and justice, nonviolent alternatives to conflict, and freedom of conscience.

Number of Internships: 8.

Type: Social service, events organizing, education.

Function/Duties: Aid in organizing workshops, other projects, outreach; publications and presentation.

Schedule: 9 months, mostly full-time.

Stipend or Pay: Expenses may be covered.

Academic Credit Offered: Per student's own arrangements with academic institution.

ELIGIBILITY: Consideration given to students, non-students, or career-changers with appropriate qualifications.

REQUIREMENTS: Interests, goals, skills, and/or experience relevant to available assignments.

APPLICATION PROCEDURE: Send inquiries *to* Internship Coordinator. *Deadline:* Ongoing.

FRIENDS COMMITTEE ON NATIONAL LEGISLATION

245 Second Street NE	**Phone:** 202/547-6000
Washington, DC 20002	**FAX:** N/A

* * *

ORGANIZATION'S ACTIVITIES: Quaker lobbying group.

Number of Internships: 3.

Type: Research, communications.

Function/Duties: Prepare and present reports and testimony on legislative issues.

Schedule: 3 to 11 months, full-time.

Stipend or Pay: 11-month research internship for a recent college grad pays $1,000 per month and benefits; other internships are volunteer.

Academic Credit Offered: Per student's own arrangements with academic institution.

ELIGIBILITY: Primarily graduate or undergraduate students and recent grads; other non-students or career-changers may be considered.

REQUIREMENTS: Strong writing and communications skills; minimum age 18; familiarity with Friends and Quaker principles.

APPLICATION PROCEDURE: Send inquiries *to* David Boynton *by* several months prior to start date.

FRONTLASH

815 16th Street NW	**Phone:** 202/783-3993
Washington, DC 20006	**FAX:** 202/637-5058

* * *

ORGANIZATION'S ACTIVITIES: National coalition of public affairs officials, educators, and youth organizations designed to promote effective political campaigns and government by educating young people and involving them in the process.

Number of Internships: Varies.

Type: Education, events organization, political.

Function/Duties: Interns within organization assist with operations; group also places youth interns with organizations related to public affairs.

Schedule: Flexible, varies; mostly summers.

Stipend or Pay: May cover expenses.

Academic Credit Offered: Per student's own arrangements with academic institution.

ELIGIBILITY: Primarily high-school and college students.

REQUIREMENTS: Interests, goals, skills, and/or experience relevant to available assignments.

APPLICATION PROCEDURE: Send inquiries *to* Internship Coordinator by as early in the school year as possible.

HERITAGE FOUNDATION

214 Massachusetts Avenue NE
Washington, DC 20002

Phone: 202/546-4400
FAX: 202/546-8328

* * *

ORGANIZATION'S ACTIVITIES: A nonprofit conservative organization that provides policy research and advocacy on a wide spectrum of foreign and domestic matters.

Number of Internships: 25; competitive positions.

Type: Summer internship.

Function/Duties: Assist foundation staff with variety of research and other activities on project basis.

Schedule: Summers, full-time.

Stipend or Pay: About $200 per week.

Academic Credit Offered: Per student's own arrangements with academic institution.

ELIGIBILITY: Primarily undergraduate and graduate students.

REQUIREMENTS: Highly competitive positions; for those whose ex-perience, goals, and views support those of the sponsoring organization.

APPLICATION PROCEDURE: Send inquiries *to* Internship Coordinator *by* as early in the school year as possible for details on requirements.

MINORITY ACTIVIST APPRENTICESHIP PROGRAM

3861 Martin Luther King Jr. Way
Oakland, CA 94609

Phone: 415/654-9611
FAX: N/A

* * *

ORGANIZATION'S ACTIVITIES: Trains and places minority group members interested in social activism with community organizations that need help with campaigns or projects.

Number of Internships: Varies; numerous.

Type: Organizing, fundraising, media interaction.

Function/Duties: After skills training and organization, work with groups around country on assignments as needed.

Schedule: 8-week program (year-round): 1 week training, 6 weeks activity, 1 week review.

Stipend or Pay: Expenses covered, plus small extra stipend.

Academic Credit Offered: Per student's own arrangements with academic institution; *Plus* training provided in skills important for any kind of social service work.

ELIGIBILITY: For activists of color, primarily aged 19 to 30.

REQUIREMENTS: Interests, goals, and/or experience relevant to program.

APPLICATION PROCEDURE: Send inquiries *to* Program Director. *Deadline:* Open.

PEACE ACTION

1819 H Street NW
Suite 640   **Phone:** 202/862-9740
Washington, DC 20006-3603   **FAX:**   202/862-9762

* * *

ORGANIZATION'S ACTIVITIES: Agency's purposes are to stop nuclear proliferation, stop conventional arms sales, and convert to peacetime economy.

Number of Internships: Varies with need.

Type: Disarmament, peace economy, and membership.

Function/Duties: Assist staff of specific departments, according to intern's skills and interests.

Schedule: Year-round, part-time (32 hours per week) internships are available.

Stipend or Pay: $50 per week.

Academic Credit Offered: Per student's own arrangements with academic institution.

ELIGIBILITY: Undergraduate students are encouraged to apply.

REQUIREMENTS: Must provide a cover letter, writing sample, list of references, and a résumé along with an application.

APPLICATION PROCEDURE: Submit full application *to* Mark Sterman *by* 6 weeks before anticipated starting date.

PRESIDENTIAL CLASSROOM FOR YOUNG AMERICANS INC.

119 Oronoco Street   **Phone:** 703/683-5400
Alexandria, VA 22314-2058   **FAX:** 703/548-5728

* * *

ORGANIZATION'S ACTIVITIES: Presidential Classroom is a nonprofit, nonpartisan civic education organization. Since 1968, the program has introduced more than 63,000 high-school juniors and seniors to the inner workings of the U.S. government. Through seminars, crossfire sessions, and site visits, the students become more aware of the way the nation's government works. Presidential Classroom's internships for college students bring outstanding young women and men from colleges and universities in this country and abroad to assist in the day-to-day administration of the program for high-school students.

Number of Internships: 12 to 16.

Type: Interns work as a team with the central staff and instructors to provide a quality program of civic education to high-school students.

Function/Duties: Interns provide logistical and administrative support to the program.

Schedule: Winter term, January to March; summer term, June to August. Interns who can provide assistance for a full program are given preference; interns who cannot stay at least 2 weeks are rarely accepted.

Stipend or Pay: No, but Presidential Classroom pays room and board.

Academic Credit Offered: Per intern's own arrangements with academic institution.

ELIGIBILITY: Interns should have completed at least 2 semesters of college courses; preferred majors: Political Science, Education, Communications, Sociology, Psychology, Hospitality Management, Business, and Liberal Arts. Adult volunteers are welcome to apply.

REQUIREMENTS: There is a 24-hour-time commitment, and the internship is both physically and mentally demanding.

APPLICATION PROCEDURE: Request application and submit *to* Internship Coordinator.

U.S.-ASIA INSTITUTE

232 East Capital Street NE   **Phone:** 202/544-3181
Washington, DC 20003   **FAX:** N/A

* * *

ORGANIZATION'S ACTIVITIES: Nonprofit organization of Americans of Asian descent as well as individuals and companies with an interest in U.S.-Asia trade and cooperation.

Number of Internships: Varies; competitive.

Type: Chan Future Leader Award.

Function/Duties: Participate actively in various activities of the Institute, including research, events, and legislative activities.

Schedule: Varies with assignment and semester.

Stipend or Pay: Yes.

Academic Credit Offered: Per student's own arrangements with academic institution.

ELIGIBILITY: Competition among Asian-American college students for internship positions.

REQUIREMENTS: Winners of competition.

APPLICATION PROCEDURE: Send inquiries *to* Internship Coordinator *by* as early in the school year as possible.

U.S. PUBLIC INTEREST RESEARCH GROUP (USPIRG)

215 Pennsylvania Avenue SE
Washington, DC 20003

Phone: 202/546-9707
FAX: N/A

* * *

ORGANIZATION'S ACTIVITIES: Nonprofit, nonpartisan public affairs research and advocacy group that conducts research, monitors public business activities, and lobbies for reforms in the areas of government, environment, and consumer affairs issues; 15 regional centers around U.S.

Number of Internships: Many hundreds nationwide.

Type: Research, surveys, editorial.

Function/Duties: Interns, summers and year-round, participate in survey-taking and other research activities and in lobbying on a local, state, and national level; some office work available in national and regional headquarters, as well as editorial assistance on PIRG newsletters.

Schedule: Full- and/or part-time; flexible hours; summers as well as school semesters.

Stipend or Pay: Some paid, some unpaid.

Academic Credit Offered: Per student's own arrangements with academic institution.

ELIGIBILITY: Primarily undergraduate students, but all others considered as well.

REQUIREMENTS: Interests, goals, skills, and/or experience relevant to available assignments.

APPLICATION PROCEDURE: Send inquiries *to* Internship Managers at headquarters or to be directed to regional headquarters. *Deadline:* Open.

YOUTH POLICY INSTITUTE

1221 Massachusetts Avenue NW
Washington, DC 20005

Phone: 202/638-2140
FAX: N/A

* * *

ORGANIZATION'S ACTIVITIES: Research organization that uses young people aged 17 to 25 to monitor and report on federal government policy concerning youth and family issues.

Number of Internships: Varies.

Type: Research, management, editorial.

Function/Duties: Work and learn to monitor, analyze, and report on public policy matters; some placed with other organizations.

Schedule: 6 to 12 months, full- and/or part-time.

Stipend or Pay: Expenses may be covered.

Academic Credit Offered: Per student's own arrangements with academic institution.

ELIGIBILITY: College students and recent graduates.

REQUIREMENTS: Interests, goals, skills, and/or experience relevant to available assignments.

APPLICATION PROCEDURE: Send inquiries *to* Executive Director. *Deadline:* Ongoing.

ZERO POPULATION GROWTH

1400 16th Street NW
Washington, DC 20036

Phone: 202/332-2200
FAX: N/A

* * *

ORGANIZATION'S ACTIVITIES: Private, nonprofit organization whose goal is population stabilization worldwide and in the U.S.

Number of Internships: Varies with availability and per project.

Type: Education, communications, research, organization.

Function/Duties: Legislative research and analysis, community organization, education, writing.

Schedule: Fall, spring, and summer semesters; hours and length flexible.

Stipend or Pay: $150 per month in summers; $400 per month other seasons.

Academic Credit Offered: Per student's own arrangements with academic institution.

ELIGIBILITY: Junior or senior undergraduate students.

REQUIREMENTS: Knowledge of and experience with legislative process; good writing skills; shared interest in issues.

APPLICATION PROCEDURE: Request application and details *from* Field Coordinator *by* several months prior to available period.

Organizations/Resources for Further Information about Internships in Public Affairs and Nonpartisan Politics

CONGRESSIONAL MANAGEMENT FOUNDATION
513 Capital Court NW   Phone: 202/546-0100
Washington, DC 20002   FAX: 202/547-0936
Helps members of Congress and their staffs to better manage their workloads; can make internship connections.

WASHINGTON CENTER FOR INTERNSHIPS AND ACADEMIC SEMINARS
514 10th Street NW   Phone: 202/624-8030
Washington, DC 20004   FAX: N/A
Sponsors internship programs in Washington-based organizations, as well as academic seminars for students and faculty. Contact as clearinghouse for D.C. internship information.

INTERNSHIP SOURCES IN SCIENCE AND RESEARCH

■■

Notes on Interning in Science and Research:

Internships are available in a variety of scientific settings. Despite the common assumption that "scientific" internships must require post-doctoral status at a university or high-intensity lab, students with scientific interests can explore the life of a scientist—and the less scientifically trained can participate in scientific activities in a variety of settings.

TIPS: 1. Yes, competition can be stiff for these openings, but worthwhile for those interested in pursuing a scientific career or for those curious about whether this is the path for them. 2. Not a scientist? Try some of the nonprofit organizations that sponsor social and other types of research.

> *For Karen Janssen, a 30-year-old mother and student in information sciences, a 6-month internship was a way to get an assurance. "Experience is very important in getting a job," she said. "Entry-level positions are getting fewer and fewer. A person with 6 months' experience will get hired over someone with no real work experience." She added that her internship had shown her that her chosen field was right for her.*

Also see entries in the *Environment, Health,* and *Business* sections.

AIR FORCE SPACE TECHNOLOGY CENTER

Kirkland Air Force Base	**Phone:** 505/844-0011
Albuquerque, NM 87117	**FAX:** 505/846-5700

* * *

ORGANIZATION'S ACTIVITIES: Oversees the work of 3 major geophysics and astronautics research laboratories and provides information to the public and to academics.

Number of Internships: Varies.

Type: Scientific, technical, and administrative.

Function/Duties: Varies with assignment—work in labs and in public information capacities.

Schedule: Varies depending on assignment.

Stipend or Pay: Yes.

Academic Credit Offered: Per student's own arrangements with academic institution, if applicable.

ELIGIBILITY: Primarily graduate students as well as post-doctoral researchers.

REQUIREMENTS: Background and education in relevant sciences.

APPLICATION PROCEDURE: Send inquiries *to* Personnel Officer. *Deadline:* Ongoing.

ARMY ENVIRONMENTAL HYGIENE AGENCY

Aberdeen Proving Ground	**Phone:** 703/695-0363
Aberdeen, MD 21001	**FAX:** N/A

* * *

ORGANIZATION'S ACTIVITIES: Defense agency that works in conjunction with Department of Energy to develop ways to clear and prevent air, water, and other pollution.

Number of Internships: Varies.

Type: Clinical research participation.

Function/Duties: Provides opportunities and support for applied clinical research and training activities in such areas as air pollution and other environmental concerns.

Schedule: 1 year, renewable.

Stipend or Pay: Yes, varies.

Academic Credit Offered: N/A.

ELIGIBILITY: Non-students—graduates who have completed bachelor's, master's, or doctoral degrees within the past 3 years.

REQUIREMENTS: Degrees in applicable science or engineering disciplines.

APPLICATION PROCEDURE: To inquire concerning details, telephone Program Director *at* 615/576-1089. *Deadline:* Ongoing.

AMERICAN ASSOCIATION FOR ARTIFICIAL INTELLIGENCE

445 Burgess Drive	**Phone:** 415/328-3123
Menlo Park, CA 94025-3496	**FAX:** 415/321-4457

* * *

ORGANIZATION'S ACTIVITIES: AAAI is the principal scientific society serving the artificial intelligence community in the United States.

The association consists of scientists, engineers, managers, consultants, programmers, academicians, and students. AAAI was founded to encourage the basic knowledge of what constitutes intelligent thought and behavior and how it can be exhibited in computers. The association's primary publication, *AI Magazine*, helps AAAI members stay abreast of significant new research, new products, and fast-breaking scientific literature across the whole field of artificial intelligence.

Number of Internships: Flexible; varies with need.

Type: Varies.

Function/Duties: Assignments as needed.

Schedule: To be arranged.

Stipend or Pay: No.

Academic Credit Offered: Per student's own arrangement with academic institution.

ELIGIBILITY: Consideration given to students, non-students, or career-changers with appropriate qualifications.

REQUIREMENTS: Interests, goals, and/or experience relevant to available assignments.

APPLICATION PROCEDURE: Send résumé and letter *to* Internship Coordinator.

BROOKHAVEN NATIONAL LABORATORY

40 Brookhaven Road   **Phone:**   516/282-2703
Upton, NY 11973   **FAX:**   516/282-3000

* * *

ORGANIZATION'S ACTIVITIES: Federal research center specializing in electronic technology and other technological development.

Number of Internships: Varies.

Type: Technician training for minorities and women.

Function/Duties: On-the-job training in electronic technology.

Schedule: 1 year.

Stipend or Pay: Work-and-learn program, earns salary.

Academic Credit Offered: Per student's involvement with associate or other degree in conjunction with program.

ELIGIBILITY: Underrepresented minority such as black, Hispanic, Native American, and/or female who is a resident alien or citizen of the U.S.

REQUIREMENTS: Basic knowledge of electronics and some technical training.

APPLICATION PROCEDURE: Send inquiries *to* Jeffrey W. Taylor. *Deadline:* Ongoing.

ENERGY, U.S. DEPARTMENT OF

Office of Energy Research
1000 Independence Avenue SW   **Phone:** 202/586-5000
Washington, DC 20585   **FAX:** 202/586-4073

* * *

ORGANIZATION'S ACTIVITIES: Government agency responsible for discovering and developing optimum energy resources and technologies.

Number of Internships: 30.

Type: Graduate student research participation program.

Function/Duties: Offers opportunity for graduate students in life, physical, and social sciences, as well as math and engineering, to participate in ongoing research in modern and extensive facilities at scientific institutions around the country.

Schedule: 1 to 12 months.

Stipend or Pay: $1,600 per month; *Plus* travel expenses reimbursed.

Academic Credit Offered: Per student's own arrangements with academic institution.

ELIGIBILITY: Students currently enrolled in graduate degree programs.

REQUIREMENTS: Faculty recommendations plus interests, goals, skills, and/or experience relevant to available assignments.

APPLICATION PROCEDURE: To inquire for details, *phone* Program Director *at* 615/576-3426. *Deadline:* Ongoing.

Number of Internships: 50.

Type: Student research participation program.

Function/Duties: Offers opportunity for college students to participate in ongoing research in modern and extensive facilities at scientific institutions around the country under guidance of Department of Energy professionals.

Schedule: 10 weeks, summer.

Stipend or Pay: $200 per week; *Plus* travel expenses reimbursed.

Academic Credit Offered: Per student's own arrangements with academic institution.

ELIGIBILITY: College junior or senior students.

REQUIREMENTS: Majors preferred: Life Science, Physical Sciences, Social Science, Math, Engineering.

APPLICATION PROCEDURE: To inquire for details, *phone* Program Director *at* 615/576-3426. *Deadline:* Ongoing.

Number of Internships: Varies.

Type: Nuclear energy and health physics fellows.

Function/Duties: Offers opportunity to those interested in pursuing graduate degrees in nuclear science or health physics to pursue high levels of research.

Schedule: 1 year, renewable.

Stipend or Pay: $14,400 per year plus monthly stipend; *Plus* travel expenses and some tuition and fees reimbursed.

Academic Credit Offered: Per student's own arrangements with academic institution, if applicable.

ELIGIBILITY: College graduates who are not currently enrolled in graduate programs but plan to pursue graduate degrees.

REQUIREMENTS: Majors preferred: Life Science, Physical Sciences, Math, and Engineering; high GPAs and faculty recommendations.

APPLICATION PROCEDURE: To inquire for details, *phone* Program Director *at* 615/576-2600 *during* senior year in college.

ENERGY, U.S. DEPARTMENT OF

Office of Environmental Restoration
1000 Independence Avenue SW   **Phone:**   202/586-5000
Washington, DC 20585   **FAX:**   202/586-4073

* * *

ORGANIZATION'S ACTIVITIES: Government agency responsible for discovering and developing optimum energy resources and technologies and managing hazardous wastes.

Number of Internships: 20.

Type: Graduate fellowship employment program.

Function/Duties: Provides fellowships and practical work experience for students pursuing master's degrees in disciplines related to environmental restoration and waste management.

Schedule: 1 to 4 years.

Stipend or Pay: Tuition and fees paid, plus $1,200 monthly stipend.

Academic Credit Offered: Per student's own arrangements with academic institution, if applicable; *Plus* potential for employment with Department of Energy.

ELIGIBILITY: Students in most engineering and science disciplines and technology management.

REQUIREMENTS: Faculty recommendations, good GPAs, appropriate career goals.

APPLICATION PROCEDURE: To inquire for details, *phone* Program Director *at* 615/576-2194 *during* January prior to enrollment.

ENGRAVING AND PRINTING, U.S. BUREAU OF

14th and C Streets NW   **Phone:** 202/874-2485
Washington, DC 20228   **FAX:**   202/874-3177

* * *

ORGANIZATION'S ACTIVITIES: The office of the U.S. Department of Treasury responsible for the production of money.

Number of Internships: Varies.

Type: Research: Technical, scientific, computer sciences.

Function/Duties: Research projects designed for development of improved techniques in producing non-counterfeitable money.

Schedule: 1 year (renewable).

Stipend or Pay: Yes; *Plus* travel expenses reimbursed.

Academic Credit Offered: Per student's own arrangements with academic institution, if applicable.

ELIGIBILITY: Some graduate students; or those non-students who have completed graduate degree within past 3 years.

REQUIREMENTS: Interests, goals, skills, and/or experience relevant to available assignments.

APPLICATION PROCEDURE: To inquire for details, *phone* Program Director. *Deadline:* Ongoing.

FOOD AND DRUG ADMINISTRATION, U.S.

Center for Drug Evaluation and Research
5600 Fishers Lane   **Phone:** 301/443-2410
Bethesda, MD 20857   **FAX:**   301/443-0755

* * *

ORGANIZATION'S ACTIVITIES: Federal government agency responsible for development and monitoring of drugs.

Number of Internships: Varies.

Type: Postgraduate research program.

Function/Duties: Participate in scientific laboratory research concerned with evaluation of drugs.

Schedule: 1 year, renewable.

Stipend or Pay: Yes; *Plus* travel expenses reimbursed.

Academic Credit Offered: N/A.

ELIGIBILITY: Professionals in life, physical, and other sciences who have completed master's or doctoral degree programs within past 3 years.

REQUIREMENTS: Professional recommendations plus interests, goals, skills, and/or experience relevant to available assignments.

APPLICATION PROCEDURE: To inquire for details, *phone* Program Director *at* 615/576-1089. *Deadline:* Ongoing.

GODDARD SPACE FLIGHT CENTER

Greenbelt, MD 20771

Phone: 301/286-6255
FAX: N/A

* * *

ORGANIZATION'S ACTIVITIES: Research center that works in conjunction with the National Aeronautics and Space Administration (NASA) to develop, study, and refine space technologies.

Number of Internships: 25 to 50.

Type: Volunteer service student intern program.

Function/Duties: Beginning during summer following high-school graduation, students work at center under supervision of a mentor, to learn disciplines firsthand.

Schedule: Anywhere from 2 weeks in summer to full academic year, depending on availability and interest.

Stipend or Pay: No.

Academic Credit Offered: Per student's own arrangements with academic institution.

ELIGIBILITY: Students beginning with senior year in high school.

REQUIREMENTS: Good academic record and interest in career in space sciences, engineering, and other related fields.

APPLICATION PROCEDURE: Send inquiries *to* Educational Programs Unit *during* senior year in high school (or work through high school counselors).

Number of Internships: 20.

Type: Visiting summer enrichment program in computer science.

Function/Duties: GSFC scientists select on-the-job work assignments for computer science students to work with and complete reports on.

Schedule: 8 weeks during the summer.

Stipend or Pay: No.

Academic Credit Offered: Per student's own arrangements with academic institution; *Plus* participate in seminars and laboratory visits.

ELIGIBILITY: Undergraduate and graduate college students and some specially selected high-school students.

REQUIREMENTS: Outstanding computer science students.

APPLICATION PROCEDURE: Send inquiries *to* Space Data and Computing Division *between* September 1 and March 1.

Number of Internships: 20.

Type: Federal junior fellowship program.

Function/Duties: Cooperative education program that allows students attending college also to work and learn in GSFC science, computer, engineering, and business administration areas.

Schedule: Varies; up to 4 years.

Stipend or Pay: Yes.

Academic Credit Offered: Per student's own arrangements with academic institution; *Plus* completion of program makes participants eligible for appointment to full-time permanent positions.

ELIGIBILITY: Undergraduate college students.

REQUIREMENTS: Successfully complete Center's selection process.

APPLICATION PROCEDURE: Send inquiries *to* Employee and Organization Development Branch *during* senior year in high school, or work through school counselors.

INDIANAPOLIS ZOO

1200 West Washington Street **Phone:** 317/630-2041
Indianapolis, IN 46222 **FAX:** 317/630-5114

* * *

ORGANIZATION'S ACTIVITIES: Center for preservation, study, and involvement with plant and animal life.

Number of Internships: Varies.

Type: Horticulture and botany.

Function/Duties: Firsthand experience in public horticulture and botanical interpretation. Become involved with everything from planting to pruning and often be responsible for own garden area. Become acquainted with many exotic species and facilitate educating the public about unique plant and animal relationships.

Schedule: A minimum of 20 hours a week.

Stipend or Pay: No.

Academic Credit Offered: Per student's own arrangements with academic institution.

ELIGIBILITY: College students.

REQUIREMENTS: Interests, goals, skills, and/or experience relevant to available assignments.

APPLICATION PROCEDURE: Submit résumé, 2 letters of recommendation, a copy of current grade transcript, cover letter, and application form. Cover letter should answer the following questions: Why are you interested in an internship at the Indianapolis Zoo? What would you like to gain from an internship? What internship opportunities interest you most? Where did you hear about the internship program? All application materials should be sent as a packet *to* Mary Kay Hood, Volunteer Coordinator. You will be contacted about an interview upon receipt of all materials.

INFORMATION TECHNOLOGY RESOURCE CENTER

59 East Van Buren
Suite 2020   **Phone:**   312/939-8050
Chicago, IL 60605   **FAX:**   312/939-8060

* * *

ORGANIZATION'S ACTIVITIES: The Information Technology Resource Center is a nonprofit organization dedicated to helping other nonprofits in their uses of computers and other technology. Facilities include a classroom, a library, and a 22-workstation computer lab equipped with both Macintosh and IBM-compatible computers. Core programs include basic information about computers, workshops that focus on common computer applications, planning sessions to assist in analyzing computer requirements, making purchase decisions, and troubleshooting. Hands-on training is offered in word processing, spreadsheet, database, desktop publishing, operating systems, and other subjects.

Number of Internships: 4 per year.

Type: Computer staff for lab and training.

Function/Duties: Assist and learn from technological professionals on staff.

Schedule: Full-time and part-time; term of at least 3 months.

Stipend or Pay: No.

Academic Credit Available: Yes.

ELIGIBILITY: College and graduate students; preferred major: Computer Science. Both career-changers and non-students with at least 2 years of college are also welcome to apply.

REQUIREMENTS: Interest, background, and/or training in developing computer and networking skills.

APPLICATION PROCEDURE: Submit résumé, and letter expressing interest, proposed period, and purpose of internship *to* Information Technology Resource Center.

THE MARITIME CENTER AT NORWALK

10 North Water Street   **Phone:**   203/852-0700
Norwalk, CT 06854   **FAX:**   203/838-5416

* * *

ORGANIZATION'S ACTIVITIES: The Maritime Center (TMC) is a $30-million nonprofit facility consisting of 20 aquarium displays, a Maritime History Hall, a rotating exhibit gallery, and an IMAX theater. TMC's mission is to educate visitors about the maritime ecosystems of Long Island Sound and the rich nautical history of New England. The animal collection, exhibited in 20 aquarium displays, consists of approximately

146 species and 1,000 individuals representing the marine communities of Long Island Sound. Internships take place within the facility or on the Norwalk Harbor of Long Island Sound.

Number of Internships: Flexible; varies with need.

Type: Aquarist internships.

Function/Duties: Helping the aquarist with daily responsibilities involving animal care; assisting in special projects and initiating individual studies on specific animals.

Schedule: No limited length.

Stipend or Pay: No.

Academic Credit Offered: Per student's own arrangements with academic institution.

ELIGIBILITY: Anyone age 16 and up.

REQUIREMENTS: Internship ideal for those students with a background in biology or marine science who wish to experience how an aquarium functions. The student will learn firsthand about the anatomy, physiology, ecology, and husbandry of the marine organisms found in the Sound.

Type: Marine research.

Ecosystems of Long Island Sound and the rich nautical history of New England. The *Research Vessel Oceanic* conducts seasonal daily study cruises for school groups and the general public. These trips explore the various marine habitats of Long Island Sound. Internships take place within the facility or on the Norwalk Harbor of Long Island Sound.

Number of Internships: Flexible; varies with need.

Type: *RV/Oceanic* internships.

Function/Duties: Aid in interpreting the various marine plants and animals collected from different habitats; collect data that would contribute to an ongoing survey of the Norwalk Harbor ecosystem.

Schedule: No limited length.

Stipend or Pay: No.

Academic Credit Offered: Per student's own arrangements with academic institution.

Type: Independent research internships.

Function/Duties: Varies by position.

Schedule: No limited time.

Stipend or Pay: No.

Academic Credit Offered: Per student's own arrangements with academic institution.

ELIGIBILITY: Anyone age 16 and up.

REQUIREMENTS: Internship is ideal for those students wishing to apply their skills and direct the interests toward focused special projects utilizing the resources at the Center.

APPLICATION PROCEDURE: *Contact* Jack Schneider at 203/852-0700.

NATIONAL AERONAUTICS AND SPACE ADMINISTRATION (NASA)

300 E Street SW	**Phone:** 202/358-8386
Washington, DC 20546	**FAX:** 202/358-0071

* * *

ORGANIZATION'S ACTIVITIES: Federal agency that manages the government's space flight centers and other research and technical development centers devoted to space science and other advanced technologies.

Number of Internships: 200.

Type: SHARP-Plus Program for Minorities.

Function/Duties: Program in conjunction with historically black colleges to provide minority students who are interested in careers in science and engineering the opportunity to work directly with an active researcher in an intensive apprenticeship program.

Schedule: Mostly summers, full-time.

Stipend or Pay: Earn-and-learn programs that provide salary to students during apprenticeships.

Academic Credit Offered: Per student's own arrangements with academic institution; *Plus* internship may ultimately lead to work with NASA.

ELIGIBILITY: High-school and some college students.

REQUIREMENTS: Career interest in science and engineering.

APPLICATION PROCEDURE: Send inquiries *to* Chief of Educational Affairs Division *by* as early as possible in the year prior to apprenticeship.

NATIONAL RESEARCH COUNCIL

300 E Street SW	**Phone:** 202/358-0000
Washington, DC 20546	**FAX:** 202/358-0071

* * *

ORGANIZATION'S ACTIVITIES: Federal agency which, in conjunction with NASA and other agencies, sponsors and coordinates variety of research programs.

Number of Internships: Varies.

Type: Resident research associateships programs.

Function/Duties: A competitive program that grants research and teaching assignments at Goddard Space Flight Center or one of 6 other federal research centers.

Schedule: 1 year or more full-time.

Stipend or Pay: Yes, regular associate's salary.

Academic Credit Offered: N/A.

ELIGIBILITY: Holders of the doctoral degree whose research proposals are judged to be most appropriate to program.

REQUIREMENTS: PhDs with full command of the English language and an outstanding research proposal.

APPLICATION PROCEDURE: Phone inquiries *to* Sally Lytch at 202/334-2766. *Deadline:* Ongoing.

NATIONAL SCIENCE FOUNDATION

1800 G Street NW	**Phone:** 202/357-9498
Washington, DC 20550	**FAX:** 202/357-7745

* * *

ORGANIZATION'S ACTIVITIES: Sponsors scientific research and education in wide variety of disciplines.

Number of Internships: 12.

Type: Research experiences for undergraduates.

Function/Duties: Work at Goddard Space Flight Center on high energy solar physics and other research projects involving NASA and other scientists.

Schedule: Full-time, summers.

Stipend or Pay: May be available to cover expenses.

Academic Credit Offered: Per student's own arrangements with academic institution.

ELIGIBILITY: Undergraduate students.

REQUIREMENTS: Majors in physics, astronomy, computer sciences, and engineering with outstanding academic records.

APPLICATION PROCEDURE: Submit academic transcript and résumé that includes a description of work experience and special interests *to* GSFC Program Administrator *by* March 1.

SCIENCE AND TECHNOLOGY ADVISORY BOARD

575 Madison Avenue	
8th Floor	**Phone:** 212/891-4191
New York, NY 10022-2597	**FAX:** 212/355-2414

* * *

ORGANIZATION'S ACTIVITIES: Helps scientists and engineers from the former Soviet Union (and other countries) to help themselves find work in their original technical specialty and to capitalize on their inventions and research results.

Number of Internships: Several.

Type: Scientific career transitions.

Function/Duties: Administrative and communications; research; working with scientific community.

Schedule: Part-time and full-time, open term.

Stipend or Pay: No.

Academic Credit Offered: Possibly.

ELIGIBILITY: Graduate students, retired professionals in human resources, marketing and finance, and career-changers.

REQUIREMENTS: Must be highly motivated.

APPLICATION PROCEDURE: Submit brief inquiry letter or telephone call *to* Dr. Stephen Rosen, c/o Celia Paul Associates, 1776 Broadway, Suite 1806, New York, NY 10019; telephone: 212/397-1020.

OAK RIDGE NATIONAL LABORATORY

P.O. Box 2009   **Phone:** 615/574-0733
Oak Ridge, TN 37831   **FAX:**   615/574-0331

* * *

ORGANIZATION'S ACTIVITIES: Major government research facility administered by the U.S. Department of Energy, which, among its other roles, offers as well as supervises a wide variety of scientific, technical, and other internship activities.

Number of Internships: 10.

Type: Technology internship program.

Function/Duties: Work with and learn from laboratory and other professionals in variety of engineering and physics specialties.

Schedule: 1 to 12 months, full- or part-time, beginning every 3 months.

Stipend or Pay: About $1,000 per month.

Academic Credit Offered: Per student's own arrangements with academic institution; *Plus* assignments geared toward each student's academic goals.

ELIGIBILITY: Undergraduate students participating in associate degree programs.

REQUIREMENTS: Recommended students in relevant disciplines.

APPLICATION PROCEDURE: Send inquiries *to* Program Manager (or phone 615/576-3426). *Deadline:* Ongoing.

Number of Internships: Varies.

Type: Postdoctoral research associates.

Function/Duties: Opportunity to work in a high-quality laboratory with support and training for a broad range of science and engineering research.

Schedule: 1 year (renewable) full- or part-time.

Stipend or Pay: Based on activities and expenses.

Academic Credit Offered: Per student's own arrangements with academic institution, if applicable.

ELIGIBILITY: Those who have completed the doctoral degree within past 5 years; others may be considered.

REQUIREMENTS: Recommended students in relevant disciplines.

APPLICATION PROCEDURE: Send inquiries *to* Program Manager (or phone 615/576-4805). *Deadline:* Ongoing.

Number of Internships: 25.

Type: Professional internship program.

Function/Duties: Opportunities to participate in energy-related research projects that correlate with academic and career goals in engineering and earth sciences, and computer technologies.

Schedule: 3 to 12 months, beginning every 3 months.

Stipend or Pay: $1,300 per month; *Plus* travel expenses reimbursed.

Academic Credit Offered: Per student's own arrangements with academic institution, if applicable.

ELIGIBILITY: Master's or doctoral candidates in appropriate disciplines.

REQUIREMENTS: Recommended students, especially those with interest in hazardous-waste management.

APPLICATION PROCEDURE: Send inquiries *to* Program Manager (or phone 615/576-3426) *by* 3 months prior to availability date.

Number of Internships: Varies.

Type: Technical editing internship program.

Function/Duties: The Laboratory's publications division offers opportunities to learn technical editing as well as some graphics expertise.

Schedule: 3 months in summer, full-time.

Stipend or Pay: Yes; *Plus* travel expenses reimbursed.

Academic Credit Offered: Per student's own arrangements with academic institution.

ELIGIBILITY: Undergraduate students enrolled at one of the U.S. historically black colleges.

REQUIREMENTS: Recommended minority students.

APPLICATION PROCEDURE: Send inquiries *to* Program Manager (or phone 615/576-1065) *by* 3 months prior to availability date.

Number of Internships: 5.

Type: Law internship program.

Function/Duties: Deal with legal aspects of energy-related techniques and procedures, national energy–related problems.

Schedule: 3 months, summers (some during academic year).

Stipend or Pay: $2,000 per month; *Plus* travel expenses reimbursed.

Academic Credit Offered: Per student's own arrangements with academic institution, if applicable.

ELIGIBILITY: Law students who have completed the first year of law school in the top third of their class.

REQUIREMENTS: Recommended students with interest in environmental law.

APPLICATION PROCEDURE: Send inquiries *to* Program Manager (or phone 615/576-3426) *by* February 15.

Number of Internships: Varies.

Type: Science and engineering research semester.

Function/Duties: Energy-related research opportunities in collaboration with laboratory scientists in engineering and earth sciences and computer technologies.

Schedule: Fall or spring semester.

Stipend or Pay: $225 per week; *Plus* travel expenses reimbursed, housing provided.

Academic Credit Offered: Per student's own arrangements with academic institution, if applicable; *Plus* regular participation in professional seminars.

ELIGIBILITY: Junior and senior college students plus a few opportunities for recent graduates or faculty/student teams.

REQUIREMENTS: Recommended students, especially those with interests and goals in scientific/technical areas of study.

APPLICATION PROCEDURE: Send inquiries *to* Program Manager (or phone 615/576-2358) in time to complete application process *by* October for spring and March for fall date.

Number of Internships: Varies.

Type: Minority student administrative summer program.

Function/Duties: Participate in administrative and business aspects of running laboratory.

Schedule: 10 to 12 weeks in summer.

Stipend or Pay: $325 per week.

Academic Credit Offered: Per student's own arrangements with academic institution, if applicable.

ELIGIBILITY: Minority junior and senior college students with 3.0 GPAs.

REQUIREMENTS: Recommended students, especially those with interests and goals in human resources, public administration, computer sciences, and managerial areas of study.

APPLICATION PROCEDURE: Send inquiries *to* Employment and Placement Manager in time to complete application process *by* February.

YERKES REGIONAL PRIMATE RESEARCH CENTER

Emory University   **Phone:** 404/727-7732
Atlanta, GA 30322   **FAX:** 404/427-7845

*   *   *

ORGANIZATION'S ACTIVITIES: The oldest primate research institute in the world, with the greatest diversity of research studies, from medical investigations of Parkinson's and other diseases to observational studies of the behavior of social groups.

Number of Internships: Numerous.

Type: Research, science, veterinary care assistantships.

Function/Duties: Interns assigned to scientists whose research interests are consistent with their own in planning and conducting research projects in behavioral biology, pathobiology, immunobiology, neurobiology, reproductive biology.

Schedule: Full-time, summers (10 weeks).

Stipend or Pay: Living-expense stipend.

Academic Credit Offered: Per student's own arrangements with academic institution.

ELIGIBILITY: Primarily graduate and upper-level undergraduate students.

REQUIREMENTS: Prefer minimum 2 years' undergraduate studies in relevant science.

APPLICATION PROCEDURE: Send résumé or curriculum vitae, letter describing educational and career objectives and significance of Yerkes experience to them, academic transcripts, 3 letters of reference, and any other relevant material *to* Dr. Larry Byrd *by* March 15.

Organizations/Resources for Further Information about Internships in Science and Research

NOTE: For further information on internships in science and research, see Resources in *Government, Environment,* and *Health* sections.

INTERNSHIP SOURCES IN SOCIAL SERVICES

■■■

Notes on Interning in Social Services:

Education, social welfare, health management, and counseling—all are fields with great career interest for the 90s; and in all, interns are in demand, especially when budgets are tight and volunteers are in short supply—and when so many groups need services.

TIPS: You can bring very hard-edged skills—accounting, computers, law— to some very soft and people-focused jobs as a way of changing career direction, or simply combining two sets of abilities and interests.

> *Sam Ford always wanted to fight against AIDS. A fundraising internship was just what Sam, an economics major, was looking for. Sam says flexibility is crucial in serving an internship. "A lot of times people go into an internship and it turns out to be different from what they initially expected," he says. "That, too, is part of the learning experience."*
>
> *Sam offers advice to anyone considering an internship: "Find an organization that is close to your heart, so that while you are working, you feel you are making a contribution to society," he says. "So even when the workload seems excessive, you don't think of it as doing it for the credits, but as doing it because you are achieving a goal bigger than that."*

Also see *Associations*, *International*, and *Health*.

ADOLESCENT COUNSELING SERVICES

4000 Middlefield Road
Suite FH
Palo Alto, CA 94303

Phone: 415/424-0852
FAX: 415/424-0854

* * *

ORGANIZATION'S ACTIVITIES: Adolescent Counseling Services is a nonprofit agency located in Palo Alto. They run three programs that reach teens and their families throughout the Bay Area. The residential treatment program, Caravan House, houses six girls at one time who cannot live at home due to parental neglect or abuse. It also runs an out-patient substance abuse program for teens and families that provides education classes, assessments, treatment and continuing care. The third program is the On-Campus Counseling Program, located in all four secondary schools in Palo Alto. Two licensed mental health professionals oversee 12 to 14 interns who provide direct services to teens and families.

Number of Internships: 12 to 14.

Type: Intern counselors on middle school or high school campus.

Function/Duties: Provide individual, group, and family counseling. May also co-teach workshops and living skills classes.

Schedule: 20 hours a week, must commit for entire school year—end of August through the middle of June (44 weeks).

Stipend or Pay: No.

Academic Credit Offered: Toward licensing for MFCC.

ELIGIBILITY: Graduate and postgraduate students; preferred majors: MFCC or Counseling Psychology. Non-students and career-changers with above qualifications welcome to apply.

REQUIREMENTS: Must be enrolled in or have graduated from a degree program leading toward MFCC licensure.

APPLICATION PROCEDURE: Submit résumé *to* Martha Chan or Penny Foc.

AFFORDABLE HOUSING ALLIANCE

Lokahi Center for Community Renewal
2331 Seaview Avenue   **Phone:** 808/946-2244
Honolulu, HI 96822   **FAX:**   N/A

* * *

ORGANIZATION'S ACTIVITIES: The Alliance is the largest organization in Hawaii concerned with affordable housing, and involved in advocacy, public education, and legislative work. The center works with "marginalized people" to solve problems related to housing.

Number of Internships: Varies.

Type: Lobbying, community development.

Function/Duties: Participate in ongoing and special projects focusing on housing discrimination, especially research monitoring compliance with the Community Reinvestment Act.

Schedule: Flexible.

Stipend or Pay: No.

Academic Credit Offered: Per student's own arrangements with academic institution; *Plus* training provided as needed.

ELIGIBILITY: Students, non-students, and career-changers welcome to apply.

REQUIREMENTS: "A passion for justice and an open mind."

APPLICATION PROCEDURE: Send inquiries *to* Steve Ito. *Deadline:* Open.

AMERICAN HUMANE ASSOCIATION

63 Inverness Drive East
Englewood, CO 80112

Phone: 303/792-9900
FAX: 303/792-5333

* * *

ORGANIZATION'S ACTIVITIES: A national nonprofit service and educational organization dedicated to protecting the health and safety of children and of animals.

Number of Internships: Varies; fairly numerous.

Type: Communications, editorial, education, research.

Function/Duties: In both children's and in animals' divisions, interns actively participate in serious projects that vary to include help with newsletters and other publications to organizing campaigns.

Schedule: Full- and/or part-time, year-round.

Stipend or Pay: Some stipend may be arranged.

Academic Credit Offered: Yes.

ELIGIBILITY: Primarily graduate and undergraduate students.

REQUIREMENTS: Students in journalism, social services, and communications especially encouraged to apply.

APPLICATION PROCEDURE: Send résumé and cover letter *to* Internship Coordinator. *Deadline:* Ongoing.

AMERICAN JEWISH JOINT DISTRIBUTION COMMITTEE

711 Third Avenue
New York, NY 10017

Phone: 212/687-6200
FAX: 212/370-5467

* * *

ORGANIZATION'S ACTIVITIES: Ralph I. Goldman Fellowship in International Jewish Communal Service.

Number of Internships: Varies; competitive.

Type: One year of work-study in overseas offices of the committee.

Function/Duties: Assist staff in service project and other activities as needed.

Schedule: Residential, full-time, one year.

Stipend or Pay: Yes.

Academic Credit Offered: Per student's own arrangements with academic institution.

ELIGIBILITY: Some graduate students or recent graduates, and some career-changers with master's degrees.

REQUIREMENTS: "In the early stages of a career with experience in the practice and/or study of communal service, showing a strong interest in international Jewish communal affairs and international social welfare."

APPLICATION PROCEDURE: Send inquiries *to* Committee Chair, in time for complete application *by* October 15.

AMERICAN NATIONAL RED CROSS

431 18th Street NW   **Phone:** 202/737-8300
Washington, DC 20006   **FAX:** 202/639-3711

*   *   *

ORGANIZATION'S ACTIVITIES: U.S. arm of international relief agency providing disaster relief as well as social services, international exchange programs, local and regional educational programs for all ages, as well as supervision of donated blood supply and other health-related services. Local chapters throughout country.

Number of Internships: Numerous.

Type: Varies widely depending on assignment, interest and locale.

Function/Duties: Varies by assignment.

Schedule: Full and/or part time, year-round availabilities, openings at local offices around country.

Stipend or Pay: Some paid.

Academic Credit Offered: Per student's own arrangements with academic institution.

ELIGIBILITY: Primarily undergraduate students, though others considered.

REQUIREMENTS: Good writing and research skills, plus interests, goals, and/or experience relevant to available assignments.

APPLICATION PROCEDURE: Send inquiries *to* Internship Coordinator. *Deadline:* Open.

ASPHALT GREEN INC

555 East 90th Street   **Phone:** 212/369-8890
New York, NY 10128   **FAX:** 212/369-2630

*   *   *

ORGANIZATION'S ACTIVITIES: Asphalt Green is a nonprofit sports, art, and education center whose mission is to promote self-esteem, to provide lifetime health, and to bring people of all ages together through this medium.

Number of Internships: Flexible; varies with need.

Type: Coaching, teaching, and clerical.

Function/Duties: Assist staff of specific departments according to intern's skills and interests.

Schedule: Year-round, full-time and part-time internships available; program is organized around fall, spring, and summer seasons.

Stipend or Pay: No.

Academic Credit Offered: Per intern's own arrangements with academic institution.

ELIGIBILITY: Students in high school and college are encouraged to apply; preferred majors: Sports, Arts, Athletic Administration. Open to non-students and career-changers. *Special Eligibilities:* Minorities, women, senior citizens, physically challenged, etc.

REQUIREMENTS: Must provide a cover letter and résumé along with an application.

APPLICATION PROCEDURE: Submit full application *to* Jan Ryan, Executive Director. *Deadline:* Open.

ATTENTION HOMES FOR YOUTH, INC.

1728 South Sixth Street   **Phone:** 217/744-7788
Springfield, IL 62703   **FAX:**   217/523-0717

* * *

ORGANIZATION'S ACTIVITIES: Group homes for adolescent males and females including: therapy, counseling, recreational activities, job coaching, independent living, pre-natal placement, case management.

Number of Internships: Varies with need; fairly numerous.

Type: Therapy.

Function/Duties: Work with kids.

Schedule: Full-time and part-time, flexible term.

Stipend or Pay: Possible, to be discussed.

Academic Credit Offered: Available; must be arranged by intern.

ELIGIBILITY: Graduate students; preferred majors: Psychology, Sociology, and related fields.

REQUIREMENTS: Must enjoy adolescents and be able to interact with clients in a positive manner.

APPLICATION PROCEDURE: Submit résumé and cover letter indicating particular interests *to* Virginia Weels, Executive Director.

THE BUSINESS/GOVERNMENT COUNCIL AND EDUCATION FUND TO END HOMELESSNESS

624 South Grand Avenue
Suite 120   **Phone:** 213/683-8094
Los Angeles, CA 90017   **FAX:** 213/683-1220

* * *

ORGANIZATION'S ACTIVITIES: Lobbyist for homeless issues, provider of educational forums including annual conference.

Number of Internships: 2.

Type: Grant-writing, conference telephoning, lobbying, and educational forums.

Function/Duties: Assist staff of specific departments according to intern's skills and interests.

Schedule: Year-round, part-time internships available.

Stipend or Pay: No.

Academic Credit Offered: Per student's own arrangements with academic institution.

ELIGIBILITY: Consideration given to students, non-students, or career-changers with appropriate qualifications.

REQUIREMENTS: Interests, goals, and/or experience relevant to available assignments.

APPLICATION PROCEDURE: Submit full application *to* Jill Karofolly, Executive Director.

CAMPHILL VILLAGE

P.O. Box 155   **Phone:** 215/935-0300
Kimberton, PA 19442   **FAX:** N/A

* * *

ORGANIZATION'S ACTIVITIES: An agricultural intentional community which includes people with developmental disabilities and offers training opportunities for biodynamic agriculture apprentices and those interested in social therapy.

Number of Internships: Varies.

Type: Agricultural, social therapy.

Function/Duties: Participate in community that aids in integration of the developmentally disabled; also help run farm and community.

Schedule: Seasonal, short-term, or ongoing depending on interests and needs.

Stipend or Pay: Living provided.

Academic Credit Offered: Per student's own arrangements with academic institution.

ELIGIBILITY: Consideration given to students, non-students, or career-changers with appropriate qualifications.

REQUIREMENTS: Interests, goals, skills, and/or experience relevant to available assignments.

APPLICATION PROCEDURE: Send inquiries *to* Internship Coordinator. *Deadline:* Open.

CATHOLIC CHARITIES USA

1731 King Street   **Phone:** 703/549-1390
Alexandria, VA 22314   **FAX:**   703/549-1656

* * *

ORGANIZATION'S ACTIVITIES: Manages, supports, and organizes a broad spectrum of health and social services for people of all faiths nationwide; provides support services for local and regional Catholic Charities groups; centers throughout the U.S.

Number of Internships: Varies; numerous.

Type: Social service, administrative.

Function/Duties: Varies according to need and locale, but in general aid in staff support as well as in direct client services.

Schedule: Varies.

Stipend or Pay: No.

Academic Credit Offered: Per student's own arrangements with academic institution.

ELIGIBILITY: Consideration given to students, non-students, or career-changers with appropriate qualifications.

REQUIREMENTS: Interests, goals, skills, and/or experience relevant to available assignments.

APPLICATION PROCEDURE: Send inquiries *to* Director of Volunteers, for information on headquarters activities and on local opportunities. *Deadline:* Ongoing.

CHILD WELFARE LEAGUE OF AMERICA

440 First Street NW   **Phone:** 202/638-2952
Washington, DC 20001   **FAX:**   202/638-4004

* * *

ORGANIZATION'S ACTIVITIES: Nonprofit organization working to enhance the welfare of children and families and to support and promote the work of social service organizations nationwide.

Number of Internships: Varies; in D.C. and in regional offices.

Type: Administrative, communications, research, fundraising.

Function/Duties: Assist professional staff with ongoing duties and special projects as assigned, depending on need and locale.

Schedule: Part-time, year-round availability, depending on locale.

Stipend or Pay: Expense stipends sometimes available.

Academic Credit Offered: Per student's own arrangements with academic institution.

ELIGIBILITY: Consideration given to students, non-students, or career-changers with appropriate qualifications.

REQUIREMENTS: Interests, goals, skills, and/or experience relevant to available assignments.

APPLICATION PROCEDURE: Send inquiries *to* Internship Coordinator for information on D.C. and other offices. *Deadline:* Ongoing.

CHILDREN'S HOPE FOUNDATION

295 Lafayette Street	**Phone:** 212/941-7432
New York, NY 10012	**FAX:** N/A

* * *

ORGANIZATION'S ACTIVITIES: A nonprofit volunteer organization whose mission is to help improve the quality of life of children affected by AIDS and the HIV virus.

Number of Internships: Varies.

Type: Communications, fundraising, administrative, social service.

Function/Duties: Assist in public relations and publications; help with volunteer coordination; provide direct service to children and families.

Schedule: Flexible.

Stipend or Pay: No.

Academic Credit Offered: Per student's own arrangements with academic institution.

ELIGIBILITY: Consideration given to students, non-students, or career-changers with appropriate qualifications.

REQUIREMENTS: Interests, goals, skills, and/or experience relevant to available assignments.

APPLICATION PROCEDURE: Send inquiries *to* Executive Director. *Deadline:* Ongoing.

CITY TEAM MINISTRIES

P.O. Box 143	**Phone:** 408/998-4770
San Jose, CA 95103	**FAX:** 408/292-9406

* * *

ORGANIZATION'S ACTIVITIES: City Team shares the gospel with more than 25,000 needy people each year through Bible clubs, a Christian camping program, a family ministry, a homeless shelter, and a recovery program for alcoholics and drug addicts.

Number of Internships: Flexible; varies with need.

Type: Volunteer and paid classifications.

Function/Duties: Planning and executing the hands-on aspects of the above programs. Interns must be born-again believers and active in a local church as well as committed to a team-approach ministry.

Schedule: Seasonal (June–August); full-time and part-time internships available.

Stipend or Pay: $900 for those who are classified as paid interns.

Academic Credit Offered: Per intern's own arrangement with academic institution.

ELIGIBILITY: Undergraduate and graduate students are encouraged to apply; open to non-students and career-changers as well. *Special Eligibilities:* Minorities are welcome and encouraged to apply; *Plus* internship may lead to employment opportunities.

REQUIREMENTS: Phone, write, or fax to request an application or additional City Team Ministries information.

APPLICATION PROCEDURE: Submit application *to* Human Resources. *Deadline:* May 15.

COMMUNITY CRISIS CENTER

P.O. Box 1390   **Phone:** 708/697-2380
Elgin, IL 60121   **FAX:**   708/742-4182

* * *

ORGANIZATION'S ACTIVITIES: A crisis intervention center which involves counseling with clients who are residents, walk-ins, and callers on a 24-hour hotline. Domestic violence program, sexual assault program, financial program, children's program, homeless program, and women/children's shelter.

Number of Internships: 6 per semester.

Type: Counseling, children's workers, financial caseworkers.

Function/Duties: Assist staff according to intern's skills and interests (i.e., counseling, advocacy, information referral, etc.). All internships require visual and auditory activity and the ability to lift small children up to 40 pounds.

Schedule: Year-round full-time and part-time internships; seasonal internships are also available (semesters).

Stipend or Pay: None.

Academic Credit Offered: Per intern's arrangement with academic institution.

ELIGIBILITY: Undergraduate (juniors and seniors) and graduate students are encouraged to apply; preferred majors: Psychology, Social Work, Sociology, Human Services, and Counseling; *Plus* internship may lead to full-time employment.

REQUIREMENTS: Must provide a cover letter and a résumé along with an application.

APPLICATION PROCEDURE: Submit full application *to* Maureen Manning-Rosenfeld. *Deadline:* Open.

COMMUNITY EMERGENCY SHELTER ORGANIZATION

1337 West Ohio Street
Third Floor   **Phone:** 312/633-0881
Chicago, IL 60622   **FAX:**   312/829-8915

* * *

ORGANIZATION'S ACTIVITIES: CESO services include consulting, training, and resource development for homeless service providers. Intern activities include research, writing, and coordination of special projects.

Number of Internships: 6 per year.

Type: Research and special projects.

Function/Duties: Assist staff of specific departments according to intern's skills and interests.

Schedule: Part-time, year-round internships.

Stipend or Pay: Negotiable.

Academic Credit Offered: Per intern's own arrangements with academic institution.

ELIGIBILITY: Undergraduate and graduate students with social service administration and social work backgrounds are encouraged to apply; open to non-students and career-changers as well. *Special Eligibilities:* Minorities, women, senior citizens, etc. are encouraged to apply.

REQUIREMENTS: Must provide a cover letter and résumé along with an application.

APPLICATION PROCEDURE: Submit full application *to* John Pfeiffer.

EMERGENCY HOUSING CONSORTIUM

440 North First Street
P.O. Box 2346   **Phone:** 408/298-9657
San Jose, CA 95109   **FAX:**   408/298-6152

* * *

ORGANIZATION'S ACTIVITIES: Homeless shelters and transitional housing for singles, families with children, and youths. Also a drop-in center for homeless youth. Provide housing, workshops, clothing, medical, job search assistance, etc., 90 days to 2 years.

Number of Internships: Varies with project.

Type: No set program—accepted as needed and as offered.

Function/Duties: All.

Schedule: Full- and part-time.

Stipend or Pay: No.

Academic Credit Offered: No.

ELIGIBILITY: College and graduate students; preferred majors: Social Work, Business, Public Administration, and Counseling. Career-changers and some non-students accepted.

REQUIREMENTS: Interests, background, and/or skills relevant to group's goals.

APPLICATION PROCEDURE: Submit letter detailing qualifications and goals *to* Rita Kemic, Director of Operations.

THE EVANGELICAL LUTHERAN GOOD SAMARITAN SOCIETY

1000 West Avenue North   **Phone:** 605/336-2998
Sioux Falls, SD 57117-5038   **FAX:** 605/336-0673

* * *

ORGANIZATION'S ACTIVITIES: Serves 240 long-term-care facilities in 26 states.

Number of Internships: Flexible; varies with need.

Type: Administrator-in-training.

Function/Duties: Learn job of a long-term-care administrator.

Schedule: Full-time, 9- to 12-month term.

Stipend or Pay: $110 to $1,600 per month based on experience.

Academic Credit Offered: Per student's own arrangements with academic institution.

ELIGIBILITY: All students. BS/BA degree or LTC administration experience preferred.

REQUIREMENTS: Interests, goals, and/or experience relevant to available assignments.

APPLICATION PROCEDURE: Send for application and submit *to* Dean Mertz.

FLORIDA EASTER SEAL SOCIETY INC.

1010 Executive Center Drive
Orlando, FL 32803

Phone: 407/896-7881
FAX: 407/896-8422

* * *

ORGANIZATION'S ACTIVITIES: A nonprofit organization affiliated with National Easter Seal Society whose mission is to provide therapeutic and recreational experiences for children and adults with disabilities, including raising funds for Camp Challenge, a 63-acre wheelchair-accessible camp.

Number of Internships: Varies.

Type: Special events.

Function/Duties: Gain hands-on experience in special events activities by assisting the agency's special events coordinator in all aspects of the program.

Schedule: Full- and/or part-time, year-round availability.

Stipend or Pay: No.

Academic Credit Offered: Per student's own arrangements with academic institution.

ELIGIBILITY: Primarily undergraduate or graduate students, but qualified non-students or career-changers are also considered.

REQUIREMENTS: Enthusiasm; all are encouraged to apply.

APPLICATION PROCEDURE: Send inquiries *to* Special Events Coordinator. *Deadline:* Ongoing.

FOX RIVER VALLEY CENTER FOR INDEPENDENT LIVING

730B West Chicago Street
Elgon, IL 60123

Phone: 708/695-5818
FAX: 708/695-5892

* * *

ORGANIZATION'S ACTIVITIES: It is the mission of the Fox River Valley CIL to enhance the options available to persons with disabilities who reside in Kane, Kendall, and McHenry counties, so they may choose and maintain individualized and satisfying life-styles. To this end, the Fox River Valley Center is the only nonresidential independent living center that offers expert, independent living services, public education and awareness, teaches advocacy, and will provide advocacy services that will allow for greater integration of persons with disabilities into the mainstream of community life. The center is staffed primarily with people with disabilities and the board of directors is to be at least 51 percent people with disabilities.

Number of Internships: Varies with need.

Type: Information and referral.

Function/Duties: Computer programmer—develop database.

Schedule: Part-time and full-time during the fall and winter.

Stipend or Pay: No.

ELIGIBILITY: Some students, recent grads, and career-changers. *Special Eligibilities:* Persons with disabilities encouraged to apply.

REQUIREMENTS: Computer skills.

APPLICATION PROCEDURE: Submit résumé and letter of intent *to* Cindy Ciancio, CEO, or Hector Palacios, Program Director.

FRESH AIR FUND

1040 Avenue of the Americas   **Phone:** 212/221-0900
New York, NY 10018   **FAX:** N/A

* * *

ORGANIZATION'S ACTIVITIES: An independent nonprofit agency that has provided free summer vacations to more than 1.6 million disadvantaged New York City children since 1877; in the 1990s, more than 10,000 children go to camps or homes in the country each summer and some 2,000 participate in year-round camping programs.

Number of Internships: Approximately 20.

Type: Social service.

Function/Duties: "Friendly Towners" and escorts assist children and families en route to visits and during stays.

Schedule: 7 to 11 weeks, summers; 35 hours per week.

Stipend or Pay: Approximately $200 per week.

Academic Credit Offered: Per student's own arrangements with academic institution.

ELIGIBILITY: College students.

REQUIREMENTS: Outgoing, organized, dedicated.

Number of Internships: Approximately 15.

Type: Recordkeeping, data processing.

Function/Duties: Keep track of children, applicants, placements, etc.; also aid in office organization.

Schedule: 7 to 11 weeks, summers; 35 hours per week.

Stipend or Pay: Approximately $200 per week.

Academic Credit Offered: Per student's own arrangements with academic institution.

ELIGIBILITY: College students.

REQUIREMENTS: Outgoing, organized, dedicated; computer skills.

APPLICATION PROCEDURE: Request application *from* Executive Director as early as possible. *Deadline:* February 15, for filing.

GIVE KIDS THE WORLD

210 South Bass Road   **Phone:** 407/396-1114
Kissimmee, FL 34746   **FAX:**   407/396-1207

* * *

ORGANIZATION'S ACTIVITIES: A nonprofit organization that gives thousands of children with life-threatening illnesses, and their families, a 6-day cost-free visit to Central Florida attractions. It operates a 35-acre resort about 10 miles from Disney World, with which it has links.

Number of Internships: 1 or more.

Type: Communications.

Function/Duties: Work with staff to perform public relations functions, as well as working with major companies that participate in project, presenting information about them as well.

Schedule: Full- and/or part-time, summers and/or year-round, depending on availability and need.

Stipend or Pay: No.

Academic Credit Offered: Per student's own arrangements with academic institution; *Plus* other nonpaid internship opportunities available through organization, including direct contact with visiting children and families.

ELIGIBILITY: Primarily undergraduate or graduate students, but qualified non-students and career-changers may also be considered.

REQUIREMENTS: Strong written and verbal communication skills, plus word processing experience; ability to take initiative and work independently.

APPLICATION PROCEDURE: Send inquiries *to* Soni Huckleberry. *Deadline:* Ongoing.

INSTITUTE FOR FOOD AND DEVELOPMENT POLICY

Food First
145 Ninth Street   **Phone:** 415/864-8555
San Francisco, CA 94103   **FAX:**   415/864-3909

* * *

ORGANIZATION'S ACTIVITIES: Independent research and education aimed at exposing the causes of hunger, poverty, and environmental degradation. Secondly, to promote development that is participatory, equitable, and sustainable. Books, articles and action alerts, as well as public speaking, radio, and newspaper interviews bring this to public attention.

Number of Internships: Flexible; varies with need.

Type: Library research, analysis, report writing.

Function/Duties: Assist staff of specific departments according to intern's skills and interests.

Schedule: Year-round, full- and part-time internships available.

Stipend or Pay: No.

Academic Credit Offered: Per student's own arrangements with academic institution.

ELIGIBILITY: Consideration given to students, non-students, or career-changers with appropriate qualifications.

REQUIREMENTS: Interests, goals, and/or experience relevant to available assignments.

APPLICATION PROCEDURE: Submit full application *to* Marilyn Borchardt.

INTERAGENCY COUNCIL FOR IMMIGRANT AND REFUGEE SERVICES

1144 10th Avenue
Suite 203
Honolulu, HI 96816

Phone: 808/735-8106
FAX: N/A

* * *

ORGANIZATION'S ACTIVITIES: A human rights and advocacy group serving as an umbrella coordinating agency for the activities of various social service agencies.

Number of Internships: Varies.

Type: Lobbying, social services.

Function/Duties: Participate in legislative monitoring and in acculturation projects for new immigrants.

Schedule: Part-time, year-round availability.

Stipend or Pay: No.

Academic Credit Offered: Per student's own arrangements with academic institution.

ELIGIBILITY: Students, non-students, or career-changers welcome.

REQUIREMENTS: Prefer multilingual people with knowledge of other cultures; either immigrants themselves or experience working with immigrants.

APPLICATION PROCEDURE: Send inquiries *to* Pat Masters. *Deadline:* Open.

LOS ANGELES CATHOLIC CHARITIES

1400 West 9th Street
Los Angeles, CA 90015

Phone: 213/251-3482
FAX: 213/380-4603

* * *

ORGANIZATION'S ACTIVITIES: Provides human services in 3 southern California counties, offering over 30 programs serving families in poverty, the homeless, children, immigrants, the elderly, and those in need of psychological counseling.

Number of Internships: Varies; fairly numerous.

Type: Professional internships in the social services.

Function/Duties: Case management, program development, community organization.

Schedule: Full-time and part-time, year-round as well as by semester; commitments from 9 months to 2 years.

Stipend or Pay: For some positions.

Academic Credit Offered: Yes. *Plus* Internships often lead to career positions.

ELIGIBILITY: Undergraduate and graduate students in social work, psychology, or early childhood education.

REQUIREMENTS: Willingness to work with all ethnic groups; minorities and bilingual and/or bicultural desirable but not required.

Number of Internships: Varies.

Type: Professional internships in gerontology program.

Function/Duties: Social work and public health case management, administrative, outreach, and fundraising.

Schedule: Full-time and part-time, year-round as well as by semester; commitments from 9 months to 2 years.

Stipend or Pay: No.

Academic Credit Offered: Yes. *Plus* Internships often lead to career positions.

ELIGIBILITY: Seniors, undergraduate and graduate students in related fields; career-changers with experience with the elderly also welcome.

REQUIREMENTS: Minorities, bilingual, and/or bicultural desirable but not required.

APPLICATION PROCEDURE: Send résumé *to* Annette Silva, LCSW, *by* about 1 month before start date of program desired.

MENNONITE CENTRAL COMMITTEE

21 South 12th Street   **Phone:** 717/859-1151
Akron, PA 17501   **FAX:**   N/A

* * *

ORGANIZATION'S ACTIVITIES: Sponsors short- and long-term social service projects overseas and in U.S. communities.

Number of Internships: Varies; numerous.

Type: Youth programs and worker-service projects offering training and crosscultural learning during service in poverty areas and disaster locations.

Function/Duties: Community organization, construction, education, support; specific assignments depend on intern's interests and skills and on community needs.

Schedule: 6 months to 2 years, depending on program.

Stipend or Pay: Room, board, and expenses paid.

Academic Credit Offered: Per student's own arrangements with academic institution.

ELIGIBILITY: Students, non-students, career-changers, and workers with any kind of special skills.

REQUIREMENTS: Active members of a Christian church (not necessarily Mennonite) committed to a nonviolent and peacemaking life style.

APPLICATION PROCEDURE: Apply *to* Personnel Department *by* about 6 months in advance of internship availability.

NATIONAL SOCIAL WORK LIBRARY

National Association of Social Workers
750 First Avenue NE   **Phone:** 202/336-8356
Washington, DC 20002   **FAX:** 202/336-8327

*   *   *

ORGANIZATION'S ACTIVITIES: A professional association library that has assembled a diverse collection of published and unpublished articles and books on social work practice and social policy issues.

Number of Internships: 1.

Type: Library technician.

Function/Duties: Collection management, database maintenance, general library duties.

Schedule: Full-time or part-time, year-round availability.

Stipend or Pay: No.

Academic Credit Offered: Per student's own arrangements with academic institution.

ELIGIBILITY: Undergraduate or graduate students or career-changers with appropriate experience.

REQUIREMENTS: Major preferred: Library Science.

APPLICATION PROCEDURE: Send inquiries *to* Library Director. *Deadline:* Open.

NATIONAL WILDLIFE FEDERATION

1400 16th Street NW

Washington, DC 20036

Phone: 202/797-6800

FAX: 202/797-6646

* * *

ORGANIZATION'S ACTIVITIES: The world's largest nonprofit, nongovernmental conservation education organization, sponsoring research, public education, and legislative and legal advocacy, among other environmental protection activities.

Number of Internships: 12.

Type: Resources conservation, social action, corporate.

Function/Duties: Grassroots development projects; also work with corporate executives toward cooperation on environmental issues.

Schedule: Full-time 6 months (January–June and July–December).

Stipend or Pay: About $300 per week plus some benefits.

Academic Credit Offered: Per student's own arrangements with academic institution.

ELIGIBILITY: Some graduate students; otherwise, college graduates with degrees and/or experience in environmentally-related sciences and social issues. *Special Eligibilities:* A completely equal-opportunity program; women and minorities are encouraged to apply.

REQUIREMENTS: These are highly competitive positions, and some related background is a plus; excellent speaking and writing skills required.

APPLICATION PROCEDURE: Send cover letter, résumé, contact information for 3 to 5 academic or professional references, and a 2- to 4-page sample of nonacademic professional writing *to* Nancy Hwa, Resources Conservation Internship Program *by* October 2 for January and *by* April 1 for July.

NEIGHBORHOOD HOUSING SERVICES OF NEW YORK CITY, Inc.

121 West 27th Street

Room 404

New York, NY 10001

Phone: 212/645-6363

FAX: 212/727-8171

* * *

ORGANIZATION'S ACTIVITIES: A nonprofit housing rehabilitation program which lends to "unbankable" but creditworthy owners of homes and small buildings for the purpose of making basic repairs. Goal is to preserve neighborhoods and affordable housing.

Number of Internships: Approximately 6 to 10.

Type: Research and various other duties.

Function/Duties: Assist staff of specific departments according to intern's skills and interests; intern must be able to type.

Schedule: Year-round, full-time and part-time internships available.

Stipend or Pay: Variable pay.

Academic Credit Offered: Per intern's own arrangements with academic institution.

ELIGIBILITY: Undergraduate (juniors and seniors) and graduate students are encouraged to apply; preferred major: Urban Planning. Open to non-students and career-changers as well.

REQUIREMENTS: Must provide a cover letter, written sample, and résumé along with an application.

APPLICATION PROCEDURE: Submit full application *to* Jay Thompson. *Deadline:* Open.

OLD FIRST REFORMED CHURCH

4th and Race Streets   **Phone:** 215/922-4566
Philadelphia, PA 19106   **FAX:** N/A

* * *

ORGANIZATION'S ACTIVITIES: Urban church that provides a wide variety of social and community services.

Number of Internships: 1.

Type: Social service.

Function/Duties: Work with homeless, with children's activities, jobs program, and other socially valuable community activities.

Schedule: One year commitment, full-time.

Stipend or Pay: Yes, plus housing and insurance.

Academic Credit Offered: Per student's own arrangements with academic institution.

ELIGIBILITY: Students, non-students, or career-changers.

REQUIREMENTS: Excellent for persons considering the ministry as a career, for those wanting a break from studies, for people desiring urban experience, or for a mature person in the midst of a life transition.

APPLICATION PROCEDURE: Send inquiries *to* Rev. Geneva M. Butz. *Deadline:* Ongoing.

OPEN HOUSING CENTER

594 Broadway
Suite 608   **Phone:** 212/941-6101
New York, NY 10012   **FAX:** 212/431-7428

* * *

ORGANIZATION'S ACTIVITIES: Since 1964, this multiracial organization has provided advocacy against housing discrimination; counseling; testing program; litigation support. Also assists low-income people to find affordable housing. They offer workshops to community organizations for empowerment.

Number of Internships: 2.

Type: Specific projects; computer database support and community work.

Function/Duties: Assist staff of specific departments, according to intern's skills and interests. Needs fixed and agreed-upon hours, enough for work to be accomplished; computer skills are required.

Schedule: Full-time and part-time internships available year-round.

Stipend or Pay: No.

Academic Credit Offered: Per intern's own arrangements with academic institution.

ELIGIBILITY: Undergraduate and graduate students encouraged to apply; preferred majors: Urban Planning, Social Work, Journalism, and Black Studies. Open to non-students and career-changers as well. *Special Eligibilities:* Women and minorities.

REQUIREMENTS: Must provide a cover letter and résumé along with an application.

APPLICATION PROCEDURE: Send complete application materials *to* Sylvia Kramer. *Deadline:* September 15.

SALVATION ARMY—CASCADE DIVISION

1785 NE Sandy Boulevard	**Phone:** 503/234-0825
Portland, OR 97232	**FAX:** 503/238-1758

* * *

ORGANIZATION'S ACTIVITIES: Regional division of national social service agency, serving low-income persons, the homeless, and the abused.

Number of Internships: 1 or more.

Type: Development, communications.

Function/Duties: Public relations writing, research; events and activities planning and organizing.

Schedule: Full- and/or part-time year-round as needed.

Stipend or Pay: No.

Academic Credit Offered: Per student's own arrangement with academic institution.

ELIGIBILITY: Graduate and undergraduate students as well as non-students and career-changers.

REQUIREMENTS: Interests, goals, skills, and/or experience relevant to available assignments.

APPLICATION PROCEDURE: Send résumé and cover letter *to* Titus Herman. *Deadline:* Open.

SAN ANTONIO FOOD BANK

4311 Director Drive   **Phone:** 512/337-3663
San Antonio, TX 78219   **FAX:**   512/337-2646

* * *

ORGANIZATION'S ACTIVITIES: A nonprofit cooperative organization acting as a collection and distribution center for usable-quality donated foods, distributed throughout 22 counties in south-central Texas through denominational and social service agencies.

Number of Internships: 1 or more.

Type: Communications, administration.

Function/Duties: Public relations functions, assist staff in ongoing activities and special events.

Schedule: Full- and/or part-time, year-round availability.

Stipend or Pay: No.

Academic Credit Offered: Per student's own arrangements with academic institution; *Plus* other types of internships often available elsewhere in organization.

ELIGIBILITY: Primarily undergraduate students, but qualified nonstudents and career-changers also considered.

REQUIREMENTS: Interests, goals, skills, and/or experience relevant to available assignments.

Number of Internships: 2.

Type: Public relations and volunteer services.

Function/Duties: Assist directors in daily events and services; if intern can communicate, written and orally, in Spanish and English, it is a plus.

Schedule: Part-time and full-time internships, year-round and/or seasonal.

Stipend or Pay: No.

Academic Credit Offered: Per intern's own arrangements with academic institution.

ELIGIBILITY: Students in high school or above are eligible to apply. Public relations and journalism majors are preferred; open to nonstudents and career-changers as well.

REQUIREMENTS: Must provide a cover letter and résumé along with an application.

APPLICATION PROCEDURE: Submit full application *to* Melody Campbell. *Deadline:* No.

SECOND HARVEST

116 South Michigan
Chicago, IL 60603

Phone: 312/263-2303
FAX: 312/263-5626

* * *

ORGANIZATION'S ACTIVITIES: The nation's largest nongovernmental, direct service feeding program—a nonprofit organization that solicits surplus groceries from the food industry and distributes it to nearly 200 food banks in 46 states that feed the local hungry through thousands of local social service agencies.

Number of Internships: Varies.

Type: Communications, administration, social service.

Function/Duties: Varies with locales; headquarters office and regional centers have variety of needs.

Schedule: Varies with locale—connect appropriate regional centers through national headquarters.

Stipend or Pay: Mostly unpaid.

Academic Credit Offered: Per student's own arrangements with academic institution.

ELIGIBILITY: Consideration given to students, non-students, or career-changers with appropriate qualifications.

REQUIREMENTS: Interests, goals, skills, and/or experience relevant to available assignments.

APPLICATION PROCEDURE: Send inquiries *to* Information Director. *Deadline:* Ongoing.

SENSES

275 State Street
Albany, NY 12210

Phone: 518/463-5576
FAX: 518/432-9073

* * *

ORGANIZATION'S ACTIVITIES: A statewide coalition that focuses on assuring the economic security of low-income New Yorkers. SENSES covers health care, housing, income security, tax, nutrition, and community economic development issues. The coalition provides policy analysis, training, and technical assistance.

Number of Internships: 3.

Type: Research, program development, writing, and organizing.

Function/Duties: Assist staff of specific department, according to intern's skills and interests; intern must be committed to social change.

Schedule: Year-round full-time and part-time internships available.

Stipend or Pay: No.

Academic Credit Offered: Per student's own arrangements with academic institution.

ELIGIBILITY: Undergraduate (juniors and seniors) and graduate students are encouraged to apply; preferred majors: Social Work, Sociology, and Political Science. Non-students and career-changers are welcome to apply.

REQUIREMENTS: Must provide a cover letter and résumé along with an application.

APPLICATION PROCEDURE: Submit full application *to* Patricia Croop. *Deadline:* Open.

TEXAS ALLIANCE FOR HUMAN NEEDS

2520 Longview
Suite #311
Austin, TX 78705

Phone: 512/474-5019
FAX: N/A

* * *

ORGANIZATION'S ACTIVITIES: "The only independent statewide multi-issue coalition of organizations concerned about low- and moderate-income Texans," serving as a clearinghouse for information, technical assistance, and materials.

Number of Internships: 1.

Type: Community organizer.

Function/Duties: Help staff and member groups with research and organization during specific campaigns; work with community groups and the press.

Schedule: As arranged.

Stipend or Pay: No; free housing may be arranged.

Academic Credit Offered: Per student's own arrangements with academic institution.

ELIGIBILITY: Students, non-students, or career-changers.

REQUIREMENTS: Must have proven organizational skill, and interests, goals, and/or experience relevant to activities.

APPLICATION PROCEDURE: *Contact* Executive Director for details. *Deadline:* Open.

UNITED JEWISH FEDERATION OF METROWEST

901 Route 10
Whippany, NJ 07981-1156

Phone: 201/884-4800
FAX: 201/884-7361

* * *

ORGANIZATION'S ACTIVITIES: United Jewish Federation of MetroWest raises funds through UJA and provides resources, coordinates programs and services for one of North America's most dynamic and sophisticated Jewish communities. As the central philanthropic address, the Federation and its beneficiary agencies strive to fulfill the communal and social service needs of the Jewish community.

Number of Internships: 3.

Type: Editorial, graphic design, and general production assistance.

Function/Duties: Research, write, and keep records according to specific department's needs. Good writing skills, designing ability (graphic arts), computer skills, and good interpersonal skills are a plus.

Schedule: Part-time, year-round interns are needed.

Stipend or Pay: $6 to $7 per hour.

Academic Credit Offered: Per intern's own arrangements with academic institution.

ELIGIBILITY: Undergraduate students with a journalism, communications, or graphic design background are encouraged to apply. Possible opportunities for non-students and career-changers as well.

REQUIREMENTS: Must provide a résumé with application.

APPLICATION PROCEDURE: Submit full application *to* Susan Milberg, Director of Marketing and Communications.

VANISHED CHILDREN'S ALLIANCE

1407 Parkmoor Avenue
Suite 200   **Phone:** 408/971-4822
San Jose, CA 95126   **FAX:**   408/971-8516

* * *

ORGANIZATION'S ACTIVITIES: VCA is a 13-year-old nonprofit organization dedicated to the prevention, location, and recovery of missing and abducted American children. They provide counseling, technical assistance, active case management, poster and photo distribution, translation services, speaker's bureau, and expert-witness testimony.

Number of Internships: 3 or 4.

Type: There is 1 in-house legal assistant internship, 1 public relations assistant internship, and 2 casework department assistant internships.

Function/Duties: Assist staff of specific departments, according to intern's interests.

Schedule: Full-time, year-round internships.

Stipend or Pay: Varies according to internship.

Academic Credit Offered: Per intern's own arrangements with academic institution.

ELIGIBILITY: Undergraduate and graduate students with social work and/or criminal justice backgrounds are encouraged to apply. Open to non-students and career-changers with 3 to 5 years related experience. *Plus* internship may lead to employment opportunities.

REQUIREMENTS: Must submit a cover letter, résumé, and 3 references along with an application.

APPLICATION PROCEDURE: Submit full application *to* Georgia K. Hilgeman, Executive Director. *Deadline:* Open.

VOLUNTEERS OF AMERICA

340 West 85th Street
New York, NY 10024

Phone: 212/873-2600
FAX: 212/769-2629

* * *

ORGANIZATION'S ACTIVITIES: A national nonprofit human service organization that provides various forms of support to the homeless, the elderly, people with AIDS, and others in need. Centers throughout the country.

Number of Internships: Varies; numerous.

Type: Communications, data processing, administrative, social services.

Function/Duties: Varies with assignment and locale; in general assist staff as needed with administrative services and direct client assistance.

Schedule: Flexible.

Stipend or Pay: No.

Academic Credit Offered: Per student's own arrangements with academic institution.

ELIGIBILITY: Consideration given to students, non-students, or career-changers with appropriate qualifications.

REQUIREMENTS: Interests, goals, skills, and/or experience relevant to available assignments.

APPLICATION PROCEDURE: Send inquiries *to* Volunteer Coordinator at headquarters or at local centers. *Deadline:* Ongoing.

WEINGART CENTER ASSOCIATION

566 South San Pedro Street
Los Angeles, CA 90013

Phone: 213/627-9000
FAX: 213/488-3419

* * *

ORGANIZATION'S ACTIVITIES: The Weingart Center is one of the nation's largest complexes providing health and human services for the homeless; widely regarded as a model for innovative partnerships with public and private agencies toward the goal of enabling homeless people to achieve economic and personal self-sufficiency.

Number of Internships: 3 or more.

Type: Development.

Function/Duties: Assist in any area of fundraising of interest to the intern, from estate planning through phoning to organizing special events.

Schedule: Full- and/or part-time, summers and/or school semesters.

Stipend or Pay: No.

Academic Credit Offered: Per student's own arrangements with academic institution.

ELIGIBILITY: Consideration given to students, non-students, or career-changers with appropriate qualifications.

REQUIREMENTS: Interests, goals, skills, and/or experience relevant to available assignments.

Number of Internships: 3 or more.

Type: Volunteer services coordination.

Function/Duties: Assist in developing and implementing a volunteer corps for service in any of the center's 20-plus service areas, and guiding tour groups.

Schedule: Full- and/or part-time, summers and/or school semesters.

Stipend or Pay: No.

Academic Credit Offered: Per student's own arrangements with academic institution.

ELIGIBILITY: Consideration given to students, non-students, or career-changers with appropriate qualifications.

REQUIREMENTS: Interests, goals, skills, and/or experience relevant to available assignments.

APPLICATION PROCEDURE: Send inquiries *to* Vice President, Development and Community Affairs. *Deadline:* Ongoing.

WORLD RELIEF CORPORATION

450 Gundersen Drive   **Phone:** 708/665-0235
Carol Stream, IL 60188   **FAX:**   708/653-8023

* * *

ORGANIZATION'S ACTIVITIES: A nonprofit group working to find homes, jobs, and health care for new immigrants, refugees, and the homeless.

Number of Internships: Varies.

Type: Direct assistance to client population.

Function/Duties: Finding shelter, food, and medical care.

Schedule: Flexible, year-round.

Stipend or Pay: No.

Academic Credit Offered: Per student's own arrangements with academic institution.

ELIGIBILITY: Students, non-students, career-changers—all are welcome.

REQUIREMENTS: Interests, goals, and/or experience relevant to available assignments; foreign language skills a plus.

APPLICATION PROCEDURE: Send inquiries *to* Intern Coordinator. *Deadline:* Ongoing.

Organizations/Resources for Further Information about Internships in Social Services

For further information about internships in the social services, *see* Resources in *Associations*, *International*, and *Health* sections.

You will find even more information in the chapter titled "Finding Further Internship Sources" (page 388)—*AND*:

Make your own service internship by starting close to home. Many religious organizations sponsor social service programs, locally, nationally, and internationally; investigate the opportunities available to members of your faith, or simply work through the local religious institution or community center that takes care of the needy in your neighborhood.

INTERNSHIP SOURCES IN ASSOCIATIONS

■■

Notes on Interning in Associations:

Membership associations numbering nearly 90,000—plus their hundreds of thousands of chapters—operate nationally, regionally, and locally in the United States. Most offer the kinds of internship opportunities listed here—in education, lobbying, publications, administration, finance, fundraising, or computer technology as well as the central focus of their group. Trade and professional organizations not only make wide use of interns—they also serve as active networks for placing interns in their member organizations.

TIPS: 1. Association internships are terrific for career-changers: if you are a member of a trade or professional group, find an internship in that field that allows you to hone the new skills you will need—communications, computers, whatever—for your new direction. Or, take one of those skills to an association representing the new career you are heading for. Do marketing or data entry for the association and make contacts while you are there.

2. Most associations and similar member organizations will offer internships if asked, but they also are terrific guides to other opportunities. See the suggestions at the end of this section for just a hint of the range of possibilities.

> *Julie, now in her second year of working at the National Academy of Public Administrators, says that her internship with the American Society of Public Administrators "was what got me my job." She credits the contacts she made at ASPA at least as much as the hands-on experience and the good references. In addition, of course, she got a lot of experience she would not necessarily have participated in as a simple entry-level employee. She found a mentor, and picked up a lot just through observation. She was also able to become a research assistant, through which she learned a great deal. Her advice? "Sure, some of it is menial—but that's the way it is in any job, so it seems pointless to get worked up about that. Instead, make the most of the other things you get to do."*

Also see: In most other sections of this book, associations are listed according to the areas of their specialties.

AMERICAN ASSOCIATION FOR ADULT AND CONTINUING EDUCATION

2101 Wilson Boulevard
Arlington, VA 22201

Phone: 703/522-2234
FAX: N/A

* * *

ORGANIZATION'S ACTIVITIES: Maintains and provides information for public, legislators, educators, and press on adult education and life-long learning.

Number of Internships: 2.

Type: Communications, editorial.

Function/Duties: Interns are needed to assist with the association's publication and with marketing and planning services.

Schedule: 10 to 20 hours per week, year-round.

Stipend or Pay: No.

Academic Credit Offered: Per student's own arrangements with academic institution.

ELIGIBILITY: Primarily junior and senior undergraduate students.

REQUIREMENTS: Interests, goals, and/or experience relevant to available assignments.

APPLICATION PROCEDURE: Send inquiries *to* Communications Director. *Deadline:* Open.

AMERICAN ASSOCIATION FOR THE ADVANCEMENT OF SCIENCE

1333 H Street NW
Washington, DC 20005

Phone: 202/326-6400
FAX: 202/682-0816

* * *

ORGANIZATION'S ACTIVITIES: With a mission "to improve the effectiveness of science in the promotion of human welfare," the AAAS sponsors programs and publications to enhance cooperation among scientists and their work, and increase public awareness of the importance of science.

Number of Internships: Varies; fairly numerous.

Type: Research, data processing, events planning, editorial.

Function/Duties: Aid staff and committees with planning programs, gathering data, editing publications, etc.

Schedule: Part- and/or full-time, year-round.

Stipend or Pay: Some internships paid; some unpaid.

Academic Credit Offered: Per student's own arrangements with academic institution; *Plus* opportunities to attend professional seminars.

ELIGIBILITY: Primarily upper-class and graduate students, but also consideration given to non-students or career-changers with appropriate qualifications.

REQUIREMENTS: Interests, goals, and/or experience relevant to available assignments.

APPLICATION PROCEDURE: Send inquiries *to* Human Resources Office. *Deadline:* Ongoing.

AMERICAN BANKERS ASSOCIATION

| 1120 Connecticut Avenue NW | **Phone:** | 202/663-5000 |
| Washington, DC 20036 | **FAX:** | 202/828-4544 |

* * *

ORGANIZATION'S ACTIVITIES: A trade association dedicated to the promotion of the banking and finance industries through communication, information, and legislative action.

Number of Internships: Varies by need.

Type: Government relations, public relations, marketing, other activities.

Function/Duties: Assist staff and committees in producing publications, conducting surveys, managing administrative matters.

Schedule: Full- and/or part-time; some summers, some year-round.

Stipend or Pay: Full-time internships are paid; part-time, unpaid.

Academic Credit Offered: Per student's own arrangements with academic institution.

ELIGIBILITY: Primarily graduate and undergraduate students.

REQUIREMENTS: Prefer business students.

APPLICATION PROCEDURE: Send inquiries *to* Human Resources Department to receive application materials for submission *by* 2 months prior to start date.

AMERICAN FEDERATION OF LABOR/CONGRESS OF INDUSTRIAL ORGANIZATIONS (AFL/CIO)

| 815 16th Street NW | **Phone:** | 202/637-5000 |
| Washington, DC 20006 | **FAX:** | 202/637-5058 |

* * *

ORGANIZATION'S ACTIVITIES: Coalition representing unions and American workers and providing information and legislative action on labor-related matters.

Number of Internships: Varies.

Type: Research, editorial.

Function/Duties: Assist professional staff members with economic analyses and with production of publications.

Schedule: Full-time, 1 year from July to July.

Stipend or Pay: Yes—about $500 per week.

Academic Credit Offered: Per student's own arrangements with academic institution, if applicable.

ELIGIBILITY: College graduates who have completed at least one year of graduate studies in relevant disciplines.

REQUIREMENTS: Interests, goals, and/or experience relevant to available assignments.

APPLICATION PROCEDURE: Request details on materials to submit *to* Human Resource Office *by* March 1.

AMERICAN HOTEL & MOTEL ASSOCIATION

1201 New York Avenue NW   **Phone:** 202/289-3100
Washington, DC 20005   **FAX:**   202/289-3138

* * *

ORGANIZATION'S ACTIVITIES: The American Hotel & Motel Association (AH&MA) represents nearly 1.4 million rooms, comprising over 10,000 hotels, motels, resorts, and inns. This represents over 60 percent of the competitive rentable rooms in the U.S. The AH&MA speaks as the trade association for the lodging industry.

Number of Internships: 3 per year.

Type: Public relations.

Function/Duties: Communications.

Schedule: Part-time and full-time, flexible term.

Stipend or Pay: No.

Academic Credit Offered: Available.

ELIGIBILITY: Undergraduate students; preferred major: Public Relations.

REQUIREMENTS: Interests, goals, background, and/or skills relevant to hospitality industry; need excellent communications skills.

APPLICATION PROCEDURE: Submit résumé *to* Jenifer Clements.

AMERICAN MANAGEMENT ASSOCIATION

135 West 50th Street   **Phone:** 212/586-8100
New York, NY 10020   **FAX:**   212/903-8168

* * *

ORGANIZATION'S ACTIVITIES: A membership and educational organization whose purpose is the enhancement of management skills through seminars and publications.

Number of Internships: 30.

Type: Data processing, editorial, marketing.

Function/Duties: Aid staff as assigned, according to interests and skills.

Schedule: Some full-time, some part-time, throughout the year in NYC headquarters, Boston office, or regional locations.

Stipend or Pay: May be arranged.

Academic Credit Offered: Per student's own arrangements with academic institution.

REQUIREMENTS: Prefer candidates with business-studies background and good communications skills.

APPLICATION PROCEDURE: Request application packet and submit with résumé and cover letter *to* Human Resources Department. *Deadline:* 2 months prior to start date.

AMERICAN PLANNING ASSOCIATION

1776 Massachusetts Avenue NW **Phone:** 202/872-0611
Washington, DC 20036 **FAX:** 202/872-0643

* * *

ORGANIZATION'S ACTIVITIES: Nonprofit nonpartisan membership organization of and for urban planners.

Number of Internships: 3 or more.

Type: Research, communications.

Function/Duties: Professional-level work in research and reporting on urban planning issues.

Schedule: Full-time in summer, part-time during school year, for 3- to 6-month stints in D.C. office or Chicago center.

Stipend or Pay: Yes.

Academic Credit Offered: Per student's own arrangements with academic institution; *Plus* may lead to career positions.

ELIGIBILITY: Primarily graduate students.

REQUIREMENTS: Prefer students in urban planning and related studies.

APPLICATION PROCEDURE: Send inquiries *to* Internship Coordinator *by* about 2 months prior to start date.

THE ASSOCIATION OF THE BAR OF THE CITY OF NEW YORK

42 West 44th Street **Phone:** 212/382-6770
New York, NY 10036-6690 **FAX:** 212/768-8116

* * *

ORGANIZATION'S ACTIVITIES: The Association is an independent organization of over 19,000 lawyers that addresses a broad range of local, national, and international public policy issues, and conducts public service and community outreach activities throughout New York City.

Number of Internships: Up to 5.

Type: Assisting the legislative program and participating in public service and community outreach activities.

Function/Duties: Research, administrative, and assistance at legal clinics.

Schedule: Part-time and full-time year-round; term of internship ranges from 2 months to 1 year.

Stipend or Pay: No.

Academic Credit Offered: Per intern's own arrangements with academic institution.

ELIGIBILITY: Students in high school, college, or graduate school are welcome; also open to non-students and career-changers.

REQUIREMENTS: Applicant must possess strong written and oral communication skills.

APPLICATION PROCEDURE: Request application by writing *to* Robin Kreitner, Director of Personnel.

BUILDING OWNERS & MANAGERS ASSOCIATION

1201 New York Avenue NW   **Phone:** 202/408-2662
Washington, DC 20005   **FAX:** 202/371-0181

* * *

ORGANIZATION'S ACTIVITIES: Trade association for companies that own or manage office buildings, providing information and advocacy for 7,000-plus members nationwide and internationally.

Number of Internships: Varies; approximately 12.

Type: Research, administration.

Function/Duties: Aid executive, research, and finance staffs in producing reports, monitoring legislative activities, running office.

Schedule: Full- and/or part-time; summers and/or year-round.

Stipend or Pay: Some internships are paid, others unpaid.

Academic Credit Offered: Per student's own arrangements with academic institution.

ELIGIBILITY: Primarily graduates and undergraduate students, but others are considered.

REQUIREMENTS: Interests, goals, and/or experience relevant to available assignments.

APPLICATION PROCEDURE: Send inquiries *to* Director of Operations.
Deadline: Ongoing.

CALIFORNIA INDEPENDENT PETROLEUM ASSOCIATION

1112 I Street
Suite #350
Sacramento, CA 95814

Phone: 916/447-1177
FAX: 916/447-1144

* * *

ORGANIZATION'S ACTIVITIES: Six hundred-plus-member non-profit trade association representing independent oil and natural gas producers and the companies that service and supply them throughout California.

Number of Internships: 4 or more.

Type: Membership recruitment, advocacy.

Function/Duties: Dependent on skills of individual.

Schedule: Full-time and part-time, open term.

Stipend or Pay: Not usually.

Academic Credit Offered: Must be arranged by intern.

ELIGIBILITY: College and graduate students; preferred major: Liberal Arts.

REQUIREMENTS: Good communications skills; computer skills a plus.

APPLICATION PROCEDURE: Submit résumé and cover letter *to* Dan Kramer.

CHICAGO FOUNDATION FOR WOMEN

230 West Superior
Suite #400
Chicago, IL 60610-3536

Phone: 312/266-1176
FAX: 312/266-0990

* * *

ORGANIZATION'S ACTIVITIES: A nonprofit women's organization providing grants to Chicago's women's and girls' programs, seeking to increase resources for women through grantmaking, fundraising, and education projects.

Number of Internships: Varies according to projects.

Type: Development/fundraising.

Function/Duties: Assist with special events and day-to-day operations of a small development office.

Schedule: At least one full-time, year-round; more as needed seasonally and/or part-time for special projects.

Stipend or Pay: Possible.

Academic Credit Offered: Yes.

ELIGIBILITY: Students at all levels, from high school through graduate school, as well as non-students and career-changers; *Plus* women and minorities are especially encouraged to apply.

REQUIREMENTS: Available to work in Chicago office.

APPLICATION PROCEDURE: Submit letter with résumé *to* Kris Torkelson, Development Director. *Deadline:* No.

DIRECT MARKETING ASSOCIATION

11 West 42nd Street   **Phone:** 212/768-7277
New York, NY 10036-8096   **FAX:** 212/768-4546

*   *   *

ORGANIZATION'S ACTIVITIES: The largest trade association in the direct-marketing field with 3,600-member companies drawn from every business segment as well as the nonprofit and public sector, DMA monitors state and federal legislative activities, sponsors ethics and consumer-service programs, conducts numerous research programs, and publishes monographs on all aspects of direct marketing as well as a national newsletter and other membership publications.

Number of Internships: Vary according to needs of individual departments.

Type: Opportunities available in each department.

Function/Duties: Determined on a departmental basis.

Schedule: Full- and part-time, year-round or per semester, according to need.

Stipend or Pay: Negotiable.

Academic Credit Offered: Per student's own arrangements with academic institution.

ELIGIBILITY: College students as well as appropriately qualified non-students and career-changers. *Special Eligibilities:* Study or experience in advertising, marketing, or other communications fields preferred.

REQUIREMENTS: Interns must be available to work during business hours in DMA New York headquarters or Washington, D.C., office.

APPLICATION PROCEDURE: Inquire concerning availabilities and procedure *to* Karen Elkins, Director of Human Resources *by* several months prior to desired internship period.

GEORGIA SOCIETY OF CPAs

3340 Peachtree Road
Suite 2750
Atlanta, GA 30326   **Phone:** 404/231-8676
                                  FAX: N/A

*   *   *

ORGANIZATION'S ACTIVITIES: Professional association for 8,500 CPAs in Georgia.

Number of Internships: 2.

Type: Communications department.

Function/Duties: Public relations.

Schedule: Full-time and part-time.

Stipend or Pay: Yes.

Academic Credit Offered: Per student's own arrangements with academic institution.

ELIGIBILITY: High school and graduate students; preferred majors: Public Relations, Journalism, and Marketing; career-changers and non-students welcome to apply.

REQUIREMENTS: Interests, goals, and/or experience relevant to available assignments.

APPLICATION PROCEDURE: Submit résumé and cover letter *to* Sylvia Small.

THE GREATER LOS ANGELES PRESS CLUB

Hollywood Palm Hotel
2005 North Highland Avenue   **Phone:**   213/874-3003
Los Angeles, CA 90068   **FAX:**   213/874-3005

* * *

ORGANIZATION'S ACTIVITIES: A social and professional association for anyone working in or involved with any of the news media, including public relations and advertising, students in these fields, and "persons of special distinction who have frequent contact with news activities."

Number of Internships: 8.

Type: Media, events, programming, management.

Function/Duties: Assist committees and staff with administration, communications, and events management, including press conferences and Awards Contest.

Schedule: Full- and/or part-time, year-round.

Stipend or Pay: No.

Academic Credit Offered: Per student's own arrangements with academic institution.

ELIGIBILITY: Consideration given to students, non-students, or career-changers with appropriate qualifications.

REQUIREMENTS: Interests, goals, and/or experience relevant to available assignments.

APPLICATION PROCEDURE: Send inquiries *to* Office Manager. *Deadline:* Ongoing.

INTERNATIONAL CITY MANAGEMENT ASSOCIATION

777 North Capitol Street NE
Washington, DC 20002

Phone: 202/289-4262
FAX: 202/962-3500

* * *

ORGANIZATION'S ACTIVITIES: Professional and educational organization with membership of over 7500 administrators of local governments, providing information and education on topics of group interest, including housing and environmental management.

Number of Internships: 15.

Type: Research, editorial, communications.

Function/Duties: Aid staff in producing publications, responding to membership inquiries, research issues, and on special projects.

Schedule: Full- and/or part-time, summers, semesters, and year-round.

Stipend or Pay: Some paid internships, some unpaid.

Academic Credit Offered: Per student's own arrangements with academic institution.

ELIGIBILITY: Graduate and undergraduate students.

REQUIREMENTS: Prefer students with majors or interests in public administration.

APPLICATION PROCEDURE: Send inquiries *to* Internship Coordinator. *Deadline:* Varies with start date desired.

METROPOLITAN WASHINGTON COUNCIL OF GOVERNMENTS (COG)

777 North Capitol Street NE
Suite 300
Washington, DC 20002-4226

Phone: 202/962-3200
FAX: 202/962-3201

* * *

ORGANIZATION'S ACTIVITIES: An independent nonprofit organization of the Washington, D.C., area's major local governments and officials, supported by contributions and grants, COG works to solve such regional issues as growth, transportation, housing, economic development, environmental quality, and public safety.

Number of Internships: Varies according to projects and available funding.

Type: Assist staff members as needed, including active participation in special projects.

Schedule: Full-time (40 hours per week) and part-time (20 hours per week) in formal summer program; fall and spring internships available on project basis.

Function/Duties: Variety of activities in areas of human services, planning, public safety; transportation planning; environmental programs; public affairs, and library.

Stipend or Pay: $7.50 per hour for undergraduate students; $8.50 per hour for graduate students; some unpaid internships.

Academic Credit Offered: Per student's own arrangements with academic institution.

REQUIREMENTS: Available during business hours to work in Washington, D.C.

ELIGIBILITY: Undergraduate and graduate students; non-students and career-changers with appropriate qualifications. *Special Eligibilities:* COG is an Equal Opportunity/Affirmative Action employer.

APPLICATION PROCEDURE: Contact Internship Coordinator about availabilities, then send résumé, cover letter, school transcript, and 6- to 8-page writing sample *to* Internship Coordinator *by* April 1 for *summer* internships.

NATIONAL ASSOCIATION OF PROFESSIONAL SURPLUS LINES OFFICES LTD.

6405 North Cosby
Kansas City, MO 64151

Phone: 816/741-3910
FAX: N/A

* * *

ORGANIZATION'S ACTIVITIES: An organization of and for specialized insurance companies that offer coverage in special-risk situations.

Number of Internships: 8.

Type: Insurance underwriting.

Function/Duties: Work at offices of member firms, assisting in various areas, sitting in on meetings, and learning underwriting hands-on.

Schedule: Summers, 10 weeks—5 weeks at a brokerage, 5 at an insurance company.

Stipend or Pay: No.

Academic Credit Offered: Per student's own arrangements with academic institution (students write reports on experiences); *Plus* 2 interns chosen to attend annual convention; 1 for a 3-week internship in London.

ELIGIBILITY: College and other students in fields associated with insurance.

REQUIREMENTS: A student must demonstrate a genuine interest in the insurance industry and be available for interview.

APPLICATION PROCEDURE: Request application materials and send with transcript and letters of recommendation *to* Tom Mulligan *by* February 1.

NATIONAL CRIME PREVENTION COUNCIL

1700 K Street NW
Washington, DC 20006

Phone: 202/466-6272
FAX: 202/296-1656

* * *

ORGANIZATION'S ACTIVITIES: Nonpartisan organization whose purpose is to educate the public and promote community involvement in preventing crimes.

Number of Internships: 8.

Type: Research, communications, editorial, administrative.

Function/Duties: Aid staff in marketing, member services, addiction prevention, development, programming, and special projects.

Schedule: Full- and/or part-time, summers, semesters, and some year-round.

Stipend or Pay: Full-time paid stipend.

Academic Credit Offered: Per student's own arrangements with academic institution.

ELIGIBILITY: Primarily college students, but consideration also given to non-students or career-changers with appropriate qualifications.

REQUIREMENTS: Interests, goals, and/or experience relevant to available assignments.

APPLICATION PROCEDURE: Send for intern packet *from* Intern Coordinator. *Deadline:* Ongoing.

NATIONAL FARMERS ORGANIZATION

2505 Elwood Drive
Ames, IA 50010

Phone: 515/292-2000
FAX: 515/292-7106

* * *

ORGANIZATION'S ACTIVITIES: Provides collective bargaining of agricultural products for farmers and ranchers.

Number of Internships: Varies; usually 3 per term.

Type: Communications and others.

Function/Duties: Assist in public affairs and other staff offices.

Schedule: Varying periods year-round, full-time or part-time.

Stipend or Pay: Negotiable.

Academic Credit Offered: Per student's own arrangements with academic institution.

ELIGIBILITY: College students or non-students with 2 years' experience in agricultural fields; career-changers also welcome; *Plus* possibility of full-time regular employment after successful internship.

REQUIREMENTS: Available to work during business hours in Ames, Iowa.

APPLICATION PROCEDURE: Submit current résumé with cover letter *to* Walter Albers, Director of Staff Development. *Deadline:* Open.

NATIONAL FEDERATION OF TEMPLE BROTHERHOODS

838 Fifth Avenue	**Phone:**	212/570-0707
New York, NY 10021	**FAX:**	212/570-0960

* * *

ORGANIZATION'S ACTIVITIES: Organization of Jewish men's groups in Reform synagogues nationwide, providing communications, support, and coordination of activities.

Number of Internships: Varies according to availability and need.

Type: Communications, public relations, clerical.

Function/Duties: Assist staff in programming, newsletter, special projects.

Schedule: Flexible; year-round, part-time, and/or seasonal.

Stipend or Pay: Possible.

Academic Credit Offered: Per student's own arrangements with academic institution.

ELIGIBILITY: Students of all levels and majors, as well as appropriate non-students and career-changers.

REQUIREMENTS: Available to work in New York office.

APPLICATION PROCEDURE: Send résumé with desired job description *to* Bradley Frome. *Deadline:* No.

NEW YORK STATE BAR ASSOCIATION

One Elk Street	**Phone:**	518/463-3200
Albany, NY 12207	**FAX:**	518/463-4276

* * *

ORGANIZATION'S ACTIVITIES: A statewide professional organization of lawyers that publishes materials for consumers; plans and organizes meetings; conducts continuing education programs; and lobbies on relevant matters in the state legislature.

Number of Internships: 12.

Type: Public relations.

Function/Duties: Write articles, news releases, edit audiotape, help organize events.

Schedule: Both full- and part-time opportunities; some summers only, others during fall and spring semesters.

Stipend or Pay: $7 per hour.

Academic Credit Offered: Yes.

ELIGIBILITY: Students—college juniors or seniors—public relations majors preferred; *Plus* many of the Association's other offices often offer a variety of internship opportunities; contact Human Resources Director at above address.

REQUIREMENTS: A two-hour written test in writing, spelling, and grammar must be passed (arrangements can be made to have it administered in locations other than Albany). Interns must be available in Albany during business hours.

APPLICATION PROCEDURE: Submit résumé with detailed cover letter *to* Bard Carr, Director of Communications and Public Affairs *by* April 15 for the fall semester, October 15 for the spring semester, and May 1 for the summer.

ORDER OF SONS OF ITALY IN AMERICA

219 E Street NE   **Phone:**   202/547-2900
Washington, DC 20002   **FAX:**   202/564-8168

* * *

ORGANIZATION'S ACTIVITIES: National office of nonprofit fraternal organization with 100,000 members nationwide provides services, programs, and publications as well as scholarships and mentor programs.

Number of Internships: 3.

Type: Public relations, program management, communications.

Function/Duties: Administrative, writing, editing.

Schedule: Full- and/or part-time, summers (May–September).

Stipend or Pay: Yes.

Academic Credit Offered: Per student's own arrangements with academic institution; *Plus* opportunities to attend meetings, seminars, events.

ELIGIBILITY: Students—Mature high school juniors through college juniors. *Special Eligibilities:* Individuals of Italian heritage.

REQUIREMENTS: Preference for those who have lived or worked in Italy or who are majoring in Italian studies.

APPLICATION PROCEDURE: Submit cover letter, résumé, transcript, writing sample, and recommendations *to* Mark Dalessandro. *Deadline:* March 31.

PENNSYLVANIA BUILDERS ASSOCIATION

412 North Second Street   **Phone:**   717/234-6209
Harrisburg, PA 17101   **FAX:**   717/234-9553

* * *

ORGANIZATION'S ACTIVITIES: A nonprofit statewide association providing marketing, promotional, educational, and legislative support to nearly 10,000 members of the residential construction industry, with 39 local chapters throughout Pennsylvania; the organization also provides educational services to members, to state agencies, and to related associations.

Number of Internships: Varies; about 5 per year.

Type: Public relations.

Function/Duties: Assist public relations director with publications, events, press releases.

Schedule: One intern each in fall and in spring semesters, 2 or 3 during the summer, 35 hours per week for 15 weeks.

Stipend or Pay: $1,800 scholarship paid at intervals during the internship.

Academic Credit Offered: Association only accepts students whose institutions have agreed to provide academic credit.

ELIGIBILITY: Students who are juniors or seniors in college; any majors are considered, but students with public relations–related experiences may receive special consideration. Other internships in the association may be available. *Plus* interns with cars receive free parking and all travel and travel-related expenses are reimbursed.

REQUIREMENTS: In addition to appropriate student status and presence in Harrisburg location, interns must possess an ability to write clearly and concisely.

APPLICATION PROCEDURE: Arrange interview *with* Debra S. Tingley, Director of Public Relations; at interview, present résumé, writing samples, and other relevant materials. *Deadline:* June 30 for fall, September 30 for winter, and April 1 for summer.

PENNSYLVANIA MANUFACTURERS' ASSOCIATION

225 State Street   **Phone:**   717/232-0937
Harrisburg, PA 17101   **FAX:**   717/232-8623

* * *

ORGANIZATION'S ACTIVITIES: Professional trade association founded in 1909 to promote the welfare and common business interests of its members and the economic prosperity of the Commonwealth of Pennsylvania and its manufacturing and service industries. Builds coalition of concerned businesspeople throughout the state to voice opinion on relevant legislative issues, and communicates these views to the legislature.

Number of Internships: Varies; fairly numerous.

Type: Research, legislative work, technical assistance, and administration.

Function/Duties: Specific duties of each internship will be determined by the projects being worked on by the professional staff; opportunity to attend seminars, workshops, hearings, etc.

Schedule: Full-time, possibly part-time (September through June), semester-long term.

Stipend or Pay: Yes; amount depends on position.

Academic Credit Offered: May be available.

ELIGIBILITY: College seniors, minimum GPA of 3.2; preferred majors: Political Science, Journalism, and Public Administration.

REQUIREMENTS: Computer word processing essential; also excellent verbal and written communications skills and previous work experience of some type.

APPLICATION PROCEDURE: Submit letter from college department head, official transcript, and letter of intent *to* Executive Director. *Deadline:* June 1 for fall semester, January 15 for spring semester.

TRI-COUNTY APARTMENT ASSOCIATION

792 Meridian Way   **Phone:** 408/297-0483
San Jose, CA 95126   **FAX:** 408/947-0819

*   *   *

ORGANIZATION'S ACTIVITIES: A nonprofit trade organization representing the rental housing industry in three California counties with a goal of promoting fairness in rental housing through educational and legislative programs.

Number of Internships: 1 or more.

Type: Various, including communications.

Function/Duties: Assist in public relations and marketing.

Schedule: Flexible.

Stipend or Pay: No, but work-related expenses are reimbursed.

Academic Credit Offered: Per student's own arrangements with academic institution.

ELIGIBILITY: Primarily undergraduate and graduate students.

REQUIREMENTS: Excellent writing skills, with some knowledge of desktop publishing.

APPLICATION PROCEDURE: Send résumé, cover letter, and writing samples *to* Communications Director. *Deadline:* Open.

UNITED JEWISH FEDERATION OF METROWEST

901 Route 10   **Phone:**   201/884-4800
Whippany, NJ 07981-1156   **FAX:**   201/884-7361

* * *

ORGANIZATION'S ACTIVITIES: United Jewish Federation of MetroWest raises funds through UJA and provides resources, coordinates programs and services for one of North America's most dynamic and sophisticated Jewish communities. As the central philanthropic address, the Federation and its beneficiary agencies strive to fulfill the communal and social service needs of the Jewish community.

Number of Internships: 3.

Type: Editorial, graphic design, and general production assistance.

Function/Duties: Research, write, and keep records according to specific department's needs. Good writing skills, designing ability (graphic arts), computer skills, and good interpersonal skills are a plus.

Schedule: Part-time, year-round interns are needed.

Stipend or Pay: $6 to $7 per hour.

Academic Credit Offered: Per student's own arrangements with academic institution.

ELIGIBILITY: Undergraduate students with a journalism, communications, or graphic design background are encouraged to apply. Possible opportunities for non-students and career-changers.

REQUIREMENTS: Must provide a résumé with application.

APPLICATION PROCEDURE: Submit full application *to* Susan Milberg, Director of Marketing and Communications.

WOMEN'S COLLEGE COALITION

1090 Vermont Avenue NW   **Phone:**   202/789-2556
Washington, DC 20005   **FAX:**   N/A

* * *

ORGANIZATION'S ACTIVITIES: A small organization providing communications and other services to women's colleges, and information about them and their activities to the press and public.

Number of Internships: 1.

Type: Public relations, office management, editorial.

Function/Duties: Assist with computer maintenance of directory, with publications, and with media relations, as well as with special projects.

Schedule: Full-time summers.

Stipend or Pay: Yes.

Academic Credit Offered: Per student's own arrangements with academic institution.

ELIGIBILITY: Primarily college students—women *or* men.

REQUIREMENTS: Interests, goals, and/or experience relevant to available assignments.

APPLICATION PROCEDURE: Send résumé and cover letter *to* Tracy Riordan *by* May 1.

Organizations/Resources for Further Information about Internships in Associations

AMERICAN SOCIETY OF ASSOCIATION EXECUTIVES
1575 I Street NW
Washington, DC 20005
Phone: 202/626-2723
FAX: 202/371-8825

Contact for information on activities of tens of thousands of U.S. associations, including those that offer or sponsor internships themselves as well as those by specialty that can provide details on internships offered by their members.

For the full scope of member groups, see:

The Encyclopedia of Associations, an annual published by Gale Research Company of Detroit. In three large volumes of fine-print descriptive listings of associations, you will be likely to find a source for internships that meet your needs. Check the reference room of your library to find that directory, as well as others that the librarian might suggest.

As an idea of the scope of possibilities, the following groups are usually open to internships, whether they have a fully established program or not.

AMERICAN ASSOCIATION OF NURSERYMEN
1250 I Street NW
Suite 500
Washington, DC 20005
202/789-2900

AMERICAN INSTITUTE FOR PROPERTY AND LIABILITY
Underwriters Insurance Institute of America
720 Providence Road
Malverne, PA 19355
215/644-2100

AMERICAN NEWSPAPER PUBLISHERS
ASSOCIATION
Box 17407
Dulles Airport
Washington, DC 20041
703/648-1069

AMERICAN PUBLIC POWER ASSOCIATION
2301 M Street NW
Washington, DC 20037-1484
202/467-2900

AMERICAN SOCIETY OF APPRAISERS
535 Herndon Parkway
Suite 150
Herndon, VA 22070-5226
703/478-2228

AMERICAN VOCATIONAL ASSOCIATION
1410 King Street
Alexandria, VA 22314
703/683-3111

ASSOCIATION FOR SYSTEMS MANAGEMENT
P.O. Box 38370
Cleveland, OH 44138
216/243-6900

DATA PROCESSING MANAGEMENT
ASSOCIATION
505 Busse Highway
Park Ridge, IL 60068
708/825-8124

FEDERATION OF AMERICAN HEALTH
SYSTEMS
1111 19th Street NW
Suite 402
Washington, DC 20036
202/833-3092

HEALTH INSURANCE ASSOCIATION
Insurance Education Program
1025 Connecticut Avenue NW
Washington, DC 20036
202/223-7780

INFORMATION INDUSTRY ASSOCIATION
555 New Jersey Avenue NW
Suite 800
Washington, DC 20001-2082
202/639-8262

INSTITUTE OF CERTIFIED PROFESSIONAL
MANAGERS
James Madison University
Harrisonburg, VA 22807
703/568-6211

INSTITUTE OF MANAGEMENT
CONSULTANTS
230 Park Avenue
Suite 544
New York, NY 10169
212/697-8262

INSTITUTE OF MANAGEMENT SCIENCES
290 Westminster Street
Providence, RI 02903
401/274-2525

INSTITUTE OF REAL ESTATE MANAGE-
MENT (IREM) OF THE NATIONAL
ASSOCIATION OF REALTORS
430 North Michigan Avenue
P.O. Box 109025
Chicago, IL 60610
312/661-0004

INSURANCE DATA MANAGEMENT
ASSOCIATION
85 John Street
New York, NY 10038
212/669-0496

MANUFACTURERS AGENTS NATIONAL
ASSOCIATION
230 16 Mill Creek Road
Laguna Hills, CA 92653
801/972-1212

MOTOR VEHICLE MANUFACTURERS
ASSOCIATION OF THE UNITED STATES
7430 2nd Avenue
Suite 300
Detroit, MI 48202-2705
313/872-4311

NATIONAL ASSOCIATION OF BANK LOAN
AND CREDIT OFFICES
1 Liberty Place
Suite 2300
Philadelphia, PA 19103
215/851-9100

NATIONAL ASSOCIATION OF CREDIT
  MANAGEMENT
8815 Centre Park Drive
Suite 200
Columbia, MD 21045
410/740-5580

NATIONAL ASSOCIATION OF INDUSTRIAL
  AND OFFICE PARKS
1215 Jefferson Davis Highway
Suite 100
Arlington, VA 22202
703/979-3400

NATIONAL ASSOCIATION OF PRINTERS AND
  LITHOGRAPHERS
Palisades Avenue
Teaneck, NJ 07666
201/342-0700

NATIONAL ASSOCIATION OF PURCHASING
  MANAGEMENT
2055 East Centennial Circle
Tempe, AZ 85284
602/752-6276

NATIONAL SOCIETY OF PUBLIC
  ACCOUNTANTS
1010 North Fairfax Street
Alexandria, VA 22314-1574
703/549-6400

SOCIETY OF ACTUARIES
475 North Martingale Road
Schaumburg, IL 60173
708/706-3500

SOCIETY FOR HUMAN RESOURCE
  MANAGEMENT
606 North Washington Street
Alexandria, VA 22314
703/548-3440

TELECOMMUNICATIONS INDUSTRY
  ASSOCIATION
150 North Michigan Avenue
Suite 600
Chicago, IL 60601
312/782-8597

INTERNSHIP SOURCES FOR
SPECIAL ELIGIBILITIES

■■■

Notes on Internships for Special Eligibilities:

Many internship opportunities, paid and unpaid, for students and others, exist for individuals with special status, such as women, minorities, and the disabled. Some of these are listed throughout the book, if an organization offers anything aside from simple "equal opportunity"—and those groups are cross-referenced on page 426.

Some groups are listed here as well, and you may find it more valuable to work through the special-interest organizations to create a network of contacts.

TIP: You may qualify as "special" even if you are not a member of the more frequently identified minority groups. Any piece of your identity— membership, heredity, specializations, employment history, education, or the like—can qualify you for some special-status opportunity. Why not take advantage of that?

> *Cary is a journalism hopeful who got two valuable internships through minority-focused programs. He is also highly qualified, and had other opportunities as well. But he recommends taking advantage of that kind of project when it is where you want to be. If the minority opportunities are not what* you *want, he suggests ignoring them. Nor can you assume you will succeed just because of special status, he notes.*
>
> *In going after internships, he recommends: "Be as professional as you can, regarding the search and the self-presentation. And in choosing, select the one that gives you greater diversity of experience."*

NATIONAL ORGANIZATION FOR WOMEN

1000 16th Street NW
Suite 700
Washington, DC 20036

Phone: 202/331-0066
FAX: 202/785-8576

* * *

378

ORGANIZATION'S ACTIVITIES: Nonprofit women's rights organization dedicated to "bring women into full participation in the mainstream of American society, NOW." Issues include abortion rights, reproductive freedom, violence against women, lesbian rights, racial diversity, and economic parity.

Number of Internships: Varies.

Type: Assistant.

Function/Duties: Varies with project.

Schedule: Full-time and part-time.

Stipend or Pay: No.

Academic Credit Offered: Yes.

ELIGIBILITY: All students, career-changers, and non-students welcome to apply.

REQUIREMENTS: Skills and/or interests relevant to organization's activities.

APPLICATION PROCEDURE: Submit résumé, cover letter, recommendation, and completed application *to* Beth Beck.

OFFICE OF MINORITY AND WOMEN INTERNSHIPS

324 South State
Suite 508   **Phone:** 801/538-8680
Salt Lake City, UT 84114-711   **FAX:**   801/538-8888

* * *

ORGANIZATION'S ACTIVITIES: This program locates internships in agencies throughout state government and helps recruit minority and nontraditional female students to apply.

Number of Internships: Flexible; varies with need.

Type: Varies.

Function/Duties: Assignments as needed.

Stipend or Pay: Usually $6.40 per hour.

Academic Credit Offered: Per intern's own arrangements with academic institution.

ELIGIBILITY: Undergraduate (sophomore–senior) and graduate students are encouraged to apply. *Special Eligibilities:* Asian-American, Hispanic-American, African-American, and women who are nontraditional students (i.e., displaced homemakers). Must be in school (enrolled at a university) and fit the above-stated ethnic/gender background.

REQUIREMENTS: Interests, goals, and/or experience relevant to available assignments.

APPLICATION PROCEDURE: Submit full application *to* Shannon Thompson, Director.

PUBLIC LEADERSHIP EDUCATION NETWORK

1001 Connecticut Avenue NW
Suite 925   **Phone:** 202/872-1585
Washington, DC 20036-5507   **FAX:** 202/457-0549

* * *

ORGANIZATION'S ACTIVITIES: PLEN is a consortium of women's colleges working to prepare women for public leadership. Through seminars, conferences, and the Internship Semester in Washington, D.C., students learn about public policy from women leaders in the field.

Number of Internships: 10 to 25 placements.

Type: Placement in interest groups, executive agencies, or Congressional offices.

Function/Duties: Assist staff of specific departments according to intern's skills and interests. Intern must have some experience doing library research and writing papers.

Schedule: Seasonal (January–May) full-time internships available.

Stipend or Pay: Depends on placement.

Academic Credit Offered: Per intern's own arrangements with academic institution.

ELIGIBILITY: Primary focus is students at women's colleges, but some programs for students with a high-school education (including students presently attending high school) and above are available. Open to non-students and career-changers as well.

REQUIREMENTS: Must provide application form and résumé along with an application.

APPLICATION PROCEDURE: Submit full application *to* Marilyn Borchardt. *Deadline:* For summer placements, mid-November.

WOMEN AND FOUNDATIONS/CORPORATE PHILANTHROPY

322 Eighth Avenue
Suite 702   **Phone:** 212/463-9934
New York, NY 10001   **FAX:** 212/463-9417

* * *

ORGANIZATION'S ACTIVITIES: This program operates in the following cities/regions: New York City, Boston, North Carolina, Minnesota (Twin Cities), and starting in 1994, San Francisco.

Number of Internships: 8 per semester.

Type: Research, writing, and grantmaking.

Function/Duties: Assist staff of specific departments according to intern's skills and interests. Intern should be committed to the goals of WAF/CP and interested in philanthropy and the nonprofit sector.

Schedule: Seasonal (2 semesters: fall and spring) part-time internships available.

Stipend or Pay: An average of $8 to $10 per hour.

Academic Credit Offered: Per intern's own arrangements with academic institution.

ELIGIBILITY: Undergraduate (juniors and seniors only) and graduate students are encouraged to apply; open to non-students and career-changers as well. *Special Eligibilities:* Program is open to women of color—African-American, Asian-American, Hispanic-American, and Native American; men of color are eligible in Boston and San Francisco.

REQUIREMENTS: Must provide an application form, writing sample, résumé, and 2 letters of recommendation.

APPLICATION PROCEDURE: Submit full application *to* (NYC) Shona Chakravartty, Director of Programs (above address); (BOSTON) Association Grantmakers of Massachusetts, 294 Washington Street, Boston, MA 02108. *Deadline:* Early June for fall; early December for spring.

Organizations/Resources for Further Information about Internships for Special Eligibilities

PLACEMENT RESOURCE

INROADS
1221 Locust Street
St. Louis, MO 63103
Phone: 314/241-7488
FAX: 314/241-9325

Formed by a coalition of major corporations with minority-development groups, this is a national organization of 37 affiliates that serves as a career development agency which "develops and trains talented minority youth in business and industry and prepares them for corporate and community leadership." In addition to placing about 4,000 qualified minorities (African-American, Latino, and Native Americans) in some 1,000 corporate internship programs, Inroads provides special training as well as personal and career guidance.

INFORMATION RESOURCES

AMERICAN ASSOCIATION OF RETIRED PERSONS
601 E Street NW
Washington, DC 20049
Phone: 800/424-3410

For those aged 50 and over, AARP offers career-change information and some internship placement connections.

BUSINESS WOMEN'S GLOBAL NETWORK (BWGN) is a national phone referral service of and for women in business. A caller simply dials (900) 73-SELECT, 24 hours a day, 7 days a week, from office or home for information on special opportunities from and for women. No extra equipment necessary— just a telephone.

THE FOUNDATION CENTER
79 Fifth Avenue
New York NY 10003
Phone: 212/620-4230

At its New York office and in sites around the country, the Center's database includes organizations offering working/learning opportunities to members of all groups. Its data is also accessible by computer.

U.S. OFFICE OF SPECIAL TARGETED PROGRAMS
Employment and Training Administration
Department of Labor
Room N4641
200 Constitution Avenue NW
Washington, DC 20210

RESOURCES FOR INFORMATION AND NETWORKING AMONG GROUPS WITH SPECIAL ELIGIBILITIES

Women's Trade and Professional Associations

AMERICAN ASSOCIATION OF BLACK
  WOMEN ENTREPRENEURS
1326 Missouri Avenue
Suite 4
Washington, DC 20011
202/231-3751

AMERICAN BUSINESS WOMEN'S
  ASSOCIATION
9100 Ward Parkway
Kansas City, MO 64114
816/361-6621

AMERICAN MEDICAL WOMEN'S
  ASSOCIATION
801 North Fairfax Street
Alexandria, VA 22314
703/838-0500

AMERICAN SOCIETY OF PROFESSIONAL
  AND EXECUTIVE WOMEN
1511 Walnut Street
Philadelphia, PA 19102
215/563-4415

AMERICAN SOCIETY OF WOMEN
  ACCOUNTANTS
1755 Lynn Field Road
Memphis, TN 38719
901/680-0470

AMERICAN WOMEN'S ECONOMIC
  DEVELOPMENT CORP.
60 East 42nd Street
New York, NY 10165
212/692-9100

AMERICAN WOMAN'S SOCIETY OF
  CERTIFIED PUBLIC ACCOUNTANTS
401 North Michigan Avenue
Suite 1400
Chicago, IL 60611
312/644-6610

AMERICAN WOMEN IN RADIO AND
  TELEVISION
1101 Connecticut Avenue NW
Suite 700
Washington, DC 20036
202/429-5102

ASSOCIATION FOR PROFESSIONAL
  INSURANCE WOMEN
c/o St. Paul Fire and Marine
456 Montgomery Street
San Francisco, CA 94104
415/774-4391

ASSOCIATION FOR WOMEN IN SCIENCE
1522 K Street
Washington, DC 20037
202/408-0742

ASSOCIATION OF PROFESSIONAL
  MORTGAGE WOMEN
P.O. Box 8613
Walnut Creek, CA 94596
510/932-6690

ASSOCIATION OF WOMEN IN
  ARCHITECTURE
7440 University Drive
St. Louis, MO 63130
314/621-3484

BLACK WOMEN IN PUBLISHING
P.O. Box 6275
FDR Station
New York, NY 10150
212/772-5951

CATALYST
250 Park Avenue South
New York, NY 10022
212/777-8900

COALITION OF LABOR UNION WOMEN
15 Union Square West
New York, NY 10003
212/242-0700

FEDERALLY EMPLOYED WOMEN
1010 Vermont Avenue NW
Washington, DC 20005
202/638-4404

FINANCIAL WOMEN'S INTERNATIONAL
  ASSOCIATION
500 North Michigan Avenue
Chicago, IL 60611
312/661-1700

INTERNATIONAL ASSOCIATION OF WOMEN
  POLICE
P.O. Box 15207
Wedgewood Station
Seattle, WA 98115
206/625-4465

INTERNATIONAL FEDERATION OF WOMEN
  LAWYERS
186 Fifth Avenue
New York, NY 10010
212/206-1666

NATIONAL ASSOCIATION FOR FEMALE
  EXECUTIVES
127 West 24th Street
New York, NY 10011
212/645-0770

NATIONAL ASSOCIATION FOR
  PROFESSIONAL SALES WOMEN
P.O. Box 255708
Sacramento, CA 25865
916/484-1234

NATIONAL ASSOCIATION OF BLACK
  WOMEN ATTORNEYS
508 Fifth Street NW
Washington, DC 20001
202/638-5715

NATIONAL ASSOCIATION OF BLACK
  WOMEN ENTREPRENEURS
P.O. Box 1375
Detroit, MI 48231
313/341-7400

NATIONAL ASSOCIATION OF INSURANCE
   WOMEN
P.O. Box 4410
1847 East 15th Street
Tulsa, OK 74159
918/744-5195

NATIONAL ASSOCIATION OF MEDIA
   WOMEN
1185 Niskey Lake Road SW
Atlanta, GA 30331
404/344-3862

NATIONAL ASSOCIATION OF MINORITY
   WOMEN IN BUSINESS
2705 Garfield
Kansas City, MO 64109
816/421-3335

NATIONAL ASSOCIATION OF WOMEN
   ARTISTS
41 Union Square West
New York, NY 10003
212/675-1616

NATIONAL ASSOCIATION OF WOMEN IN
   CONSTRUCTION
327 South Adams Street
Ft. Worth, TX 76104
817/877-5551

NATIONAL ASSOCIATION OF WOMEN
   LAWYERS
750 North Lake Shore Drive
Chicago, IL 60611
312/988-6186

NATIONAL CONFERENCE OF WOMEN'S
   BAR ASSOCIATIONS
P.O. Box 77
Edentown, NC 27932-0077
919/482-8202

THE NATIONAL FEDERATION OF BUSINESS
   AND PROFESSIONAL WOMEN'S CLUBS,
   INC.
2012 Massachusetts Avenue NW
Washington, DC 20036
202/293-1100

NATIONAL FEDERATION OF PRESS WOMEN
P.O. Box 99
Blue Springs, MO 64015
816/229-1666

NATIONAL FORUM FOR EXECUTIVE
   WOMEN
1101 15th Street NW
Suite 400
Washington, DC 20005
202/857-3100

NATIONAL LEAGUE OF AMERICAN PEN
   WOMEN
1300 17th Street NW
Washington, DC 20036
202/785-1997

NATIONAL NETWORK OF WOMEN IN SALES
P.O. Box 578442
Chicago, IL 60657
312/577-1944

NATIONAL WOMEN'S ECONOMIC ALLIANCE
605 14th Street NW
Suite 900
Washington, DC 20005
202/393-5257

NATIONAL WOMEN'S EMPLOYMENT AND
   EDUCATION
8781 Rockefeller Center Station
New York, NY 10175
212/842-1200

9 TO 5—NATIONAL ASSOCIATION OF
   WORKING WOMEN
614 Superior Avenue NW
Suite 852
Cleveland, OH 44113
216/566-9308 or 800/245-9TO5

WOMEN CONSTRUCTION OWNERS AND
   EXECUTIVES
P.O. Box 883034
San Francisco, CA 94118
415/468-1920

WOMEN ENTREPRENEURS
1275 Market Street
San Francisco, CA 94103
415/929-0129

WOMEN EXECUTIVES INTERNATIONAL
TOURISM ASSOCIATION
136 East 56th Street
New York, NY 10022
212/759-5268

WOMEN IN DATA PROCESSING
P.O. Box 22818
San Diego, CA 92122
619/569-5615

WOMEN LIFE UNDERWRITERS
CONFERENCE
1922 F Street NW
Washington, DC 20006
202/331-6008

WOMEN'S DIRECT RESPONSE GROUP
224 Seventh Street
Garden City, NY 11530
212/503-4938

WOMEN'S NATIONAL BOOK ASSOCIATION
160 Fifth Avenue
New York, NY 10010
212/675-7804

Minority Opportunities Directories

AFFIRMATIVE ACTION REGISTER
Affirmative Action, Inc.
8356 Olive Boulevard
St. Louis, MO 63132
314/991-1335

DIRECTORY OF CAREER RESOURCES FOR
MINORITIES
Ready Reference Press
P.O. Box 5169
Santa Monica, CA 90405
310/474-5175

DIRECTORY OF MINORITY PUBLIC
RELATIONS PROFESSIONALS
Public Relations Society of
America
33 Irving Place
New York, NY 10003
212/228-7228

DIRECTORY OF SPECIAL PROGRAMS FOR
MINORITY GROUP MEMBERS
Garrett Park Press
P.O. Box 190F
Garrett Park, MD 20896
301/946-2553

Minority Professional Organizations

AMERICAN INDIAN SCIENCE AND
ENGINEERING SOCIETY
1085 14th Street
Suite 1506
Boulder, CO 80302
303/492-8658

ASIAN-AMERICAN JOURNALISTS
ASSOCIATION
1765 Sutter Street
San Francisco, CA 94115
415/346-2051

ASSOCIATION OF BLACK CPA FIRMS
1101 Connecticut Avenue NW
Washington, DC 20036
202/857-1100

BLACK WOMEN IN PUBLISHING
P.O. Box 6275
FDR Station
New York, NY 10150
212/772-5951

INTERRACIAL COUNCIL FOR BUSINESS
OPPORTUNITY
51 Madison Avenue
New York, NY 10010
212/779-4360

LATIN BUSINESS ASSOCIATION
5400 East Olympic Boulevard
Suite 237
Los Angeles, CA 90022
213/721-4000

NATIONAL ASSOCIATION OF BLACK
ACCOUNTANTS
900 Second Street NE
Washington, DC 20002
202/682-0222

NATIONAL ASSOCIATION OF HISPANIC
JOURNALISTS
National Press Building
Suite 634
Washington, DC 20045
202/662-7145

NATIONAL ASSOCIATION OF MINORITY
ENTREPRENEURS
322 West Jefferson
Suite 301
Dallas, TX 75208
214/943-7198

NATIONAL ASSOCIATION OF MINORITY
WOMEN IN BUSINESS
2705 Garfield
Kansas City, MO 64109
816/421-3335

NATIONAL ASSOCIATION OF NEGRO
BUSINESS AND PROFESSIONAL
WOMEN'S CLUBS
1806 New Hampshire Avenue NW
Washington, DC 20009
202/483-4206

NATIONAL BANKERS ASSOCIATION
127 C Street NW
Suite 240
Washington, DC 20001
202/783-3200

NATIONAL BLACK M.B.A. ASSOCIATION
111 East Wacker Drive
Suite 600
Chicago, IL 60601
312/644-6610

NATIONAL BLACK POLICE ASSOCIATION
1100 17th Street NW
Suite 1000
Washington, DC 20036
202/457-0564

NATIONAL CONFERENCE OF BLACK
LAWYERS
2 West 125th Street
New York, NY 10026
212/864-4000

NATIONAL COUNCIL FOR EQUAL BUSINESS
OPPORTUNITY
1221 Connecticut Avenue NW
4th Floor
Washington, DC 20036
202/293-3960

NATIONAL HISPANIC BUSINESS GROUP
730 Fifth Avenue
New York, NY 10459
212/333-8738

NATIONAL ORGANIZATION OF BLACK LAW
ENFORCEMENT EXECUTIVES
1221 Pennsylvania Avenue SE
Washington, DC 20003
202/546-8811

NATIONAL SOCIETY OF BLACK ENGINEERS
344 Commerce Street
Alexandria, VA 22314
703/549-2207

NATIVE AMERICAN COMMUNICATION AND
CAREER DEVELOPMENT
P.O. Box 1281
Scottsdale, AZ 85252-1281
602/483-8212

SOCIETY OF HISPANIC PROFESSIONAL
ENGINEERS
5400 East Olympic Boulevard
Suite 120
Los Angeles, CA 90022
213/725-3970

SOCIETY OF SPANISH ENGINEERS,
PLANNERS AND ARCHITECTS
P.O. Box 75
Church Street Station
New York, NY 10017
212/292-0970

TRADE UNION WOMEN OF AFRICAN
   HERITAGE
530 West 23rd Street
New York, NY 10011
212/929-6449

UNITED INDIAN DEVELOPMENT
   ASSOCIATION
9650 Flair Drive
El Monte, CA 91731
818/442-3701

Organizations Promoting Careers for People with Disabilities

FEDERATION OF THE HANDICAPPED, INC.
154 West 14th Street
New York, NY 10011
Phone: 212/727-4200

Its purpose is the vocational rehabilitation of the disabled.

GOODWILL INDUSTRIES OF AMERICA, INC.
9200 Wisconsin Avenue
Bethesda, MD 20814
Phone: 301/530-6500

A leading nonprofit provider of vocational rehabilitation and employment services for disabled adults.

HUMAN RESOURCES CENTER
201 Willets Road
Albertson, NY 11507
Phone: 516/747-5400

A nonprofit organization composed of five coordinated units: Vocational Rehabilitation, Human Resources School, The Employment Research and Training Center, Abilities, Inc., and Industry-Labor Council.

INTERNATIONAL CENTER FOR THE
   DISABLED (ICD)
340 East 24th Street
New York, NY 10010
Phone: 212/679-0100

An international organization dedicated to the rehabilitation of disabled persons; the provision of job-skill education, training, and placement services; and research and professional education.

JOB OPPORTUNITIES FOR THE BLIND
   (JOB)
National Federation of the Blind
1800 Johnson Street
Baltimore, MD 21230
Phone: 800/638-7518

The nationwide job listing and job referral system of the NFB.

NATIONAL REHABILITATION INFORMATION
   CENTER (NARIC)
8455 Colesville Road
Suite 935
Silver Spring, MD 20910
Phone: 800/34-NARIC

An outstanding resource: a clearinghouse for information and referrals for vocational and other rehabilitation resources, including ABLEDATA, a national computerized databank.

IV. FINDING FURTHER INTERNSHIP SOURCES

■■■

Extend your individual internship search through networking; seek out assistance from the many organizations that are sources of general information on interning. Included in this section are a number of such umbrella groups, placement services, and clearinghouses.

You can succeed at interning by creating your own opportunities within your profession or your community, but you can also work with specialist organizations that have expertise and a track record of success at developing and promoting internships of all kinds. The following groups provide either expert information on interning, specific guidance and placement for internships, or both.

INFORMATION

NATIONAL SOCIETY FOR INTERNSHIPS AND EXPERIENTIAL EDUCATION
3509 Haworth Drive, Suite 207
Raleigh, NC 27609
(Do not phone)

Nonprofit organization "to support the use of internships and other forms of experiential learning as an integral part of education. NSIEE is concerned with the integration of academic, career, and personal development of learners through internships and experiential education programs in all their forms."

ACCESS

Access: Networking in the Public Interest is a national non-profit organization that since 1985, has served as the nation's only comprehensive clearinghouse of information regarding employment opportunities in public and community service.

Access also offers public service employment publications that provide job-seekers with updates of available paid positions and internships of all levels in public service organizations throughout the country.

Its *Non-Profit Organization Search* is a service that provides job-seekers with a list of up to 100 nonprofit organizations that fit specific criteria. This list is a networking tool which can be used alone or as a supplement to *COMMUNITY JOBS: The Employment Newspaper For The Non-Profit Sector.*

Phone: (617) 720-5627 or (617) 720-1318

PLACEMENT PROGRAMS

DYNAMY
27 Severn Street
Worcester, MA 01609-2129
Phone: 508/755-2571
FAX: 508/755-4692

Dynamy, founded in 1969, is in its 23rd year as an urban experiential education program. Seventeen- to 22-year-old students from all over the country come to Dynamy, in Worcester, Massachusetts. Dynamy enrolls between 30 and 40 interns each year for service in regional nonprofit groups.

ENERGIZE ASSOCIATES
5450 Wissahicken Avenue
Philadelphia, PA 19144
Phone: 215/438-8342

Specializes in placements with social service and volunteer groups.

THE WASHINGTON CENTER
514 Tenth Street NW
Suite 600
Washington, DC 20004
Phone: 202/624-8000
FAX: 202/624-8058

Undergraduates, recent graduates, and graduate students in all academic disciplines from accredited institutions of higher education around the globe are eligible to apply for Washington Center programs, which offer internships in all fields. If your school has appointed a campus liaison, your application must be approved by the liaison before you apply to The Washington Center (TWC). Fees: About $2,000/semester.

An internship applicant must be a second-semester sophomore or above at the time s/he participates in a TWC program, and have a GPA of 2.5 or higher (on a 4-point scale), unless approved by the campus liaison. You must arrange for credit through the campus liaison or academic advisor at your school.

A Minority Leaders Fellowship program is also offered, through application to college or university presidents. The Washington Center is committed to equal opportunity for all. Of 250 participants, about 20 percent of placements are on Capitol Hill, about 30 to 35 percent in the executive branch, and the remainder in national associations.

The Independent Sector Internship Program provides opportunities for students to study and be a part of the unique mission of the nonprofit sector. Its Environmental Internship Program focuses on how to develop workable strategies to manage environmental problems better.

OTHER USEFUL ORGANIZATIONS FOR INFORMATION AND NETWORKING

ACTION AGENCY
1100 Vermont Avenue NW
Suite 8100
Washington, DC 20525
Phone: 202/606-5108

A government-sponsored clearinghouse.

CAMPUS COMPACT: THE PROJECT FOR PUBLIC COMMUNITY SERVICE
Brown University
25 George Street
Providence, RI 02912
Phone: 401/863-1119

A clearinghouse for community-service internships.

CAMPUS OUTREACH OPPORTUNITY LEAGUE (COOL)
386 McNeal Hall
St. Paul, MN 55108-1011
Phone: 612/624-3018

A student organization to support and promote student involvement in community service.

PARTNERSHIP FOR SERVICE-LEARNING
815 Second Avenue
Suite 315
New York, NY 10017-4594
Phone: 212/986-0989

A consortium of colleges, universities, service agencies, and religious organizations committed to internship opportunities for students and recent graduates.

ASSOCIATIONS OF NONPROFIT ORGANIZATIONS

Nonprofit organizations remain the richest source of internships. To explore them—including those that aren't listed anywhere else—use the following affiliations as resources:

The National Council for Nonprofit Associations at 1828 L Street NW, Suite 505, Washington, DC 20036, has member associations in every state; phone: 202/785-3208.

Alaska
ASSOCIATION OF NONPROFIT
  CORPORATIONS
P.O. Box 100956
Anchorage, AK 99510
Phone: 907/349-7787
FAX: 907/349-7993

Arkansas
NONPROFIT RESOURCES, INC.
500 Broadway
Suite 302
Little Rock, AR 72201-3342
Phone: 501/374-8515
FAX: 501/374-6548

California
CALIFORNIA ASSOCIATION OF NONPROFITS
P.O. Box 1478
Santa Cruz, CA 95061-1478
Phone: 408/458-1955
FAX: 408/458-9486

Colorado
COLORADO ASSOCIATION OF NONPROFIT
  ORGANIZATIONS
1600 Sherman Street
Suite 210
Denver, CO 80203
Phone: 303/832-5710
FAX: 303/894-0161

Connecticut
CONNECTICUT HUMAN SERVICE
880 Asylum Avenue
Hartford, CT 06105
Phone: 203/522-7762
FAX: 203/520-4234

Delaware
DELAWARE ASSOCIATION OF NONPROFIT
  AGENCIES
613 Washington Street
Wilmington, DE 19801
Phone: 302/762-9240
FAX: 302/652-3945

District of Columbia
WASHINGTON COUNCIL OF AGENCIES
1001 Connecticut Avenue NW
Suite 925
Washington, DC 20036
Phone: 202/457-0540
FAX: 202/457-0549

Florida
FLORIDA ASSOCIATION OF NONPROFIT
  ORGANIZATIONS
7480 Fairway Drive
Suite 206
Miami Lakes, FL 33014
Phone: 305/557-4650
FAX: 305/821-5228

Illinois
COUNCIL OF ILLINOIS NONPROFIT
  ORGANIZATIONS
522 East Monroe Street
Suite 503
P.O. Box 255
Springfield, IL 62705-0255
Phone: 312/435-1155

Kansas
KANSAS ASSOCIATION OF NONPROFIT
  ORGANIZATIONS
P.O. Box 363
Lindsborg, KS 67456
Phone: 913/227-3443
  or 316/686-1133

Maryland
MARYLAND ASSOCIATION OF NONPROFIT
  ORGANIZATIONS
22 Light Street
Baltimore, MD 21202-1075
Phone: 410/727-6367
FAX: 410/727-1914

Massachusetts
MASSACHUSETTS COUNCIL OF HUMAN
  SERVICE PROVIDERS
34$\frac{1}{2}$ Beacon Street
Boston, MA 02108
Phone: 617/742-3236
FAX: 617/742-2551

Michigan

MICHIGAN LEAGUE FOR HUMAN SERVICES
300 North Washington Square
Lansing, MI 48933
Phone: 517/487-5436
FAX: 517/371-4546

Minnesota

MINNESOTA COUNCIL OF NONPROFITS
2700 University Avenue West, #250
St. Paul, MN 55114
Phone: 612/642-1904
FAX: 612/642-1517

New Hampshire

GRANITE STATE ASSOCIATION OF
NONPROFITS
125 Airport Road
Concord, NH 03301
Phone: 603/225-0900
FAX: 603/225-4346

New Jersey

CENTER FOR NONPROFIT CORPORATIONS
15 Roszel Road
Princeton, NJ 08540
Phone: 609/951-0800
FAX: 609/951-8770

New York

COUNCIL OF COMMUNITY SERVICES
901A Madison Avenue
Albany, NY 12208
Phone: 518/489-4791
FAX: 518/589-5212

North Carolina

NORTH CAROLINA CENTER FOR
NONPROFIT ORGANIZATIONS
4601 Six Forks Road
Suite 524-A
Raleigh, NC 27609-5210
Phone: 919/571-0811

Pennsylvania

DELAWARE VALLEY COUNCIL OF
AGENCIES
125 South 9th Street
Suite 302
Philadelphia, PA 19107
Phone: 215/956-2335
FAX: 215/351-0779

Utah

UTAH NONPROFIT ASSOCIATION
183 West 1700 South
Salt Lake City, UT 84115
Phone: 801/485-9146

Washington

NORTHWEST REGIONAL FACILITATORS
East 525 Mission Avenue
Spokane, WA 99202-1824
Phone: 509/484-6733
FAX: 509/483-0345

INDEXES TO INTERNSHIPS

The following seven indexes have been compiled in order to make it easier for readers to pinpoint internship opportunities to suit their individual needs. The initial index supplies an alphabetical listing of the organizations sponsoring internships and is followed by an index to groups offering information on internships beyond what appears in the book listings. The remaining indexes provide alphabetical lists of internship sponsors classified by type of work offered, by U.S. regional locations, by whether pay or a stipend is offered, by internships welcoming non-students and career-changers, and by groups stressing readiness to employ those with special eligibilities.

ORGANIZATIONS OFFERING INTERNSHIPS

Organizations Providing Additional Information on Internships

▪▪

INTERNSHIP SPONSORS LISTED BY TYPE OF WORK OFFERED

■■■

EDUCATION

Adler Planetarium,   146
Adolescent Counseling Services,   331
Affordable Housing Alliance,   332
Agriculture, U.S. Department of,   207, 233
Agriculture, U.S. Department of/Office of
   International Trade,   262
American Cancer Society,   241
American Horticultural Society,   147
American Hotel & Motel Association,   361
American Humane Association,   333
American Slavic Student Internship Service
   (and Training Corp.)(A.S.S.I.S.T.),   264
Anasazi Heritage Center,   148
Art Institute of Chicago,   11
Asphalt Green Inc.,   334
Associate in Rural Development,   266
Attention Homes for Youth, Inc.,   335
Audubon Naturalist Society,   183

B'nai B'rith Hillel   153
Bishop Museum,   13
Borderlinks,   268
Boston Museum of Fine Arts,   14
Boston Museum of Science,   154
Brookhaven National Laboratory,   317
Brooklyn Botanic Garden,   155
Brooklyn Museum,   14

Capital Children's Museum,   15
Central Hudson Gas & Electric Corp.,   47
Chicago Botanic Garden,   156
Chicago Children's Museum,   16
Children's Museum of Boston,   156
Children's Museum of Indianapolis,   157
Citizen Action Fund Inc.,   305
Cloisters,   157
Common Cause,   306
Community Crisis Center,   339
Craft and Folk Art Museum,   18

Dahlem Environmental Education
   Center,   160, 186
Dallas Arboretum,   161
Denver Zoological Foundation,   162

Earthwatch,   187
Emergency Housing Consortium,   340
Environmental Defense Fund,   187

Fellowship of Reconciliation,   307
Fresh Air Fund,   99, 343
Frontlash,   308

Holden Arboretum,   163
Houston Museum of Fine Arts,   23

Indianapolis Zoo,   163, 190, 322
International Development, U.S. Agency for,
   218, 261
Institute of International Education
   (IIE),   277

J. Paul Getty Museum,   21
The Job Corps,   232

Kohl Children's Museum,   165

Longwood Gardens,   167
Los Niños,   283

Maritime Center at Norwalk,   167, 323
Mennonite Central Committee,   284, 346
Merck Forest and Farmland Center,   193
Metropolitan Museum of Art,   26
Moter Marine Laboratory,   193
Multifaith AIDS Project of Seattle,   252
Museum of Photographic Arts,   27

National Research Council,   325
New York State Theatre Institute,   28

Opera Company of Philadelphia,   29
Oregon Coast Aquarium,   173

Peace Corps,   232
Peace Valley Nature Center,   197
Pennsbury Manor,   174
Philadelphia Academy of Natural
   Sciences,   175
Philadelphia Institute of Contemporary
   Art,   31

San Diego Museum of Art,   32
Sanefreeze,   288

FINANCE

MANAGEMENT PRACTICE

RESEARCH

SERVICE PROFESSIONS

TECHNICAL PROFESSIONS

INTERNSHIP SPONSORS LISTED BY U.S. REGIONAL LOCATIONS*

■■

MIDDLE ATLANTIC

Accuracy in Media, Inc., 79
Agriculture, U.S. Department of, 207, 233, 262
AIDS Support Group, 239
American Association for Adult and Continuing Education, 359
American Association for the Advancement of Science, 359
American Bankers Association, 360
American Council for an Energy-Efficient Economy, 182
American Federation of Labor/Congress of Industrial Organizations (AFL/CIO), 360
American Friends Service Committee, 261
American Hotel & Motel Association, The, 361
American Institute of Ultrasound in Medicine, 242
American Legislative Exchange Council, 207
American National Red Cross, 242, 334
American Planning Association, 362
American Rivers, 183
American Security Council, 263, 301
American Society of Hospital Pharmacists, 243
AMTRAK (National Railroad Passenger Corporation), 42
Arena Stage, 11
Army Corps of Engineers, 208
Army Environmental Hygiene Agency, 316
Association for International Practical Training (AIPT), 267
Audubon Naturalist Society, 183

BASF Corporation, 44
Beijing-Washington, Inc., 267
Bread for the World, 269
Brookings Institution, 155, 303
Building Owners & Managers Association, 363

Camphill Village, 336
Capital Children's Museum, 15
Caplan/Capozzi, 89
Carrying Capacity Network, 184
Catholic Charities USA, 337
Central Intelligence Agency, 210, 270
Challenge International, 304
Chamber of Commerce of the United States, 211
Child Welfare League of America, 337
Chol-Chol Foundation for Human Development, 272
Commerce, U.S. Department of, 213, 233, 273
Common Cause, 306
Concern, 222
Congressional Budget Office, 212
Congressional Management Foundation, 229, 314
Cooperative House Foundation, 273
Corporation for Public Broadcasting, 94
Council for a Livable World, 307

Delmarva Power, 52
Democratic National Committee, 214

Energy, U.S. Department of, 214, 234, 318
Engraving and Printing, U.S. Bureau of, 320
Export-Import Bank of the U.S., 275

Federal Home Loan Mortgage Corp., (Freddie Mac), 55
Friends of the Earth, 189
Friends Committee on National Legislation, 308
Frontlash, 308

Gannett Company, Inc., 100
Goddard Space Flight Center, 321

Heritage Foundation, 309
Housing and Urban Development, U.S. Department of, 216, 234

*NOTE, however, that these are headquarters offices that in many cases have branches or affiliates elsewhere.

MIDDLE WEST

North Central

Northeast

Dance in America,   18
Dance Theater Workshop,   19
David Finley Jr. Fine Arts,   19
Deloitte & Touche,   53
Dera & Associates,   97
Direct Marketing Association,   365
Dunhill Personnel Systems,   53

Earthwatch,   187
Environmental Defense Fund,   187
Ernst & Young,   54

Farm Sanctuary,   189
Farrar, Straus & Giroux,   98
Fellowship of Reconciliation,   307
Foundation for a Civil Society,   276
Foundation for Independent Video and Film
   (FIVF),   20, 99
Franklin Furnace Archive,   20
Fresh Air Fund,   99, 343

General Foods USA,   56
Geraldo,   101
Green Century Capital Management,   57
Gould, William J., Associates, Inc.,   247
Guggenheim Museum,   21

Headline Communications,   102

Impression Impact,   102
International Labor Organization,   280
International Radio and Television Society
   (IRTS),   144
International Workcamps,   283

Jacob's Pillow Dance Festival,   20, 103
Jewish Chautauqua Society,   165
John Wiley & Sons,   60, 104

Leukemia Society of America,   250
Lincoln Center for the Performing Arts,   24
Lobsenz-Stevens, Inc.,   110

Mallory Factor Inc.,   112
Manhattan Theatre Club,   25
Medical Care Development, Inc.,   252
Merck Forest and Farmland Center,   193
Merrill Lynch Inc.,   64
Metropolitan Museum of Art,   26
Montel Williams Show,   114

National Audubon Society,   194
National Federation of Temple
   Brotherhoods,   370
NBC-TV,   116
Neighborhood Housing Services of New
   York City, Inc.,   348
New York Open Center,   170
New York State Bar Association,   370
New York State Theatre Institute,   28
Newsweek,   119
92nd Street Y,   170

Open Housing Center,   349

Pearl Theater Co.,   30
Performing Arts Resources, Inc.,   30

Planned TV Arts,   122
Porter/Novelli,   123
Public Relations Journal,   124
Public Relations Society of America,   143

Quaker United Nations Office,   287

Random House Publishing,   68, 125

Sage Marcom, Inc.,   127
Samuel Goldwyn Co.,   127
Scholastic, Inc.,   71, 129
SENSES,   352
South Street Seaport Museum,   177
Stack Marketing Communications,
   Inc.,   131
Stanley Works,   69
Sterling Hager Inc.,   131
Student Conservation Association,   200

Technoserve,   290
Teleway,   72
Translink Communications,   134

United Nations Association of the USA
   (UNAUSA),   290
United Nations Children's Emergency Fund
   (UNICEF),   291
United Nations Institute for Training &
   Research,   291
US Committee for UNICEF,   292

Volunteers of America,   355

Wadsworth Atheneum,   36
Waldenbooks Headquarters,   73
Wheelock College,   140
WKXL AM & FM,   136
WNET-TV,   137
WNYC Radio and TV,   137
Women and Foundations/Corporate
   Philanthropy,   380
Worldteach,   297

Yeshiva University Museum,   37, 180

NORTHWEST

Lost Valley Educational Center,   192

Multifaith AIDS Project of Seattle,   252

Northwest Folklife,   171

Register-Guard,   125

Salvation Army,   350
Sealaska Corporation,   71
Seattle/King County News Bureau,   130
Space Needle Corp.,   68

Westin Hotels and Resorts,   74
Weyerhauser Company,   75
Windermere Services Company,   75

INTERNSHIP SPONSORS OFFERING PAY, STIPEND, OR SUBSIDY

■■

Internship Sponsors for Non-students and Career-Changers

INTERNSHIP SPONSORS
FOR CANDIDATES WITH
SPECIAL ELIGIBILITIES*

*See also the section on special opportunities, page 378.